# Feminist Theology from the Third World

Other Related Titles:

*Feminist Theology: A Reader*
edited by Ann Loades (SPCK, W/JKP 1990)

*Voices from the Margin: Interpreting the
Bible in the Third World*
edited by R. S. Sugirtharajah (SPCK 1991)

*A Reader in African Christian Theology*
edited by John Parratt (SPCK 1987)

*Readings in Indian Christian Theology 1*
edited by R. S. Sugirtharajah and
Cecil Hargreaves (SPCK 1993)

# Feminist Theology from the Third World

A READER

EDITED BY

## Ursula King

SPCK/Orbis Books

First published in Great Britain 1994
Society for Promoting Christian Knowledge
Holy Trinity Church
Marylebone Road
London NW1 4DU

Second Impression 1996

First published in the USA 1994
Orbis Books
Maryknoll, New York
ISBN 0-88344-963-3

Cataloging-in-Publication Data for this book
is available from the Library of Congress

British Library Cataloguing-in-Publication Data

A catalogue record for this book is available
from the British Library

ISBN 0-281-04736-7

Typeset by Pioneer Associates Ltd, Perthshire
Printed in Great Britain by
The Cromwell Press, Melksham, Wiltshire

# Contents

Acknowledgements      viii

Preface      xi

Introduction    *Ursula King*      1

## PART ONE: Doing Theology from Third World Women's Perspective

1 *Mercy Amba Oduyoye* (Ghana)    Reflections from a Third World Woman's Perspective: Women's Experience and Liberation Theologies      23

2 *Mexico Conference*    Final Document on Doing Theology from Third World Women's Perspective      35

3 *The Ecumenical Decade of Churches in Solidarity with Women* (1988-98)      45

4 *Ivone Gebara* (Brazil)    Women Doing Theology in Latin America      47

5 *Indian Theological Association*    Theologizing in India—A Feminine Perspective      60

6 *Kwok Pui-lan* (Hong Kong)    The Future of Feminist Theology: An Asian Perspective      63

7 *Delores S. Williams* (USA)    Womanist Theology: Black Women's Voices      77

8 *Ada María Isasi-Díaz* (USA)    The Task of Hispanic Women's Liberation Theology—*Mujeristas*: Who We Are and What We Are About      88

## PART TWO: Women's Oppression and Cries of Pain

9 *Ranjini Rebera* (Sri Lanka/Australia)    Challenging Patriarchy      105

10 *Marianne Katoppo* (Indonesia)    The Church and Prostitution in Asia      114

# Contents

11  *Yayori Matsui* (Japan)   Violence Against Women in   124
    Development, Militarism, and Culture

12  *Swarnalatha Devi* (India)   The Struggle of *Dalit*   135
    Christian Women in India

13  *Bette Ekeya* (Kenya)   Woman, For How Long Not?   139

14  *Roxanne Jordaan* and *Thoko Mpumlwana* (South   150
    Africa)   Two Voices on Women's Oppression and
    Struggle in South Africa

15  *Mercy Amba Oduyoye* (Ghana) and *Roina Fa'atauva'a*   170
    (Samoa)   The Struggle about Women's Theological
    Education

16  *Asian Women's Consultation on Justice, Peace, and*   177
    *Integrity of Creation*   Letter Addressed to the
    Women of the World

## PART THREE: The Bible as a Source of Empowerment for Women

17  *Rigoberta Menchú* (Guatemala)   The Bible and   183
    Self-Defense: The Examples of Judith, Moses,
    and David

18  *Elsa Tamez* (Mexico)   Women's Rereading of the Bible   190

19  *Reflections on Biblical Texts*   202
    Matthew 15.21-8   The empowering of women
    Luke 1.26-45   Reversing the natural order
    Luke 1.26-55   The Magnificat
    Mark 16.1-11   Who will move the stone?

20  *Grace Eneme* (Cameroon)   Women as Living Stones   214

21  *Raquel Rodríguez* (Puerto Rico)   Open Our Eyes   220

22  *Jean Zaru* (Israel)   The Intifada, Nonviolence,   230
    and the Bible

23  *Kwok Pui-lan* (Hong Kong)   Worshipping with Asian   236
    Women: A Homily on Jesus Healing the
    Daughter of a Canaanite Woman

## PART FOUR: Challenging Traditional Theological Thinking

24  *Marianne Katoppo* (Indonesia)   The Concept of   244
    God and the Spirit from the Feminist Perspective

## Contents

25 *Chung Hyun Kyung* (Korea)   To Be Human Is to           251
   Be Created in God's Image

26 *Anonymous Poem* (India)   "God as Food for              259
   the Hungry"

27 *Teresa M. Hinga* (Kenya)   Jesus Christ and the         261
   Liberation of Women in Africa

28 *Singapore Conference*   Summary Statement on            271
   Feminist Mariology

29 *Ivone Gebara* (Brazil) and *María Clara Bingemer*       275
   (Brazil)   Mary—Mother of God, Mother of the Poor

30 *Betty Govinden* (South Africa)   No Time for Silence:   283
   Women, Church, and Liberation in Southern Africa

## PART FIVE: A Newly Emerging Spirituality

31 *Workshop Reflection*   From Barrenness to               303
   Fullness of Life: The Spirit as Enabler

32 *María Clara Bingemer* (Brazil)   Women in the           308
   Future of the Theology of Liberation

33 *Luz Beatriz Arellano* (Nicaragua)   Women's            318
   Experience of God in Emerging Spirituality

34 *Mary John Mananzan osb* (Philippines)   Theological    340
   Perspectives of a Religious Woman Today—Four
   Trends of the Emerging Spirituality

35 *Aruna Gnanadason* (India)   Women and Spirituality      351
   in Asia

36 *Mercy Amba Oduyoye* (Ghana)   The Empowering            361
   Spirit of Religion

37 *Naomi P. F. Southard* (USA)   Recovery and              378
   Rediscovered Images: Spiritual Resources for
   Asian American Women

38 *Chung Hyun Kyung* (Korea)   Come, Holy Spirit—          392
   Break Down the Walls with Wisdom and Compassion

Notes                                                       395

Bibliography                                                413

Index                                                       426

# Acknowledgements

**WCC**: Ranjini Rebera, "The Feminist Challenge" and Raquel Rodriguez, "Open Our Eyes" from *The Power We Celebrate: Women's Stories of Faith and Power*, edited by Musimibi R. A. Kanyoro and Wendy Robins, copyright© 1992 World Council of Churches; Marianne Katoppo, "The Church and Prostitution in Asia" and "The Concept of God and the Spirit from the Feminist Perspective" from her book *Compassionate and Free: An Asian Woman's Theology*, copyright© 1980 World Council of Churches; "The Magnificat" and "Worship" from *We Cannot Dream Alone: A Story of Women in Development* by Ranjini Rebera, copyright © 1990 World Council of Churches; Hyun Kyung Chung, "Come Holy Spirit—Renew the Whole Creation" from *Signs of the Spirit*, edited by M. Kinnamon, copyright © 1991 World Council of Churches; Bette Ekeya, "Woman for How Long Not?", Grace Eneme, "Who Will Move the Stone?", and Marie Assaad, "Reversing the Natural Order" from *New Eyes for Reading: Biblical and Theological Reflections by Women from the Third World*, edited by J. S. Pobee and Bärbel von Wartenburg-Potter, copyright © 1986 World Council of Churches; "Ecumenical Decade of Churches in Solidarity with Women" from *WCC 1988 Resource Book: Prayers and Poems, Songs and Stories*, copyright © 1988 World Council of Churches. Reprinted by permission of World Council of Churches.

**Verso**: Rigoberta Menchú, "The Bible and Self-Defence: The Examples of Judith, Moses, and David" from *I, Rigoberta Menchú: An Indian Woman in Guatemala*, edited and introduction by E. Burgos-Debray, copyright © 1984 Verso. Reprinted by permission of Verso.

**SCM**: Chung Hyun Kyung, *The Struggle to Be the Sun Again*, pp. 47-51, 72, copyright © 1990 SCM. Reprinted by permission of SCM Press Ltd.

**Augsburg Fortress**: Ada María Isasi-Díaz and Yoland Tarango, "Solidarity: Love of Neighbor in the 1990s" from *Hispanic Women: Prophetic Voice in the Church*, copyright © 1992 Augsburg Fortress. Reprinted by permission of Augsburg Fortress Publishers.

**Skotaville**: Roxanne Jordaan, "Black Feminist Theology in South Africa" from *We Are One Voice: Black Theology in USA and South*

# Acknowledgements

*Africa*, edited by S. Maimela and D. Hopkins, copyright © 1989 Skotaville Publishers. Unable to contact the publisher.

**Cluster Publications**: Thoko Mpumlwana, "My Perspective on Women and Their Role in Church and Society" and Betty Govinden, "No Time for Silence: Women, Church and Liberation in South Africa" from *Women Hold Up Half the Sky: Women in the Church in Southern Africa*, edited by Denise Ackermann, Jonathan Draper, and Emma Mashini, copyright © 1991 Cluster Publications. Unable to contact the publisher.

**Journal of Feminist Studies in Religion**: Ada María Isasi-Díaz, "Who We Are and What We Are About" in *Journal of Feminist Studies in Religion, vol 8, number 1*, copyright © 1992 Journal of Feminist Studies in Religion. Reprinted by permission of the Journal.

**Pacific Journal of Theology**: Tessa Mackenzie, "Roina Pioneers Theological Education for Samoan Women" in *Pacific Journal of Theology, series II, number 4*, copyright © 1990 Pacific Journal of Theology. Reprinted by permission of the Journal.

**The Asia Journal of Theology**: "Letter Addressed to the Women of the World", "Consultation on Justice, Peace and Integrity" in *The Asia Journal of Theology, vol 2, number 1*, copyright © 1988 The Asia Journal of Theology; Kwok Pui-lan, "Worshipping with Asian Women: A Homily" in *The Asia Journal of Theology, vol 1, number 1*, copyright © 1987 The Asia Journal of Theology; Naomi P. F. Southard, "Recovery and Rediscovered Images: Spiritual Resources for Asian American Women," in *The Asia Journal of Theology, vol 3, number 2*, copyright © 1989 The Asia Journal of Theology. Reprinted by permission of the Journal.

**The Auburn News**: Kwok Pui-lan, "The Future of Feminist Theology: An Asian Perspective" in *The Auburn News*, Fall 1992, copyright © 1992 The Auburn News. Used by permission of the periodical.

**LADOC**: María Clara Bingemer, "Women in the Future of the Theology of Liberation" in *LADOC (Latin American Documentation), vol 20, number 6*, copyright © 1990 LADOC. Used by permission of LADOC.

**Asian Women's Resource Center for Culture and Theology**: *Singapore Report: Asian Women Doing Theology*, copyright © 1987 Asian Women's Resource Center for Culture and Theology; "Who Will Move the Stone" (June 1989), copyright © 1989; Yagori Matsui, "Violence Against Women in Development, Militarism, and Culture (Winter 1991), copyright © 1991; Aruna Gnanadason, "Women and Spirituality in Asia" (Winter 1989) copyright © 1989 from *In God's Image*, edited

## Acknowledgements

by Sun Ai Lee Park, copyright © 1982, 1989, 1991 Asian Women's Resource Center for Culture and Theology. Used by permission of the Asian Women's Resource Center for Culture and Theology.

**HarperCollins:** Mercy Amba Oduyoye, "The Empowering Spirit of Religion" and Ada María Isasi-Díaz, "The Bible and *Mujerista* Theology from *Lift Every Voice: Constructing Christian Theologies from the Underside*, edited by Susan Brooks Thistlethwaite and Mary Potter, copyright © 1990 HarperSanFrancisco. Used by permission of HarperSanFrancisco (a division of HarperCollins).

**Indian Theological Association, Bangalore:** *Socio-Cultural Analyses in Theologizing*, edited by Kuncheria Pathil, copyright © 1987 Indian Theological Association. Used by permission of the Association.

**ISPCK:** Swarnalatha Devi, "The Struggle of *Dalit* Women in India" from *Towards a Dalit Theology*, edited by M. E. Prabhakar, copyright © 1989 ISPCK, Delhi. Used by permission of SPCK, London.

# Preface

This Reader brings together very different women's voices from many parts of the so-called "Third World." The context and background of the book, and of feminist theology in the Third World, are explained in the Introduction. An earlier publication, *With Passion and Compassion: Third World Women Doing Theology* (eds. Virginia Fabella and Mercy Amba Oduyoye, Orbis Books, 1988), contained theological reflections from the Women's Commission of the Ecumenical Association of Third World Theologians (some of which have been reprinted here), whereas the extracts in this book are based on a much wider and more diverse range of sources. These sources reflect differences in experience and setting, in multiple networks and methods of working, and in the style of writing. In addition to theological articles written by individual women, there are also some collectively produced pieces—for example, important conference statements that reflect the dynamic interaction and shared thinking among different groups of women—and, furthermore, there are personal testimonies, poems, and public addresses. It has not been my aim to analyze each contribution in detail, but I have prefaced each by a brief comment that explains the larger context and theme, provides references to comparable material elsewhere, and invites readers or groups who use this book to listen attentively to a particular woman's voice and engage in critical dialogue with it.

You may ask why I as a white woman living in the First World have edited an anthology of Third World women. I cannot speak on their behalf—and do not attempt to do so—but I have had the opportunity to encounter many women's voices, and consider it important to draw attention to them. It is not only through traveling that I have met many Third World women, or through sharing their ideas at theological conferences and reading their work, but also through living in India for five years—where my interest in the Third World first gained its full momentum. Although I now live and work in the West, I have many contacts and friends among women in the Third World, through whom I learn a great deal that challenges and enriches me deeply. I now see the development of feminist theology very much in a crosscultural, global perspective and have been fortunate in having had access to many different sources—often more easily available in the West than in most other parts of the world (this is also discussed in the Introduction). I wanted to give space and visibility to many different women, their experiences, and reflections, and thereby show the great diversity and richness of feminist theology in the non-Western world.

My selection of texts is a personal one, and another woman would no doubt have chosen differently. So much material is becoming available now that it is impossible to be comprehensive in one's choice. However, under the heading of the five chosen themes I have provided significant, and to some extent representative, examples. In each case, had space permitted, these examples could have been accompanied by many other women's voices.

You may notice a certain preponderance of Asian contributions, and there are several reasons for this. It is not only that I have something of an experientially rooted bias toward Asia, but also that this immense continent perhaps possesses greater variety than any other. To date, Asian feminist theologians seem to have written more than women from Africa or Latin America. Strong evidence of this is provided by the existence of the Asian feminist theological journal *In God's Image*, which is already over ten years old. This journal is certainly unique among women theologians of the Third World. Yet, in spite of it, Asian women's theological work is generally less well known than that of Latin American women who have long been associated with liberation theology. It is also no coincidence that Asian women's voices speak so strongly and so movingly about spirituality: Asia is the continent that challenges us most with its religious pluralism and its ancient spiritual traditions.

## *Preface*

Many women have helped me to compile this book—too many to list all of them here. However, I would like to thank most warmly all my friends and sisters who have encouraged and assisted me in bringing this project to completion. I would like to dedicate this book especially to the many courageous black and white women of South Africa whom I met during my visit in April 1993 and who were inspiring partners in dialogue. May the publication of this book help to ensure that Third World women's voices are listened to more widely.

*Ursula King*
*Bristol, July 1993*

❖    ❖    ❖

# Introduction

URSULA KING

☐ Feminist theological voices have been heard in North America and Europe since at least the late 1960s. The development of the steadily growing field of feminist theology in Western countries has often been described, but the emergence of feminist theology in the Third World is much less known. It began more recently and includes contributions from many different women around the globe whose voices deserve much attention. If we listen carefully to them, we can discern both a greater diversity of approaches and a greater unity of themes than are found among feminists in the First World.

These voices come from Africa, Asia, and Latin America; they also come from women in minority groups in the USA and include women in South Africa, Palestine, and the Pacific. The work of individual women theologians has been published in article and book form, mainly in the USA but also in Asia, yet so far none of the existing collections has surveyed the full range of feminist theology from the Third World nor discussed its wider context, history, and main themes. One of the best-known introductions available is *Inheriting our Mothers' Gardens: Feminist Theology in Third World Perspective* edited by Letty M. Russell, Kwok Pui-lan, Ada María Isasi-Díaz, and Katie Geneva Cannon.[1] Although it emphasized the need for a global network "in which women of all colors, cultures, and continents share their stories for faith and struggle,"[2] most of its contributions are concerned with what feminist theology means to women of color living in the USA. The present book makes available the contributions of women from the Third World by providing a selection of texts from a wide range of sources that will introduce the reader to the oppressive (and

1

also challenging) experiences, the lively debates, and critical theological reflections of Christian women around the globe. My anthology was planned as a companion volume to the Reader on *Feminist Theology* edited by Ann Loades (SPCK and Westminster Press, 1990) and it complements this earlier publication by showing how the critical theological work of Western women has seeded new creative growth of considerable originality and challenge among women from the Third World. It also shows how, through numerous contacts and connections between women theologians around the world, feminist theology has now acquired a truly global dimension.

The need for contextuality is often emphasized in feminist theology, that is to say, attention must be paid to the wider context of events and ideas, so that they are not interpreted in isolation from one another. This need for contextuality, while being attentive to the particular and specific at the same time, is also required for the understanding of feminist theology itself. I therefore propose to set the voices of the women from the Third World into both their larger context, and also their more specific one, by clarifying important connections and concepts, and through describing historical developments as well as the web of contemporary networks and common themes.

**Feminist theology and the Third World: some clarifications**

The term "Third World" has always been problematic—and is even more so now, given the profound political transformations and economic upheavals of recent years. While the First World of Western capitalist democracies still exists, the Second World of Eastern communist countries is disintegrating before our very eyes and the Third World of so-called "developing countries" is deeply affected by the changes in the First and Second Worlds. Sometimes people speak of the "Fourth World" with reference to the poor in all countries, and these are often especially the women whom others refer to as the "Two-thirds World" because women outnumber men in the global population. The term "Fourth World" is also understood to refer to those who lead Third World lives in First World countries—for example, members of specific minorities and aboriginal people. After considerable reflection I have decided to retain the term

"Third World," not only because it is currently still widely used (as, for example, in publications such as the journal *Voices from the Third World*), but, more importantly, because it is part of the self-description used by the feminist theologians of the Women's Commission of the "Ecumenical Association of Third World Theologians," usually abbreviated as EATWOT. However, as used in this volume, "Third World" does not primarily refer to fixed geographical locations; instead, it is used with more fluid boundaries, for it is also applied to women minorities who are usually, but not always, women of color. The term can also apply to women who live on the margin in societies of great wealth such as, for example, in the USA, South Africa, Israel, Japan, New Zealand, or Australia.

Feminist theology in Third World countries has developed as a result of women's association with ideas, institutions, publications, and people in the First World, as has been the case with feminism in general. As Kumari Jayawardena has pointed out in her book *Feminism and Nationalism in the Third World*,[3] the growth of feminism around the world does not mean that the movement for the emancipation of women and their full participation in society has been imposed from the outside. On the contrary, women from the Third World stress the importance of their own struggle and efforts to achieve their own liberation while participating in movements for the political and economic liberation of their own countries.

I mentioned earlier that feminist theology, after originating in the West, has been seeded in the Third World with the result that it is now growing in different soils, all producing rich harvests of their own. While Third World feminist theology is diverse and different from feminist theology in the First World, it also shares a number of similar characteristics. Feminist theology is deeply rooted in women's experience; it is marked by commitment and oriented toward personal and social transformation, toward praxis, and in turn much theological reflection arises out of such praxis. Feminist theology has been called an advocacy theology concerned with the liberation of women from oppression, guided by the principle of seeking to achieve the full humanity of women. In a Third World context feminist theology expresses itself as a liberation theology in a much stronger sense, as it develops within situations where the

3

oppression of women and the denial of their full humanity often occurs on a much larger scale and to a much greater degree than in the First World.

Feminist theology is always dynamic and pluralistic. It includes and expresses the voices, experiences, and approaches of many different women in very different situations and societies. It is not a systematically developed body of received knowledge handed down in traditional institutions of learning. On the contrary, the emphasis is very much on "doing theology," on theology in the active mode, for it means suffering and seeking, listening and speaking, voicing and questioning, encountering and sharing, responding to and being responsible for action. To use a traditional distinction, the process of theologizing occurs inductively rather than deductively.

The term "feminist theology" can be understood both in a broader and more narrow sense. It has been applied to the work of Jewish and Christian feminists and also to writings on new forms of feminist spirituality. I do not use the term in this wider sense, but apply it more narrowly as referring to the experience and reflection of Christian women from the Third World. However, these women belong to many different Christian churches and work closely together in an open, ecumenical, sisterly spirit.

All feminist theology has an experiential and experimental quality about it, evident even in its language and style, in its stories, poems, prayers, artwork, and new liturgies. Through these different forms of expression it seeks to accomplish both a negative and a positive task. Its negative task is the critique of and struggle against all forms of oppression resulting from patriarchy, sexism, and androcentrism; its positive task is one of reform and reconstruction, of a reinterpretation of the Christian tradition, especially the Bible and the core symbols and teachings of Christianity in the light of women's experience, and with a critical attitude toward the socially and historically constructed notion of gender. This implies a radical questioning of what different cultures and religions have traditionally held a woman's place and role to be. Feminist theology has also become more complex since black feminist consciousness emerged in black women's struggle against the sexism of black men and the racism of white women. These issues, first debated in the USA but now also widely discussed by Third World women, highlight how gender, race, and class are closely intertwined and have to be critically reflected upon in theological thinking.[4]

Feminist theology anywhere, whether in the First or Third World, would never have come about without women's full access to theological education up to the highest academic level. Since the beginning of the women's movement in the nineteenth century, women struggled to gain this access, but they were given it only late and often grudgingly. Apart from a few exceptions, women in the Western world generally gained access to the formal study of theology only after the Second World War. Yet there are still theological institutions, including some in the Third World, that will not admit women to theological studies. However, where openings have occurred, women have availed themselves eagerly of these new educational opportunities, so that now in many university theology faculties, divinity schools, and theological seminaries at least half the currently enrolled students are women. This trend is even visible among the small number of Christians in China.[5]

Without full theological training—initially this meant full training in traditional, androcentric forms of theology—women would not have become fully theologically literate, and thereby capable of critiquing and deconstructing existing theologies from within. This importance of theological education up to the highest Ph.D. level is of great significance in the development of feminist theology, both in the USA and Europe, and also elsewhere around the world. Theological education is an important initial catalyst, but once women have become theologically empowered, feminist theology flourishes more through informal networks, including many women working at grassroots level rather than in the context of traditional academic theology teaching. However, the importance of theological training is widely recognized, as is evident from the fact that women in several countries of the Third World have formed associations of "theologically trained women."[6] Not all these women would necessarily describe themselves as "feminists," a label developed in the West—and one that some women feel does not describe their work adequately. Others speak freely of "feminist theology," but it must be kept in mind that the boundaries to this term are fluid and not always clearly definable among the different women doing theology in the Third World.

The voices of women included in this book are all expressed in English, yet they come mostly from women for whom this is not their first language. Thus we must be aware of the problem of cultural and linguistic translation, and even more of the oppression of language—something that is experienced deeply by at least some women for whom English is associated with the painful memory of colonialism and its accompanying exploitation. This is by no means only a memory of the past, as for many women from the Third World this oppression is part of their contemporary experience, further reinforced by the capitalism and neo-colonialism of Western culture. There is no easy way out of this dilemma of language. Women who are seeking to voice their own experiences and reflections have to do this in their own languages for their own people (otherwise real change and transformation cannot occur), but in order to connect with one another, work together, and strengthen women around the world, there must also be a common, shared language so that such women can be more widely heard and become effective. At present, this language is most often English, and it is in English that many Third World women theologians write, speak, and publish. It is from their publications in English that I have chosen the selection of texts found in this volume. As a white Western woman (whose first language isn't English either), I am deeply aware of the complex and sensitive issues raised by presenting and introducing the work of women from the Third World whose experiences are not mine. I cannot speak on behalf of my sisters, but, in some small way, I may be able to make them more visible and give their large chorus of voices a wider hearing.

My own attention to the plight and power of their lives first came into focus when I lived in India in 1965–70, and this focus has been increasingly strengthened through several subsequent visits there, to Southeast Asia, the Far East and South Africa. More recently, I was also able to meet several Third World women theologians from Asia, Latin America, and the USA at the Annual Meeting of the American Religion, where I was thrilled to hear them speak personally about their work. Together with my students, I have studied their writings and indirectly shared some of their experiences and ideas. We have found this deeply challenging, sometimes truly disturbing, but also greatly enriching, affirming, and empowering. It is from this experience and perspective that I would like to share the following reflections on the significant stages in the development of Third World feminist theology as it has occurred until now. When I refer to feminist theology in the Third World, I am now primarily thinking of Asia, Africa, and Latin America, but I shall also say something about women from minority groups in the First World.

**The historical development of Third World feminist theology: some crosscultural connections**

The emergence of feminist theology in the Third World has to be seen in a larger crosscultural context. Which are the most significant moments, contacts, and connections that have contributed to the implanting of feminist theological ideas *within* different cultures and helped the diffusion of feminist thinking *across* and *between* cultures around the globe? The importance of theological education and academic training for women has already been mentioned. Several Third World countries possess well-established institutions of advanced theological education, but it is not always easy for women to get either access to or funding for such training (which is still mostly under the control of male church authorities in the different denominations). Great is the lament of some women who still suffer exclusion from both education and leadership in the work of their churches. However, quite a few leading Third World women theologians have received their advanced theological training in the First World, with doctorates from well-known universities in the USA or Europe, and supported by scholarships from ecclesiastical and academic institutions in the West where, in addition, they have held teaching posts, at least on a temporary basis. When returning to their own countries and cultures, these women can and do play a key role in the development of new feminist theological thinking.

However, by no means all feminist theologians of the Third World travel by this route. A large proportion of women work from within an ecclesiastical context in their own churches, and their degree of church activity and commitment frequently distinguishes them from the less community-oriented, more individualistically working feminist theologians of the West. They are often sisters in religious orders (among Roman Catholics), ordained women ministers (of different Protestant churches), teachers in religious schools and colleges, or church workers with different kinds of professional expertise.

Feminist theology in the Third World must be understood within the larger context of both feminist theology *and* liberation theology as well as that of a distinct Third World theology. Another important factor in the development of feminist theological thinking and praxis is the initiative taken by several Christian world organizations in promoting women's activities and critical reflection, leading to the transformative experience of consciousness-raising. The diffusion of feminist thinking across different cultures in association with the work of many Christian churches clearly demonstrates the profoundly ambivalent double dynamic of religion as both an oppressive force in people's lives, and a liberating one. On the one hand, women are still being oppressed by patriarchal religious institutions. On the other hand, these very institutions, at a different level, help to bring about the transformation of women's lives and thought, which in turn cannot but lead to fundamental changes within these institutions themselves.

Examples of such active initiatives among women, of the art of midwifery or bringing to birth, can be found among others in the work of the World YWCA, the World Christian Students' Federation (WCSF), the Christian Conference of Asia (CCA), and especially of the World Council of Churches (WCC). The last plays a particularly active role which, because of its wide influence and importance, I shall describe in some detail.

The WCC brings together the worldwide diversity of Christian churches, but from its center in Geneva it also functions as a global institution. From among its many activities, the following WCC-initiated events can be signaled as particularly significant for the development of feminist consciousness among Christian women worldwide:

(1) In 1974 the WCC organized a consultation in West Berlin dealing with "Sexism in the 1970s" attended by about 170 women from 50 different countries around the globe. This was a new departure, which led to some important insights among the women present.[7] Although the WCC had already established a Department of Co-operation of Women and Men in Church and Society in 1955, its concerns rarely went beyond questions of women's ordination and participation in the Church. Only when an African woman, Brigalia Bam, took charge of this Department in 1967 did global issues of women's development and women's rights as human beings come onto the agenda. Sexism gradually became recognized as a deficiency in human relations, an evil to be resisted and uprooted, and this led to the Berlin conference. At first, however, member churches of the WCC considered sexism as a non-theological, secular issue; only later was sexism recognized as a challenge to the Church worldwide.[8]

(2) Also in 1974, the WCC Sub-Unit on Women in Church and Society established a worldwide "Programme on Women and Rural Development," which involved education, leadership development, and skills training—and was later described by Ranjini Rebera from Sri Lanka "as an attempt to deal with the inequalities within the global village that continue to treat women as a faceless component in the process of development." Between 1974 and 1988 some 230 programs were funded around the globe,[9] which placed development within the context of the empowerment of women, created a new awareness and new openings at grassroots level, and helped to forge solidarity between women in rural and nonrural areas. In 1988 the WCC organized an evaluation conference of these programs that brought together fifteen women participants from different churches around the world whose stories and project evaluation, accompanied by biblical and theological reflections as well as women's liturgies, have been edited by Ranjini

9

Rebera in *We Cannot Dream Alone: A Story of Women in Development*[10] (some excerpts from this are reprinted in this Reader).

(3) In 1978-81 the WCC undertook a worldwide study on "The Community of Men and Women in the Church." This was known as the "Community Study," and many women and men from the Third World took part in it. Following its last conference in Sheffield/England in 1981, this study is also known as "The Sheffield Report"; it focuses on issues of identity and sexuality, the role of scriptures and structures, and the challenges of inclusiveness as a principle of community building.[11]

(4) The United Nations Decade for Women (1975-85) had culminated in an international women's conference in Nairobi (1985). Following it an African Methodist bishop suggested the launch of a churches' decade for women at a WCC central committee meeting, as the churches had not been sufficiently aware of the UN Decade and the position of women had not improved in many churches over the ten previous years. This subsequently led the WCC to declare 1988-98 as the Ecumenical Decade of the Churches in Solidarity with Women. The importance of this step for Christian women is considerable, since the WCC suggested to its member churches three areas for particular consideration: women's full participation in church and community life; women's perspectives on, and commitment to, justice, peace, and integrity of creation (this falls into a wider program of the WCC's work); women doing theology and sharing spirituality. It is the last area in particular that is important for the development of feminist theology in the Third World.

The Ecumenical Decade has been launched and marked in different ways by different member churches. It has led to a sense of joy and empowerment, especially as its purpose for women has been described in terms of empowering, affirming, giving visibility, enabling churches, and encouraging action and dynamic movements. The WCC has also published a resource book[12] and study materials for women; these will affect the awareness of church women worldwide at the level of their local communities. A particular highlight and affirmation of the Ecumenical Decade of the Churches in Solidarity with Women is the decision of the Anglican Church in England, arrived at in November 1992, to ordain women. This historic decision, taken at long last after many years of struggle, will certainly have an affirming and empowering effect on those women in the churches who are still struggling to achieve full participation in the work of their communities.

In many parts of the Third World the WCC has acted as an enabler for women: it has provided a supportive network, financial and human resources, and many opportunities through workshops, conferences, publications, and places of study—all of which have helped the theological development of women in different countries. At the same time, these developments are closely interconnected with the development of Third World theologies, initially solely undertaken by male theologians who gave little attention to women. Male theologians from different Third World countries met up with each other at international conferences, not least at some of those organized by the WCC, and eventually decided to form their own organization, the Ecumenical Association of Third World Theologians (EATWOT), founded in Tanzania in 1976.

At first, women theologians were hardly present at EATWOT meetings, but they soon came to represent a third of its membership. EATWOT held three major assemblies in countries of three different continents (Ghana 1977, Sri Lanka 1979, Brazil 1989). Each conference had a different focus influenced by the continent where the meeting took place: Africans stressed indigenization; Asians focused on religious pluralism; Latin Americans stressed class analysis. In addition to these differences in emphasis, though, there were many similarities: including a stress on liberation as the central core of the Christian gospel, the need to reread the Bible in the light of the hermeneutical privilege of the poor, and a rejection of the dominant theologies of Europe and the USA. These are all themes that subsequently influenced the discussions of feminist theologians from the Third World and are reflected in their work.

11

## Introduction

EATWOT initially excluded theologians from minority groups in the USA, but later these became eligible for membership. In 1981 EATWOT organized a meeting in New Delhi that was attended by fifty theologians who described the irruption of the Third World into theology as a historical event. Through meeting in India there was also the additional irruption of the non-Christian world into their theological thinking. When the African woman theologian Mercy Amba Oduyoye was asked to reflect on this situation, she spoke about the presence of women as "the irruption within the irruption," especially after Marianne Katoppo, author of the first Asian woman's theology, *Compassionate and Free: An Asian Woman's Theology* (WCC Publications, 1979), drew the meeting's attention to the need to watch our language about God and before God. From now on, the network among women theologians of the Third World began to emerge and gain increasing visibility and momentum. At the next EATWOT conference in Geneva in 1983, when Third World theologians—after seven years' of dialogue among themselves—came together with progressive theologians from Europe and the USA in order to assess their mutual concerns and discuss the role of the Church in the liberation struggles of the poor, the issue of sexism came fully to the fore. The women theologians present realized that they were faced with an additional twofold struggle: they had to challenge both the sexism of male Third World theologians and the racism of white women from the First World. The women therefore founded their own Women's Commission of EATWOT (not a "Commission on Women" as some of the men had wished), and set plans in motion for their own national, regional, continental, and intercontinental consultations. It is planned that these are to be followed by a future conference where Third World women theologians will meet for dialogue with women theologians from the First World in Costa Rica, December 1994.

This is not the place for a detailed history of the many different conferences organized by women theologians from EATWOT in different countries and regions, but it is important to know that three continental conferences were held, one in Latin America (Buenos Aires/Argentina: October 30–November 3, 1985), one in Asia (Manila/Philippines: November 21–30,

1985), two in Africa (for Anglophone Africa at Port Harcourt/ Nigeria: August 19-23, 1986, and for Francophone Africa at Yaoundé/Cameroun: August 3-9, 1986). These were followed by an intercontinental conference for women theologians from all three continents, held at Oaxtepec/Mexico (December 1-6, 1986). The Final Statement of each conference and a selection of papers from each continent can be found in Virginia Fabella's and Mercy Amba Oduyoye's *With Passion and Compassion: Third World Women Doing Theology* (Orbis Books, 1988).[13] Papers from the Latin American conference have been edited separately by Elsa Tamez from Costa Rica under the title *Through Her Eyes: Women's Theology from Latin America* (Orbis Books, 1989), whereas papers from the Asian conference in Manila, together with papers from a later conference in Singapore in 1987, have been edited by Virginia Fabella and Sun Ai Lee Park and published under the title *We Dare to Dream: Doing Theology as Asian Women* (Hong Kong, 1989).[14] I will refer to these publications in the selection of texts later in this book.

There is more information available on Asian women's theology than on developments elsewhere. Much of this is a result of the journal *In God's Image (IGI)*, the only regularly published feminist theological journal in Asia, begun in December 1982. In addition to its many stimulating articles, it also contains much information about the different conferences of Third World women theologians. Founded and edited by Sun Ai Lee Park, a poet, ordained minister, and theologian from Korea who described herself as a "theologically trained housewife who refused to be wasted," *IGI* has been published from Singapore, Hong Kong, and now Seoul where Sun Ai Lee Park has also located the Asian Women's Resource Center for Culture and Theology. Her journal has been described as "a theological sanctuary where women who were theologically orientated could share their reflections on the spiritual dimensions of life without male censorship."[15]

Asian women are in the vanguard of feminist theological development in the Third World. Not only did Marianne Katoppo from Indonesia write the first "Asian Woman's Theology," as already mentioned, but many different associations of women theologians exist in the different countries of Asia.[16] Several Asian women have described the process of the emergence of Asian feminist theology and spirituality, first Sr. Mary John Mananzan from the Philippines in the book *Women and Religion* (1988),[17] then Elizabeth Tapia, also from the Philippines, in her Ph.D. on "The Contribution of Philippine Christian Women to Asian Women's Theology" (1989),[18] followed by the discussion in the doctoral work of the Korean woman theologian Chung Hyun Kyung, now published in book form as *Struggle to be the Sun Again: Introducing Asian Women's Theology* (1990).[19]

Chung's work has raised a great deal of interest, not least because she gave a highly controversial plenary address on "Come Holy Spirit—Renew the Whole Creation" at the 1991 WCC Assembly in Canberra.[20] In her book she clearly points out that three organizations helped to develop Asian Christian women's theology: the Women's Desk of the Christian Conference of Asia that developed from 1980 onwards and has been fully established since 1982;[21] the Women's Commission of EATWOT founded in 1983, and the journal *In God's Image*. This is a clear example of the structural and organizational links that helped to develop feminist theology in one part of the Third World. To experience something of the vitality, the struggle, the depth of suffering, and the strength of hope present in contemporary Asian women's theology, I can do no better than recommend Chung's book *Struggle to be the Sun Again*, and also the many articles in the journal *In God's Image*—although these may be more difficult to find.

Given the religious pluralism of Asia, where Christians represent only 3% of the overall population,[22] Asian women have also pioneered a consultation on interfaith dialogue with women of other faiths in Kuala Lumpur/Malaysia in 1989.[23] The experience of interfaith encounter and dialogue, and the need to respond to the spiritual riches of the indigenous traditions of different cultures, is something that several feminist theologians of the Third World are well aware of. It is a theme that finds increasing attention in their reflections.[24]

Feminist voices from the Third World do not only come from women in Asia, Africa, and Latin America, but also from women belonging to African-American, Hispanic/Latino and Asian-American minorities in the USA — as well as from women in South Africa[25] and Palestinian Christian women of the Intifada. This is clear evidence, if evidence is needed, that feminist theology is not simply a white, Western, middle-class phenomenon, as some of its critics would have it. The prophetic critique of feminist theology and its call for liberation can empower women everywhere. Christian women around the world are linked and connected with one another in a truly cross-cultural and global network.[26]

Black American Christian women have taken up the term "womanist," referring to a black feminist or feminist of color, to articulate their own experience and distinguish their theology from that of the majority of white Christian feminists in the USA. Womanist theology has been described by Delores S. Williams, one of its important representatives, as "a vision in its infancy,"[27] but black women theologians have already produced more writings than the women of other minorities. Spanish-speaking women in the USA, whose cultural and historical roots are in Cuba, Mexico, Puerto Rico, or Latin America, describe their theological work as Hispanic, Latino, or *mujerista* theology, born of feminism, Hispanic culture, and the struggle for liberation. Ada María Isasi-Díaz, co-author of the first book on Hispanic women's theology[28] and the main contact person for the newly founded Instituto de Teologia Hispana, the Hispanic Theology Institute at Drew University/New Jersey, has described *mujerista* theology as a communal theology done by groups of Hispanic women throughout the USA who experience themselves as living in exile, as a remnant which is not an integral part of American society, and whose mission it is to challenge the oppressive structures of society and non-liberative theologies.

Womanist and *mujerista* theologians are voices from the margin, and so are Asian American theologians who, for lack of a common language, have not been able to name themselves as a distinct and separate group who share yet other experiences of the struggle against exploitation and oppression. Since 1984 there has existed an Asian Women's Network on the East Coast of the USA and there is also the group of Asian American

Women in Ministry and Theology. Some of their members live permanently in the USA, while others move regularly between their Asian country of origin and the West. This is another example of the many crosscultural connections between feminist theology in the Third and First World.

Another such connection becomes apparent when one considers where Third World theology is published and who makes the voices of Third World women known. While feminist material is circulated in indigenous languages, as well as in English, in different countries of Asia, Africa, and Latin America, the widest distribution of works by Third World women theologians written in or translated into English occurs through the publishing houses of the USA, Britain, and also the WCC in Geneva. Particular mention must be made of the contribution of Orbis Books[29] from Maryknoll, New York, which has published some of the pioneering texts of feminist theology from the Third World. Some of the important material published by the WCC has appeared in their challenging collection "The Risk Book Series," a title that indicates the pioneering and innovative nature of women's theological work. Like other theologies on the margin, it breaks through traditional boundaries and explores new ways of being as self, in society, community, and Church. This quality of risk, adventure, and exploration is expressed with an authentic voice in the texts selected for this Reader, drawn from such a variety and wealth of materials that it is impossible to be comprehensive. Moreover, this quality is also evident when examining some of the major themes that thread like a common pattern through Third World feminist theologies in spite of all their differences.

### Some common themes of feminist theology from the Third World

Women's theology from the Third World, like all feminist theology, puts great emphasis on *doing* theology. It is theology as an activity, as an ongoing process rooted in praxis, interdependent with and compassionately committed to life, justice, and freedom from oppression. It is not theology as a reified, academic subject with watertight categories, clear boundaries, and sharp intellectual definitions totally separate from people's experience. Of course it includes a tremendous intellectual effort, much powerful and creative thinking, but this is part of, and arises from, the ongoing process that is life as lived, experienced, struggled through, wrestled with, and celebrated.

This means that there are no sharp boundaries between women's voices coming out of academic institutions and other women's voices speaking out in the community at large. There is a fluidity and continuity between the stories and reflections of all these women, a common participation in one another's experiences. This is overwhelmingly evident when one reads the articles found in the journal *In God's Image* from Asia, or the collections of Latin American and African women's voices, or some of the reflections by womanist and *mujerista* theologians. The diversity of these voices and of their location in quite different contexts, as well as the commonality of certain patterns of experience from which these different women speak, is also clearly visible in the texts selected for this Reader.

There would be no sharing of the process of theologizing if there were not first of all a sharing of the depth of *oppression*, *suffering*, and *struggle*, however different the situations are in which these occur. The concreteness of this struggle is vividly felt when one reads biblical reflections, poems, prayers, homilies, and theological essays by women from Africa, Asia, Latin America, and from the many minority women around the world—whether it is about the plight of the poor, rural women, women laborers, oppressive customs and marriage structures, sexual exploitation or genital mutilation, prostitution or sex tourism in Asia, or the oppressively hierarchical structures of the churches and their traditional ideas about women's confined roles. But besides the sharing of oppresssion, suffering, and struggle, there is also a sharing of *hope*, of a new, empowering vision born out of the sense of *solidarity* among women. This solidarity finds strong expression in Third World feminist theology as solidarity with poor women, rural women, black women, all minority women, and women of color, and for some there is also the solidarity between Third World and First World women, and between women of different faiths.[30]

17

## Introduction

The new consciousness of women, the ability to articulate their pain, analyze their situation, express their protest, and seek radical change has given them the possibility of envisioning different ways of being for their communities and for themselves. Women have birthed *a new vision* nurturing hope, strength, and extraordinary courage. This inspiring vision is an imaginative leap forward into alternative possibilities and forms of existence born out of the audacity and determination to dream. The *metaphor of dreaming*, not in the sense of idle unreality but as a step forward into new realms of existence, is found more than once in the writings of women from the Third World. "We dare to dream," as one book title says, and yet women "cannot dream alone," as is expressed by that of another. Women have to be connected with one another in a new network across the world, a strong web of mutual support that may then enable them to shape a new community for women, men, and children, and for the Christian churches.

The theme of *church-as-community* is very strong among women from the Third World, much more so than one finds among feminist theologians in the First World, for the simple reason that the church communities are often the first context in which women become enabled and encouraged to speak. One might also say that, in spite of all their oppressive constraints, church communities can become living laboratories where the fire for women's transformation and new dreaming is first lit. The community theme is also so central because of the different social and cultural traditions of Third World women's experience, their sense of and responsibility for extended kin, their respect for and veneration of ancestors, their palpable sense of being part of a much larger community, and that includes a closeness with and reverence for all forms of life on earth.

Yet another important theme often expressed by Third World women is that of a new sense of *empowerment*. This implies a new understanding of power where power is not practiced in a dominant, hierarchical mode as "power over." Such power is finite and cannot be shared; only some people can have it, while others remain without it. But power understood as "enabling power," as empowerment, can be shared, and it can grow and increase so that all who participate in it are strengthened and affirmed without excluding or diminishing anyone. Third World women have become empowered to speak to one another, to their communities, and to us; they are responding to the challenge of their own situation and are taking on the responsibility and awesome task of bringing about much-needed change by initiating it themselves. As Sr. Mary John Mananzan has said, women's struggle gives concreteness to their new visions and in turn "it is the vision that gives direction to women's struggles."[31]

The theme of *liberation* is more concrete and vivid in Third World feminist theology than in that of the Western world, although there are continuities and connections here too. The theologies of Third World women also share many features with other liberation and Third World theologies,[32] where religion is a source of empowerment and social change,[33] gives a voice to the voiceless, and helps to develop a new sense of responsibility, solidarity, and community. This greater sense of community among Third World women theologians is also expressed through newly created organizational structures of cooperation and collaboration in conferences and publications, made possible through the EATWOT Women's Commission and other agencies. Through this network, Third World feminist theologians sometimes speak with a better coordinated voice than Western feminists, who frequently, though not always, tend to work in a more individualistic way.

When the EATWOT Women's Commission was founded in 1983, it was suggested that all theologically trained women in Asia, Africa, and Latin America should concentrate their work in the following areas:

(1) the analysis of women's oppression in society and Church;
(2) the social analysis of each respective country, involving economic, political, and socioreligious factors;
(3) theological reflection bearing first on a hermeneutical analysis of the Bible, complemented by other sources such as myths, folklore, legends, and indigenous religions, and then followed by further reflections on theological themes and their implications for women. The suggested themes were God-talk, Christology, Mariology, pneumatology, and emerging forms of spirituality.

## Introduction

Feminist theologians from the Third World have written on all these themes, and on others too. Given the need for selection and the importance of the topics listed in the three areas, I have chosen to arrange the many different voices from Christian women around the world into five sections: Part One: Doing Theology from Third World Women's Perspective; Part Two: Women's Oppression and Cries of Pain; Part Three: The Bible as a Source of Empowerment for Women; Part Four: Challenging Traditional Theological Thinking; Part Five: A Newly Emerging Spirituality. It is here perhaps, in the newly emerging forms of spirituality, that the explorations into interfaith dialogue and the discovery of the rich spiritual resources of indigenous cultures will eventually be judged to be most significant. The suggested areas of work that women theologians from the Third World have now pursued for at least ten years also fall into the larger context raised at earlier EATWOT conferences, that is to say, the context of the class struggle focused on by Latin Americans, the context of indigenization for Africans, and that of religious pluralism and interfaith dialogue for Asians.

Feminist theology from the Third World is a theology of struggle and hope. It is marked by anguish and a sense of pain, but also by a freshness and vibrant vitality fed by the quest and determination to seek the full humanity of women—and ultimately that of all people: women, men, and children. It is a listening theology attentive to women's suffering and oppression, but, as Chung Hyun Kyung has said, it is above all a theology that is woman-affirming, life-affirming, and cosmos-affirming.

Feminist theology from the Third World is so rich and diverse that it consists of a wide range of different perspectives and voices. Space does not allow for more than a small selection of this diversity in this Reader. Material for further reading is listed in the substantial bibliography at the end of the volume.

The different women's voices from the Third World selected for this Reader express a new vision and the resolute will to create a new society and Church, more just and more humane to women and to all who are poor, suffering, and exploited. I hope these voices will speak to you as stirringly and strongly as they did to me.

## PART ONE

# Doing Theology from Third World Women's Perspective

---

□ *The introduction has outlined the crosscultural context and historical development of feminist theology in the Third World. This theology has emerged during the last fifteen years and it shares many features with liberation theologies from the Third World. The emphasis is very much on doing theology from within the context of women's experience and of their struggle for liberation. It is a theology that involves much anguish and demands a high cost of commitment to personal and social transformation. Many women find it difficult to articulate their struggle and write about it, but they are helped by new networks and by new organizational structures created by Christian women around the world. These empower other women to come forward and participate in the task of collaboration, of transformative social praxis, and of critical reflection.*

*There is now so much material available in print in the form of books, conference reports, articles, and whole journals that it is impossible to provide a comprehensive survey of all the theological discussions among women in different parts of the Third World. It is not even possible to include a separate voice from each of the major parts of the Third World on each theme in this Reader. I had to be highly selective in the choice of contributions, for otherwise there would have been too much material for one volume. I have tried to include as many different voices as possible in order to convey a sense of the urgency, passionate commitment, vitality, and the dynamic spirit that empowers Christian women to speak out and theologize from the depths of their own experience. However, for each woman speaking on one particular topic several others could have been* quoted, speaking with equal vigor and conviction on some of the central issues of feminist theology.

The first two chapters give readers an insight into how the process of theologizing among Third World women began and was subsequently strengthened through a series of consultations among women theologians.

❖   ❖   ❖

*In chapter 1, the African woman theologian Mercy Amba Oduyoye from Ghana discusses how women's theological reflection irrupted as a new event within the larger context of Third World theology, whose own irruption into the dominant theology of the First World became manifest at the 1981 EATWOT conference in New Delhi.\* Mercy Amba Oduyoye has extensive ecumenical experience and is currently Deputy General Secretary of the World Council of Churches as well as a Methodist lay preacher.*

# 1  MERCY AMBA ODUYOYE

# Reflections from a Third World Woman's Perspective: Women's Experience and Liberation Theologies

## A tale of two halves

Once there lived on earth Half and Half, each of them only half a human being. They spent all their time quarreling and fighting, disturbing the rest of the village and trampling upon the crops. Every time a fight began cries went up to Ananse Kokroko: *Fa ne Fa reko o!*[1] "They are at it again, Half and Half are fighting." So one day ·God came down, brought Half and Half together, and a whole human being appeared.

This fable, rich with the imagery of the desirability of unity and peace, is my image of what is happening to male/female relationships in our world. The question is, "What kind of unity and peace, and at what expense?" Today we begin to be aware of concepts such as unity in diversity, difference in sameness

---

\* *See Virginia Fabella and Sergio Torres, eds.,* Irruption of the Third World: Challenge to Theology, *Maryknoll, NY: Orbis Books, 1983. Mercy Amba Oduyoye's essay is found on pp. 246-55. For other contributions by Mercy Amba Oduyoye, see chapters 15 and 36 of this* Reader.

and sameness in difference, unity within difference, and more will come, as we search for language with which to express this experience.

But not all are prepared to see difference within unity. I was talking with a German woman recently on the use of the term "Third World," which she does not like and which some Third World persons too have declared anathema. She told me about a poster used by Bread for the World; it states that we have only "one world." We do have one *earth*, granted, but it is also true to say that we live in *different* worlds. The world of the rural woman in Ghana has little in common with that of the rural woman in Germany, nor does the world of the white woman in South Africa bear comparison with that of her black compatriot.

In our desperate attempts at "being one" and being "at peace," we forget how God put an end to the ideology of the Tower of Babel, replacing it later with the more meaningful and community-building diversity of Pentecost—life in the Spirit of God as opposed to the mentality of "let us . . . make a name for ourselves" (Gen. 11.3–4) and build structures that will never be changed. To strive for unity in diversity is a task we cannot evade—and there are no shortcuts.

In EATWOT our recognition of this fact prevents us from embarking on the construction of a single Third World theology. In spite of our common experience of exploitation and oppression, we have recognized that sources and manifestations vary, and so does experience. Yet we are united in our reading of biblical motifs and imagery—the Exodus, the Magnificat, the proclamation from Isaiah that Jesus read at Nazareth. Women too have been reading the Bible and cannot come to these experiences except through their own experience. Hence the "irruption" at New Delhi, on which I have been asked to reflect.

### The irruption within the irruption

The person who sleeps by the fire knows best how intensely it burns, so runs an Asante proverb. The irruption of women in Church and society is an integral part of the voice of the earth's voiceless majority that is beginning to penetrate the atmosphere and disturb the peace of the principalities and powers that hold the structures of our so-called one world in their hands.

It sounded like a joke to some when Marianne Katoppo of Indonesia, author of *Compassionate and Free*,[2] called the attention of the session to the necessity to watch our language about God and before God. It was not intended as comic relief; it was the irruption within the irruption, trumpeting the existence of some other hurts, spotlighting women's marginalization from the theological enterprise and indeed from decisionmaking in the churches.

EATWOT had come face to face with the fact that the community of women and men, even in the Church and among "liberation theologians," is not as liberating as it could be. That "irruption" could only have come from a woman. But why at New Delhi and not before? The answer is simple; the process of involving women in meaningful roles in EATWOT did not begin at the initial stages. So until Virginia Fabella undertook the assignment of program coordinator, EATWOT was virtually a male enterprise.

It was Virginia Fabella in her role as coordinator who explained EATWOT to me and urged me to get involved in the enterprise. Talking to me of the concerns of the association she repeated several times, "it is our responsibility to get more women involved." Whether or not this was part of her official mandate as coordinator, she did get more women and encouraged their contribution with "don't disappoint the women." My experience is that it has always taken women to ensure the representation and voice of women, at least in the Church and other related bodies. Of course not every woman in EATWOT was called in by a woman.

The theory of our unity and equality in Christ often pales in the structures we create, thus the necessity for more visibility demanded by and for women. It is also a fact that even when "a place" has been found for the contribution of a woman, it is often on women, or so-called women's issues: home and family, children and education. The concerns and experience of women as women are yet another *locus* for liberation theology. The presence and contribution of women as women have not been fully appreciated or respected. This was the problem in Delhi. The outburst came not because women were being treated as mere spectators at the meeting, but because the language of the meeting ignored our presence and therefore alienated some of the women present. But language was not the only issue; it was an index of other deep-seated criteria for assigning roles. Even the periods of relaxation were painful at least to me, as I listened to African misogynist fables being enjoyed by all and sundry.

To some the "outburst" was uncalled for. After all, from Dar es Salaam to Delhi women have not been absent from EATWOT meetings, and never have they been prevented from contributing. Conceived at Louvain, it seems to have had an all-male genesis and could have become an all-male enterprise but for the presence of Sister Virginia Fabella, who coordinated the study process through the journey from Dar es Salaam to Delhi.

The general pattern, however, has given the impression that women do not form a legitimate part of the human community but are beings who are to be benevolently listened to and then passed over. Occasionally a woman will beat men at their own games and have to be admitted to contribute to central issues. It happens in politics and theology. Women are supposed to feel flattered when it is said of them "she is as good as a man," "she can hold her own against any man." These are simply indications of the male-oriented nature of our common consciousness.

It was such language that sparked off the feminism discussion at Delhi. Yet more glaring perhaps was the fact that none of the formal papers was assigned to a woman. Presumably we were dealing with more "central issues," which, until Delhi, did not specifically include sexism and therefore no "competent" woman could be discovered.

That session became for me one more example of the manifestation of the entrenched mind-set of Christians, both women and men, which hinders listening to a rereading of the Bible especially by a woman. Just point out that in none of the Gospel narratives was "the woman who was a sinner" identified as a prostitute, or as Mary of Magdala, and you might have a minirevolt on your hands. Women's sinfulness has to do with their sexuality. Thus gender has become one of the challenges to our attempts at building a community in which a person can function as a human being, helped rather than hampered by his or her sex.

Among theologians working for the liberation of theology so that it may serve God's liberating work among "the poor of the land," I was shocked to discover that some saw the "irruption" of women upon the Christian theological scene and their call for a clean-up of the language of theology and its effects on church practices, especially in liturgy, as one big joke. Part of the agenda of New Delhi was to assess EATWOT's contribution to the renewal of theology in the Third World and to plan for the future. Will sexism-in-community become an issue for Third World theology?

There have been several international meetings at which Third World representatives have said that antisexism is not their priority. At times they have even said it is not an issue in their world, where men and women *know their place* and *play their role* ungrudgingly and no one feels suffocated by society's definition of femininity and masculinity. Issues of sexism are supposed to belong to a minority of disgruntled, leisure-saturated, middle-class women of the capitalist West. The few Third World women who speak that language are just allowing themselves to be coopted. The fact is that sexism is part of the intricate web of oppression in which most of us live, and that having attuned ourselves to it does not make it any less a factor of oppression. Most Third World women, being literally close to the earth and to the maintenance of their race against classist and racist aggression, have opted to find complete fulfillment in this sacred duty and why not? But that does not mean an approval of sexism. Brigalia Bam puts the choice this way:

> To understand that while you are preoccupied with, say, equality or abortion rights, your sister is anxiously awaiting her husband's release from South African police detention is consciously to accept responsibility for *her* freedom in her terms. What is important for you may be merely incidental for her by comparison with the suffering she experiences because of the color of her skin. . . . I am not saying that the

issues which affect us as middle-class women are unimportant, but I am saying that, if we have platforms, we must also speak on behalf of others who have no platform. . . . *We simply have no place for our freedom if there are still black women working like slaves under the impossible conditions of racial injustices.*[3]

Third World theologians, women and men, occupied with the study and exposure of sexism as a factor of oppression, and those attempting to discover community-building concepts from Christianity and other religions, should take their full place in EATWOT. The struggle for a wholesome and life-expanding community of women and men in Church and society is bound to be enhanced by viewing feminism in theology as a theology of relationships, and a Third World perspective on it will be a contribution to the global effort. Feminism is anything but the imperialist ploy some would like us to take it for. There may be a lot of red herrings to come, but feminism is certainly not one of them. It is a fact of experience, not a thesis.

The experiences that have informed the doing of theology in the context of EATWOT have been mainly socioeconomic and political and have led largely to the analysis of the roots of classism and racism. The religio-cultural concerns of Africa and Asia and of the indigenous peoples of the Americas have been marginal. This I believe has been one of the reasons why sexism, often anchored on religio-cultural perceptions, had not surfaced before. It will be interesting to see how the recognition of "anthropological poverty" as a negative factor in the struggle for full humanity will deal with the sexist elements in African culture. The same applies to our commitment to study seriously the role of other religions in this quest, bearing in mind that the same religion can be used to alienate as well as to liberate. What has religion done with the full humanity of women?

EATWOT has a structure and an atmosphere suited to liberation discussions, for within the membership and among the participants at its conferences are women and men who have personal experiences of various types of oppression and who are therefore equipped to see the interrelatedness of the struggle for liberation. To deal with "women's issues" in isolation and, even worse, to assign only women to do that job will be unrealistic. Overcoming sexism in theory and practice will demand the joint search of women and men, not only in a conference taking up that challenge but wherever sexism appears in other areas of emphasis. It is not necessary that we should all speak with one voice on the preoccupations of feminist theologians or any other concerns, but as seekers after the truth we are duty-bound to examine them. Conflicting perceptions will be the seeds out of which a clear vision of the new humanity will emerge.

EATWOT claims to work in the context of the challenges of reality to theology. As such, the feminist claim that "the male-dominated patterns of culture and social organization" oppress women in society and manifest themselves in the life and theology of the Church has to be examined. This is not simply a challenge to the dominant theology of the capitalist West. It is a challenge to the maleness of Christian theology worldwide, together with the patriarchal presuppositions that govern all our relationships, as well as the traditional situation in which men (male human beings) reflected upon the whole of life on behalf of the whole community of women and men, young and old.

Because EATWOT has recognized that it is premature to consider the emergence of a synthesis called Third World theology, in spite of the various common oppressions and convergences of understanding, there is still room for further, in-depth probes to be undertaken. The events and deliberations of Delhi confirm this conclusion, for there it became clear that we cannot assume that African men and African women will say the same things about African reality. But also just as African men do not speak with one voice on Africa, so African women should not be expected to speak with one voice. The diversity we are dealing with ought to be fully recognized and as many experiences as possible incorporated into EATWOT, provided they are anti-domination and foster full participation and mutual critical relationships and cooperation—the things that unite us in EATWOT. In this way the experience of "women and other outsiders to traditional theological discussions may become occasions for discovering new dimensions of unity."[4] EATWOT is clearly a newcomer as far as sexism is concerned.

## The story of a desk

One of the several roads along which the concern for unity of the Church has led the World Council of Churches (WCC) is the establishment of "a desk" called the "Cooperation of Men and Women in Church and Society." To trace this journey is to understand better the struggles of the WCC to take women seriously in its structures and in those of the member churches. It is also to get a valuable insight into how crucial the factor of sexism is in our search for the unity and renewal of Church and the human community at large.

The factor of sexism appears right from the beginning and is a study of how women have always had to announce themselves before men would recognize their presence. It was the efforts of women that led to the French Reformed Church's asking that the subject of women in the Church be put on the agenda for the WCC Amsterdam assembly.[5] Here also began the strategy of women's preassembly consultations, for it became clear that women needed them in order to contribute effectively to the concerns of the whole council.

The founding assembly of the WCC at Amsterdam in 1948 had this to say: "The church as the Body of Christ consists of men and women created as responsible persons to glorify God and do his will." But the same assembly recognized that "this truth, accepted in theory, is too often ignored in practice." It appears that once more it would have been ignored by the founding fathers of the WCC if church women and the YWCA had not organized to ensure that the role of women in the church be explicitly taken up by the nascent council. It was both realistic and prophetic that the concerned women of the time saw the issue as that of "women in relationship with men" and placed it squarely on the table of the WCC rather than on that of the YWCA. It is a community issue.

This was also highlighted by the late D. T. Niles, a well-known figure in the ecumenical movement, who by comparing men/women relationships in Sri Lanka and northern India at a meeting in 1953 led the participants to the realization that in studying the contribution of women one is simply aiming at redressing a balance. Nor was it to "suggest the promotion of noncommunicating parallel groups acting autonomously within the larger church."[6] The result was that when eventually "a desk" was created it was to deal with "the cooperation of men and women in church and society." It was through the efforts of this "desk" that the WCC is now studying "The Community of Women and Men in the Church," which had its origin in the West Berlin 1974 consultation on "Sexism in the 1970s" — organized by the "desk." The findings of this study will be another source for further research and even more important for strategies for implementation of our longing for community.

The World YWCA and the World Student Christian Federation have had to face the theory and practice of how the common humanity of women and men should govern our interaction in human community. Issues that have surfaced through the efforts of these ecumenical bodies have been political, economic, sociopolitical, and legislative, as well as psychological, cultural, and theological. Space limitations prevent the giving of samples from all fields, but, inasmuch as EATWOT has listed as one of its program goals to support women's quest for equality "in and through theology," here are a few theological issues chosen at random from various stages of the search:

(1) Examination of the language, imagery, and symbols of Scripture, worship and theology in reference to God.

(2) The representation of Christ in the ordained ministry in relation to the ordination of women.

(3) Christian *diaconia* and ordination to sacramental ministry.

(4) Evidence in Scripture and tradition with regard to the participation of women and men in the Church.

(5) The importance of cultural traditions in the shaping of community in the Church. Mariology and the Magnificat.

(6) The authority of Scripture.

(7) Theological anthropology: toward a theology of human wholeness.

31

The global perspectives of these issues should not hide the concerns of specific situations, which one finds in the documents available in the WCC, especially as illustrated by the statement from Third World participants at Sheffield, which provoked a very intense dialogue within that consultation.[7]

## Unpicking the web of oppression

Does the feminist movement have any meaning in Africa? The accepted position is that it does not. This was the general tone of the religious studies conference that took place at the University of Ibadan in 1974. The theme was "Women from the Perspective of Religion." A paper, "Continuity and Change in the Status of Women," given by Folanke Solanke, a Nigerian legal luminary, ended with: "Ladies and gentlemen, there is no need for confrontation." There was loud and sustained applause. She had hit at the reason for wanting to isolate Africa from the sexism debate, and the opinion columns of Nigerian dailies in the International Women's Year confirm this.[8]

From April 26 to 30, 1976, at the Conference Centre of the University of Ibadan, a national conference was held. The theme was "Nigerian Women and Development in Relation to Changing Family Structure." Professor Ogunseye, in her keynote address, expressed the same sentiment: "I hope the popular belief that there is a conflict between the sexes will not be allowed to surface and mar the discussions." But should we not rather bring popular belief to the surface in order that we may examine it critically?

There is yet another way of avoiding this so-called conflict. B. Onimode, an economist, in his paper "Capitalist Exploitation, Women and National Development," quotes Samora Machel as pointing out that "the antagonistic contradiction is not between women and men, but between women and the social order." Therefore, Onimode continues, "men and women should unite to fight the exploitative society they have together created." This would be my own focus, except that it leaves the women who believe that "the hand that rocks the cradle rules the world" to rest content, for if this saying holds good, then women have exactly the world they want. Here I part company with some of my sisters. I did a study of Akan proverbs in which I attempted to demonstrate that women fall victim to linguistic imagery that socializes them to accept *their place* in society and to view with caution any call for more space.

In the process of the noble, and I believe necessary, battle to maintain the institution of the family, women's personal development is curbed because "their domestic labors are *required* by the male folk to make their own participation and progress in the modern labor force possible and comparatively easy." Dr. Aboyade, from whose contribution to the conference I have just quoted, also points out that an unmarried woman is considered a social failure. Should we not reexamine our assumptions about marriage and family life?

There are therefore voices from Africa that would suggest that we too have a problem, and not one that was created only by the arrival of Islam and Christianity, but is an integral part of our African worldviews. F. Solanke, quoted above, was present at the conference and in her paper "Legal Rights of Nigerian Women in Decision-Making" made the following recommendation: "We should call for more research . . . and encourage the Obas [kings] and the aged men and women to speak candidly on these matters in order to have a clearer picture of the traditional role of Nigerian women."[9]

A similar situation exists in Asia, as was stated in a press release issued by a consultation held in Bangalore in August 1978: that "cultural and traditional structures along with misinterpretation of Scripture have kept women in subordinate roles both in the church and in society was the consensus opinion expressed by all papers that were read."

By now it ought to be quite clear that I welcome "the irruption" and the move of EATWOT to be involved in these struggles. Those who will examine our language, proverbs, myths, and fables cannot exalt our African culture into one that backs up the woman who seeks a fuller participation in her community, or for that matter the man who finds so-called feminine roles fulfilling. But this may be discovered to apply in various degrees to the cultures represented in the Third World. The Chinese ideograms translated below illustrate the power of language and symbolism over our lives:

33

(1) Three women together means noisiness, badness.

(2) Woman under a roof means peace.

(3) Woman combined with littleness means exquisite, whereas a young woman and a man means wickedness because *she* seduces the man.[10]

The word "feminism," which jars on the ears of so many, and the expression "feminist theology," which sounds like some kind of heresy, have been occasioned by women's experience of how Christian anthropology and upbringing have required them to be content with being subsumed. Those who speak out do so from a Jeremian cloud, which threatens to consume them. It becomes for them the sin of omission. No, persons labeled feminists, rather than being shunned or feared, are to be welcomed as persons who seek to define more realistically what it means to be human. This has to be a common search, of women and men, of the northern and southern hemispheres; all have to bear their part of this responsibility.

The way forward is a "new community of men and women," not reversal; participation, not takeover or handover. Feminism in theology springs from a conviction that a theology of relationships might contribute to bring us closer to human life as God desires it. In the same way as most accepted traditional Western theological categories went without question until they were examined in the light of the peculiar contexts of the Third World, so Christian women have begun to see that from their experience they cannot confess the same sins or affirm the same reading of the Christian faith. Is this not what a liberating theology is about, a hermeneutic that enables us to get the most out of the confrontation of texts and contexts as well as their interaction?

To benefit fully from this hermeneutical figure of eight requires that women's experience, hitherto marginalized, should become a part of the "community of interpretation,"[11] not only of Scripture but of the whole Christian tradition. We pray fervently for the Holy Spirit to lead us to the truth and we thank God for each step taken toward God's will for our human community.

□ *Third World women theologians became more visible when they grouped themselves together in 1983 as a separate Women's Commission of EATWOT. During the following years they organized regional and national consultations, followed in 1985 by continental conferences held in Latin America, Asia, and Africa (described in more detail in the introduction to this Reader). An important milestone was the intercontinental Women's Conference held in Oaxtepec, Mexico, in December 1986. Its final document sets out the process and contents of Third World women's theology and concludes with recommendations for further work. It also expresses how women are committed to a ministry of theology that they undertake with both passion and compassion. The full text of the final document is reproduced in chapter 2.* *

# 2 MEXICO CONFERENCE

# Final Document on Doing Theology from Third World Women's Perspective

An intercontinental conference of women theologians from the Third World was held in Oaxtepec, Mexico, December 1-6, 1986. The theme of the conference was "Doing Theology from Third World Women's Perspective." The conference was sponsored by the Ecumenical Association of Third World Theologians (EATWOT) as part of its commitment to total liberation and the achievement of full humanity for all, women and men alike.

* *Together with the conference declarations of the earlier continental conferences held in Africa, Asia, and Latin America, this final document is printed in Virginia Fabella and Mercy Amba Oduyoye, eds.,* With Passion and Compassion: Third World Women Doing Theology, *Maryknoll, NY: Orbis Books, 1988, pp. 184–90.*

Planned to operate in three stages, the women's project sought:

(1) To broaden our understanding of women's situation in our respective socioeconomic, political, and religio-cultural realities.

(2) To discover the vital aspects of women's experience of God in emerging spiritualities.

(3) To reread the Bible from Third World women's perspective in the light of total liberation.

(4) To articulate faith reflections on women's realities, struggles, and spirituality.

(5) To deepen our commitment and solidarity to work toward full humanity for all.

The first two phases of the study took place on the national and continental levels. The present meeting provided a forum of exchange among the women on their findings of the study in their respective continents. Twenty-six delegates from seventeen countries of Africa, Asia, and Latin America took part in the conference.

Mexico—where an affluent minority and a poor majority exist side by side, where signs of its colonial past and neocolonial present were everywhere evident, where "machismo" is still a given—offered a suitable venue for our theological reflections from the perspective of Third World women.

In their address of welcome, the Latin American women pointed out that even though the nameless concubine of the Levite in Judges 19 did not speak out against the oppression meted out to her, her cut-up body did. Everyone who saw the outcome of this atrocity was enjoined "to reflect, take counsel and speak." So Israel stood together united to act for justice. This story moves us to ponder the oppression of women, to discuss it, and then give our verdict, acting as Deborah, the judge, would have done, confident that today is the Day of Yahweh (Judg. 4).

## Process

One of the notable features of this meeting was the atmosphere of serious study, sisterhood, and friendliness that prevailed throughout. Worship times saw all the delegates praying together, in the typical styles of each continent, to the God of all nations. The themes (reality of oppression and struggle of women; vital aspects of women's experience of God in emerging spiritualities; women and the Church; women and the Bible; women and Christology) were presented by skilled panelists from each of the three continents. The open forum that followed each panel presentation gave the participants a chance to question, clarify, or comment on the issues raised.

Variations in the dynamics of the meeting included role-playing, audio-visual presentations, a fishbowl session, small-group discussions, and mural painting by all. Informal exchanges outside the formal sessions strengthened the spirit of friendship and solidarity.

## Contents

The panel on each theme brought out some rich commonalities and differences:

(1) In all three continents, the oppression of women is affirmed as a hard and abiding reality of life, though this varies in form and degree from place to place. Women have an irreplaceable role in society, yet our contribution is not acknowledged, nor are we accorded equal rights with our male counterparts. This oppression is felt in all sectors of life: economic, social, political, cultural, racial, sexual, religious, and even within the family itself. Having become conscious of our human rights and of the injustices perpetrated against us in all these sectors, as women we are teaming up and organizing various liberating movements and projects to help ourselves.

Some of these movements are motivated by Christian faith; we are aware that our liberation is part and parcel of the liberation of all the poor and oppressed as promised by the gospel. Our efforts are rooted in Scriptures. Being created in God's image demands a total rupture with the prevailing patriarchal system in order to build an egalitarian society.

This liberating process happens differently in the three continents. In Latin America, women organize themselves around survival strategies. In Africa, the rebirth of women takes place in their struggle to overthrow the oppressive elements in traditional African cultures and religions and the evils of colonialism. In Asia, the struggle is centred in rediscovering the pride of being woman, in building womanhood and humane communities, and in fighting against political, economic, and sexual injustices.

Nevertheless, we have perceived a common perspective in the three continents. The women's struggle is deeply connected with the efforts of all the poor and the oppressed who are struggling for their liberation in all aspects of life.

(2) Among the efforts being made toward liberation from oppression, theologizing emerges as a specific manner in which women struggle for their right to life. Our theologizing arises from our experience of being discriminated against as women and people of the Third World. The emerging spiritualities we perceive in the three continents show that spiritual experience rooted in action for justice constitutes an integral part of our theology. As women we articulate our theology in prayer and worship, in our relationship with our neighbor in whom God lives, and in our ongoing struggle as one with the poor and the oppressed.

Spiritual experience for women of the Third World thus means being in communion with all those who fight for life. This is our motivation for doing theology, which is done with the body, the heart, the mind, the total self—all penetrated by the Holy Spirit. Compassion and solidarity are main elements of this spirituality and this theology, and this is expressed in action: organized, patient, and loving action. The divergences in action are due to religious and cultural differences among the continents, to the diversities within the various regions in each continent, and to the varied ways the different churches assimilate these new experiences.

(3) The Bible plays a vital role in the lives of women and in our struggle for liberation, because the Bible itself is a book about life and liberation. This liberation is rooted in God's action in history, particularly in the Christ-event. The Gospels restore to women our human dignity as persons loved and

cherished by God. New methods of reading the Bible are emerging in the three continents. In Latin America, the poor have rediscovered the Bible and, in it, the liberating God, and this has allowed women, who are part of the poor and oppressed, to capture the spirit of the text while distancing themselves from the letter. In Asia, where Christians are a minority, the Bible is read in the context of interfaith dialogue as well as in the context of concrete life struggles. In Africa, there is some evidence of openness to new ways of reading the Bible. The fact that there are now some women biblically trained gives us hope that the Bible will be read and interpreted from the perspective of women, especially since the situation of African women has elements similar to that of women in the Old Testament.

In reading the Bible, we women face the constant challenge of interpreting texts that are against us. There is great commonality in considering these texts in their cultural contexts and epochs, not as normative, but as peripheral and not touching the heart of the gospel. The essentially patriarchal nature of the Bible and the interpretations that reinforce the oppressive elements should be acknowledged and exposed.

We participants felt that instead of rejecting the Bible wholesale, as some women do, we should "mine" deeper into it, rejecting all the patriarchal crusts that have obstructed its true meaning over the centuries, and highlighting those neglected elements that portray women as individuals in their own right as well as God's co-workers and agents of life. It was considered imperative to highlight Jesus' relationship with women and his countercultural stand with respect to them. Emphasis should also be laid on God as lover and giver of life, as well as liberator of all the oppressed. The Bible is normative and authoritative insofar as it promotes fullness of life for each person (John 10.10).

(4) In all three continents, women constitute a vital and dynamic force within the Church. Our strong faith and numerous services of love keep the Church alive, especially among the poor and the marginalized. Yet though we constitute a strong labor force within the heavily institutionalized Church, we are powerless and voiceless, and in most churches are excluded from leadership roles and ordained ministries. This deplorable condition urgently calls for sustained efforts to

discover new ways of being Church, of being in the world as the visible presence of God's reign, and of the new creation.

As the New Testament *ecclesia* started with women who were active participants in all areas of its life and mission, we, as women of the Third World, are rediscovering our distinctive role and place in the renewed Church today. Our faith in the power of the cross and the resurrection empowers us to live out the vision of God's new creation, where no one is subordinated or enslaved, but where free people take part in God's liberating project to build a true community and a new society. In Latin America and in parts of Africa, a hopeful sign is the increasing leadership roles played by women in basic ecclesial communities. In all Third World continents, the presence of women who stand for justice in all its forms is both challenging and conflictive. But this is the way in which the Church will be able to rediscover its true identity.

(5) Christology has appeared to be central to women's theology. In the person and praxis of Jesus Christ, women of the three continents find the grounds of our liberation from all discrimination: sexual, racial, social, economic, political, and religious. By reflecting on the incarnation, that is, the life, death, and resurrection of Jesus, we have come to realize the need to contextualize our Christology in the oppressed and painful realities of our continents. This means that Christology is integrally linked with action on behalf of social justice and the defense of each person's right to life and to a more humane life. Hence in Africa, Christology has to do with apartheid, racial discrimination, militarism, deficiency syndromes that come in foreign-aid packages, and genocide perpetrated through family-planning programs. In Asia, with the massive poverty, sexual exploitation, and racial, ethnic, caste, and religious discrimination, Christology incorporates the efforts to draw out the humanizing elements in the other religions. In Latin America, where poverty and oppression often give rise to a tendency to use religion to reinforce a passive and fatalistic attitude to life, Christology is necessarily connected with the preferential option for the poor. In short, to Christologize means to be committed to the struggle for a new society.

We remark also that many Christians in our continents are

seeking to see in Jesus' suffering, passion, death, and resurrection a meaning for their own suffering. This explains the great devotion our people have to the mysteries of the passion and the cross. Nevertheless, we have a mission to announce that Christ brought a new life for humanity and that this was the whole point of his suffering. Suffering that is inflicted by the oppressor and is passively accepted does not lead to life; it is destructive and demonic. But suffering that is part of the struggle for the sake of God's reign or that results from the uncontrollable and mysterious conditions of humankind is redeeming and is rooted in the Paschal Mystery, evocative of the rhythm of pregnancy, delivery, and birth. This kind of suffering is familiar to women of all times, who participate in the pains of birth and the joys of the new creation.

(6) The passionate and compassionate way in which women do theology is a rich contribution to theological science. The key to this theological process is the word "life." We perceive that in the three continents women are deeply covenanted with life, giving life, and protecting life. The woman in our streets always appears surrounded and weighed down with children: children in her body, in her arms, on her back. Thus, even physically, she extends and reaches out to other lives, other human beings born from her body, sustaining their lives. In doing theology, we in the Third World thus find ourselves committed and faithful to all the vital elements that compose human life. Thus without losing its scientific seriousness, which includes analyzing the basic causes of women's multiple oppression, our theologizing is deeply rooted in experience, in affection, in life. We as women feel called to do scientific theology passionately, a theology based on feeling as well as on knowledge, on wisdom as well as on science, a theology made not only with the mind but also with the heart, the body, the womb. We consider this as a challenge and an imperative not only for doing theology from women's perspective, but also for all theology. The Latin American theology of liberation has already discovered that the rigid, cold, and purely rationalistic theology of the West thirsts to be combined with spiritual flexibility and creativeness. *"Minjung* theology" and other efforts of contextual theology in Asia, as well as black theology

and other emerging theologies in Africa, are also finding their way to a theological reformulation that is firmly and deeply rooted in human life, where the Holy Spirit lives and acts. Thus our theology is people-oriented, not something done in an ivory tower, apart from people.

As women, we have a contribution to make in the effort of Christian communities to rethink and rediscover new expressions of their Christian faith. Moreover, since religious pluralism is a reality in our different situations, we, as Christians and as theologians, need to dialogue and work with women of other faiths, convinced that in other religious traditions there too we meet Christ.

In the task of doing theology, our common goal is to bring a new dimension to the struggle for justice and for promoting God's reign, a dimension that is not ours, but is given to us both by the voices of our people clamoring for justice, and by God, who inspired and convoked us here. Humanity as a whole, not only women, stands to benefit from the whole endeavor.

### Recommendations

Our rich and intensive reflections and exchanges during these past days inspired many possible lines of action, both personal and communal. However, we have made the following specific recommendations:

(1) That the Women's Commission continue its program of consultations on the national and continental levels.

(2) That the Women's Commission establish a network among the women of the three continents for information-sharing and solidarity work.

(3) That EATWOT initiate a dialogue between the Women's Commission and the male members of the Association for greater understanding and more effective collaboration toward the attainment of our common goal of achieving full humanity for all.

(4) That EATWOT create a joint commission on the Bible, which will:

(a) encourage and organize conferences on the Bible,

(b) provide materials for biblical formation,

(c) facilitate the exchange of personnel and materials.

(5) That EATWOT publish in three languages (English, French, and Spanish) an official bulletin containing works of its members, with adequate contribution from women.

(6) That each region of the Women's Commission express its continuing support of and solidarity with the struggles of Southern Africa and Central America and direct part of its theological effort to their situations.

## Conclusion

At the end of our days together, we feel identified with the woman in John 12 and Mark 14, who makes a passionate prophetic action in proclaiming Jesus as Messiah, anointing him with the royal ointment. John portrays the woman anointing Jesus' feet, perhaps to show that she is a real disciple, washing Jesus' feet as Jesus himself washed the disciples' feet.

This woman's action is a passionate and compassionate action—passionate, because by anointing Jesus with so expensive a perfume she shows her extreme love for him; compassionate, because her action gives Jesus the opportunity to direct the community's attention to the poor and to exhort its solidarity with them.

Jesus approves the woman's action and says that it would be proclaimed wherever the Good News is preached. The Gospel states that the fragrance spread by her gesture filled the house. As women theologians of the Third World, we are called to do the same. As we commit our lives to the ministry of a passionate and compassionate theology, we shall spread the fragrance of the Good News to all four corners of the world.

❖    ❖    ❖

## Feminist Theology

☐ *There are many commonalities and differences in women's situations around the globe. In addition to their own consultations and networks, women theologians of the Third World also draw strength and encouragement from the WCC's declaration of "The Ecumenical Decade of Churches in Solidarity with Women"; this has initiated programs and workshops for women in its member churches around the world. The participation of women in the work of the WCC since its first Assembly in 1948 has to be critically examined, as Anna Karin Hammar has done in her article "After Forty Years—Churches in Solidarity with Women?"* (Ecumenical Review, *vol. 40, nos. 3-4, 1988, pp. 528-38), where she writes: "Many have given up hope regarding the institutional church. Women gather in women-church, and women and men gather in new communities, searching for a home for their spirituality and commitments. Some stay in the institutional church and exercise a 'critical solidarity' with it, trusting its potentials for liberation and change through intentional planning and commitment to a biblical vision of church, a community of equals responding to the call of God and the needs of people" (p. 538).*

*The history of women's involvement in the WCC has been told by Susannah Herzel in her book* A Voice for Women: The Women's Department of the World Council of Churches *(Geneva: WCC Publications, 1981), and there is much in this history to take inspiration and encouragement from. Women in the Third World in particular have been given much support and help, although there is still a long way to go before women enjoy equal participation in all activities of the member churches and in the central work of the WCC itself. The work of the Ecumenical Decade of Churches in Solidarity with Women is an important step in this direction, and its aims have often been outlined. The text in chapter 3 is taken from the WCC's own resource book on the Ecumenical Decade (1988).*

# 3

# The Ecumenical Decade of Churches in Solidarity with Women (1988-98)

The Ecumenical Decade of Churches in Solidarity with Women (1988-98) aims at:

- empowering women to challenge oppressive structures in the global community, their country and their church;
- affirming—through shared leadership and decisionmaking, theology and spirituality—the decisive contributions of women in churches and communities;
- giving visibility to women's perspectives and actions in the work and struggle for justice, peace, and the integrity of creation;
- enabling the churches to free themselves from racism, sexism, and classism; from teachings and practices that discriminate against women;
- encouraging the churches to take action in solidarity with women.

❖    ❖    ❖

☐ *Theological writings by women from Africa, Asia, and South America are listed in detail in the bibliography of this Reader. Selections from each continent can be found in the book* With Passion and Compassion: Third World Women Doing Theology *(1988) (eds. Virginia Fabella and Mercy Amba Oduyoye) from which the following chapter (chapter 4) by Ivone Gebara, a Roman Catholic sister from Brazil, has been chosen (pp. 125-34).* With Passion and Compassion *also includes a helpful survey on women in Africa by Rosemary Edet and Bette Ekeya, entitled "Church Women of Africa: A Theological Community" (pp. 3-13). The most recent work by African women theologians is* The Will to Arise: Women, Tradition, and the Church in Africa *(1992) (eds. Mercy Amba Oduyoye and Musimbi R. A. Kanyoro) and an extract from this is found in chapter 27 of this Reader. In chapter 4, Ivone Gebara, a Roman Catholic sister from Brazil, reflects on the characteristics of feminist theological activity in Latin America.*

*In chapter 5, I have included another brief report from one of the workshops held at the Annual Meeting of the Indian Theological Association. This report is unusual in that a group of women and men theologians worked out a statement together on doing theology from a women's point of view; this was published in 1987.\* This document shows the process of consultation that is taking place in a particular region and theological association. More detailed information on women in the Indian churches is given in Jessie Tellis-Nayak's article "The Women's Movement and the Church in India" (*In God's Image, *December 1987–March 1988, pp. 32-41) and the development of feminist theology in India is described by Aruna Gnanadason in "Feminist Theology: An Indian Perspective" (*The Asia Journal of Theology, *vol. 2/1, 1988, pp. 109-18, also reprinted in the journal* In God's Image, *December 1988, pp. 44-51).*

*Feminist theology finds a rich response in the Indian subcontinent. Its specific focus is the condition of women in India; whereas, larger issues affecting the development of feminist theology in Asia as a whole are being considered in chapter 6. Here Kwok Pui-lan, a Chinese Anglican woman theologian from the University of Hong Kong, discusses feminist theology in the context of Asian cultural diversity and in its relation to religious pluralism and interfaith dialogue. Kwok Pui-lan wrote this chapter when she was a Visiting Theologian at the Auburn Theological Seminary, New York, and it was first published in* The Auburn News, *Fall 1992, pp. 1–9. Since then, she has been lecturing at the Episcopal Divinity School in Cambridge, Massachusetts. Other publications by her include a book on* Chinese Women and Christianity 1860– 1927 *and several articles found in the bibliography of this Reader. With Letty Russell and others, she is also one of the co-authors of* Inheriting Our Mothers' Gardens: Feminist Theology in Third World Perspective.

# 4  IVONE GEBARA

# Women Doing Theology in Latin America

The expression "women doing theology" is new, as is the explication of what the expression means. Previously, there was never any mention of sexual difference with regard to those who wrote theology, since it was obvious that the task was something proper to men. Today it would seem that the matter is no longer obvious, and the gender of the authors must be specified. Gender is understood not only as a biological difference prior even to birth, but especially as a cultural dimension, that is, as a stance or an aspect that affects the production of other cultural values, of other kinds of human interrelationship and other ways of thinking.

The fact that women have entered the world of economic

---

* *The Workshop Report is found in K. Pathil, ed.,* Socio-Cultural Analyses in Theologizing, *Bangalore: Indian Theological Association, 1987, pp. 179–82.*

47

production and, more broadly, into politics and culture and the consequences for change in society and in the various churches deserves deeper reflection in its own right. Such a deepening would go beyond the scope of our contribution, since right now we have another aim.

I am going to devote my attention especially to the question of the task of theology, emphasizing some points of reflection on what has already been said, and I shall continue my reflection beyond issues that are properly theological.

## What characterizes the way women do theology?

In order to sketch a response to this question, we must first explain what we understand today by the theological activity of women. I should make it clear that my starting point is the Latin American context and, more specifically, the situation in northeastern Brazil. Placing myself at that starting point is crucially important, since it conditions my reflection as a woman out of a particular socioeconomic, political, and cultural situation. This situation shapes my being and my acting, my seeing and my feeling, my speech and my silence.

To speak or write from northeast Brazil is to situate myself in a region where misery and exploitation take on extremely dehumanizing forms and where most of the people, and especially women, are its victims. This region is the victim of internal and external contradictions of the capitalist system and is marked by various kinds of contrasts: (1) by economic and social contrasts: a few large-scale property-owners, most people landless, very high unemployment; (2) by political contrasts: power of the "colonels"—sugar-mill owners, industrialists, and politicians—alongside the lack of decisionmaking power on the part of millions of people in the northeast; (3) by cultural contrasts: utilization of popular culture to serve the dominant culture, machismo, and subjection of women.

As we know well, these contrasts entail enormous social consequences, reducing most of the people to subhuman living conditions. It is out of this situation, which sustains my being and my reflection, that I can speak of women's theology. I recognize that I am a woman who lives in privileged conditions,

conditions that give me enough space to reflect, to speak, and even to write. I speak of the woman that I am myself, and of others, the poor women of my region, in an effort to move over into their world on the basis of my option for our liberation, as well as on the basis of our common human condition as women.

As I see it, the theological task is multiple and varied. There is nothing new about such a statement. What may be new is the fact of explicating it from the starting point of the situation of women. Hence I speak of different theological tasks.

*Shared experiences*

There is a way of doing theology that starts with shared experience from oral transmission, from the simple fact of sharing life. I believe this way of doing theology is what is most representative of the popular milieus. Many women are especially gifted with a deep intuition about human life and are able to counsel, to intuit problems, to express them, to give support, to propose solutions, and to confirm the faith of many people. They explain biblical passages on the basis of their experience and respond to doctrinal questions by simplifying them and setting them on the level of existential reality. Some of these women are illiterate. That would pose problems for a more academic doing of theology, but it does not hinder the exercise of this ministry. This activity is sapiential; it springs from life, and life is its reference point. It is received as a gift from God and handed on as a gift.

Discourse dealing with the important issues in life is the heart of every theology. God's life is related to the life of humankind, and the life of humankind is related to God. All subsequent systematizing, all thematizing, all connecting of ideas, is vitally linked to this most basic aspect.

With regard to this primordial religious experience, it is important that we take note of the function of women in Candomblé,[1] especially in northeast Brazil. I draw attention to this point simply to underscore the fact that even in machistic cultures like our own, in Candomblé the woman has a special place in carrying out religious tasks. The "Mother of the Saint" is "queen" in her own territory. She is the recipient of the wish of the saint, male or female; she transmits or presides over and coordinates religious ceremonies. Generally speaking, this sort of thing does not take place in Christian churches, although one can cite some similar nonofficial functions: counselors, prayer leaders, faith healers, and providers of other services deeply connected to the religious dimension of human life. In some Protestant churches, female priestly ministry is allowed, but it is not exercised at all among the popular sectors in northeast Brazil.

## Efforts of popular catechists

The theological efforts of the so-called popular catechists, who are responsible for more systematic initiation into Christian doctrine, especially among children and young people, can be one of repeating written materials, things learned in their own childhood, or ideas imposed by priests. One can also find a dimension of impressive creativity, which has a strong influence on the life of children and young people. Today in Latin America one can speak of a "revolutionary role" played by many catechists who open themselves clearly and effectively to the problems of their people and who have shown that they can both take an active role in popular movements and pass on to children and young people a Christianity characterized by the struggle for justice, a high value placed on life, and the sharing of goods. In so doing, they provide alternatives to this consumerist and individualistic society.

## Catholic sisters

The theological effort of Catholic sisters among the popular sectors is a kind of work that became significant in Brazil, especially during the 1970s. The "migration" of sisters to popular milieus, and the fact that young people in those areas have taken on religious life while remaining to serve in those milieus, have strengthened and continue to strengthen a consciousness and militancy in the popular organizations as well as a reading of Christian faith whose starting point is the problems and hopes of our people.

The presence of these sisters has stimulated and motivated a rereading of the Bible as the history of a people to whom we are linked by religious tradition and from whom we must learn fidelity to life, and in particular fidelity to a book that tells us about Jesus and Mary, figures who set in motion a new way for people to relate to one another.

Something new is happening in the people's theological expression. There seems to be a before and an after, that is, the presence of these sisters often seems to establish the context that enables the poor to experience certain elements of change in the way they formulate and live their religion. The image of a God committed to the liberation of the poor, of a Mary closer to women's problems, of a Jesus who is less remote and whose words are understandable in our own situation—these are just examples of the enormous change that gradually takes place.

## Doing theology from daily life

The theological activity of women who teach in theology departments and institutes is a ministry not limited just to courses, but also involves advising the various groups and movements in the Christian churches. Above and beyond the academic theological formation, which both men and women receive in higher institutions of learning where men are the majority, there is something quite special in the way that women do theology. The elements of everyday life are very intertwined with their speaking about God. When women's experience is expressed in a Church whose tradition is machistic, the other side of human experience returns to theological discourse: the side of the person who gives birth, nurses, nourishes, of the person who for centuries has remained silent with regard to anything having to do with theology. Now she begins to express her experience of God in another manner, a manner that does not demand that reason alone be regarded as the single and universal mediation of theological discourse. This way of doing theology includes what is vital, utilizing mediations that can help to express what has been experienced, without exhausting it, a discourse that leads to the awareness that there is always something more, something that words cannot express.

What is vital cannot be expressed through formal mediations. It can be done only through those mediations that are proper to a sapiential discourse in which relationships with others express the diversity and complexity of human situations and challenges. Theological speech is expressed in the kind of prophecy that denounces the present, in songs of hope, in lament, in the form of counsel. It is as though the aim were to bridge the gap between speech and reality, the distance that the formal ·and idealist discourse of religion has imposed on us for a long time. It is as though we were discovering, very powerfully and starting from our own situation, the mystery of the incarnation of the divine in the human, not just because "we have been told," but because we experience it in the confines of our lives as women.

The experience of this theological activity is still in its early stages. In Brazil there are not many published works to confirm it and make it known. There is only what I regard as most basic and prior to theological elaboration: faith and its expression based on an encounter with the experience of the oppression of women as an experience of the oppression of the poor. This expression has been more oral and more direct, and has proved to be effective.

At this point, I am limiting myself to taking note of this kind of activity. Further on, I shall seek to explain some characteristics, intuitions, and efforts involved in this activity.

### Historic contexts

The different theological activities spelled out above take place on different levels and in different situations, characterized by various kinds of conditionings. At this point, I propose that we reflect on some "historic contexts" and some characteristics that, I think, are proper to women doing theology in Latin America during these last few years. The basis on which I point to these contexts and their characteristics is my own observation and the way I exercise this ministry, which is confirmed by the practice of a few of my colleagues and by the reception given by the audience I address.

I cannot avoid speaking about my own experience. In a vital

way it makes me what I am. My theological experience is the product of my relationship with people, of mutual influences, of my philosophical and ideological stance, situated in time and space. The faith I have received from my childhood onward, the difficult and twisting path of my life, the discoveries I have made, the past and the present, have all left their mark on my experience of theology.

It is hard to draw a line between the subjective and the objective, or a line between what I say about others and what I say about myself. In life, such things are mixed together and interconnected, and we risk killing something vital within them if we try to "divide the waters" too precisely. Every "theory" includes something very personal, something deeply involved with the one who elaborates it, something that is part of the very desire to know and change the world. To speak either as a single person or universally seems to show or reflect something that we experience in the everyday reality of our life within our different social and cultural conditionings: the partial nature of our perception and the partial nature of our interpretations.

Thus it is within the boundaries of my subjectivity/objectivity and within the limits of my experience and observation that I set forth the following three historic contexts and three characteristics.

## Irruption of history into women's lives

When we speak of the irruption of history into the lives of women—and especially the theological expression of their faith—we do not mean the entrance of women into history; they have always been present. What we have in mind is something qualitatively different and new, that is, the irruption of historic consciousness into the lives of millions and millions of women, leading them to the liberation struggle by means of an active participation in different fronts from which they had previously been absent. It is as though a strong wind had begun to blow, opening eyes and loosening tongues, shifting stances, enabling arms to reach out to new embraces and hands to take up other tools, impelling feet to take other steps, raising the voice so its song and its lament might be heard. Woman begins to take her place as agent of history. The fact is that with her activity and new stance toward what happens in life, a new awareness is clearly coming into being. Participation in labor unions, neighborhood movements, mothers' groups, and pastoral leadership all manifest a change in the consciousness and in the role women play today. Entering into history in fact means becoming aware of history, entering into a broader meaning, in which women are also creators or increasingly want to be forgers of history.

### Discovering causality within women's experience

In connection with history, one can speak of the causality of things. The condition of women is the result of an evolution: it has been different, and it can be different. Their present state can be partly explained on the basis of historic causes. The discovery of the causes of the oppression of the poor and, among them, of the oppression of women, has changed women's understanding of themselves as persons individually and corporately. Woman is not marked for an unchangeable fate, nor is she the object of alien wills that shape her existence. Despite the conditions inherent in human existence, she can conquer spaces in which to express her word and her being. This new historic moment of hers is pregnant with future, a moment that announces a Good News that is both present and yet to be lived in its fullness.

It is worth noting that the discovery of causality within women's experience bears the characteristic marks of the particular way in which they perceive and approach the problems of life. No one single cause is absolutized but, rather, the causes are multiple. This way of looking at matters is obedient to their perception, as women, in its complexity, diversity, and mystery.

### Entering the labor force

The fact that more and more women are entering the world of paid labor, and the world of work and struggle for survival, has awakened them to struggle in other areas where human destiny is also at stake.

Entering the labor force has changed the expression of women's faith. From their previous horizon of home and family, women have opened out to a broader reality. God is no longer one who addresses a world limited to the activities of home and family; God becomes the one who addresses socioeconomic and political challenges in the new militancy of Latin American women. The image of God is no longer that of the father to whom one owes submission; rather, God is basically the image of what is most human in woman and man, seeking expression and liberation. A working woman said, "God is the force that won't allow me to surrender to the will of those who oppress my people."

Women's entry into the struggle of the world of paid labor has thus brought about a change in the way they relate. Obviously, this is not the only factor, but it seems important to remind ourselves of it, since it tends to be forgotten or left as a purely accidental aspect within a traditionalist or reactionary theological vision.

## Characteristics of feminist theological activity in Latin America

### Living realities and theological elaboration

Feminist theological expression always starts from what has been lived, from what is experienced in the present. Consequently it rejects an abstract type of language about life and those matters deeply affecting human relationship. That is why there is a growing effort to clear the field of old theological concepts in order to discover what vital realities they correspond to, and to what extent they really do so. Living realities are the takeoff point for theological elaboration; they are rational symbols that arose in a particular period, the product of a series of conditions, and they were able to bring together rationally certain experiences of reality. It is urgent that we get to know them and discover their meaning for today, and for our history. In their theological work, women seek to retrieve existential realities, to let them speak freely, to allow them to become reorganized on the basis of our context today, and only subsequently to connect them to a prior tradition.

This way of proceeding represents an attempt to restore to theological language its capacity for touching some vital centers of human existence. In other words, to some extent this procedure means returning the poetic dimension of human life to theology, since the deepest meaning in the human being is expressed only through analogy; mystery is voiced only in poetry, and what is gratuitous is expressed only through symbols.

Purely rational concepts do not take into account the meaning, desire, flavor, pleasure, pain, and mystery of existence. Given their own history, women are bolder in questioning concepts, and they have a creative curiosity that opens new paths and allows new understandings. This new mode makes possible a kind of theological creation in community. That is, the new formulation gathers a broader number of experiences and is not narrowed to a formulation or a text with individual "authorship."

This is a "new way" of expressing something after it has been heard, lived, and felt many times and in many ways, so that people recognize themselves when they hear it spelled out, and they feel invited to a deeper reflection on the questions that life poses. It is their own issues that they see reflected on, questioned, or clarified so that the reflection proposed touches most deeply the questions and doubts present in the lives of millions of people.

*Recreating tradition*

In women's theological discourse, the theological tradition shared by the different churches does not function as a legitimizing justification that we need only to go on repeating. If we do repeat, it is because that is what today's situation demands, because it does touch the roots of our existence, because to some extent it responds to the problems that ongoing history sets before us. In this sense, what is normative is primarily the present, what calls out today; tradition is viewed in terms of the present. Thus the tradition of Christian communities in the past is continually recreated, and one may even speak of fidelity to that tradition to the extent that both today and yesterday are faithful to the Spirit of God manifest in history and demanding absolute respect for life. The past is not only information, but enlightenment, teaching, and witness for the present to the extent that it relates to the question of being human.

## Human complexities

The theological work of women reflects an ability to view life as the locus of the simultaneous experience of oppression and liberation, of grace and lack of grace. Such perception encompasses what is plural, what is different, what is other. Although this way of looking is not the exclusive property of women, we must say that it is found to an extraordinary extent among women. In popular struggles, in which women have played a very important role, this ability to grasp in a more unified way the oppositions and contradictions, the contrasts and differences as inherent in human life, has been a characteristic feature of the way in which women live and express their faith. Such behavior enables them to avoid taking dogmatic and exclusive stances, and to perceive or intuit the real complexity of what is human.

## The tapestry of human life

In addition to these factors or characteristics of the theological work of women, we cannot fail to recall the inestimable contribution of the social sciences—anthropology, psychology, and different theories about language—as elements that have been changing, directly or indirectly, women's understanding of themselves. These same elements have contributed to the emancipation of women's power in the social dimension of human relations and in the way these relations are organized.

All these contributions form part of the tapestry woven by women expressing and reflecting human life as this century ends. The threads, colors, flowers, and other designs—all taken together, interconnected, and linked to each other—are forming the embroidery of life while the artists themselves are beginning to appear, to show their faces in public, to demand respect and appreciation. It is also worth noting that the international women's movement, in its expressions and organizations, has played a role in opening up the oppressed situation of Brazilian women so they could be aware of the situation of women in different areas of the world. For example, the resistance of the Madres de Plaza de Mayo in Argentina, and of our sisters in Bolivia, Nicaragua, and El Salvador, has become well known and has led to solidarity and energy, which has confirmed us in the struggle, even though our contexts are different.

The persistence of women in the struggle for life and the restoration of justice have been linked together and lived out as expressions of faith, as the presence of God in the struggles of history. Many women see in these developments the expression of their desire to struggle for a more human world, in which certain values presently dormant may be aroused, where people can accept affection, where life may triumph over the powers of death.

## Basic ecclesial communities

Finally, I want to take particular note of the work of women in basic ecclesial communities. No doubt this work has been present throughout this reflection, but I cannot avoid dealing with it more fully at this point, before concluding my thoughts. I am not going to describe what women do in basic ecclesial communities. That would fill a long essay, and besides it is well known to all of us.

I would simply like to emphasize how their active role is prefiguring within the Christian churches a new way of organizing ministries. Even though these ministries are not sanctioned by church officials, they are recognized by the poorest, those to whom this service is especially directed. The new element in this service is found in the way it responds to a certain number of the community's vital needs and in the fear that it is generating in those who are in charge of the churches and who are gradually losing their former prestige. Women's ministry is shaking up men's ministry, challenging their practice and the exercise of their authority. This is taking place, not because of some decision taken by women to make it happen, but because of the nature and quality of their service and of the new social role that they are winning in the world. To the extent that women actively move onstage in the churches, their organizations, institutions, and expressions must be revised to meet the challenges continually posed by today's world.

### In conclusion: my hope for the future

Theological formulations that are extremely machistic, privileges of power over what is sacred, and the need for male legitimation for things to "happen" in the churches are beginning to be affected by the clashes that hint of the future. Such a statement in no way intends to replace the "masculine" model with the "feminine" one, but to anticipate a new synthesis in which the dialectic present in human existence can take place, without destroying any of its vital elements.

This is my hope: The day will come when all people, lifting their eyes, will see the earth shining with brotherhood and sisterhood, mutual appreciation, true complementarity. . . .

Men and women will dwell in their houses; men and women will eat the same bread, drink the same wine, and dance together in the brightly lit square, celebrating the bonds uniting all humanity.

# 5 INDIAN THEOLOGICAL ASSOCIATION

# Theologizing in India — A Feminine Perspective

(1) There is a spoken and unspoken male perspective in all theology, in the Church, and in society at large. How do we go about changing this so that a richly human perspective emerges that would incorporate the unique contributions of both men and women? For this, an effort should be made to uncover the power constellations in theology, in the Church, and in society that deny to women all participation in decision-making.

To begin with, we sought out specific areas of feminine experience in India that have an effect on theologizing too.

These are:

- the pronounced social preference for the human male,
- the dowry system and all its implications,
- the growing numbers of female abortions and the existence of female infanticide (amniocentesis to discover sex),
- language and symbolism used to legitimate male domination,
- family roles and customs,
- women stereotyped as sex object and temptress,
- female slave trade and prostitution,
- rape,
- media stereotypes of women (television, video, cinema, novels, children's storybooks),
- job discrimination against women, unjust wages for women, and sexual harassment in the workplace,
- no title to property for women and, when married, no title to income or even her own family name,

- clerical domination in the Church over the religious women in general and the dependent status of diocesan congregations of sisters in particular.

(2) Given this fact that an Indian woman belongs to a society that considers women to be almost valueless, how can she contribute to the theological enterprise?' How can she do theology if she does not exist? What resources has she to do theology if she does not have enough to eat? How can she speak prophetically if she has no voice? What practical possibility is there for her to do theology if her only place is in the home? Can she even recognize God as existing and caring for her and her sisters? These questions were asked in the process of trying to discover a direction for changing the male perspective in theology and allowing a richly human perspective to emerge. Some concrete strategies for action are proposed as a result of this questioning:

(a) Women must articulate their unique vision of reality. They need to stimulate and encourage each other to do this in speaking, writing, poetry, music, painting, sculpture, cinema, etc.

(b) Jesus gave a full initiation to Mary to leave aside the household tasks in order to be introduced into a reflective listening. To make it possible for women to contribute, they need a basic theological training and to belong to a theologizing community.

(c) For this to happen, men in general will have to make the necessary adjustments with regard to gender roles, and husbands in particular will have to make adjustments within the family.

(d) Indian spirituality perceives a complementarity of female/male images in the representation of God and reality. A feminine perspective in theology has to take this seriously. Women's respect for life and their potential for motherhood give them a special sensitivity to ecological and environmental issues, and suggest the possibility of a special female contribution in this area.

(e) Attitudinal changes in both women and men must be brought about by:

- a constant process of conscientization, beginning in the family and continued in schools, parent-teacher associations, pre-marriage courses, and general catechesis,
- coeducation at all levels including seminaries,
- a proper (holistic) formation of priests and sisters,
- a courageous and outspoken stand by men-theologians in support of women,
- an end to the reinforcement of female stereotypes in male preaching,
- participation in and listening to women's groups,
- a critical look at the male and female stereotypes, encouraging the masculine potentialities in women and feminine potentialities in men.

(3) Power and decisionmaking within the Church is entirely in the hands of the clergy. This fact results in the exclusion of women, and indeed the greater part of the people of God, from ministries for which they are called, about which there is no doctrinal debate, and which must be given official recognition. We submit that women must also be admitted to the ordained ministry. In matters of sexual morality, especially when they relate directly to women, women must make themselves heard, be listened to, and actively consulted by male moral theologians and the magisterium, and be encouraged to increase their competency in moral theology. In all matters of ecclesiastical administration and finance, participation in the decisionmaking must be clearly set down in terms of percentage, i.e., on every council/board 50% must be women. The kind of cooperation in social, political, liturgical, and pastoral action that exists between priests and sisters in some parts of India must be extended to the whole Indian Church and to *lay* women and men as well. The Indian Theological Association must extend personal invitations to all suitably qualified women in India to participate in the annual meetings and become its members.

# 6  KWOK PUI-LAN

## The Future of Feminist Theology: An Asian Perspective

In the summer of 1988, more than a hundred scholars, theologians, and religious activists gathered at Maryknoll, New York, to celebrate the sixtieth birthday of Gustavo Gutíerrez, and the fifteenth anniversary of the publication in English of his classic, *A Theology of Liberation*. From Asia, Africa, Latin America, and North America, these people came as oppressed people, as Jews, as blacks, and as women, from all over the world to discuss the work of Gutiérrez and the future of liberation theology.[1]

If a forum for the future of feminist theology were to be held in 1993 on the occasion of the twentieth anniversary of the publication of Mary Daly's *Beyond God the Father*, we don't know whether the author would like to discuss feminist theology since she has identified herself as post-Christian. Some of the Afro-American and the Latino women theologians might also hesitate to join a discussion of "feminist" theology. Moreover, sisters from Asia, Africa, and Latin America would be unwilling to come if feminist theology is preoccupied with the issues of the First or Second World. Other religious feminists, such as Jewish, Muslim, Buddhist, and Goddess-worshippers would be watching carefully what the Christian feminists have to say on the uniqueness of the Christian faith.

This is a very ambiguous situation that leaves us sometimes in a quandary. The point is that it is often easier to talk about the liberation of the poor and the marginalized than about the liberation of women. Not only do men have different points of view on the subject, we women argue passionately among ourselves about the goals and strategies of women's liberation. In fact, this is to be expected. Why should we assume there is a "universal" approach to the liberation of more than half the world's population? Would it not be a kind of cultural hegemony if there should be just one way of doing feminist theology?

I certainly do not have a crystal ball to prophesy what the future of feminist theology would look like. But as an Asian woman theologian, who has followed attentively these debates and who has tried to articulate theology from my own cultural context, I have a few observations to make on some of the most important issues that feminist theology needs to address in the near future. In the past, Asian Christians, let alone Christian women, have seldom been invited to help set the theological agenda. We are seen more as "missiological objects" of Christian mission, rather than as "theological subjects," expected to participate in the dialogue.[2] I welcome this opportunity to lift up Asian women's voices in Christian theology and to share with you our views on the *problématique* of feminist theology.

I will try to discuss four clusters of issues: cultural and racial diversity, religious pluralism, Jewish-Christian dialogue, and the language of the erotic.

### Cultural and racial diversity

The seventh Assembly of the World Council of Churches, held in Canberra in 1991, brought together 4,000 Christians from all parts of the world. The Assembly will always be remembered as one held in the shadow of the Gulf War. But it will also be remembered as the Assembly in which the issue of "syncretism" created such a controversy among participants that the worldwide Church was implicated. The icon of that Assembly is a young woman theologian from Asia, Professor Chung Hyun Kyung of Korea, burning a scroll after she had invoked the spirits of people who died in Hiroshima and Nagasaki, in gas chambers in the Holocaust, in Kwangju, Tiananmen Square, and Lithuania.

Professor Chung was one of the plenary speakers invited to address the Assembly theme, "Come Holy Spirit, Renew the Whole Creation."[3] Accompanied by music, slides, dance, drums, and rituals, Chung powerfully told the stories of the han-ridden spirits of the Korean people. "Han" means resentment, anguish, bitterness, and brokenheartedness as a result of injustice. In her passionate and spirit-filled presentation, Chung freely employed religious symbols and concepts from her culture to articulate her deep anguish as an Asian and as a woman. Her paper raised a lot of issues, including "inculturation, creation, inclusiveness, interreligious dialogue, syncretism, discernment of the limits of diversity, and pneumatology," as one commentator put it.[4]

Chung's presentation clearly called for a paradigmatic shift in doing theology, as she tried to address the multiple oppression of women living under sexism, classism, and racism. For some time, feminist theologians have critiqued the patriarchal bias of Christian doctrines and practices, recovered useful traditions from reexamining women's religious history, and reconstructed models of God-talk that take into consideration women's experiences. These efforts were chiefly made by women theologians of European and American descent and focused primarily on white women's experience. It is only fairly recently that the daring and breathtaking voices of women from Asia, Africa, and Latin America are being heard. These newcomers challenge the established "order of things" and raise the significant issue of cultural and racial diversity in feminist theological discourse.

Female theologians in Asia have not conjured up another name for the kind of theology they are doing because there is no common language we can use together. Many would prefer to call their work Asian women's theology, instead of feminist theology, because the term "feminist" carries connotations of a militant, man-hating, and separatist stance of some women in the West. The term "feminism" is translated as "women's rights movement" in the Chinese language, which carries a significant political overtone not found in other terms. I myself continue to use the term "feminist" because I do not think any group should have a monopoly on the use of it.

Asia is the home for over half of the world's population. Divided into seven major linguistic zones, Asian people have lived for centuries in a multiracial, multicultural, and multireligious world. From Japan to Indonesia, and from the Philippines to Inner Asia, people live in different sociopolitical realities and divergent cultural worlds. Asian mental constructs, approaches to reality, ways of life, and spirituality are in many ways radically different from those of people in the West. Asian women theologians must try to decipher the cultural codes of the people, delve into the rich resource of Asian traditions, and learn to speak the language of poor women in that continent before they can construct a theology that touches the Asian soul.

The affirmation of diversity and multiplicity in feminist theology is based on our beliefs that gender is historically conditioned. There is not an "abstract" woman, nor is there an "abstract" man. Women living in the Third World, or as minorities in the First and Second World, often find that they have multiple and simultaneous identities as a result of their double or triple oppression.[5] In fact, many white women are becoming more keenly aware that they too have the double identities of both the oppressors and the oppressed. As women struggling for liberation, it is important that we should be aware of these multiple identities and allow them to interplay with each other in naming who we are and in shaping our religious faith.

The racial and cultural diversity in feminist theology should not separate women from one another, but challenge us to be accountable not just to our own community but other communities as well. Living in the cosmopolitan city of Hong Kong, I am conscious of the tensions of cultural conflicts as well as the genuine possibility of "crossing" the boundaries to see the viewpoints of others. In the modern world where advanced technology, mass media, intercultural exchange, and the market economy have brought the different cultures much closer than before, no one could afford to live in a tribal village anymore. Our destinies as members of the human species are intertwined, and our multiple identities often overlap with one another.

Poor and oppressed women in the Third World, women of color in America, indigenous people all over the world are historically forced to live in more than one culture: the dominant culture of the oppressors and the subversive culture of resistance. We have learned to speak many tongues, and we live in differently constructed worlds. We know what diversity is and we are not frightened by multiplicity. When we hear the fresh theological insights from other groups of oppressed women, we rejoice and celebrate with them, knowing that a new key has been struck, and a new breakthrough has been made. A few days ago, I was talking about Asian feminist theology with a church group when I met a native American woman. As she came up and thanked me for my presentation, I told her I am eagerly waiting for the native American contribution to the feminist theological symphony. Moreover, with other women of color, Asian women have challenged white women to stop using a "universal" language as if they could represent us. The lifting up of every voice, the celebration of diversity, the affirmation of plurality, help us to see glimpses of the amazing grace of God in all cultures and all peoples.

**Religious pluralism**

Asia is the birthplace of all major religions in the world. As a tiny minority making up less than 3% of the vast population of Asia, Christians live in a religious environment with conflicting claims to truth, colorful religious festivals and rituals, and alternative forms of spirituality. Living in this enchanting world of gods and goddesses, Asian women theologians recognize the need to address the issues of religious pluralism and interfaith dialogue. We can only speak about our Christian identity in relation to, and not in spite of, these indigenous traditions of our motherland. We are happy to know that these are not just our parochial issues, for many leading theologians in the West, including some feminist theologians, have recognized religious pluralism as a crucial theological issue.[6]

It is significant to note that except for the first centuries, the dominant self-understandings of Christianity were conversion, crusade, and mission. From a crosscultural perspective, the self-understandings of Confucianism, Buddhism, Taoism, and other Asian religions are quite different, except perhaps for Islam. For example, in China, Confucianism was the major cultural tradition, but when Buddhism was introduced, it was thoroughly sinicized. In the eleventh and twentieth centuries, the interpenetration of Buddhism, Taoism, and Confucianism gave birth to a new philosophical system: neo-Confucianism. Through the centuries, Chinese people lived in the multireligious worlds of Confucianism, Buddhism, and Taoism, and most of the time these traditions existed peacefully together.

Theologian Marjorie Hewitt Suchocki has made the connection between religious imperialism and sexism in Christianity. Insofar as the masculine experience has been universalized to define what is fully human in Christian thought, there seems to be a parallel when one religion is absolutized as the norm for others. Religious imperialism, like sexism, operates in a "superiority-inferiority" syndrome, where the value and dignity of the "other" is not respected.[7] Challenging white male supremacy in Christian thinking and practice, feminist theologians must collectively begin to redefine our Christian identity without using such expressions as "uniqueness," "special revelation," "highest fulfillment," or "outside the Church, no salvation."

For a very long period of its history, the institutionalized Christian Church has adopted a vehemently exclusivist position in talking about truth, revelation, the Bible, and Christ. When missionaries arrived in Asia, Africa, and Latin America, trying to convert the people, they condemned our ancestors, trashed our gods and goddesses, and severed us from our indigenous cultures. Many missionaries, both male and female, accused indigenous traditions of being oppressive to women, without the slightest recognition of the sexist ideology of Christianity. Although the missionary age is a bygone era, there are still many people in the West, including women, who believe that Islam, Shintoism, or Buddhism must be more patriarchal than the Christian religion. Non-Christian women in the Third World have found such presumptuous beliefs deeply troubling. They have refused to be labeled "victims" for our complacent Christian conscience. Riffat Hassan, an Islamic feminist, has said that she is very tired of Western women trying to "sympathize with Islamic women without even knowing what Islamic feminists want."[8]

While the exclusive position is blatantly imperialistic, the inclusivist position is even more ambiguous and dangerous.

The inclusivist position affirms the centrality of Jesus Christ, but acknowledges that truth and wisdom can be found in other traditions. As a rule, the other traditions are allowed to have a place if they can be nicely fitted in pigeon-holes, such as "general revelation," "unknown Christ," "theocentrism as against Christocentrism." If Christian thinkers, such as Langdon Gilkey and David Tracy, cannot even make up their minds whether Buddhism sounds more like Whitehead, Hegel, Dewey, or postmodern thinkers like Gilles Deleuze and Jacques Derrida, how can Christians rush to give Buddhists, Taoists, or Hindus such honorary titles as "anonymous Christians," or "latent Christians."[9]

In working for justice, women of color have always found any inclusivist attitude to be patronizing because it tends to overlook real differences. African-American women, for example, have been told by white women that their struggles can be taken care of if they participate in the feminist movement. On the other hand, they are told by black men that their oppression can be overcome only if they join the black men to fight against racism. Over and over again, African-American women feel that they are not really included because they have to struggle against sexism, racism, and classism. Similarly, Buddhist feminists, Islamic feminists, and Hindu feminists feel they are not included if they are just tokens in the dialogue, or if their issues are never given priority.

More recently, there is the suggestion of a third way when some theologians have finally "crossed the Rubicon" to speak of a pluralistic theology of religions. Some Asians must have secretly rejoiced or sighed with relief that they have finally got the idea. We Asians have lived in a religiously pluralistic world for centuries and we have always believed that truth is more than a few propositional statements. In Western symbolic logic, the opposite of "A" is "negation A," and the two must be mutually exclusive. The yin-yang philosophy in oriental thinking understands that "A" and "negation A" are correlated, interdependent, and interpenetrating. The Buddhist logic is even more radical for it insists that all reality is neither one nor many but is not-two (non-duality), in an attempt to overcome dichotomy in our thinking.

As women participating in interfaith dialogue, this pluralist understanding allows us to meet each other and share our religious heritage with honesty and integrity. We need not pretend that our religion is infinitely superior to yours, and we need not feel ashamed to pinpoint the oppressive beliefs and practices that are deeply entrenched in our particular traditions. In the statement issued by the first Asian women's consultation on interfaith dialogue in 1989, it is clearly stated that "as a result of religious discrimination, women of all religions continue to be marginalized and discriminated against at the societal level. And societal prejudices in turn influence religion in a cyclic fashion."[10] And as women trying to transform the world religions for the sake of our own salvation, we have an obligation to empower each other by sharing what lies beyond patriarchy in our own traditions.[11]

### Jewish-Christian dialogue

At the Asian women's consultation on interfaith dialogue, a Jewish woman came all the way from the USA to attend the meeting. While studying at the Harvard Divinity School some years ago, I made a special effort to go to a Jewish synagogue near Harvard to listen to a lecture by Professor Judith Plaskow. Her lecture, entitled "Toward a Jewish Feminist Theology," has been elaborated and developed into a book.[12]

As an Asian woman reading the work of Jewish feminists, I share the anguish and pain when one looks back to critical points or holy moments of one's history and finds that women were excluded. It is a bitter memory marked by scars, wounds, and hurts that are hard to heal and difficult to live with. One feels betrayal, anger, and sometimes even despair. This memory, though painful, is so much a part of one's identity that one cannot easily give it up or trade for something else, as Plaskow has powerfully testified: "I am not a Jew in the synagogue and a feminist in the world. I am a Jewish feminist and a feminist Jew in every moment of my life."[13]

The encounter and dialogue between Jewish feminists and Third World women has barely begun, and much needs to be done in the future. In the work of women theologians of the Third World, the issues of anti-semitism and the Holocaust were rarely discussed. Sometimes there is a naïve assumption that since they do not belong to the white race, they are exempted from the collective guilt. In the attempt to find some security in their Christian identity, many continued to emphasize that Jesus was a feminist, while condemning Jewish culture as irredeemably patriarchal. There is little effort to recognize the leadership roles of Jewish women in their synagogues, then and now, nor the kind of transformation going on in Judaism as a result of the feminist critique.

On the other hand, Third World women as gentiles or pagans are painfully aware of the ethnocentrism, rejection, and disdain of Jews toward the outsiders. The exclusive Christian claims can be traced in part to this Jewish legacy, as Wilfred Cantwell Smith and others have noted.[14] Without blaming the Jews for killing the goddesses,[15] it is important for us to reflect on the circumstances leading to the emergence of monotheism with its predominant androcentric symbolism and the historical implications thereafter. Just as Christians are challenged by outsiders to critically reexamine their self-understanding as Christians, Jewish feminists are also called to look at their Jewish identity with sensitivity to the plight of the gentiles. The painful memory of being excluded from their own tradition and the tragedy of the Holocaust should enable Jewish feminists to speak out for others who are oppressed and excluded, including the Palestinians living in the occupied territories.

Jewish, Christian, and other religious feminists must move ahead to break barriers and build bridges without dwelling on past guilt and pain. The ultimate challenge for all of us is to create a sociopolitical reality, a cultural matrix, and a way of speaking about God, Tao, Allah, or Nothingness so that we can all live, and live abundantly. The ancient wisdom preserved in the book of Ruth in the Hebrew Scriptures offers us fresh insights to address the brokenness of our world. The covenant between Naomi and Ruth, two women of different races and religions, exemplifies the deepest commitment and solidarity between persons. "Entreat me not to leave you or to return from following you; for where you go I will go, and where you lodge I will lodge; your people shall be my people, and your God my God" (Ruth 1.16). In the highly volatile situations of the world

71

where people, and especially women, suffer from religious and racial conflicts such as in the Middle East, Ireland, and Sri Lanka, the wisdom of Ruth should continue to guide us and motivate us to work for justice that is inclusive of all the peoples concerned.

### The language of the erotic

Ever since the African-American poet and writer Audre Lorde published the classic article "The Uses of the Erotic: The Erotic as Power,"[16] feminist theologians such as Rita Nakashima Brock and Carter Heyward have been excited about the possibility of talking about God and the power of the erotic.[17] But strangely enough, the language of the erotic is noticeably missing in the theological construction of African-American women, and feminist theologians from other parts of the world also find it difficult to speak about the power of female sexuality.

In the fall of 1991, the American public had the chance to see on television how Professor Anita F. Hill, a law professor at the University of Oklahoma, made allegations with vivid details that Judge Clarence Thomas, nominee for Associate Justice of the Supreme Court, had sexually harassed her when she worked for him some ten years ago. Professor Hill said that she was deeply embarrassed, humiliated, and hurt when those incidents occurred. African-American women theologians and ethicists are not inclined to use the language of the erotic in their religious imagination because their bodies were sold and their sexuality institutionally controlled during slavery. As Delores Williams has said, during the period of slavocracy, "many white males turned to slave women for sexual pleasure and forced these women to fulfill needs which, according to racist ideology concerning male–female relations, should have been fulfilled by white women."[18] When their bodies were defiled and used for the lust of the white oppressors, the language of the erotic had also been stolen from them for a long time.

Asian women find it embarrassing to talk about sex and the erotic not only because decent women are not supposed to raise those issues in public, but also because many of our sisters are working as prostitutes in the hotels, nightclubs, bars, disco joints, and cocktail lounges in the big cities like Manila, Bangkok, Taipei, Hong Kong, and Seoul. The international human flesh trade as a result of sex tourism has brought in much needed foreign cash for so-called economic "development." On the other hand, it has led to the degradation of women, venereal diseases, exploitation by pimps, bribery of the police, and a host of other social problems.[19] In the Philippines, some 7,000 registered hospitality girls used to service the airmen at the American Clark Air Base, and there were more than 20,000 prostitutes, waitresses, street walkers catering to the sexual appetites of American servicemen at the naval bases in Olongapo City.[20] According to a recent report by the United Nations, among the 400,000 prostitutes in Thailand, more than 60%, or 250,000, are HIV positive.[21] Behind each of these figures is a human body mutilated, defiled, and transgressed.

The tragic situation of prostitutes in Asia calls for responses from women's organizations, civic groups, and churches. In the Philippines, GABRIELA, a national organization of women's groups, has worked for the provision of alternative jobs for prostitutes, the punishment of users of, and traffickers of, women and children, and more stringent laws against vice establishments involved in the flesh trade.[22] In Thailand, women's groups established New Life Centers for prostitutes, and several organizations, such as the Foundation for Women, Empower, and the Association for Promotion of the Status of Women, have demanded changes of existing laws relating to prostitution.[23] Women in Japan have also worked in solidarity with Korean and Filipino women to demonstrate against Japanese involvement in sex tourism.[24] The magnitude of the international flesh trade and the courageous action of these women's groups challenge us to rethink the connection between the language of the erotic, the control of the female body, and power over women in its naked and symbolic forms.

Women theologians in Asia, listening to the outcry of prostitutes, have tried to address the sexual abuse and exploitation of women. Elizabeth Dominguez, a scholar of the Hebrew Scriptures from the Philippines, reread the Bible through the eyes of the prostitutes. For example, in Genesis 38 the story of Tamar whose husband died without a male heir is recounted. Tamar disguised herself as a prostitute to have sexual relations with her father-in-law so that she could conceive a son. Although it is a sad thing that Tamar was bound by duty to continue the patrilineal line, the story concludes that Tamar is proved to be more righteous than her father-in-law. In Joshua 2, the prostitute Rahab was remembered as one who negotiated with the Israelite conquerors, resulting in bringing security to the family. In the New Testament, Jesus discussed profound theological issues with the Samaritan woman at the well (John 4); and the unnamed woman could be considered a prostitute by the standards of that time. Even more striking is when Jesus said, "Let him who is without sin cast the first stone," in the story of the woman caught in adultery. The religious leaders, Pharisees, Sadducees, and Scribes must have been terribly embarrassed when Jesus proclaimed that "Thieves, prostitutes and harlots will go to heaven ahead of you."[25]

Many of us today would not be comfortable discussing sexuality and few would try to imagine what the gospel according to the prostitutes would be. While the French feminists are talking about *jouissance,* and some lesbians are trying to break the taboo to talk about passionate love and relationships among women, many women have yet to find a language to speak about pleasure of the body, female sexuality, and the power of the erotic because the yoke of "compulsory heterosexuality" is still heavy upon us. But many of the metaphors of Christianity come out of the familial context and sexual relationships between persons, such as the Father and the Son, the Church as the bride of Christ, and Adam and Eve as the first couple. The experiences of women, whose sexuality has been controlled and who suffer violence to their bodies, challenge some of these "beloved" images and should be taken up as a serious theological issue in our feminist reconstruction.

When I look back to the twenty years since the publication of *Beyond God the Father,* I rejoice that we have such a plurality of voices and multiplicity of images and symbols. Feminist theology will continue to have a future if the kind of work that we are doing stimulates, encourages, and motivates women and men to struggle against all forms of oppression, to seek justice, and to love ourselves and others. Feminist theology will not have a future if we hear only the white women's voices which try to prescribe a "universal feminism" for everybody. More awareness of the contextual and embodied nature of God-talk will help us value various formulations and approaches from different historical and cultural contexts.

Historically, there have been multifaceted and multilayered traditions in the Bible and in the Church. The Hebrew Scriptures and the New Testament can certainly be read from the Jewish, Christian, or even the Babylonian, Egyptian, or Assyrian perspectives. Similarly, the history of the Church can be examined from the points of view of the privileged, the powerful, and men, and also from the oppressed, women, and those who are excluded and abandoned. As one particular perspective contributing to our global discussion on feminist theology, Asian Christian women lift up many questions and issues for the feminist theological agenda because of our experiences of Christianity in a multicultural and multireligious context. In fact, all feminist theologians must be more sensitive to the multiplicity of cultures and the different religious worlds women live in. As Rosemary Radford Ruether points out eloquently: "We should see ourselves in need of becoming multicultural in religious understanding, entering deeply into perhaps two or three cultural configurations of religion and being able to experience our own life renewed through them in different ways. . . . But this cultivation of the ability to enter in depth into several symbolic cultures gives us a basic sympathy for the possibilities of truth in all religions."[26] If feminist theologians of all colors continue to articulate the voice of the oppressed, to integrate theory with practice, and to be more sympathetic to women's needs in different faith communities, there will be a bright future for feminist theology.

❖    ❖    ❖

## Feminist Theology

□ *Kwok Pui-lan has expressed the multicultural and multireligious content in which feminist theology occurs today. Feminist theology is increasingly involved with many different kinds of dialogue, a theme also present in Delores S. Williams's discussion of the womanist theology that has been developed by black women in the USA. The term "womanist" describes "a black feminist or a feminist of color." African-American women often find themselves at the margin of society where they experience a double oppression: that of being a woman and of being black. Black feminists have often criticized the racism of white feminists (see the roundtable discussion "Racism in the Women's Movement," in the* Journal of Feminist Studies in Religion, *vol. 4/1, 1988, pp. 93-114, and also Susan Brooks Thistlethwaite,* Sex, Race and God: Christian Feminism in Black and White, *London: Geoffrey Chapman, 1990). Yet they possess a rich religious history of "sisters of the spirit" from which they can draw strength and encouragement for their lives today. The courageous lives of black women of the nineteenth century, as described, for example, in William L. Andrews's book* Sisters of the Spirit *(Bloomington: Indiana University Press, 1986) provide black women with powerful inspiration for theologizing today. Ethicist Katie Geneva Cannon has developed* Black Womanist Ethics *(Atlanta: Scholars Press, 1988; see also Cheryl Sanders, "Christian Ethics and Theology in Womanist Perspective,"* Journal of Feminist Studies in Religion, *vol. 5/2, 1989, pp. 83-102), whereas the theologian Jacquelyn Grant has examined the womanist response to Jesus (see her study* White Women's Christ and Black Women's Jesus: Feminist Christology and Womanist Response, *Atlanta: Scholars Press, 1989).*

*In chapter 7 Delores Williams explains the origin and meaning of the word "womanist" and describes briefly how womanist theology and method work.\**

---

*\* This chapter is taken from Judith Plaskow and Carol P. Christ, eds.,* Weaving the Visions: New Patterns in Feminist Spirituality, *New York: HarperCollins, 1989, pp. 179-86.*

# 7 DELORES S. WILLIAMS

# Womanist Theology:
# Black Women's Voices

DAUGHTER:   Mama, why are we brown, pink, and yellow, and
            our cousins are white, beige, and black?
MOTHER:     Well, you know the colored race is just like a
            flower garden, with every color flower repre-
            sented.
DAUGHTER:   Mama, I'm walking to Canada and I'm taking
            you and a bunch of slaves with me.
MOTHER:     It wouldn't be the first time.

In these two conversational exchanges, Pulitzer Prize-winning
novelist Alice Walker begins to show us what she means by the
concept "womanist." The concept is presented in Walker's *In
Search of our Mother's Gardens*, and many women in Church
and society have appropriated it as a way of affirming
themselves as *black*, while simultaneously owning their connection with feminism and with the African-American community, male and female. The concept of womanist allows
women to claim their roots in black history, religion, and culture.

What then is a womanist? Her origins are in the black folk
expression "You acting womanish," meaning, according to
Walker, "wanting to know more and in greater depth than is
good for one . . . outrageous, audacious, courageous and willful
behaviour." A womanist is also "responsible, in charge, serious."
She can walk to Canada and take others with her. She loves, she
is committed, she is a universalist by temperament.

Her universality includes loving men and women, sexually or
nonsexually. She loves music, dance, the spirit, food and
roundness, struggle, and she loves herself. "Regardless."

Walker insists that a womanist is also "committed to survival and wholeness of entire people, male and female." She is no separatist, "except for health." A womanist is a black feminist or feminist of color. Or as Walker says, "Womanist is to feminist as purple is to lavender."

Womanist theology, a vision in its infancy, is emerging among African-American Christian women. Ultimately many sources — biblical, theological, ecclesiastical, social, anthropological, economic, and material from other religious traditions — will inform the development of this theology. As a contribution to this process, I will demonstrate how Walker's concept of womanist provides some significant clues for the work of womanist theologians. I will then focus on method and God-content in womanist theology. This contribution belongs to the work of prolegomena — prefatory remarks, introductory observations intended to be suggestive and not conclusive.

## The meaning of womanist

In her definition, Walker provides significant clues for the development of womanist theology. Her concept contains what black feminist scholar Bell Hooks in *From Margin to Center* identifies as cultural codes. These are words, beliefs, and behavioral patterns of a people that must be deciphered before meaningful communication can happen crossculturally. Walker's codes are female-centred and they point beyond themselves to conditions, events, meanings, and values that have crystallized in the African-American community *around women's activity* and formed traditions.

A paramount example is mother–daughter advice. Black mothers have passed on wisdom for survival — in the white world, in the black community, and with men — for as long as anyone can remember. Female slave narratives, folk tales, and some contemporary black poetry and prose reflect this tradition. Some of it is collected in "Old Sister's Advice to her Daughters," in *The Book of Negro Folklore*.

Walker's allusion to skin color points to an historic tradition of tension between black women over the matter of some black men's preference for light-skinned women. Her reference to black women's love of food and roundness points to customs of female care in the black community (including the Church) associated with hospitality and nurture.

These cultural codes and their corresponding traditions are valuable resources for indicating and validating the kind of data upon which womanist theologians can reflect as they bring black women's social, religious, and cultural experience into the discourse of theology, ethics, biblical and religious studies. Female slave narratives, imaginative literature by black women, autobiographies, the work by black women in academic disciplines, and the testimonies of black church women will be authoritative sources for womanist theologians.

Walker situates her understanding of a womanist in the context of nonbourgeois black folk culture. The literature of this culture has traditionally reflected more egalitarian relations between men and women, much less rigidity in male–female roles, and more respect for female intelligence and ingenuity than is found in bourgeois culture.

The black folk are poor. Less individualistic than those who are better off, they have for generations practiced various forms of economic sharing. For example, immediately after Emancipation mutual aid societies pooled the resources of black folk to help pay for funerals and other daily expenses. *The Book of Negro Folklore* describes the practice of rent parties which flourished during the Depression. The black folk stressed togetherness and a closer connection with nature. They respect knowledge gained through lived experience monitored by elders who differ profoundly in social class and worldview from the teachers and education encountered in American academic institutions. Walker's choice of context suggests that womanist theology can establish its lines of continuity in the black community with nonbourgeois traditions less sexist than the black power and black nationalist traditions.

In this folk context, some of the black female-centered cultural codes in Walker's definition (e.g., "Mama, I'm walking to Canada and I'm taking you and a bunch of slaves with me") point to folk heroines like Harriet Tubman, whose liberation activity earned her the name "Moses" of her people. This allusion to Tubman directs womanist memory to a liberation tradition in black history in which women took the lead, acting as catalysts for the community's revolutionary action and for social change. Retrieving this often hidden or diminished female tradition of catalytic action is an important task for womanist theologians and ethicists. Their research may well reveal that female models of authority have been absolutely essential for every struggle in the black community and for building and maintaining the community's institutions.

The womanist theologian must search for the voices, actions, opinions, experience, and faith of women whose names sometimes slip into the male-centered rendering of black history, but whose actual stories remain remote. This search can lead to such little-known freedom fighters as Milla Granson and her courageous work on a Mississippi plantation. Her liberation method broadens our knowledge of the variety of strategies black people have used to obtain freedom. According to scholar Sylvia Dannett, in *Profiles in Negro Womanhood*:

> Milla Granson, a slave, conducted a midnight school for several years. She had been taught to read and write by her former master in Kentucky . . . and in her little school hundreds of slaves benefited from her learning. . . . After laboring all day for their master, the slaves would creep stealthily to Milla's "schoolroom" (a little cabin in a back alley). . . . The doors and windows . . . had to be kept tightly sealed to avoid discovery. Each class was composed of twelve pupils and when Milla had brought them up to the extent of her ability, she "graduated" them and took in a dozen more. Through this means she graduated hundreds of slaves. Many of whom she taught to write a legible hand [forged] their own passes and set out for Canada.

Women like Tubman and Granson used subtle and silent strategies to liberate themselves and large numbers of black people. By uncovering as much as possible about such female liberation, the womanist begins to understand the relation of black history to the contemporary folk expression: "If Rosa Parks had not sat down, Martin King would not have stood up."

While she celebrates and *emphasizes* black women's culture and way of being in the world, Walker simultaneously affirms black women's historic connection with men through love and through a shared struggle for survival and for productive quality of life (i.e., "wholeness"). This suggests that two of the principal concerns of womanist theology should be survival and community building and maintenance. The goal of this community building is, of course, to establish a positive quality of life—economic, spiritual, educational—for black women, men, and children. Walker's understanding of a womanist as "not a separatist" ("except for health"), however, reminds the Christian womanist theologian that her concern for community building and maintenance must *ultimately* extend to the entire Christian community and beyond that to the larger human community.

Yet womanist consciousness is also informed by women's determination to love themselves. "Regardless." This translates into an admonition to black women to avoid the self-destruction of bearing a disproportionately large burden in the work of community building and maintenance. Walker suggests that women can avoid this trap by connecting with women's communities concerned about women's rights and well-being. Her identification of a womanist as also a feminist joins black women with their feminist heritage extending back into the nineteenth century in the work of black feminists like Sojourner Truth, Frances W. Harper, and Mary Church Terrell.

In making the feminist-womanist connection, however, Walker proceeds with great caution. While affirming an organic relationship between womanists and feminists, she also declares a deep shade of difference between them ("Womanist is to feminist as purple is to lavender"). This gives womanist scholars the freedom to explore the particularities of black women's history and culture without being guided by what white feminists have already identified as women's issues.

But womanist consciousness directs black women away from the negative divisions prohibiting community building among women. The womanist loves other women sexually and nonsexually. Therefore, respect for sexual preference is one of the marks of womanist community. According to Walker, homophobia has no place. Nor does "Colorism" (i.e., "yella" and half-white black people valued more in the black world than black-skinned people), which often separates black women from each other. Rather, Walker's womanist claim is that color variety is the substance of universality. Color, like birth and death, is common to all people. Like the navel, it is a badge of humanity connecting people with people. Two other distinctions are prohibited in Walker's womanist thinking. Class hierarchy does not dwell among women who ". . . love struggle, love the Folks . . . are committed to the survival and wholeness of an entire people." Nor do women compete for male attention when they ". . . appreciate and prefer female culture . . . value . . . women's emotional flexibility . . . and women's strength."

The intimations about community provided by Walker's definition suggest no genuine community building is possible when men are excluded (except when women's health is at stake). Neither can it occur when black women's self-love, culture, and love for each other are not affirmed and are not considered vital for the community's self-understanding. And it is thwarted if black women are expected to bear "the lion's share" of the work and to sacrifice their well-being for the good of the group.

Yet, for the womanist, mothering and nurturing are vitally important. Walker's womanist reality begins with mothers relating to their children and is characterized by black women (not necessarily bearers of children) nurturing great numbers of black people in the liberation struggle (e.g., Harriet Tubman). Womanist emphasis upon the value of mothering and nurturing is consistent with the testimony of many black women. The poet Carolyn Rogers speaks of her mother as the great black bridge that brought her over. Walker dedicates her novel *The Third Life of Grange Copeland* to her mother ". . . who made a way out of no way." As a child in the black Church, I heard women (and men) give thanks to God for their mothers ". . . who stayed behind and pulled the wagon over the long haul."

It seems, then, that the clues about community from Walker's definition of a womanist suggest that the mothering and nurturing dimension of African-American history can provide resources for shaping criteria to measure the quality of justice in the community. These criteria could be used to assure female-male equality in the presentation of the community's models of authority. They could also gauge the community's division of labor with regard to the survival tasks necessary for building and maintaining community.

### Womanist theology and method

Womanist theology is already beginning to define the categories and methods needed to develop along lines consistent with the sources of that theology. Christian womanist theological methodology needs to be informed by at least four elements: (1) a multidialogical intent, (2) a liturgical intent, (3) a didactic intent, and (4) a commitment both to reason *and* to the validity of female imagery and metaphorical language in the construction of theological statements.

A multidialogical intent will allow Christian womanist theologians to advocate and participate in dialogue and action with *many* diverse social, political, and religious communities concerned about human survival and productive quality of life for the oppressed. The genocide of culture and peoples (which has often been instigated and accomplished by Western white Christian groups or governments) and the nuclear threat of omnicide mandate womanist participation in such dialogue/ action. But in this dialogue/action the womanist also should keep her speech and action focused upon the slow genocide of poor black women, children, and men by exploitative systems denying them productive jobs, education, health care, and living space. Multidialogical activity may, like a jazz symphony, communicate some of its most important messages in what the harmony-driven conventional ear hears as discord, as disruption of the harmony in both the black American and white American social, political, and religious status quo.

If womanist theological method is informed by a liturgical intent, then womanist theology will be relevant to (and will reflect) the thought, worship, and action of the black Church. But a liturgical intent will also allow womanist theology to challenge the thought/worship/action of the black Church with the discordant and prophetic messages emerging from womanist participation in multidialogics. This means that womanist theology will consciously impact *critically* upon the foundations of liturgy, challenging the Church to use justice principles to select the sources that will shape the content of liturgy. The question must be asked: "How does this source portray blackness/darkness, women, and economic justice for nonruling-class people?" A negative portrayal will demand omission of the source or its radical reformation by the black Church. The Bible, a major source in black church liturgy, must also be subjected to the scrutiny of justice principles.

A didactic intent in womanist theological method assigns a teaching function to theology. Womanist theology should teach Christians new insights about moral life based on ethics supporting justice for women, survival, and a productive quality of life for poor women, children, and men. This means that the womanist theologian must give authoritative status to black folk wisdom (e.g., Brer Rabbit literature) and to black women's moral wisdom (expressed in their literature) when she responds to the question, "How ought the Christian to live in the world?" Certainly tensions may exist between the moral teachings derived from these sources and the moral teachings about obedience, love, and humility that have usually buttressed presuppositions about living the Christian life. Nevertheless, womanist theology, in its didactic intent, must teach the Church the different ways God reveals prophetic word and action for Christian living.

These intents, informing theological method, can yield a theological language whose foundation depends as much upon its imagistic content as upon reason. The language can be rich in female imagery, metaphor, and story. For the black Church, this kind of theological language may be quite useful, since the language of the black religious experience abounds in images and metaphors. Clifton Johnson's collection of black conversion experiences, *God Struck Me Dead*, illustrates this point.

The appropriateness of womanist theological language will ultimately reside in its ability to bring black women's history, culture, and religious experience into the interpretive circle of Christian theology and into the liturgical life of the Church. Womanist theological language must, in this sense, be an instrument for social and theological change in Church and society.

Regardless of one's hopes about intentionality and womanist theological method, questions must be raised about the God-content of the theology. Walker's mention of the black womanist's love of the spirit is a true reflection of the great respect African-American women have always shown for the presence and work of the spirit. In the black Church, women (and men) often judge the effectiveness of the worship service not on the scholarly content of the sermon nor on the ritual nor on orderly process. Rather, worship has been effective if "the spirit was high," i.e., if the spirit was actively and obviously present in a balanced blend of prayer, of cadenced word (the sermon), and of syncopated music ministering to the pain of the people.

The importance of this emphasis upon the spirit is that it allows Christian womanist theologians, in their use of the Bible, to identify and reflect upon those biblical stories in which poor oppressed women had a special encounter with divine emissaries of God, like the spirit. In the Hebrew Testament, Hagar's story is most illustrative and relevant to African-American women's experience of bondage, of African heritage, of encounter with God/emissary in the midst of fierce survival struggles. Kate Cannon, among a number of black female preachers and ethicists, urges black Christian women to regard themselves as Hagar's sisters.

In relation to the Christian or New Testament, the Christian womanist theologian can refocus the salvation story so that it emphasizes the beginning of revelation with the spirit mounting Mary, a woman of the poor: (". . . the Holy Spirit shall come upon thee, and the power of the Highest shall overshadow thee . . ." Luke 1.35). Such an interpretation of revelation has roots in nineteenth-century black abolitionist and feminist Sojourner Truth. Posing an important question and response, she refuted a white preacher's claim that women could not have rights equal to men because Christ was not a woman. Truth asked, "Whar did your Christ come from? . . . From God and a woman! Man had nothin' to do wid Him!" This suggests that womanist theology could eventually speak of God in a well-developed theology of the spirit. The sources for this theology are many. Harriet Tubman often "went into the spirit" before her liberation missions and claimed her strength for liberation activity came from this way of meeting God. Womanist theology has grounds for shaping a theology of the spirit informed by black women's political action.

Christian womanist responses to the question "Who do you say God is?" will be influenced by these many sources. Walker's way of connecting womanists with the spirit is only one clue. The integrity of black church women's faith, their love of Jesus, their commitment to life, love, family, and politics will also yield vital clues. And other theological voices (black liberation, feminist, Islamic, Asian, Hispanic, African, Jewish, and Western white male traditional) will provide insights relevant for the construction of the God-content of womanist theology.

Each womanist theologian will add her own special accent to the understandings of God emerging from womanist theology. But if one needs a final image to describe women coming together to shape the enterprise, Bess B. Johnson in *God's Fierce Whimsy* offers an appropriate one. Describing the difference between the play of male and female children in the black community where she developed, Johnson says:

> the boys in the neighborhood had this game with rope . . . tug-o'-war . . . till finally some side would jerk the rope away from the others, who'd fall down. . . . Girls . . . weren't allowed to play with them in this tug-o'-war; so we figured out how to make our own rope—out of . . . little dandelions. You just keep adding them, one to another, and you can go on and on. . . . Anybody, even the boys, could join us. . . . The whole purpose of our game was to create this dandelion chain—that was it. And we'd keep going, creating till our mamas called us home.

Like Johnson's dandelion chain, womanist theological vision will grow as black women come together and connect piece with piece. Between the process of creating and the sense of calling, womanist theology will one day present itself in full array, reflecting the divine spirit that connects us all.

☐ *Like their African-American sisters, Hispanic women in the USA struggle to liberate themselves and to name their own specific struggle. Hispanic women experience themselves as living in exile, on the margins of a dominant, oppressive, white society, but through working in groups they have developed a communal theology of liberation; this must be understood in the wider context of Hispanic theology within the USA as a process of enablement for Hispanic women. In their ongoing struggle, Hispanic women have sought a way to name themselves and, encouraged by African-American women who describe themselves as "womanist," they have created the new term* mujerista *to encourage Hispanic women and explain their struggle.*

*The wider context of Hispanic theology is presented by Allan Figueroa Deck, ed., in* Frontiers of Hispanic Theology in the United States *(Maryknoll, NY: Orbis Books, 1992), where two contributions discuss different aspects of Hispanic women's liberation theology: María Pilar Aquino, "Perspectives on a Latina's Feminist Liberation Theology" (pp. 23–40) and Gloria Inés Loya, "The Hispanic Woman:* Pasionara *and* Pastora *of the Hispanic Community" (pp. 124–33). The first book entirely devoted to Hispanic women's theology is the jointly produced English–Spanish work by Ada María Isasi-Díaz and Yolanda Tarango,* Hispanic Women: Prophetic Voice in the Church *(Minneapolis: Fortress Press, 1992). Originally published in 1988, it does not use the term* mujerista *because it had not been invented at that time. I have chosen an extract from this book (pp. 103–7) because it describes the task of Hispanic women's liberation theology in some detail. This is followed (on p. 97) by another extract from a roundtable discussion in the* Journal of Feminist Studies in Religion *(vol. 8/1, 1992, pp. 105–9); this explains the term* mujerista *in depth because the discussion was undertaken in order to get Hispanic women scholars to appropriate and use this new term.*

*Ada María Isasi-Díaz's description of the content of her work and her commitment is a fitting introduction to Part Two of this Reader. Chapter 8 first shows the way she describes herself in Susan Brooks Thistlethwaite's and Mary Potter's* Lift Every

Voice *(San Francisco: HarperCollins, 1990, pp. 31-2), and then gives a description of the task of Hispanic women's liberation theology, followed by a discussion of the term* mujerista.

## 8   ADA MARÍA ISASI-DÍAZ

# The Task of Hispanic Women's Liberation Theology— *Mujeristas*: Who We Are and What We Are About

I am a Cuban activist theologian struggling to develop a *mujerista* theology that is rooted in and has as its source the experience of Hispanic women. I have lived away from my country most of my adult life because of circumstances beyond my control and I think of myself as living in exile. This is the context within which I have struggled to find my voice and my mission. I now know that finding my voice has been part of my mission, a mission that now calls me to struggle to create a platform in the theological world for my voice and the voices of my Hispanic sisters.

As a *mujerista* I do not see myself as part of a minority group, a marginalized group. It is a fact that at present *mujeristas*, as well as all Hispanics, have no way of influencing the society in which we live; our values and ideals are not part of the norm of society. As a *mujerista* I believe that we need to change radically the society in which we live. Simply influencing society will not result in the changes that are needed to bring about peace with justice in our world. That is why we *mujeristas* understand ourselves along the lines of the biblical concept of the "remnant." Like the biblical remnant we are not an integral part of society. Our mission is to challenge oppressive structures that refuse to allow us to be full members of society while preserving our distinctiveness as Hispanic women.

We also apply this understanding of ourselves as a remnant to our theological task and to our role as theologians. We see *mujerista* theology as a distinctive contribution to the theological enterprise at large which challenges particularly nonliberative theological understandings. For us theology is a praxis—a liberative praxis having as its goal the liberation of Hispanic women, which cannot take place at the expense of any other oppressed group. As *mujerista* theologians we straddle the academic theological world and the Hispanic women's community. Hispanic women are indeed my community of accountability. But I am an academically trained theologian and wish to maintain a dialogue with all liberation theologies. Therefore, *mujerista* theology must be understandable both to Hispanic women and to liberation theologians. Our theological method must be a liberative praxis; at the same time we must be able to explain our methodology in such a way that it impacts, in no matter how limited a degree, upon the whole theological world.

For me the struggle is life, *la vida es la lucha*. To do *mujerista* theology is an intrinsic part of my struggle for liberation. To do *mujerista* theology is to attempt to live life to the fullest, to be about justice and the self-determination of all peoples. To do *mujerista* theology is to believe that God stands in solidarity with us, Hispanic women.

**The task at hand**

The task of Hispanic women's liberation theology is to further the liberation of Hispanic women. Liberation is an ongoing process that involves three levels of meaning of one complex process:

> In the first place, liberation expresses the aspirations of oppressed peoples and social classes, emphasizing the conflictual aspect of the economic, social, and political process which puts them at odds with wealthy nations and oppressive classes . . .
>
> At a deeper level, liberation can be applied to an understanding of history. Man [*sic*] is seen as assuming

conscious responsibility of his [*sic*] own destiny. . . . In this perspective the unfolding of man's [*sic*] dimensions is demanded—a man [*sic*] who makes himself [*sic*] throughout his [*sic*] life and throughout history.[1]

Third, liberation enables Hispanic women to deal with their religious understandings and practices in such a way that they recognize them as the source of their presence and action in history. Liberation enables Hispanic women to articulate what they have often lived "unconsciously": it is their sense of the divine in their lives that gives them strength for the struggle—a struggle that is not a part of life but life itself.[2]

Undoubtedly, because of the different levels of meaning in the process of liberation, Hispanic women's liberation theology is a subversive praxis. It does not accommodate itself to Church or academic structures, but rather seeks to change them so that Hispanic women will be able to participate fully in them. As a praxis, Hispanic women's liberation theology has to insist on the reflective moment, which is so important in the ongoing process of critical awareness. Without this critical awareness, there is no conscientization and, therefore, no possibility of liberation. Reflection is also intrinsic to self-definition. Only by a firm grasp of who they are—their religious and cultural roots—and who they want to be—their hopes and dreams of liberation—can Hispanic women begin to be self-determining. Furthermore, the possibility of being self-determining depends partially on being able to influence the norm. That will never happen without reflection, without a critical awareness that will enable them to lay aside "all forms of false consciousness . . . and learn to discern what is of perennial value in their own cultural traditions."[3]

### The theologians

Hispanic women's liberation theology as a praxis is done by the community and not just by one or two persons. Hispanic women protesting the lack of city services in the South Bronx, emptying a bag of trash on the desk of the city official who could order the garbage to be picked up more frequently in the area where the women live—that is doing Hispanic women's liberation theology. A woman struggling in a meeting controlled by Hispanic men to pass a resolution that would insure a certain percentage of women in each of the delegations to an important national meeting—that is doing Hispanic women's liberation theology. Four women testifying in front of a group of Roman Catholic bishops about the oppression of Hispanic women in Church as well as in society, finishing their presentation by giving each of the bishops a stone and telling them, "We have asked for bread and you have given us stone. Put these stones on your altars when you celebrate Eucharist and remember us Hispanic women, struggling for our liberation and the liberation of our people"—that is doing Hispanic women's liberation theology.

But the reflection that led to such actions, reflection about self-identity, about our participation in making decisions that affect us and our families, about our willingness to risk—doing such reflection is also doing Hispanic women's liberation theology. Meeting after an action to analyze what has been done, to evaluate how each one involved performed assigned tasks, to hold accountable those who have participated in a community action/project—participating in such meetings is doing Hispanic women's liberation theology. To gather, to reflect on how the nature of Hispanic women's involvement either reflects or goes against important values and religious understandings—such reflection is doing Hispanic women's liberation theology.

Hispanic women's liberation theology as a praxis is done by the community, each one contributing to the process of doing theology according to her own gifts: combining her natural ability, opportunity, and her generosity for the good of the community. All gifts are of equal value. No gift is better than another one; no gift is more valuable, more holy, more worthy of respect than another. At a given moment, because of a particular need, one gift might be more useful than another, but that does not make it more important. To place the gifts of the people of the community in any hierarchical gradation is to do violence to the community. One of the intrinsic elements of the community is an equalization of power. To see anyone's gift as

91

more important is to do away with equality, is to permit the use of individual gifts for claiming power over the rest of the community. Anyone using her gift in such fashion has destroyed the gift because it is not being used any longer for the common good; gifts are gifts only insofar as they are used for the good of the community.

In any community there is a great variety of gifts. Some of the members of the community have the gift of gathering the folk; others are the physical and/or spiritual nurturers of the group; others are powerful speakers; and others are prophets listening to the hidden hopes of the people and proclaiming them. Some can move the community to prayer and worship; others are leaders of action; others quietly pursue the common good by being always ready to participate; others are writers; and others are teachers/learners—enablers. Among the latter are those who enable the group in the reflective moment of praxis, who lead the community in reflecting on the "moods and motivations" that move the community, who enable the community to understand that its daily struggle for survival is not separate from its religious understandings, sentiments, beliefs. The Hispanic women with this gift of enablement, as well as those with the gift of gathering what the community is saying, writing it down, and making it known are indeed "theological technicians."

"Theological technicians" are those who are "in possession of certain technical competences in exegesis, social sciences, languages, archaeology, or history and who offer(s) these findings in these different fields to the real theologians to help them in the act of interpreting reality from . . . [their] perspective . . ."[4]

Theological technicians, as well as other members of the community with specific knowledge, must not hoard what they know—often a ploy used to achieve privileged status within the community. On the contrary, theological technicians should make it their goal to help others learn these same skills so as to enrich the community and its praxis.

What is the task of the theological technician who is the enabler? First, enablers of the reflective moments have to understand their task very clearly so as not to objectify the group and set themselves up as the authority. The task of the enabler is to lead the participants in the group "to grasp the knowledge we all have."[5] The enabler has to both see herself and be seen as a member of the group. She might suggest the questions—some of the questions, the starting questions—but she also has to be willing to share with the group, to become vulnerable in order to learn with the group, from the group. The enabler has the responsibility of insisting on critical reflection. It is not a matter of just telling stories, of just relating what happened; it is a matter of coming to understand the reasons behind the events in the lives of Hispanic women. Only then will a critical consciousness be developed by the group as a whole and by each of the members of the group in particular. The enabler has to push the group continually to make the connections between what different members of the group are saying, between what they are saying and their religious understandings and actions, between the understandings of this group and those of other groups. Finally, the enabler has to be sure that the reflection of the community is gathered and recorded, as it is of great importance for that community to continue to deal with what they have surfaced during the time spent together; in the same way, the reflection of the community is important for other communities also struggling for liberation. The reflections of the community need to be given a voice in order to claim a place as part of the norm of society.

The recorder/writer, whether or not she is the enabler, also has to be a member of the group. Unless she is an intrinsic member of the community and understands that her own liberation is linked to the liberation of the community about which she is writing, she runs the risk of objectifying the group, of using what the community has said to make her own individual points. The recorder/writer, therefore, has a most important task; she is accountable to the community for saying what the community has said and not making the community say, through her writings, what it did not say. At the same time, she is also accountable to the community for making what the community has said understandable to the other communities of struggle and even to the dominant group in order to challenge it. Thus, because her writing is addressed to several audiences, the task of the recorder/writer is enormously complicated. How can the material speak to Hispanic women and the Hispanic community at large and, at the same time, say something to and/or be understood by theological communities of other cultures and oppressed groups? Regardless of which community she is addressing, the recorder/writer must keep in mind at all times that her main community of accountability is the community of Hispanic women.

How does the recorder/writer deal with the issue of making both audible and understandable the voice of the community instead of thinking that she is "being" or is "giving" a voice to the community? In order not to lose the truth and vitality generated by the process, the writer needs to understand the process not as a consultation, but as *doing* theology. The material gathered should not be violated by imposing the writer's analysis and theological constructs on it and/or using the material gathered from the reflection of the community as examples to back up what the writer wants to say.

In order not to fall into this objectification of the reflection of the community, the writing process needs to follow certain criteria:

- The writer needs to write in a very simple way, using extensive direct quotes from what the community has said.[6] The analysis should be geared to explaining what the women have said.
- The material needs to be organized rather than systematized according to some preconceived construct. It is not a matter of imposing a systematic grid on it, but of organizing it so that its meaning is readily accessible and reflects accurately the community's reflection.
- The organization should be around central words/ideas that are repeated often in the conversation and carry emotional weight. Two important keys to this emotional weight are: When do the women cry? When do they speak in English and when in Spanish? Both the expressions of emotion and the choice of language give most important clues as to what is intrinsic to the women's lives and what are foreign, nonorganic understandings.

- The relationship among these frequently repeated central ideas/words has to be carefully considered. Do they relate dialectically, sympathetically, controversially?
- The imagery used by the women has to be central in the writing. The imagery should stand on its own; its interpretation should neither overwhelm it, simplify it, nor adapt it.[7]

Once the recorder/writer has finished her task, the material should be reviewed by a representative number of the women who have participated in the praxis. This is done in order to ensure faithfulness of the written word to the understandings and experiences of the group. If the group members cannot relate directly to what has been written, the writing needs revision. Second, they must see what has been written as their own. The litmus test for this will be the future use of the written material by the community. Third, the community doing theology needs also to decide how it wants to use what has been written—is it best to use it only internally or would it be a good strategy to go public with their reflections? If the material is going to be made public, it needs to be studied by members of other communities who stand in solidarity with Hispanic women to ensure that what has been written is a voice that can be understood but cannot be used against these other communities of struggle.

To claim that the community of Hispanic women is the real theologian and to insist that those academically trained are but theological technicians—organic theologians themselves insofar as they are members of the theologizing community—these are intrinsic elements of Hispanic women's liberation theology. The community of Hispanic women is the true theologian; in no way does Hispanic women's liberation theology attempt to minimize or see the task of the community as less important or less central to the process of doing theology than the task of the theological technicians.[8] This does not mean that there might not be a proper place and function for academic theology—a theology done by technicians for a community of which they are not a part or a "general" theology based on the belief that the technician's understandings are "objective" and, therefore, universally valid. Frankly, to affirm or deny the existence or importance of such a theology is irrelevant to Hispanic women. This is made evident by the fact that many Hispanic women have lived their religion mostly outside the official churches with which academic theology deals and that they have ignored the language of such a theology. Such irrelevance is a warning to academic theologians about claiming to be "voice of the voiceless."[9]

*Evaluating the task*

The task of the writer as described in the previous section includes what constitutes an evaluation for Hispanic women's liberation theology: submitting the text to the community of Hispanic women in order for them to see if it is faithful to their experience, if they can understand what is being said. Does the language adequately disclose "an authentic dimension of [their] experiences as selves"? Is what is being said true? Does it explain "how a particular concept (e.g., time, space, self, or God) functions as a fundamental 'belief' or 'condition of possibility' of all [their] experience"?[10] Does it clearly and unequivocally explain the religious dimension of the moods and motivations that move them to action and give them reason for hope? Is what has been written an appropriate understanding of their sense and experience of Christianity?[11]

Though this analysis by Hispanic women is the core and deciding factor in the evaluation of Hispanic women's liberation theology, it also requires an evaluation by people outside the community in order to ascertain if what has been written can be understood clearly by the other receiving communities. Persons from other oppressed groups standing in solidarity with Hispanic women—those willing to understand not only with the head but also with the heart, willing to enter into the experience of Hispanic women as much as they can—are the ones, besides Hispanic women, to critique, to evaluate what has been written. The task is not to judge whether it is right or wrong but, again, to ascertain that what is being said will be grasped adequately by others. It is important for questions pertaining to strategy to figure in their critique. Given the way of presenting the material, is it going to gain some attention, a foot in the door? Is it going to impact society at large at least in a small way?

This is extremely important because, since the task of Hispanic women's liberation theology is the liberation of women, doing theology has to operate at the three levels of meaning included in the sense of liberation. Is Hispanic women's liberation theology contributing to the political, economic, and social liberation of Hispanic women? Is it enabling Hispanic women to assume conscious responsibility for their own history? Does it elucidate, explain how their religious understandings and their "Christianity" motivate them to action?[12]

Hispanic women's liberation theology has been born. As a process and a praxis, it is always being birthed by Hispanic women who struggle for liberation and for whom *la vida es la lucha* (life is the struggle). But Hispanic women's liberation theology also does the birthing—it births hope and a vision of the future in which all peoples will be free because Hispanic women are free.

❖    ❖    ❖

MUJERISTAS: WHO WE ARE AND WHAT WE ARE ABOUT

The decades of the 1970s and 1980s have clearly established the existence of a multiplicity of theologies. What has made this plurality possible is the unmasking of the so-called objectivity of theology. All theology is subjective because one of its main elements is the historical circumstances of the theologian along with the community of faith to which she or he relates. The theology I have been involved in articulating is born out of my experience and that of other Hispanic women living in the USA. For the last fifteen years those of us who struggle against ethnic prejudice, sexism, and in many cases, classism, have been at a loss as to what to call ourselves. The majority of Hispanic women have simply called ourselves *cubanas, chicanas,*

97

*puertorriqueñas*, and most probably will continue to do so. Some of us have called ourselves *feministas hispanas*. Though *feministas hispanas* has been an appellation riddled with difficulties, we have felt the need for a name that would indicate the struggle against sexism that is part of our daily bread, while also helping us identify one another as we struggle for our survival within Hispanic communities and US society as a whole. But using *feminista hispana* has required long explanations of what such a phrase does *not* mean.[13]

*Feministas hispanas* have been consistently marginalized in the Anglo feminist community because of our critique of its ethnic/racial prejudice and lack of class analysis. Though Anglo feminists have worked to correct these serious shortcomings in their discourse, in my experience their praxis continues to be flawed.[14] *Feministas hispanas* have also been rejected by many in the Hispanic community who consider feminism a concern of Anglo women. Yet Hispanic women widely agree with an analysis of sexism as an evil within our communities, an evil that plays into the hands of the dominant forces of society and helps to repress and exploit us in such a way that we constitute a large percentage of those in the lowest economic stratum. Likewise Hispanic women widely agree that, though we make up the vast majority of active churchgoers, we do the work but do not participate in deciding what work is to be done; we do the praying but our understanding of the God to whom we pray is ignored.

Hispanic women understand how sexism works in our lives and we struggle against this oppression daily. In spite of our understanding and struggle, however, we have not had a way to name ourselves. To name oneself is one of the most powerful human acts. A name is not just a word by which one is identified. A name also provides the conceptual framework, the point of reference, the mental constructs that are used in thinking, understanding, and relating to a person, an idea, a movement. In our search for a name of our own, we have turned to our music, an intrinsic part of the soul of our culture. In our songs, love songs as well as protest songs, we are simply called *mujer*. And so, those of us who make a preferential option for *mujeres* are *mujeristas*.[15]

*Creating a name of our own—beginnings*

The task at hand is to create the meaning of *mujerismo*. We want to start by recognizing that for *mujerismo* to become a term that refers to the struggles of Hispanic women against oppression, the meaning of the term has to remain open, in flux—alive! Those of us who have come up with the term and have been the first to use it wish to encourage Hispanic women to appropriate this term, fully aware of the fact that such a process also includes adaptation. We have no intention of ever claiming exclusive authority to decide that what others mean by *mujerismo* is not correct, that a given person should not be called a *mujerista*. But we do believe we have the responsibility of establishing certain flexible parameters of meaning for these terms and of insisting on organic development rather than artificial changes. This is why instead of using a definition, we have chosen to use descriptions; instead of establishing criteria, we have chosen to indicate context; instead of demanding correct usage we have chosen to explain our methodology. We do not ask others to conform to our understanding and use of the terms *mujerismo* and *mujerista*. But we do ask those who use these terms to participate in constructing, rather than rejecting, this world of meaning, and to engage in this task openly, fueled by the desire and need for our liberation as Hispanic women.

We come to the task of establishing parameters from a religious perspective—not only because we are theologians, but also because of the centrality of religion in the Hispanic culture. It is particularly Christianity, and within Christianity, Roman Catholicism, that continues to be the faith tradition to which the majority of Hispanic women relate. We will attempt to deal with these terms in language that is accessible to our Hispanic community. Some may consider this language lacking in precision. But for us the most important thing is to contribute to the struggle of Hispanic women. Though we believe that we must impact the world of ideas and the academic world as part of this struggle, we choose clarity to our main community of accountability over academic correctness and linguistic precision.

This discussion has already provided much information about

*mujerismo*. But, to be more explicit: a *mujerista* is a Hispanic woman who struggles to liberate herself not as an individual but as a member of a Hispanic community. She is one who builds bridges among Hispanics instead of falling into sectarianism and using divisive tactics. A *mujerista* understands that her task is to gather the hopes and expectations of her people about justice and peace. In the *mujerista*, God chooses to once again lay claims to and revindicate the divine image and likeness of women made visible from the very beginning in the person of Eve. The *mujerista* is called to gestate new women and new men—Hispanics who are willing to work for the common good, knowing that such work requires us to denounce destructive self-abnegation.[16]

## Mujerista *theology*

Because the term *mujerismo* was conceived by a group of us working from a religious perspective for the liberation of Hispanic women, the first application of this term has been to our theological task. Such an application further illumines how we have used the term *mujerismo*.

*Mujerista* theology, which includes both ethics and theology, is a liberative praxis: reflective action that has as its goal liberation. As a liberative praxis, *mujerista* theology is a process of enablement for Hispanic women insisting on the development of a strong sense of moral agency, and clarifying the importance and value of who we are, what we think, and what we do. Second, as a liberative praxis, *mujerista* theology seeks to impact mainline theologies that support what is normative in Church and, to a large degree, in society.

How does *mujerista* theology accomplish this two-pronged liberative praxis? A first task of *mujerista* theology is to enable Hispanic women to understand the many oppressive structures that strongly influence our daily lives. It enables us to understand that the goal of our struggle is not to participate in and to benefit from these structures, but to change them radically. In theological and religious language this means that *mujerista* theology helps us to discover and affirm the presence of God in the midst of our communities and the revelation of

God in our daily lives. We must come to understand the reality of structural sin and find ways of combating it because it effectively hides God's ongoing revelation from us and from society at large.

The second task of *mujerista* theology is to help us define our preferred future: What will a radically different society look like? What will be its values and norms? In theological and religious language this means that *mujerista* theology enables Hispanic women to understand the centrality of eschatology in the life of every Christian. Our preferred future breaks into our present oppression in many different ways. We must recognize those eschatological glimpses and rejoice in them and struggle to make those glimpses become our whole horizon. Third, *mujerista* theology enables Hispanic women to understand how much we have already bought into the prevailing systems in society—including the religious systems—internalizing our own oppression. *Mujerista* theology helps us see that radical structural change cannot happen unless radical change takes place in each and every one of us. In theological and religious language this means that *mujerista* theology assists us in the process of conversion, helping Hispanic women to see the reality of sin in our lives. Further, it enables us to understand that to resign ourselves to what others tell us is our lot and to accept suffering and self-effacement is not necessarily virtuous.

To coin a new term is not complicated but to have it become common usage is another matter. What moved us to create the terms *mujerismo* and *mujerista* was our experience in the struggle for our liberation as Hispanic women. We felt a strong need to have a name of our own. And as community, allowing ourselves to be inspired by one of the best expressions of the soul of our culture, our music, we birthed these terms. Now we eagerly wait for all Hispanic women to add their understandings to the meaning of *mujerismo* so that we all, as Hispanic women struggling for liberation, will be able to call ourselves *mujeristas.*

☐ *In her chapter on "The Bible and* Mujerista *Theology," in Susan Brooks Thistlethwaite's book* Lift Every Voice, *Ada María Isasi-Díaz sums up once again the basic characteristics of* mujerista *theology (pp. 261-2).*

There are certain basic aspects of *mujerista* theology that must be shared with the reader:

(1) *Mujerista* theology is Hispanic women's theology.

(2) *Mujerista* theology is a *mestizaje* (hybrid) born of the intersection of feminism, Hispanic culture, and the struggle for liberation.

(3) *Mujerista* theology is a communal theology; the theologizing has been and is being done by groups of Hispanic women throughout the USA. Two of us who have academic theological training have served as theological technicians, articulating and synthesizing the theological understandings of the community. As full members of the theologizing community, we have afterwards met with some of the other women in the theologizing community and asked them for a critique of what we have written.

(4) In the category of Hispanic women we include women whose cultural and historical roots are in Cuba, Mexico, and Puerto Rico, but who at present live in the USA. They now see their lives linked to this country and have a sense of being part of the resident Hispanic community in the USA.

(5) When we refer specifically to Hispanic women, we are not claiming that we are unique, but that we are distinct. Therefore, some of what we say about Hispanic women may very well be true of Hispanic men and some of it may be true about women in general.

❖     ❖     ❖

# PART TWO
# Women's Oppression and Cries of Pain

☐ *The starting point of Third World women's theology is their own experience of economic, social, political, and ecclesiastical exploitation and oppression. In many ways the powerful reality of patriarchy is not unlike that experienced by women elsewhere, but it expresses itself in harsher, starker forms. Women in the Third World often face abject poverty and extreme forms of exploitation; they are treated as cheap labor, migrant workers, and are victims of international trafficking in connection with prostitution. Much violence against women in Third World countries is also associated with militarism and development, as it is with long-established social structures and taboos about women's sexuality and bodily functions—often deeply rooted in traditional religious teachings. (Women in the member churches of the WCC have undertaken a comparative study of these issues; the results are found in Jeanne Becher, ed.,* Women, Religion and Sexuality: Studies on the Impact of Religious Teachings on Women, *Geneva: WCC Publications, 1990.) Today, the consciousness of many women has been raised and their voices are now crying out loudly against their situation of injustice and oppression. Theirs is a new strength, a vision, and a hope that women's life can be different. Women's cries of pain ring through the following pages, but also their faith and hope that women can, and must be able to, realize their full humanity as promised by the Christian gospel.*

*The forms of oppression are many, and numerous examples can be given of the powerlessness of women, whether in Asia, Africa, or South America. There are many women who now speak out about their experiences and that of their sisters, and they show us how women are becoming empowered in a new way. Christian women find a new empowerment through reading the Bible with new eyes and reinterpreting Christian stories in a new light. This is visible in some of the following passages that focus primarily on women's oppression and pain, but the strength of women's faith and their source of empowerment will become even more evident in Part Three, which deals with "The Bible as a Source of Empowerment for Women."*

❖   ❖   ❖

□ *Chapter 9 was originally part of a chapter entitled "The Feminist Challenge", contributed by the Sri Lankan Ranjini Rebera, now living in Australia, to a book on women's stories of faith and power (see Musimbi R. A. Kanyoro and Wendy S. Robins, eds.,* The Power We Celebrate, *Geneva: WCC Publications, 1992, pp. 37–50). Ranjini Rebera reflects on the power of patriarchy and on women's power to challenge it.*

# 9  RANJINI REBERA

# Challenging Patriarchy

It is easy to see the human face of patriarchy in oppression and the exploitation that women are subjected to in the economic areas of life. But when it comes to social issues, patriarchy can take many guises. From the rejection of the female fetus even before the baby is born to the giving in marriage, to the gender-specific role in a home, women know and experience the reality of patriarchy.

In Asian society there is still a myth that women are treated as goddesses and that motherhood is sacred. It is an image that should bring dignity and freedom to women, but the reality is the very opposite. If women are being treated like goddesses, how is it that our countries need to legislate to protect the rights of women? Why is it that despite such legislation, women have little or no property rights and women have little or no economic status in our countries? If motherhood is sacred, why are mothers treated with scorn and oppressed? Laws granting maternity leave in most countries do not state that this benefit is only for married mothers. But the practice discriminates between the wed and the unwed. Motherhood seems sacred only in the context of marriage, in other words, the protection of a man is required to sanctify the reproductive ability of women!

Furthermore, the reproductive functions of women are still considered unclean. They serve one purpose alone: to give birth, preferably to a male child.

A society that, despite legislation, operates on the basis of patriarchy cannot be called a just society. Power resides with the powerful, and patriarchy is powerful. All the legislation in the statute books will not eradicate the control of patriarchy until women become aware not only of their rights, but also of the images and symbols they have inherited from childhood. Embedded in these images are the controls of patriarchy. "Girls are weak. Boys are strong." "Girls are silly. Boys are sensible."[1] And so it goes on. Interestingly, just as consumerism is targeted at women and is perpetuated mainly by women, so is patriarchy. We teach our children in the home, in our schools, through community activities, that male is superior, that male is right. Often we do this unconsciously because we have internalized these images from our childhood. Once these images are embedded in both women and men, it is inevitable that society reflects the same norms and principles. A grown woman believes she is weak and silly. A grown man believes he is strong and sensible.

A woman's low image of herself then becomes the source through which society exploits its women. Whether it be through economic exploitation or through social exploitation, the low image that most women have of themselves is crucial to the kind of acceptance women tolerate when social oppression takes place. Violence against women is a good example. With the rising level of consciousness created by women's groups, violence against women, especially physical violence, has come into the open. A start has been made, and rape is not talked of in the same hushed tones as in years past. But it is interesting that most laws governing rape still favor men rather than the victim, who is a woman. As Padmini Swaminathan writes, "Rape, not kidnapping and seduction, have been made offenses not to protect the person of the woman, but to protect the rights of a man against violation of another."[2]

This kind of violence, evident in countries such as Sri Lanka, gains its satisfaction through the raping and killing of women and children. Domestic violence in the form of dowry deaths and bride burning are other expressions of this form of violence. Dignity and the right to sovereignty do not seem to be valid for women. So gentle, caring women become victims of violent societies that have grown to accept violence as the norm. Physical, economic, and psychological violence continues to form the fabric of our society. At a series of forums on "Violence and the Community" held in Canberra, Australia, an Asian woman talked of the pain of academic violence. She described the pain that women suffered in the name of academic advancement. Husbands pursue academic goals and academic advancement at the cost of family life and sometimes at the cost of a wife's career. Another form of this violence against women is evident in the fast-growing trade of prostitution.

Most societies still consider sexuality and women as synonymous. Sexuality is still linked to temptation and sin, and female sexuality has always been the property of men. A woman has no right to enjoy her sexuality; it is something she offers to the man. With this kind of imagery embedded in our psyche, it is not difficult to see how and why women become easy victims of prostitution. It is often the only way in which they can earn a living. When society closes the door to economic survival in the workforce, then a woman's body and her sexuality become the only tools of trade left. Today these realities are learned at increasingly younger ages. Young children, male and female, are encouraged to prostitute themselves in countries such as the Philippines, Sri Lanka, and Indonesia. In Thailand, prostitution is the second highest income earner of the country, next to the export of rice. Yet the woman who plies this trade is exploited at every step. Not only does she expose herself to venereal diseases, unwanted pregnancies, and illegal abortions, but today she runs the very real risk of contracting AIDS. Financially, too, she is exploited, and the money she earns is seldom hers. What she gets is what's left over after her earnings have been divided among the night club owner, the tour operator, the local guide, and any others involved in bringing her business. The money she then earns could well be sent to the family she has left behind or to meet medical bills or to educate siblings. The majority of women who become prostitutes do so not because they enjoy this kind of lifestyle (which is what most middle-class people like to believe), but because they have no other option for survival.

The hope for giving necessary protection to women who are forced into prostitution becomes slimmer as Third World governments look to tourism as the quickest way to earn much-needed foreign exchange. Prostitution is one of the "baits" on the hook that draws the tourists into a country to spend their dollars. The assumption is that tourists will empty their purses in our countries. The reality is that tourism benefits the tourist's country of origin as much as, if not more than, the country being visited. How does this happen? Take Thailand and the German tours that were prolific at one time. Most Germans would buy their tickets in Germany and travel on a German airline. Once in Bangkok, most of them would live in the larger hotels. These hotels would be furnished with imported furnishings so that the tourists' standards for comfort would be met. So companies in Japan and Taiwan benefit through the trade. Finally, the amount spent by the tourists in Thailand is rarely as much as the government would like us to believe. Therefore, neither social nor economic benefits result from prostitution or tourism. The stark reality is that social injustice and economic injustice seem to form the cornerstones of our society. The position of women in society is a sad indictment of our social systems. The old saying is proved true again: You can judge the degree of civilization by the social and political position of the women in that country.

The question then is, How does one build a just society, in which women share in the use and distribution of power? Do the Christian community and the institutional Church have a role to play in building a just society? My young friend, Maria, standing before a group of male church leaders and being condemned for going to the aid of a victim of violence, doesn't see any hope for the institutional Church, and its role in building a just society. Women being called by God to serve as ministers of the Word and being denied that right in some churches, purely on the grounds of gender, do not see a role for the institutional Church in building a just society. The institutional Church, which seems to spend so much time and money in acquiring property, constructing concrete cathedrals, and conducting litigation, will not have the vision or the credibility to help construct a just society. Any institution that accepts patriarchy as its model and patriarchal images as its symbols and its vision will have little credibility in the process of building a just and equal society.

## Hidden power

To me the greatest hope for women lies in rebuilding and restructuring society through collective actions by women themselves. I believe that women can, and will, change society. That is not rhetoric. It is the reality and it is also the most logical direction for society to turn, and is beginning to happen.

Collective action is powerful and can change structures. Collectivity is not a new concept, though; it is evident in all societies throughout history. Collective action is the basis of the success of movements that have changed the course of history. Women in the lower socioeconomic groups are realizing the impact of collective action through self-help groups and cooperatives that are growing in number in Third World countries. Since women are still nonpersons in most economic systems and women's work outside the home is seen as secondary to their role as mothers and caregivers, the formation of collectives and self-help cooperatives empowers women gradually to rethink their own acceptance of roles. This awareness gives women the strength and the vision needed to challenge the structures that keep them imprisoned.

Collectivity has other offshoots. It strengthens the voice of women. A woman alone needs tremendous courage and resources to change her situation. Women together can articulate their needs more forcefully and more clearly. Satyarani, the mother of a victim of a dowry death in India, enlisted the help of a women's collective to fight for justice when the offender got off without punishment. When asked why she didn't organize a demonstration soon after her daughter's death, she said:

> I didn't know about these demonstrations. Otherwise I would never have let the hundreds of women of my community who came to mourn the death of my daughter sit around crying

with me. We would have gone together and demonstrated outside their house, put pressure on the neighborhood to socially ostracize the family and got justice for ourselves.[3]

Satyarani is a leading organizer of antidowry demonstrations today, a woman who discovered the strength of collective articulation and collective action.

Collective action is often easy to accept within a situation such as economic or social oppression, especially in the lower socioeconomic level of society. It is harder for women who belong to the middle-income level. They have to contend with status, with custom, and with culture much more than women living in low-income communities. Most of them have been molded to believe that collective action is Marxist or feminist or even "unwomanly." I do accept that it is difficult for some women to take part in demonstrations and to align themselves with groups that lobby for social and economic reform, but this is not the only way to bring about a just society.

Women in the middle socioeconomic group are beginning to realize the need for being informed. They are beginning to learn that economics and legal issues are not for economists and lawmakers alone. They are beginning to realize that they need to know about the debt crisis, which is creating an economic structure that is exploiting them as well as those in the sweatshops and those exploited by social evils such as prostitution. Women are beginning to realize that they can analyze the teachings of patriarchal religions that would keep them under bondage. Women, more and more, are becoming aware of their own right to think for themselves and to make choices for themselves. Women are beginning to realize that being vocal is not only demonstrating in street marches, but it is also taking a stand for themselves in the home, in the community, in the workplace, and in religious institutions.

Collective action is not only the prerogative of society outside the Church. It is so within the Church as well. Unfortunately, until recent years it has been hidden within layers of patriarchy. But it is there, and women theologians and biblical scholars are beginning to recognize and articulate it. The Gospel stories record images of a strong collective of women. The phrase "a

110

group of women" appears many times in the Jesus narratives. The strongest evidence of this group was at the foot of the cross. The women stood in solidarity with each other in a situation that must have been frightening and bewildering to them. Their collective support empowered them to keep going when there seemed to be no hope. Later, when the disciples refused to believe Mary's report of her encounter with the risen Christ, a group of women went back to the empty tomb. Women believing in women. The growth of the women-church movement is the continuation of collective action within the Church. Rosemary Radford Ruether writes: "For the first time the vision of the church as an exodus community from patriarchy is being developed by feminist Christians."[4]

### Reconstruction — the challenge to women

Economic and social systems built on patriarchal images and in patriarchal molds are destroying this planet. The global economic and environmental crises affect the lives of all of us. They affect the lives of the children who will inherit the world we hold in trust for them. We have a responsibility to them, and we have a responsibility to each other. That is what collectivity is about. Our lives and our actions are interlinked, and unless each of us is committed to building a just society, the process will be longer and more painful for all of us.

It is not my intention to polarize the sexes, to create an all female community and ideology. But I do believe that the strength of women to change and create a just society lies in our ability to recognize our own gifts and strengths. Once we take that step, then we need to support each other as we struggle to change the economic and social structures that hold both women and men in bondage.

About five years ago, two young Indian men strayed into a rural women's workshop I was conducting. It happened through a process of miscommunication. With the permission of the group, however, the two men stayed for the five-day workshop. Just before the workshop concluded, one of them said (as earnestly and as fervently as only a young university graduate can), "Madam, socialism has failed India. Communism has

111

failed India. I believe the answer for India is feminism." I replied, "Bless you, my son! Go, spread the message!"

The feminist reconstruction of our society is to me the strongest hope for our planet. The patriarchal model has failed, and matriarchy is not the answer either. But I believe that feminism can and must be taken seriously if a just society is to be built. If feminism becomes another ideology, it will fail as well. However, if feminism can continue to challenge patriarchal structures and provide alternatives at the same time, if feminism can lead to an honest analysis of patriarchy and an honest analysis of women's role in perpetuating it, if feminism can continue to help women develop new perspectives, not just about women and women's issues, but about any issues that concern human living, then feminism will never become another ideology or another "ism."[5]

Feminism has the potential and the power to reconstruct our society. By beginning with women's experiences and women's stories, by affirming the nurturing, the caring, the healing, and the dreaming that women bring to society, feminism challenges the structures that keep us imprisoned. It also challenges the acceptance of patriarchy as the norm for humankind. This is the vision and the challenge to which we, as women, are called today.

❖　　❖　　❖

## Women's Oppression and Cries of Pain

□ *Much of women's pain is a result of different forms of sexual exploitation, and prostitution is a particularly iniquitous example of such exploitation. The* Concise Oxford Dictionary *laconically defines a prostitute as a woman "who offers her body to indiscriminate sexual intercourse especially for hire." This is a typical example of a male-centered perspective, because the definition implies that the woman makes a conscious choice of offering her body and is to be blamed for her action, and the necessary collaboration of men in this matter is not mentioned. The true situation is quite the opposite, however, for in reality many women are sold into prostitution against their will and it is mainly men who benefit financially from this.*

*Prostitution is a particularly difficult social problem in Asia, especially in Thailand, the Philippines, Taiwan, and Japan. This is connected with the presence of large foreign military bases and the development of what has been called "sex tourism" on a large scale. There is also much trafficking of Asian girls between different Asian countries, linked to the desperate search for labor and employment. In seeking such employment in a different country whose language they may not even speak, many girls finish up in prostitution — where they can sometimes earn more money than in other low-paid jobs.*

*A certain number of women prostitutes come from Christian families, especially when they are from the Philippines, the only country in Asia that is 92% Christian. A particularly shocking example of the interdependence between religion and the exploitative treatment of women comes from Thailand, where it is known that some poor families sell their daughters into prostitution in order to raise the necessary money for covering the expenses of ordaining their sons as Buddhist monks. The Asian continent is marked by the poverty of its masses, surrounded by pockets of affluence, but this poverty stands also in stark contrast to the pluralistic richness of the Asian religious and cultural traditions. Asia is immense; it is the most extensive of all continents with 58% of the world's population, yet overall it only has a minuscule Christian presence of 3%. The position of women varies from country to country, but it is often low. Women are the poorest among the poor, the most oppressed among the oppressed, or the "minjung" among the*

113

*"minjung" as the Korean woman theologian Chung Hyun Kyung calls them, the "dalit" among the "dalit," the most downtrodden and broken, as is said in India. Feminist theology in Asia has to be seen in this overall context of oppression, an immense struggle against dominant sociopolitical realities and powerful cultural traditions. Such theology is a cry, a plea, an invocation where "God weeps with our pain" as Kwok Pui-lan has written (see her article in* The East Asia Journal of Theology, *vol. 2/2, 1984, pp. 228–32).*

*When in 1979 Marianne Katoppo wrote her small pioneering book on an Asian woman's theology, entitled* Compassionate and Free, *she devoted a whole chapter to the "Socio-Political Realities" of Asian women; this drew attention to the economic, educational, political, legal, and sexual exploitation of women. In chapter 10 the section on prostitution is reproduced, followed by a case study.*

## 10   MARIANNE KATOPPO

# The Church and Prostitution in Asia

Prostitution is one of the burning issues in Asia today; there is a very real link between tourism and prostitution. It is also linked to the presence of foreign military bases and transnational companies.[1]

Where tourism has become an integral part of the country's economic program, one should not be too surprised if there is no great enthusiasm to search for viable alternative occupations for the prostitutes.

The Church does not exhibit an attitude of love and acceptance to the prostitutes. More often it is one of judgment and self-righteousness. Recently a pastor was suspended from service in his church for having had the audacity to marry a prostitute. She was in the so-called high-class bracket, and cynical tongues said that the real reason for the pastor's suspension was the embarrassment felt by some of the church members to whom she might have been more that just a casual acquaintance.

The double standard is, of course, as old as the Church Fathers. Augustine—who didn't exactly lead a saintly life prior to his conversion—couldn't refrain from crying: "Remove prostitutes from human affairs, and you will unsettle everything because of lust." He was, of course, referring to the *man*'s lusts. It was a well-known fact that women, i.e., the respectable ones, didn't have any.

In referring to this passage, Thomas Aquinas, the greatest of Roman Catholic theologians, said: "Prostitution in the cities is like the sewage system in the palace. Do away with it, and the palace will turn into a place of filth and stink." The Provincial Council of 1665 in Milan was of the same opinion.

It is interesting to see how Jesus dealt with prostitutes. Perhaps it is not admissible to say that Mary Magdalene, commonly accepted as the first person Jesus revealed himself to after his resurrection, was a prostitute. The woman at the well in Samaria (John 4) definitely was, though, yet Jesus treated her as a person, not as an object: a safety-valve for male passion, or part of a sewage system.

An appalling disregard for the dignity of women is also manifested in the Council of Konstanz, 1414-18. This council is mainly remembered for its indictment of John Hus, who was burned at the stake for heresy. All church history books record this.

Less attention is given to something else, which is equally revealing to the kind of church renewal the gentlemen of the council had in mind—namely, the fact that the number of prostitutes who came to Konstanz during this time was equal to the number of delegates to the council.

Actually, it must be said that the reputation of the clergy at the time was so bad that the farmers, seeking to protect their wives and daughters from seduction, refused to appoint spiritual counselors who didn't promise to take concubines, if they didn't have any to start with—a situation that inspired the Bishop of Konstanz to levy a special "concubine-tax" from the priests in his diocese.

### Consent or exploitation?

The present secular society is one in which practically everything has been transformed into commodities, including human relationships. Sex, as one of the most intensive forms of relationships, has turned into a prime commodity.

In many Asian countries, tourism (hence, prostitution) is one of the most lucrative sectors of the nation's economy. Evidence for this is found in the *Far Eastern Economic Review*, which devoted three whole pages in its issue of March 2, 1979, to prostitution in Asia. The article is called "For Singles, Swingers and Others (After Dark)," and is sprinkled with cute remarks that are no doubt intended to show the liberated attitude of the writer. As Enrique Dussel has said: "It is just as bad to say cute things about women as it is to say things against them."

The *Review* is obviously more concerned with economy than with ethics. "*Kisaeng* are traditionally recreational *creatures* [Katoppo's italics] trained to serve and entertain men," says the article, referring to the swinging life in Korea. "Asia's lights o' love are mostly young, pretty, gay and a welcome change from the hard-faced crones found in the West."

W. S. Rendra, the well-known Indonesian poet, wrote a poignant poem about Maria Zaitun (Mary Olive), a prostitute who was no longer "pretty and gay"; though still young, she was dying of venereal disease on the city garbage-heaps—or, as the *Review* would have put it discreetly, "one of the indispositions Captain Cook's sailors are said to have introduced to the East."

Since then, American GIs have done their share: "Vietnam Rose" is a particularly resistant strain of "one of those indispositions." It became resistant because they could not be bothered to take the whole course of antibiotics. The GIs have gone home, but the disease lingers on.

An SCM report has estimated that 60% of the women in some areas of Indonesia are prostitutes. Generally, they are driven by economic necessity. Living in conditions of extreme poverty, they are ruthlessly exploited. This is a prime example of the way women tend to bear the burden of double exploitation because of their sex in an underdeveloped exploited country.

But prostitution exists, the argument goes, with the consent of the prostitutes. Some men claim self-righteously that it is even necessary for the economic survival of the women, so they are really doing a Good Thing—an attitude that is reflected in the above-mentioned article in the *Far Eastern Economic Review*: "In Manila, 'hospitality girls' from one of the small bars . . . in a gesture of gratitude to some of their favoured clientele, put up a makeshift shrine decorated with the photographs of their top three (journalist) patrons."

As Mary John Mananzan pointed out: "Even when done with the consent of women, the fact that the consent is extracted or even just conditioned by a weakness or position of disadvantage makes the act an act of exploitation."

She goes on to distinguish between the "peaceful" form of sexual exploitation and the violent forms. The former is based on the recognition that the female possesses something of value to the male, which she can be coerced to surrender for a good that appears to her to be, at least for the moment, greater than this value she possesses. The violent forms of sexual exploitation can be traced further back to man's structural capacity for forcible entry into the woman's correspondingly structural vulnerability. In other words: rape, which man comes to see as "a vehicle of his victorious conquest of the woman [being] the ultimate test of his superior strength, the triumph of his manhood."[2]

This possibility of coercion in the exchange of values or the power of intimidation by a superior strength makes sexual exploitation doubly exploitative, and this in Third World situations that are compounded by economic, political, and social coercion.

Since the 1960s there has been a remarkable leap in the tourism industry in most Asian countries—take, for example, the Philippines. From being a minor item in the nation's economy, it became the fifth largest dollar-earning industry by the 1970s, according to the statistics on travel and tourism for

1965-75, published by the statistics division of the Department of Tourism.

In the Philippines, says the *Far Eastern Economic Review*, sex provides a major incentive to the traveler. Whereas in the past Japanese all-male tour groups took night tours in buses which returned to the hotel with double the original number of passengers, a first-class (*sic*) hotel now offers a room package which includes a female companion. For the more discriminating, there are also co-eds, fashion models, movie starlets, or teen-age boys.

It should be noted that the women included in the package deals normally get only 15-20% of the fee paid by the clients.

Perhaps there are no sufficient indicators to measure the moral degradation that prostitution brings with it. But it is clear that a country that considers tourism as a pillar of its economic development does so at the expense of human dignity, and especially at the cost of the exploitation of its women.

These are the modern human sacrifices, who are devoured daily—not by the tribal gods of old who craved human blood for the sake of cosmic balance, but by the Anti-God, by Mammon, for the sake of GNP.

**Moral pollution**

The presence of foreign military bases is also a factor responsible for prostitution. Angeles and Olongapo in the Philippines are two examples. The dehumanization and corruption, especially among Philippine women, that is brought about by these bases underline the social cost to the country, apart from the military and political implications.

Olongapo, a town of nearly 200,000 people (the home of the Subic Bay Naval Base), is also the working ground of 16,000 prostitutes, of which 10,000 are licenced. There are several thousand illegitimate children of US servicemen.

During the Vietnam war, Olongapo had the reputation of being a wide-open area for the GIs' R & R (= Rest and Recreation).

This is one aspect of the war that has not been adequately discussed: the social death of a whole community. This is far worse than physical destruction. Willfully or not, through the

Vietnamese war the Americans destroyed what was most precious to the Vietnamese (and, in the same way, to the people of Olongapo, for example), namely: family, friendship, their manner of expressing themselves.[3] From persons, people have turned into objects, commodities, statistics. They become non-persons.

What right does one nation have to make another nation its battleground or its playground? As long as the policies of Asian nations are so determinedly export-oriented and foreign-control-led, this question will continue to be asked.

Yet another factor in the rise of prostitution in Asia is the mushrooming of industrial establishments everywhere, as a result of the incentives to foreign investments.

Aside from ecological pollution, these establishments give rise to moral pollution. In Indonesia, there are the so-called "contract-wives," i.e., the women who live with the contracted foreign workers only for the period of their contracts. An analogue for this may be found in the colonial period, when many Dutchmen kept *nyais* (mistresses) during the period of their stay in the region. Children of such unions were legitimized and sent to Holland, if so lucky—although that almost invariably meant they never saw their mothers any more. Otherwise, when the father declined responsibility, the child often grew up with its mother's relatives, facing all the unpleasantness that is the fate of illegitimate children of such a mixed ancestry even today.

Young girls are employed as maids, laundrywomen, and cooks of the foreign workers. Most of the time they are expected to become their mistresses as well, and very few are in a position to make formal complaints, firstly, because of the fear of being fired, and secondly, because of the inherent shame attached to sexual violation. To these girls, it is literally a fate worse than death. Often, it's the first step toward prostitution, since the girl feels so ashamed and so despised that she thinks nothing much worse can happen to her now.

## CASE STUDY

A prostitute

Jakarta Utara (north) is one of the five cities making up the metropolitan district of Greater Jakarta (estimated at 6 million inhabitants).

Tanjung Priok, the harbour, used to be Indonesia's main gateway to the world in the days before air travel. It also used to be the area where prostitution flourished most.

Today, prostitution is localized—not legalized—in the area known as Kramat Tunggak. About 3,000 women live in 150 houses, separated from the main street by a high wooden fence. The houses are neatly and conspicuously numbered. About eight women live in each house, together with the madam and her protector. Each woman has her own room, and each house has its sitting room, including a bar. Sanitation facilities are better than average. Generally, there are framed photographs of the women on the wall of the sitting room. The customer points out the woman of his choice, and the madam then gives him the key to her room. The fee is around Rp. 3,000 = US $5, of which the madam takes the lion's share. There are also special "all night" reductions.

Inem is a young girl in her teens. Her father was the pastor in the small East Javanese village where she comes from. A few years ago, the whole family was transmigrated to Kalimantan (Borneo). Inem didn't want to go with them; besides, her brother wanted her to join him in Jakarta, "to get an education."

Inem's parents consented. Her brother kept his promise and sent her to school. He gave her a good home, and she was quite happy to be with him.

One day he was killed in a traffic accident. His wife, Inem's sister-in-law, said that she couldn't be expected to take responsibility for someone else's offspring. Not only did she turn Inem out of the house, she also contrived to have her become a prostitute.

Inem is now one of the 600 Christian women living in the Kramat Tunggak compound. In Indonesia, one is obliged to state one's religion in the Kartu Penduduk (Civil Registration Card).

Some Ursuline nuns discovered the proportionately high rate of Christians among the inhabitants of the complex. They applied for permission to start a program that would involve Bible studies, general knowledge, and physical education.

Permission was granted, but at first they were not allowed to enter the compound. They had to conduct all their classes in the clerk's office across the road.

The prostitutes are not allowed to leave the compound without permission. Even crossing the road proved to be not without complications. The madams would say: "How do I know you're really going to school with those holy women, and not off to some rendezvous with a man?" So the women would have to pay their usual commission first, before obtaining permission from the madams.

It wasn't until the Ministry of Social Welfare intervened that the madams stopped harassing the women who attended the classes. Soon the nuns were also allowed to hold their program within the compound itself, taking different houses in turn. The attitude of the madams varied. On the whole, they seemed to be willing to cooperate only for fear of rebuke from the ministry.

When we talked with the madam of Inem's house to make enquiries about the possibility of holding the classes there, she was very sociable, insisting that we have some refreshments with her. She kept saying that, although she was not a Christian herself, she had great respect for people who were religious. She never discouraged them from performing their religious duties. For example, it happened to be the month of Ramadhan—the fast of the Muslims—and she did not stop her girls from fasting, although it inevitably affected their work. She said that she always encouraged the girls to broaden their interests, and to get as much education as possible, "so they can serve the country in better ways."

It was not immediately clear in what context she applied the word "better." Apparently, she had been a prostitute herself. This seems to be the only "good" future a prostitute can aspire to: becoming a madam—unless she has the good fortune to get married to a man who does not exploit her. Some prostitutes marry several times: usually, when their savings have gone, so has the man.

"She's such a bright girl, is Ina," said the madam, patting Inem on the back. Apparently she felt Ina sounded more sophisticated than Inem. "I keep telling her to try to get back to school. She's always carrying her Bible with her, reading it whenever she gets the chance."

When we had left the house, we asked Inem, who was allowed to walk us to the gate: "What would you like to do in the future?"

She just smiled.

❖　　　❖　　　❖

## Women's Oppression and Cries of Pain

☐ *Marianne Katoppo wrote the words in chapter 10 in 1979. Since then, much more has become known about violence and discrimination against women. The Asian journal of feminist theology,* In God's Image, *has published in its ten years of existence numerous articles dealing with prostitution, female genital mutilation, and other forms of sexual violence against women. In June 1990 it carried an article by the Japanese woman journalist, Yayori Matsui, entitled "Asian Migrant Women Working at Sex Industry in Japan Victimized by International Trafficking," where the author says: "I am here to make heard the painful voices (cries) of victimized migrant women of Asia." In her view, the Japanese economic "miracle" has been achieved "at the expense of countless women both inside and outside Japan. One of Japan's most serious social problems is an expanding sex industry—this is the other less publicized side of the economic prosperity."*

*In 1991 another article was published wherein Yayori Matsui linked violence against women with several aspects of development, militarism, and culture in the Third World. A shortened version of this is found in the next chapter (for the full text see* In God's Image, *vol. 10/4, 1991, pp. 22-8). In her earlier book,* Women's Asia *(London: Zed Books, 1989), Yayori Matsui tells us how she comes from a family environment "of shared religious values such as the equality of human beings before God"; therefore it was a profound shock to her when she first discovered racial discrimination as a student in the West and then, on her return journey home, the abject poverty of Asia. As a result, she felt that the idea of human equality before God can perhaps only be applied to white Westerners.*

*Yayori Matsui became a journalist and feminist activist and worked as a Singapore correspondent for a Japanese paper in the period 1981-5. During this time she visited eighteen Asian countries and became aware of the oppression of Asian women that resulted from the social, political, and religious factors that she describes in her book. For her, women are truly "the last colony." The new colonialism of First World countries can be seen most clearly through the eyes of women. Yayori Matsui is co-founder of the "Asian Women's Association," which examines the relationship between Japanese and other countries from the point of view of women, especially with regard to such issues as sex tourism, Japan–South Korea relations, war responsibility, Japanese multinationals, and the exploitation of women as cheap labor.*

*But is the solidarity of Japanese women with other Asian and Third World women possible, she asks in her book. Japanese women play the double role of being both victims and oppressors, because they are discriminated against in their own society and at the same time benefit from the exploitation of other Asian women. Part of Matsui's article is reprinted in chapter 11.*

## 11  YAYORI MATSUI

# Violence Against Women in Development, Militarism, and Culture

I am a journalist, a former Asia correspondent based in Singapore, and a feminist activist, co-founder of the Asian Women's Association. I come to you from Japan, not the country of the rising sun but the country of the rising daughters, because Japanese women are breaking out of the stereotypical image of calm, docile women who are happy to serve their menfolk.

It is not only in the political realm that Japanese women have begun to take action. Last year was marked by the beginning of various new and dynamic grassroots campaigns focusing on violence against women. In Osaka, the second largest city in Japan, a "stop the rape" campaign was organized following news reports of a woman trying to rescue another woman who was being sexually harassed by two men in a crowded subway train. The would-be rescuer was dragged from the train and raped by the two men she had confronted.

In Tokyo, various feminist groups together formed a "Network Against Violence to Women" that has examined a number of cases of such violence; for example, the prostitute who was charged with the murder of a sadistic customer, and the case of a bar hostess who was charged with the murder of a drunken man who sexually harassed her. The networking group had tried to change the attitude of the judiciary and the general public as well. Instead of blaming victimized women, they are urged to prosecute the men who victimize them.

Anti-sexual harassment campaigns erupted nationwide after a woman in Fukuoka, a large city in southwest Japan, filed the first sexual harassment suit against her former editor. She was constantly humiliated and insulted by his verbal attacks on her private life. A feminist coalition against sexual harassment was organized, and it received more than 6,500 replies from all over the country to enquiries about incidents of sexual harassment.

"Media watch" is another growing activity in feminist groups because of the large volume of sex and violence for sale through many different media. Morning and evening, 10 million issues of sports newspapers and several million copies of tabloids, all filled with pornographic photos, comics, and stories, are read by untold numbers of men. There are hundreds of so-called "comic" magazines filled with sex and violence, and one of the largest that is aimed at young men has a monthly circulation of 5 million. Some such magazines are even directed toward young teenage girls. Hundreds of thousands of cheap novels with descriptions of brutal rapes of women every three pages or so are published annually. All of this is despicably insulting to women.

Japan has become an economic superpower with a huge trade surplus, extensive foreign investment, important overseas assets, and a dispenser of economic aid to underdeveloped countries. Such rapid economic growth has been accompanied, however, by a comparable growth in the sex industry, an inseparable part of the whole. The huge demand for female workers in this profitable industry cannot be met by available Japanese women only. Thus the shortage of young women as workers in the sex industry has been filled during the past decade by migrant women from neighboring Asian countries.

Some people estimate that now nearly 100,000 women come to Japan every year. While 70% of them are Filipina, Thai women are increasing, followed by Taiwanese, Koreans, and Malaysians.

A blatant example of international trafficking, these women are brought here and, in most cases, forced into prostitution. This flesh trade and other facets of the sex industry are almost entirely controlled by the *yakuza* (the Japanese Mafia), or the *boryokudan*, violence-prone gangs. The women are "imported" at a cost of around $7,000 and sold to brothels and bars for $10,000 to $15,000, depending largely on their looks. In order to cover the buyer's cost, the women are forced to earn as much as possible by prostitution, and if they resist they face physical violence. During a three-year period beginning in 1986, 1,200 Asian migrant women sought refuge and assistance at HELP, a women's shelter in Japan, because of human rights violations such as physical violence, psychological abuse, drug use, non-payment of wages, and so on.

A number of tragic cases of victimized women have been reported over the past few years. One, the "Lapin case," occurred in Nagoya, a large city between Osaka and Tokyo. In 1988 four Filipina women, aged twenty-one to twenty-six, were employed at the snack bar Lapin (a brothel, really), where they were forced into prostitution daily. When they tried to escape they were brutally punished. One managed to get away as far as Osaka, but she was forcibly returned to Nagoya by a Lapin employee, and raped by him at a hotel. In December 1988 the owner placed iron bars over the windows to prevent escape, and, when one of the women made an attempt to do so, the owner ordered that she be raped by male employees. She was confined in a room called the "monkey box" (migrant Asian women are sometimes called "monkeys"), and raped repeatedly by two men while other men watched.

The list of sexual abuses and human rights violations of Asian migrant women in Japan is endless, but I shall stop here for now. Let me direct your attention to the situation of such women in their home countries.

Several months ago I attended a conference "Child Prostitution and Tourism" in Chiang Mai in northern Thailand. I was shocked to learn of the number of young prostitutes under sixteen years of age in Thailand: perhaps as many as 800,000 according to the Children's Rights Protection Center. Thai economic development is so dynamic and fast that it almost reaches the level of the newly industrialized economies. In spite of this, rural poverty is persistent and consumerism penetrates even into very poor villages in remote areas.

Expanding tourism, promoted by the Thai government, creates more demand for prostitutes and, under such circumstances, in many villages in northern Thailand more and more poor farmers are selling their daughters to the sex industry in Bangkok and other tourist resorts. The price of a girl is from 5,000 to 10,000 baht (around US $500 to $1,000) and the cash the farmers get or the money their daughters earn after paying back debts is usually spent on building or repairing houses, buying a motorbike or agricultural machinery, or on other such consumer goods.

It was especially painful to see young hilltribe girls, not only from the northern Thai border, but also from Myanmar, Laos, and other neighboring countries, sold to brothels. Last year I saw two hilltribe sisters, thirteen and fourteen years old, at the Emergency Home in Bangkok. I was told that they had each been forced to take at least ten customers a day. Their bodies, so tiny and fragile, had been abused by big men, foreign tourists, and foreign military men.

In Japan recently, I saw a child pornographic magazine, a special issue on Thai prostitutes, that included a series of photos of a fifteen-year-old virgin hilltribe girl from Myanmar being raped and abused.

European pedophiles, preferring even younger girls of about ten to fourteen years old, come to Southeast Asia in large numbers. They are not allowed to abuse children in their own countries, and they find it relatively easy to buy a very young girl in a Third World country.

Should sexual violence against poverty-stricken and totally powerless young girls be allowed on the grounds of the right to act according to one's sexual preference? I must say "no" because it is a violation of the young girl's human rights.

Then, is violence against women increasing or not? From my observation it is definitely increasing and disturbingly so, both personal and domestic violence as well as structural violence.

Why? What are its causes? An African sister said that violence against women is rooted in three things: poverty, war, and culture. I would like to discuss with you three major causes of this violence as I see them: development, militarism, and culture. First of all, development is a great problem. The type of development that has been pursued for the past three decades has widened the gap between rich and poor, both globally and within nations. This kind of development has destroyed nature and reinforced men's domination over women because it has been promoted by, and favors, the interests of the industrialized world, particularly the transnational corporations.

In the First World, competitive money-oriented economic systems, new technology, consumerism, and other inhuman social structures that result from a lifestyle of overdevelopment, all contribute to and converge in increasing violence against women at home, at the workplace, and in faraway places.

On the other hand, in the Third World where three out of four human beings on the earth live, people suffer from debilitating poverty because of underdevelopment. Here in this part of the world women are victimized by men who are so poor, and frustrated because of it, that they tend to express their feelings in cruel ways.

Both overdevelopment and underdevelopment can be called "male development" and it most definitely is "male." There are many women's groups now at work, searching for alternative development models in order to create a new society: one that is free from violence, oppression, and discrimination.

I would like to mention several issues that indicate a causal relationship between development strategy and violence. It should go without saying that poverty is the key issue in most Third World countries, and it is equally true that it is always the weakest sector of society—the poor and the women—that is most affected by violence. On Malaysian plantations where the legacy of British colonial rule still has its influence, and where the so-called "culture of poverty" is deeply rooted, Indian male workers live oppressed lives and compensate for this by oppressing their women. And the women become the victims of severe beatings, harassment, and even rape. And now a new

128

colonialism is manifested in the restructuring policy being imposed on the impoverished Third World by the World Bank and the International Monetary Fund.

The worldwide increase of street children is caused partly by family violence in urban slum areas; the children run away from homes where wife beatings and incest are everyday events.

The north-south unjust and unequal economic system lies behind various forms of violence against women, and women in the Third World see clearly the link between personal physical violence and their socioeconomic situation.

Another problem of development is consumerism, which begins in the First World and spreads to the Third World. Giant transnational advertising companies provoke the materialistic greed of the masses in both First and Third World countries. Commoditization of women is usually accompanied by violence, as in forced prostitution.

Technology is also a development issue that affects women. Transnational corporations with advanced technology are operating in Third World countries far away from oversight committees and home offices. It happens, however, that these corporations often use their new technologies without the safety precautions that would be required in their home countries.

A second cause of increasing violence against women is militarism. History tells us that military aggression has always been accompanied by rape and other forms of sexual abuse. When the Japanese Imperial Army invaded China and Southeast Asia between 1930 and 1945, Japanese soldiers not only raped the women in their path of conquest, but carried away many thousands of young Korean women as *Chongshindae*, or "battlefield prostitutes." Korea was a colony of Japan at that time, and the helpless plight of these abused women was inexpressible. They were forced to serve sexually thirty to forty soldiers each day. As Japan was forced to withdraw its troops near the end of the war, these women were abandoned in the jungles and on other battlefields, and some were even killed. We Japanese women learned of this shameful atrocity only after the war ended, and we have pledged to prevent this from ever happening again.

The United States Army in Vietnam in the 1960s and 1970s

was no better behaved than the Japanese army during World War II. Many books have been written by former US servicemen about their experiences there. Their testimonies to the rape of village women during their "search and destroy" missions, and accounts of purchasing prostitutes in Saigon (now Ho Chi Minh City), are painful reading. To do so produces immense anger at both the inherent racism and sexism that are always present.

I have visited Vietnam several times to find the people there struggling to survive under terrible economic conditions. But the most shocking and depressing experience was to see the victims of Agent Orange, a chemical defoliant sprayed by the US military on crops and jungle areas from 1965 to 1970 to reduce the opportunity for ambush and expose enemy troop movements. The herbicide contains a highly toxic substance, dioxin, which is a carcinogenic and mutagenic poison, and women who have been exposed to it suffer most horribly. Not only cancers and so-called "mole" pregnancies, but unbelievable fetus malformations such as absence of brain matter or no eyeballs, two heads, three legs, and various other reproductive organ complications occur with some frequency. Nearly twenty years after the Agent Orange spraying, the women who were poisoned when they were children continue to produce malformed children of their own.

Such a chemical disaster resulting in death or horrible damage to vast numbers of people on such a scale as this had never happened before, and the US government has refused to make amends for introducing this terrible means of modern warfare that, in my view, is clearly a crime against the Vietnamese people, particularly the women. We cannot and we must not discuss violence against women by militaristic actions without considering the victimization of women by chemical warfare.

Even though the US military presence in Asia was reduced following the Vietnam war, US bases still remain in many countries, and prostitution around these bases—for example, in Okinawa in Japan, the Philippines, and South Korea—is dreadful.

In Olongapo City in the Philippines, adjacent to the largest US naval base in the world, Subic Bay, nearly 20,000 women offer sexual services at some 300 Rest and Recreation establishments. These women, some of whom are very young, come from economically depressed areas all over the country. A few years ago, twelve girls, ranging in age from ten to sixteen, were hospitalized because of severe complications of venereal disease, and when an Irish priest working in Olongapo City reported this terrible abuse to the media he was intimidated and threatened by the US military authorities, with the support of the local government.

The situation around the US bases in Okinawa, an island in southwest Japan, is much the same, except that Filipina women have replaced the local women. Because of the stronger yen, the price of sex with a Japanese woman is too expensive for the GIs. In darkened clubs Filipinas dance on the stage as watching servicemen drink beer, and video projections of sex and violence run continuously in the background. In unlit corners some of the men are being sexually serviced. In this kind of environment, fueled by alcohol and exposure to violence, the phenomenon of soldiers belonging to an oppressed class in their own culture expressing their frustrations in brutal sexual assault on prostitutes can be observed.

Today, in many Third World countries under military dictatorship, women who oppose, or who criticize and resist, even those women who are named feminist activists, suffer imprisonment, sexual torture, and sometimes execution—all without trial.

Regional or local war is another serious issue related to militarism and the violence against women it engenders. In the decade of the 1970s, military expenditures in the Third World tripled, and most of the purchased weapons came from the First World. During the 1980s, in the Third World alone, more than ten wars have been fought, producing countless refugees.

It must be said that violence against women is also a peace issue. We women must work harder to realize reconciliation among hostile nations in order to improve the lives of women in those nations.

I will look briefly at a third factor inherent in the problem of violence against women. That is, how patriarchal culture, religion, and tradition have institutionalized violence against women, and how fundamentalism and communal tension perpetuate or aggravate it today.

Historically, most world cultures have had cruel forms of violence against their women. In Europe, for example, witch hunting caused the horrible deaths of about 9 million women between the fifteenth and seventeenth centuries.

From the twelfth century until early in the present century, the painful practice of footbinding was widespread in China, rendering the women helpless slaves, treated as property, as objects of sexual pleasure.

Another type of maiming of the female body is genital mutilation, of female circumcision. The purpose is to control women's sexuality, and to deprive women of sexual pleasure. Rooted in ancient times, this inhuman practice affects some several million women in more than thirty countries today.

Traditions of institutionalized violence against women abound in India, and they are fed by commercialism and technology. Sati, or "widow-burning," still occurs. Sati means that the wife is burned alive on the funeral pyre of her deceased husband. Banned by the British in 1829, nevertheless only three years ago an eighteen-year-old woman was killed in a Sati rite and glorified by fundamentalists. So-called "dowry deaths" are not infrequent. This is caused by the husband's side demanding more expensive and ever-increasing consumer goods from the bride's family. Unable to pay, the woman is burned to death or forced to burn herself. This kind of violence seems to be on the increase because of modernization, consumerism, and the cult of materialism.

Sex determination technology is causing the deaths of more and more female fetuses—a new problem resulting from advances in medical techniques in a patriarchal culture where women are devalued. Female infanticide is a dreadful violence against baby girls and is not uncommon; the mortality rate for female children in India is much higher than for males. The current population ratio of women to men is 930 to 1,000, and has continued to decrease since the 1960s. India is a true illustration of the suffering of women from merciless violence in a peculiar combined type of development: Hindu patriarchal tradition and Western modernization.

In Islamic countries like Pakistan, fundamentalism is growing, with a negative impact on women there. In such countries, women who do not follow the Islamic traditions face physical attacks and legal prosecution. Communal violence is increasingly serious in India, Sri Lanka, and other countries. In the name of culture, women are being raped and killed.

As we have seen, violence against women occurs in many places and takes many forms. It moves from the domestic scene to the state, the military, and the transnational agencies; from mutilation, and maiming, to murder. Clearly, this can be classified as human rights violations but, unfortunately, human rights activist groups do not realize this.

On the other hand, in most countries in Asia, Latin America, and Africa, women are beginning to fight back in an effective variety of ways: the establishment of crisis centers and shelters, counseling services, networking, changing laws, demonstrations, consciousness-raising activities that empower, and challenging male-oriented education systems.

What I want to share with you, and appeal to women in the West, is that we need to have a global perspective, a structural analysis, and long-term strategies. We must begin by listening to the voices and sharing the pain of the most victimized and oppressed women in our own countries and particularly in the Third World. It is my confirmed belief that sisterhood should be not only a grassroots reality, but a global vision. We must act locally, we must think globally, to eliminate violence against us women.

❖  ❖  ❖

☐ *Another voice from an Asian country, but with a different culture from that of Japan, is that of the Christian* dalit *woman of India.* Dalit *means "broken," "downtrodden," and refers to the effects of oppression. In a wider sense the word would include all oppressed people, but in India it is currently applied to the outcasts and untouchables who make up almost one-fifth of the Indian population—which Mahatma Gandhi had earlier described as "Harijans" or "children of God."*

*The* dalit *movement emerged during the 1980s as a general liberation movement of the poor and oppressed in India. The majority of Indian Christians are originally of* dalit *origin and the Church is still beset by many caste issues. It is estimated that among the 20 million Christians of India, at least 15 million are* dalits*—particularly among the rural and urban poor. A movement of rising consciousness and increasing struggles of all* dalits *against dehumanization and deprivation has developed. In connection with this, a "Christian Dalit Liberation Movement" has been formed as an all-India forum to fight against caste discrimination and for social justice both within and outside the churches. Out of this struggle a* dalit *theology is emerging that includes voices by and on* dalit *women, who are said to be* "dalit *among* dalits," *"firewood" and fuel of society, "exploited, hungry, weak," whose bodies are but "bony cages."*

*Several poems and brief reports of the book* Towards a Dalit Theology *(ed. M. E. Prabhakar, Delhi: SPCK, 1989) deal with Christian* dalit *women. One poem by the South Indian woman Theresamma on "Dalit Women Society's Firewood" ends*

> *We are not prostitutes,*
> *We are toilers with self-respect,*
> *We are dalit women proud,*
> *We are the providers for humanity,*
>
> *Did God ordain our fate?*
> *Will men decide our lives?*
> *Are we faggots for burning in the funeral pyre?*
> *No, we will rise and free ourselves.*

*What follows in chapter 12 is a brief description of the struggle of Christian* dalit *women in one of the Indian states, Andhra Pradesh, taken from* Towards a Dalit Theology *(pp. 152-4), based on a conference devoted to this subject.*

## 12  SWARNALATHA DEVI

# The Struggle of *Dalit* Christian Women in India

I am grateful to the organizers of the Christian Dalit Liberation Movement for giving me a chance to share with you my especial concern about the Christian *dalit* women's issue in Andhra Pradesh.

Most Christian women in Andhra are *dalits*. They are mostly daily wage earners, seasonal workers, migrant workers, underemployed, and underpaid. Some 90% of them are below the poverty line.

The other day someone in this conference [on *dalit* theology] raised a question: "Do the *dalits* need liberation? Or do *we* think they need liberation?" Let me share with you two examples of Christian *dalit* women before we attempt to answer this.

The first example is as follows. On the evening of November 3 I was at the Guntur railway station to catch a train to Madras to attend this conference. There I saw at least 400 Christian *dalit* women, each with a heavy headload of a bag (with utensils and clothes) and two or three children with each of them, rushing to get into the train along with their men. They prayed before they boarded the train, as a group, as a community. They were migrating to other places for agricultural work, leaving their homes and hearths. In the new places they have to live under trees or in open places or sometimes in the cattle sheds. During this period they virtually live under the pleasure and the will of the landlords and middlemen. They will continue to pray and sing and struggle. This scene reminded me that I was going to Madras to talk about these very women and to formulate theology for them, and I began to laugh at myself. I was reminded about their Christian faith.

They are the ones who are the givers to the Church.

They are the ones who are the cross-bearers of the congregation.

They are the ones who are the torch-bearers of the faith. They practice *dalit* theology in their day-to-day life, whereas we are struggling to formulate *dalit* theology. What a contrast it is!

The *dalit* Christian women's aspirations and theological understanding of God is very well revealed in a famous Telugu devotional song sung by each and every *dalit* Christian woman in Andhra. It is as follows:

In distress and at all times
We'll praise you, mighty God,
O, our Redeemer and Salvation.

Here in this song the *dalit* Christian woman expresses her faith in God, the Liberator and Redeemer.

Now let me ask you whether *dalit* women are in need of liberation or whether we are pretending to be capable of liberating them.

The second example is this. In July 1985 at Karamchedu village, nine Christian *dalit* men were brutally murdered by the landlords. The Christian *dalit* women who were the mothers, wives, and sisters of these victims courageously started to lead the movement against the landlords from Chirala Church compound. When Ms. Anne Grace Bai, a community organizer of RICE, Guntur, met them to discover their future plans, they said in one voice, "How can we go back to Karamchedu and face the *ryots* who, regardless of our own employers, fell upon us, like beasts, molested and humiliated us. We will not go back to our homes stained by our blood and teardrops. We have been buried alive, and we will continue to shout from our living tombs. We will go everywhere, and speak to anyone and do

everything to help our *dalits*. We have nothing more to fear."
At every stage of their struggle they prayed to God and
continued their struggle because they believe that he will
liberate them.

These two instances tell us that the *dalit* Christian women
are very strong in their faith, in their commitment, and in their
efforts. So let us not break our heads in formulating *dalit*
theology. The call that was given to Moses by God is being
given to you and to me today. God said, "The cry of the *dalits*
(Israel) has come to me and I have seen the oppression with
which the caste people (Egyptians) oppress them. Come! I will
send you to the *dalits*, that you may bring forth my people out
of oppression."

So . . .

There is a Cry, Let us listen
There is a Call, Let us respond
There are committed ones
Let us communicate the strategy.

Therefore, *dalit* theology must have the following three
aspects:

Listening to the People's Cry
Responding to the People's Cry
Strategizing the People's Commitment.

❖ ❖ ❖

☐ *The experience of the discrimination, subjection, oppression of, and violence against women takes different forms in different cultures. The contemporary struggle of the poor against all forms of oppression makes visible what Elsa Tamez in her introduction to women's theology in Latin America has called "the power of the naked" (see her book* Through Her Eyes, *Maryknoll, NY: Orbis Books, 1989, pp. 1–14). Women's voices from Latin America have been heard for longer than those from Africa, but a new publication makes women's theological work from that continent more accessible now. In the collection of essays edited by Mercy Amba Oduyoye and Musimbi R. A. Kanyoro,* The Will to Arise: Women, Tradition, and the Church in Africa *(Maryknoll, NY: Orbis Books, 1992), the oppression of women —caused by many aspects of traditional African ritual, sexuality, marriage, polygamy, and widowhood, as well as some practices of the Christian churches —is well brought out. The difficulties faced by the Christian widow in African culture is also discussed in Chris I. Ejizu's article "African Widows: An Agonistic Definition,"* The Asia Journal of Theology, *vol. 3/1, 1989, pp. 174–83. The important contribution that African Christian women make to the churches is usefully discussed by Rosemary Edet and Bette Ekeya in "Church Women of Africa: A Theological Community," in Virginia Fabella and Mercy Amba Oduyoye, eds.,* With Passion and Compassion: Third World Women Doing Theology, *Maryknoll, NY: Orbis Books, 1988, pp. 3–13.*

*Chapter 13 is a discussion of women in African culture by Bette Ekeya, entitled "Woman, For How Long Not?", and it comes from John S. Pobee and Bärbel von Wartenberg-Potter, eds.,* New Eyes for Reading: Biblical and Theological Reflections by Women from the Third World, *Geneva: WCC Publications, 1986, pp. 59–67.*

❖  ❖  ❖

## 13  BETTE EKEYA

# Woman, For How Long Not?

---

Here I am going to reflect on the fact that, although Jesus' Good News has indeed been preached to my people, one section of these people remains poor, captive, blind, downtrodden, and unaware that the Lord's favor rests upon them. This group is African women. The coming of the missionaries, about a century ago, should indeed have been very good news to the African woman, but now, besides the cultural norms and taboos that bound her and held her in subjection, two other oppressive elements have been added to her world: the loaded interpretation of certain biblical passages, and the predominantly male church ministries and institutions.

### The African culture

Rather than generalize on African culture in this section, I will give a brief description of the life and social position of the woman among the Iteso, although most of what I am going to say can be applied to the African woman in general.

The Iteso live in the Teso district of Uganda and in parts of the Bukedi district of eastern Uganda. They are the second largest ethnic group in that country. A small group of the Iteso of Bukedi district were cut off from their Ugandan kin by the colonial Kenya-Uganda border. The Kenyan group is a very small minority. Christianity was preached to the Iteso by the Mill Hill missionaries of St Joseph and by the Church Missionary Society. The Kenyan Iteso are predominantly Roman Catholic. I will confine my remarks to the impact of Roman Christianity upon the Atesot woman.

The Iteso whom the early missionary encountered were a

people who believed in one God called *Akuj*. This Akuj was believed to live *kuju*—far above in the sky. Akuj it was who created the world and everyone in it and continued to take care of them. Akuj could be invoked at any time, anywhere, when the need to invoke him arose, although in times of national crises communal prayers and sacrifices were offered. On these occasions, religious specialists called diviner prophets-cum-priests officiated. The religious life of the Iteso people was not confined to special religious times, though; rather, as with all African peoples, religion permeated all of life.

One aspect of Iteso religion that largely concerned women was what was called domestic rituals. It was in the domestic sphere that woman's life was concentrated. The highest aspiration of an Atesot woman was to marry and have children. Toward the fulfillment of this, she was carefully raised and trained. Her father made a careful choice as to who should marry her when she came of age.

The marriage of a young girl was a painstaking affair which stretched over a period of time, a gradual undertaking that consisted of several stages. Two extended families or clans participated in it: the future husband's clan and that of the future bride's father. It was a covenant of two communities whose external symbol was *Asuti*: that is, the transfer of an agreed-upon quantity of livestock from the family of the boy to that of the girl. *Asuti* legalized the marriage and helped to guarantee its success and stability.

Marriage for a young Atesot girl meant leaving her father's homestead, abandoning her father's clan rituals, and going to live in a strange home with strange clan rituals. It was a major transition in her life, and to ease her passage from one state of life to another—more complex—one, she went through rituals of incorporation. These rituals initiated her into the married state and incorporated her into her husband's clan. There were the rituals of anointing her with the oil of her husband's clan which constituted her wedding ceremony, her ritual introduction to all the various domestic chores she was henceforth to perform, rituals accompanying her first pregnancy. At the successful birth of her first child, rituals were performed to welcome her child into the community and at the same time cleanse her from the process of childbirth, which had rendered her ritually unclean. With the birth of her first child, the young girl ceased to be a child and became a mother. More rituals were performed to mark this transition. Other rituals were performed to ensure the health and survival of her children.

Apart from incorporating her into the clan of her husband and into the married state, the rituals that an Atesot woman underwent and participated in were also designed to give her the necessary spiritual strength, and protection against the myriads of malevolent spiritual forces with which the world was believed to be inhabited. Some of these forces operated in the form of spiritual possession and in witchcraft, sorcery, and evil magic. Children were especially vulnerable in the face of these forces, and so the woman needed rituals that she could perform to ward off these forces from herself and from her children. Except in cases requiring the special intervention of healing specialists, these rituals were organized and performed only by women. The young woman learnt the significance of the various rituals as she learnt to grow and operate in her new state, and in time she too became a specialist in performing them for the wives of her sons. No man ever dared to legislate, discuss, change, or officiate in these domestic rituals. This was where woman was supreme.

Iteso society, like African society in general, treated the woman with an accepted cultural dichotomy. As long as she was the mother of healthy children, sons and daughters proportionately, her place in the home and in her society was assured and honored. Both her father's clan and that of her husband did everything possible to make her marriage work. She could not be arbitrarily dismissed or divorced, for the legally married woman always belonged where she was initially married. She could go *ekurumane*, that is, be "held," be "married" somewhere else, but should she wish to return, the cultural laws obligated the first husband to take her back. Polygamy was an accepted form of marriage and all wives in polygamous marriages were legal wives.

Outside of the home, the woman had no real influence on society, and her rights were never equated with those of the man. While still in her parents' homestead, it was her father and brothers who had almost absolute rights over her. Her husband was chosen for her, her marriage was necessary to bring her brothers the bridewealth that would eventually become the *asuti* for their wives. It was the man who married her. She it was who gave up her clan taboos to adopt those of her husband, and henceforth she became identified with his people. Children were always members of their father's clan. In the event of a marriage breaking up, the woman was never given custody of the children. When children turned out well, her husband got the credit. When children grew up into bad characters, the fault was wholly their mother's. Should her marriage remain childless the fault was hers alone. A childless woman was perhaps the most miserable of women.

In every period of her life the Atesot woman had to live in the shadow of a man, and her existence was defined and given legal sanction by men. It was marriage and motherhood that gave her complete fulfillment as a person. The single woman, fully self-sufficient, was an anomaly. It was considered an abnormality and a curse for a woman to remain a resident of her father's homestead all her life. Such a decision on her part was believed to bring ill-luck to her father's homestead. When her husband died, she could not inherit his property. If she was a young widow, her husband's next of kin inherited from her. If she was past child-bearing, she could elect to be housed and fed by one or another of her married sons.

Within traditional Iteso society, a woman lived quite a happy and contented life because there was nothing to challenge the cultural norms under which she operated. Then along came Christianity with its promise of the Good News of salvation. Missionary Christianity came to the Iteso in the form of Roman Catholicism and Anglicanism (CMS), both very traditional and rather conservative, particularly in their understanding of morality and in their understanding of the place of women in society in general, and in particular in the Christian community. The "Good News" that missionary Christianity brought to the African woman was more in the field of education than in spiritual transformation. It is indeed true that Jesus Christ has been introduced, but the Good News that the person of Jesus Christ should be and wants to be for the African woman remains hidden from the majority of them. The minority who have encountered Jesus Christ in the manner of the New Testament women (like the Samaritan woman, John 4.2-11), the woman caught in adultery (John 8.2-11), the woman with the hemorrhage (Luke 8.40ff.), for example, are those women who are "saved," in religious life, in good Christian marriages and in canonically recognized lay organizations. These can claim to have encountered the Christ who, notwithstanding the existing cultural and religious laws that forbade any public communication between women and rabbis, reached out to women who had been declared social outcasts and gave them new hope and a feeling of wellbeing.

Two main reasons that hinder women from personally meeting Jesus Christ fully may be examined: the way certain passages of Scripture have been and continue to be interpreted to the detriment of women, and the predominantly male-oriented church ministries and institutions.

### Interpretation of certain passages of Scripture

One teaching that has hurt a certain percentage of African women and placed them outside the salvation community is the interpretation of Matthew 19.4-6. This passage presents Jesus' interpretation of marriage as divinely instituted and monogamous (cf. Gen 2.18-24). Iteso men who wanted to become Christians were told to send away their wives and choose only one with whom they could contract the sacrament of matrimony. Iteso traditional marriage, which was culturally legal and binding, was not recognized by the Church. Those unfortunate women who were not chosen to become Christian wives were declared concubines and their children bastards. The once happily married women found themselves abandoned and homeless, for they could not return to their fathers' homesteads. Some were no longer women in their prime who could remarry.

For a while, this strategy seemed to work. Those who adhered to the form of marriage that the Church insisted upon were those whose livelihood was dependent on missionary employment. For a man employed by missionaries to take another wife was to risk his job. When, later on, the government took over the task of employing most people, many men in monogamous marriages became polygamous. Currently, the major factor that is making polygamy difficult is the high cost of living. The majority of marriages contracted by the average Iteso of the rural area tend to follow traditional marriage lines, even when they are not polygamous.

Another church teaching that has served to emphasize the subservient position of women is the interpretation given to Colossians 3.1a and Ephesians 5.22a: "Wives, be subject to your husbands." What is implied in Ephesians 5.21, "Be subject to one another out of reverence for Christ," is usually ignored or downplayed. The fact that men should love their wives with a sacrificial love is hardly ever highlighted. By emphasizing woman's subjection to man in marriage, the Church has directly given men the excuse for laxity and tyranny in their dealings with their wives. Laxity here means the tendency men have of being unfaithful to their wives. They are of the opinion that women should be faithful because they must be submissive to men. Women are expected to practice a higher morality than men. Women have been blamed for their husbands' unfaithfulness; for, the argument goes, if a man goes after other women then the wife must be lacking in some way. This argument is too one-sided. It does not take into consideration the fact that in marriage, frustrations, lack of fulfillment, be it sexual or personal, could be caused by either the man or the woman. Of course no man could ever tolerate his wife's unfaithfulness because it is considered a direct affront to his authority.

The Church's emphasis on the subjection of the wife to her husband in marriage has given many men an excuse for being tyrannical to their wives, even to the extent of physically assaulting them. It is of course natural to discipline one who is one's subject and the subject is expected to accept the discipline as part of her position. In marriage, as the Church presented it to our people, woman is the subject who can and often should be so disciplined. The fact of the complementarity of the man and woman in marriage has not become an integral part of the teaching of the Church. In a very subtle way the Church encourages woman to endure the hardships of marriage even to the point of accepting an impossible marriage relationship as a necessary martyrdom.

Traditional Iteso society had provisions for preventing excessive cruelty to wives. A court of elders often met to settle serious cases of incompatibility in marriage. Church marriage has no such provisions, especially with its emphasis that marriage is an affair between two parties only. Always there is the underlying view that it is woman's lot to suffer in marriage because the Bible says so (1 Tim. 2.14; Gen. 3.16). Was it not the woman who, after all, brought evil and disorder into the world by her sin? She should therefore take what life metes out to her and accept it as part of her atonement for causing man to sin. Often this interpretation of the story of the Fall is taken literally, with complete disregard of the historical and cutural setting of the story. The revolutionary interpretation to it that Jesus gave by his own example is totally ignored.

Jesus Christ had every reason to perpetuate the subjugation of women. As a Jewish rabbi, he must have been aware of the practice the male Jews had of thanking God each day that they were not created slaves, gentiles, or women. But in his own relationship with women, he chose to ignore the traditional Jewish attitudes and instead treated women with compassion and complete acceptance. For his pains he earned the reputation of being the friend of sinners. To those women who encountered Jesus of Nazareth in his lifetime, he must have been really Good News.

These interpretations of the Bible have only confirmed to the woman that her apparent low status is in accordance with the divine will and the natural order from the beginning. When Christ's relationship with women is discussed, and whenever related passages are expounded by preachers, Christ's own full acceptance of women is discussed in very low key. A sermon on the woman who washed the feet of Jesus with her tears manages to ignore Christ's love for the woman as a person and instead concentrates on her abject sinfulness. Christ is portrayed as pitying women as morally weaker vessels, for after all if he fully accepted them as equal with men why did he not include them among the twelve apostles? The story of Mary, from whom seven demons had been cast out, as being sent by the risen Christ to announce the Good News of his resurrection to his brothers is invariably ignored. But she was the first apostle of the resurrection.

## Church ministry

The ministry of the Church is a predominantly male enterprise. Only men go through ministerial training and only men get ordained as priests. The ministerial training that priests undergo removes them culturally and physically from the people they are preparing to minister to. By the time a man completes his training he has become a stranger to his people. The people regard him as someone outside and above their ordinary lives. Very often he has no way of touching the lives of the people.

During their priestly training, one overriding indoctrination is in the area of sexual morality. Moral decadence becomes equated with having any kind of intimacy with women. Sexual abstinence or celibacy is regarded as part and parcel of priesthood. The future preachers of the Good News of Christ's salvation are warned in no uncertain terms to avoid women. Woman is portrayed as the archenemy of a priest's holy vocation. Women are to be treated objectively and formally. Young women are to be especially shunned because of their terrible power to confuse the heart and head of a young man. Sermons have been preached from the pulpits on Sundays that castigated young girls who dared to have anything to do with seminarians. African priests leaving the seminary are generally quite ignorant of how to approach women as people. They feel safe with religious and married women, but are at a loss with young unmarried women. Should a priest seduce a young woman, his sin is nicely covered up by his bishop, while the young woman is as good as tried, condemned and executed, psychologically and spiritually.

The traditional woman had her domestic rituals that sustained her. Missionary Christianity, combined with inevitable cultural changes, has tended to belittle, if not prohibit outright, the performance of these rites. They were dubbed demonic or superstitious. Their spiritually healing power for the woman whose whole life was full of special difficulties was never fully appreciated. No alternatives were given and consequently a vacuum was created that has never been filled. For example, whenever there was serious illness, especially psychosomatic illness, a woman could go to a traditional healer who was very well versed in diagnosing such illnesses. These healers prescribed a healing ritual that usually involved a healing of relationships, for this was the common cause of such illnesses. After performing these rituals of healing, the patient was cured.

The Church has no real effective healing ministry that corresponds to this sort of thing. The coming of Christianity and Western civilization has caused an upheaval in the world of the African woman. Her way of life was disrupted if she had contracted a polygamous marriage. Christianity condemned the traditional healers as diabolical. It condemned all of African culture as pagan. The African had to adopt Western ways in order to become a Christian: naming ceremonies, dressing and etiquette, education, recreation, and even burials—all had to be "Christian."

The tensions caused by these changes are considerable. Christianity did not remove the African from the African world, which conflicted with the new world of Christianity. The ministry of healing was often confined exclusively to physical ailments. Hospitals healed the body, but often left the spirit and psyche ailing. For spiritual healing, one could go to a priest, but the priests did not understand the psychosomatic illnesses that troubled people, particularly women. Few women ever feel free to consult a priest.

There is an increase in the number of African women who find themselves unmarried and outside the convent. Most of these women are educated and professionals in their chosen fields. For one reason or another they could not conform to the kind of life that society defines as acceptable. Many of them would have wanted to give their lives to the service of the Church, but the Church, as already pointed out, does not readily welcome them in ministry. A great many of these women find themselves in the very difficult position of single motherhood, widowhood, broken marriages, or in unfortunate liaisons with men. It should be a very natural thing for a single mother to find welcome acceptance in the Church; instead, their state of single parenthood is considered a permanent state of sin. Having fallen before, they are given little or no encouragement to get up and live among people who understand and are morally supportive. If anything, fingers are pointed at them as people who must be avoided and whose terrible example must not be imitated. A man who sins and then confesses is more readily forgiven and accepted than a woman who, out of loneliness or weakness (or cleverly seduced), finds herself a single mother.

The single woman faces the terrible ordeal of becoming a social misfit; she risks becoming turned in on herself. It is extremely difficult for such a woman to get the seemingly necessary spiritual guidance of a priest: few priests can appreciate the life of a single woman, and frequent visits to a priest, however innocent they may be, will be misconstrued. These women find it difficult to encounter the Christ who came to give liberty to captives. In their lonely struggle to cope, they often cannot experience Christ as a person who cares for them.

For the majority of African women, the Good News that is the person of Jesus Christ is still inaccessible. Unless church structures radically change and allow women to receive the liberty that the Son of God died to make available, there can be no real transformation of people's lives.

❖ ❖ ❖

## Women's Oppression and Cries of Pain

☐ *Although Bette Ekeya's discussion of African women is largely based on her experience in Kenya, when speaking about African women we must be aware of women's special situation in Southern Africa, especially under the regime of apartheid in the Republic of South Africa. Over recent years a growing number of women have raised their voices and begun to develop a feminist theological vision. The first academic conference on feminist theology, where women and men reflected together on women in Church and society, was probably the one held at the University of South Africa in Pretoria in September 1984 (see W. S. Vorster, ed.,* Sexism and Feminism in Theological Perspective, *Pretoria: University of South Africa, 1984). Reflecting on their double oppression of sexism and racism, black women have developed new perspectives of black feminist theology in South Africa.*

*In chapter 14 two black women describe their struggles. The first extract comes from a longer chapter on "Black Feminist Theology in South Africa," in Simon Maimela and Dwight Hopkins, eds.,* We Are One Voice: Black Theology in USA and South Africa, *Braamfontein: Skotaville Publishers, 1989, pp. 51-9. Its author is the Reverend Roxanne Jordaan, a minister in the Congregational Church of Port Elizabeth, South Africa, from where she went to Vanderbilt University in the United States to work for a theological doctorate. A shorter and somewhat different version of this chapter can also be found in Denise Ackermann, Jonathan Draper, and Emma Mashinini, eds.,* Women Hold Up Half the Sky: Women in the Churches in Southern Africa *(Pietermaritzburg: Cluster Publications 1991, pp. 122-8).*

*In the second extract, Thoko Mpumlwana tells us about her upbringing in South Africa, her experience as a minister's wife, and her own theological training and understanding of black feminist theology. It is taken from her chapter entitled "My Perspective on Women and their Role in Church and Society," in* Women Hold Up Half the Sky *(pp. 369-85) mentioned above. Its author is a high school teacher closely involved in community development; she is also a member of the Social Responsibility Department of the Order of Ethiopia.*

## 14 ROXANNE JORDAAN AND THOKO MPUMLWANA

# Two Voices on Women's Oppression and Struggle in South Africa

"BLACK FEMINIST THEOLOGY IN SOUTH AFRICA"—
by Roxanne Jordaan

Being black is synonymous with being oppressed and being exploited. In South Africa, and in all other places in the world, it means to earn less than what is humanly sufficient to eat, to be housed, and to be schooled properly. It is to see the desolation and hopelessness all around you, but never to give up hope. To be black is to experience total disbelief in the face of army rifles and the military, but not to be silenced by this fear and keep on believing. To be black in South Africa is to smell the stench of injustice from the armpits of mine workers, of domestic servants, and of factory workers. To be black is to be faced very often by a board stating "whites only" outside a very beautiful park, and not to feel your humanness diminished. It is to be thrown into prison for saying that you cannot and never will stand under the authority of an unjust system; and being prepared to be imprisoned without ever standing trial.

Furthermore, it is being employed in backbreaking, low-paid jobs or never to have a job, but still to have the inborn desire to want to work. In South Africa, it is to see a pregnant woman and a four-year-old child killed in cold blood by South African riot police; shots ripping through their bodies, but not giving up the fight. It is to be restricted in your movements, in your speech, in your worship, but still have the freedom to sing the Lord's song. It is to be uprooted from your dwelling place and to be placed in temporary tents, having your family wiped out in the cold face of death by the cold of the night but still have the warm will to live. It is being. It is black. It is living.

Moreover, added to this atrocious way of life is the position of the oppressed and exploited black woman in her own community. Admittedly both black and white women suffer from a denial of independence and dignity, but no white woman knows the inhuman intentions of racial oppression. So black women in South Africa have an added burden caused by the effects of exploitation and oppression. Black women are the lowest-paid workforce in South Africa. In boom times they are hired at low wages and fired during recession periods. They form 70% of the unemployed community. They have to cook, wash, clean in their own homes after a very hard day's work. They form 60% of the church members, but are labeled as the weaker, subordinate, non-thinking people by their oppressed and exploited black men. Women can raise the funds, but are not allowed in the Church to decide how the funds are to be spent. With the rise of political violence in South Africa, more women have been raped by white troops in the townships and along the roadside than ever before. There are times when women fight side by side with their men in street wars against the army, yet they have no say in the decisionmaking body of the liberation struggle. Black women have to leave suckling babies behind and all their nurturing instincts would be wrenched from their bodies. Still they must go out to find work in a big city, very often only to become prostitutes.

The very beginnings of humankind are challenged. We live in the face of these demoralizing, dehumanizing conditions. It takes a superhuman being to just survive. And we, black women, have indeed survived. These dehumanizing situations are totally out of line with what God intended us to be at creation, for God gave dominion over all the earth to both male and female, with no specific color attached to it either. God used Moses to deliver the people of Israel, but it was Moses' mother who defied Pharaoh's orders. Consequently she saved a child and eventually she saved the house of Israel. And isn't it also wonderful that God so designed the body of the woman that it would bear Christ the Liberator? Mary was not only concerned about her spiritual well-being when the angel of the Lord spoke to her. For instance, we read in Luke 1.51-3 in the Magnificat that Mary speaks about the political oppression of her people. Here she says that the mighty will be thrown from their throne.

### Black women's experience and black theology

Thus the greatest event in the life of God's people was performed through an agent, a woman. Yet despite this, the rise of black theology did not initially consider the feminist aspect of *divine* liberation. However, I was very inspired by Professor James Cone's acknowledgment of his own weaknesses when he was shaken into the reality of accepting how black theology, in essence, had to reevaluate the legitimacy of its liberation claims. Specifically he realized that any form of liberation that does not address itself to the emancipation of the whole person should be seriously challenged for misrepresenting the concept of liberation. For no person can be free when part of that which gives you your humanity is in chains. A part of the wholeness of black womanness is also caught up in black theology and, more specifically, black feminist theology.

Now I do not want to contend that men who oppress us women, and especially black men who oppress us black women, will be violently washed away. We love you and it makes the struggle more difficult. Yes, I do not wish you to be washed away. But I believe that male domination over female submission is not God ordained. We have to rectify this incorrect relation in the black community. Therefore we must use reconciliation together with repentance on the side of the oppressor and exploiter. Reconciliation together with repentance between black male and black female takes place in a just fashion. Each one of us has to recognize that one is not the enemy of the other. Rather we must focus on the real enemy of racist classism. In this situation, black women suffer the worst oppression and exploitation. Now God is no neutral God. Accordingly, it could then be claimed, and I do not want us to debate this issue, that God is supposed to be on the side of the black woman. God is supposed to be a black woman. This might be so; it may not be so.

## Black feminist theology's origins

Above all, black women are prepared to accept God's granting dominion to all people over the earth. Black feminist theology in South Africa has only just begun, though it was written on the table long before people consciously got together to articulate the development of black feminist theology. Yet with the birth of the Johannesburg-based Institute for Contextual Theology (ICT) toward the latter part of 1981, black feminist theology deliberately got off the ground. During this time, an exciting new era began to evolve in our communities. As the crisis erupted in our country, more women were taking up positions as equals with our men on the battlefield and at the drawing table. And at this point, we tried to sit down to really reflect on what was happening to us as oppressed women and to the black community as a whole.

But despite our involvement in the liberation struggle, women still had to be the slaves in our own homes. Black women, then, started getting together and added to the general thrust of black theology, a black feminist theology. However, it did not develop as a countermovement, but as an integral part of black theology. Unfortunately in 1985, black men at a black church leaders' ecumenical consultation held in South Africa laughed at the cries and distress of black feminist theologians. They laughed at what were real feelings of people. But nobody ever laughs at jokes about black people. Yet the cries and the anger of the women were real. The disappointment of realizing the insensitivity of other oppressed people was sad, but not disheartening. For a black woman is never disheartened. We cannot afford to lose heart.

For instance, when I was a student at the Federal Theological Seminary (supposedly one of the most progressive black-oriented theological schools in South Africa), some new students would not participate in communion at the Lord's table when I served them. To add insult to injury, when my husband and I decided to have a baby and my tummy grew big with child, even those black men who initially received communion from me refused because I was no longer "clean." Thus we also find male seminary students, male church members, and male pastors acting extremely oppressively. But again, black women cannot afford to lose heart.

As the political crisis heightened in our country, the awareness of total liberation grew and women became more intensely aware of our position in the Church and Church-related organizations. Specifically, we realized that our destiny as black women would be determined by how much we were prepared to fight a war for total liberation. In Luke 4, we read the famous words of Jesus saying: "I have come to preach Good News to the poor, to proclaim release to the captives . . ." Sometimes Jesus' proclamation seems to be related only to men. But our experience tells us that the captives in South Africa (e.g., the poor, the blind, the oppressed) are women too, specifically black women. So Jesus died for all of us and rose for all of us.

Admittedly, black feminist theologians in South Africa are not highly "qualified." We are not all trained pastors. But black feminist theology is preached in the bushes of Nyanga in Cape Town. Black feminist theology is lived in the streets of downtrodden Soweto. It is lived in the shacks and preached in the shacks throughout South Africa. Black feminist theology is preached in the tents of forced removal townships. Black women in South Africa are involved at the grassroots developmental level of a theology from both our intellectual capacity as well as from our inner strength and from our gut feelings. For this reason, we find that black feminist theology does not differentiate itself from liberating political tendencies. They all work together; for the political oppression and exploitation gave birth to black feminist theology.

Slowly but surely a theology challenging the inferior position of women has emerged. Black women are on the way to rediscovering our tremendous power as black women in South Africa. Obviously there are still many who have not blossomed from their germinating period. But within the liberation movement and especially in black feminist theology, the ground has been tilled and now we shall work until the rains of justice shall fall from the heavens and breathe life into its once dormant receptors, heralding in a new way of awareness from the shackles of our oppressed bodies.

When white people came to South Africa, they had the Bible and we had the land. But now we find that they have the land and we have the Bible. This is why we have black theology. Thus black feminist theology does not intend to disqualify oppressed men from the saving grace of Jesus Christ. On the contrary, black women condemn white settlers for stealing the land from black men as well. Black feminist theology simply attempts to have black men view the struggle in a holistic way. Certainly all of the oppressed have to be set free to make the struggle a just struggle.

Indeed, we have the Bible and the oppressors have the land. Yet it is from the soil of Africa that we blacks were called into a community with God. Because we have been called on the soil of Africa, that is where we have a relationship with God. But what kind of relationship can we have with God now that we have no soil? The soil has been taken from us. Even the wealth of the soil in the homelands, which are part of South Africa, is controlled by the racist regime. Moreover, this loss of our land for the Bible affected both men and women. For example, men were forced to leave their homes to go to cities to find jobs, and poverty therefore became a way of life. Women took control over the whole household and ran the affairs of the family. It was only when money ran short or when there was extreme illness that the women would go to the cities to join their husbands.

Yet nothing much has been written in the theologies of a believing people about such brave women. In contrast, books upon books have been written about great black men all depicting their struggle for survival. But women still have a greater struggle for survival. Black women in South Africa today know what it is like to nurse those injured in the streets as the struggle for liberation continues. We know what it is like to care for children not our own. The Bible teaches us a gospel of caring and sharing. Sometimes, as black people who do not have, we find it difficult to preach the gospel of caring and

155

sharing. Yet black women know what it is like to cry at the grave of some unknown comrade; not having personally known that person, but to have been involved with the spirit of that person for liberation. Black women in South Africa know what it is like to form support groups of victims of the system. In a word, through our own experiences, black women in South Africa are laying the foundation of a theology that makes God relevant to all people—a black feminist theology of liberation.

"MY PERSPECTIVE ON WOMEN AND THEIR
ROLE IN CHURCH AND SOCIETY"—
by Thoko Mpumlwana

## Personal history

In my family there were three of us children: two boys and myself. Therefore I had to learn to trust my own abilities as the only girl. Born in Melmoth, Zululand, I spent most of my early years in rural areas of Natal, though I also had a taste of urban life in my pre-teen years.

### Family

My father was a minister with the United Congregational Church. My mother was qualified as a teacher, but could not teach. I never got to ask her, but now I think it was because we had to move to so many areas. Also, it was taboo for clergy wives to work. They were supposed to *support* their husbands in their ministry and be available when people called for them. They were also expected to lead the women's organizations (*manyanos*) in their churches.

My family was very religious, and as children we grew up in that family environment. But the poverty, suffering, and injustice that I saw being practiced by people in the Church made us question whether the Church really practiced the gospel. As children still under our parents' authority we were churchgoers, but I myself had not been nourished by the Church. The Church to me exploited my father, who sometimes earned as little as R5.00 a month—yet expected him to meet all his missionary obligations and still bring up his family. Within the same Church were missionaries and ministers for whom the Church provided adequate housing facilities and stipends. I saw a Church that did not really care. There were lots of questions about God that I asked myself, and yet dared not ask my father who would have seen them as blasphemous.

My mother developed budgeting skills and would sell this and that to supplement my father's income. My mother was a powerful woman, a dedicated mother, and yet cared about other people's problems. While she respected my father in the traditional sense, she would challenge him as his equal too!

## Schooling

I started school in a new township school at Kwa-Mashu, which was a new black township in Durban of people just moved from Cato Manor and other "mixed areas" around Durban. Kwa-Mashu also had an influx of migrant workers who lived in newly built hostels. My higher primary schooling was at a rural area on the Natal South Coast, a place called Bangilizo in Hibberdene. It was a so-called Bantu Community School. Memories of the conditions of that school still haunt me, yet we were all (teachers, community, and all) wearing masks of satisfaction with conditions: three classes in one room with no windows. Standard 1 was an unfinished dark storeroom. There were few desks. Some had to sit on the floor. The teachers' cottages were small mud houses. Yet here I am, a full-blown person today.

My high-school life was spent at a church boarding school for girls in Inanda Seminary. That's where I really got my sociopolitical nourishment, even though that probably wasn't the purpose of the high school. Inanda was a Roman Catholic missionary school that inculcated important values in us, e.g., leadership, self-confidence, and pride in ourselves. Perhaps that's why I refuse to allow anyone to make me feel smaller than I am. We had no boys to bully us or to do things for us!

At Inanda we were not really taught politics, but we were made to see that life is broader and more complicated than we thought it was. I remember at matric that we had two wonderful teachers in history and English. I got my political awareness and initiation, or rather analysis of my sociopolitical experience, from history and English lessons. Our history teacher helped us to see that history did not start with 1652, and he always reminded us that history was written according to the interpretation, if you like ideology, of the historian. We were therefore encouraged to critique opinions of historians based on our own interpretations.

## Church.

I grew up in the Church and was involved in a young girls' organization. There is a lot we learnt from this organization—but we also grew up to know that boys could be free not to be in any organization, but girls had to be organized for their own protection!

When I became a young woman, at age about twenty, I started to drift away from the Church for the following reasons:

- I had been exposed to a more meaningful expression of love for my neighbor in politics. The Church shied away from politics, therefore I also stayed away from what I regarded as a heaven Church where people scream, shout, and cry about their sins and hardships yet do nothing to address the real issues.
- The way the Church had treated my father, who to us was a humble and committed Christian, made me despise the institutional Church. In particular in the late 1970s in King Williamstown, my father was treated like dirt by church people simply because of who he was or his style of leadership. The unjust treatment of my family and the failure of the wider church leadership to support him angered me.
- I felt that the institutional Church takes a lot from you, especially if you are selfless, and it gives suffering or nothing in return. You are promised a greater reward in heaven.

*Marriage*

In the second year of my married life, my husband Malusi went through a conversion experience that shocked me. I realized that something supernatural had happened to him, but still I resisted any involvement in the Church. By this time I'd moved from my family church to his family church: the Order of Ethiopia with its Anglican style and African traditional background.

It all got worse for me. I resisted any involvement until Malusi went to college to, as he said, "test his vocation"! I hated the idea of leaving my job in order to *follow* him. Malusi and other friends ministered to me until I saw that the Church I was rebelling against was just an institution, and that the God I needed to serve was the God that worried when there is suffering, hunger, distress.

My involvement in my Church was mainly in the area of social responsibility and later women's ministry through which I believed God used us to show love and concern for us. I allowed God to use me as an instrument of peace and love. This teaching was therefore not contrary to my political commitment. The history of Ethiopianism strengthened my commitment to serve God through serving others.

My experience as a priest's wife has been exciting on the one hand and unfair on the other. I'll mention a few examples. Your husband ceases to be yours: you share him day and night with others. You are expected not to complain or demand *your* time. That's taken as "pulling your husband by his nose" and is taboo.

You have to change your lifestyle to suit the demands of others. I had to give away my tracksuits and pants because a priest's wife cannot wear trousers. Men, and old men in particular, do not respect a woman who does not cover her hair at all times, especially in church. I had to change to accommodate that if my husband's ministry was to succeed.

As a priest's wife you are expected to be a leader of the women's *manyano*. If not, you are regarded as a deviant, a social misfit, who is a stumbling block in the ministry of your husband. Sometimes they put you in this position to evade the responsibility of providing leadership themselves, and so that they can direct their criticisms to you.

Despite the disadvantages mentioned above, being a priest's wife may help you develop skills and leadership abilities that you would not have developed otherwise. You are able to get to know a number of people, exciting people too.

## Becoming aware of racism

It is actually very difficult to say what my first experience of racism and sexism was, because I grew up in a society so unjustly structured that it became part of life. Let me make a painful admission; I grew up in a liberal Church that practiced racism. I could not understand how my family could live in such poverty, when in the same Church white counterparts lived reasonably comfortably.

But there was one humiliating experience that shocked me as a young rural girl and opened my eyes. Ministers of religion are highly respected in our communities. My father belonged to the old stock of clergy who put on their clerical shirts at all times. One day he went to Umzinto, those days our nearest town, and did not come back with the afternoon (and only) bus. We were all worried, but because we had neither a phone nor a car within our reach we spent the night without him. In the morning Mother went to search for him in town. She checked hospitals and finally the police station. There was my father under arrest because he had forgotten to pay his poll tax on time. Although I was young and could not get answers to some political questions I had around this issue, I became convinced that there was something evil in our country if an honest man like my father could spend a night in jail for tax. Could the same have happened if my father were white? But our parents protected us from the harsh realities of life. We were never given a full explanation as children.

## Growing awareness of sexism

Sexism? The irony of sexism and perhaps racism is that one is not conscious of it unless the consciousness is aroused to those inequalities and discriminations. I may have been a victim of sexism throughout my upbringing, but could have accepted it as part of life.

It was when I got married that I suddenly felt awkward about some of the accepted roles that married women were expected to play at home. Somewhere at the back of my mind I hated washing, cooking, ironing, cleaning the house and so on, while my husband didn't see it as his role to help. I hated my new role, but I thought there must be something wrong with me because other wives seemed content with the status quo. So on Sundays my husband would wake up and go to church, leaving me with an unmade bed, a bath full of dirty water, clothes lying about. When he came back he would bring people for lunch, and he would read the *Sunday Times* while I dished up for them.

Our stay at the seminary changed our pattern. We appreciated each other more, and Malusi was awakened to the fact that housework and childrearing was his role as well as mine. Because I was working and studying, sometimes he found himself having to do things he had never done before. Among the women I met at college, the issues of sexism and exploitation of women would come up in discussions. And I'd always believed that I had more talents to use than being chained to the housework or a subordinate role.

My first real experience of an extreme case of sexism was in Cape Town in about 1987 when I went to visit a friend whose son had just come out of an initiation school. Traditionally men sit around the kraal to drink together as men. Women do not go anywhere near them. The kraal is regarded as a sacred place where only men enter, or at least only older women. But in the townships the situation is different. I entered through the front door having properly knocked. I was properly dressed for the occasion with a *doek* on my head. In the sitting room were men drinking beer and whiskey and eating meat; they chased me out like a leper, a person with an infectious disease. I was hurt, humiliated, felt degraded, unwanted, and angry. I was going there excitedly ready to support my friend and here were these men, most of whom I didn't know, treating me like dirt. Did they know who I was?

## Women in the Church

Women should be able to do everything that they are gifted and called to do in the church without being hindered by biological factors. If a woman is gifted to decorate the church with flowers let it be, but if a man is equally gifted to play that role, why not? The same applies to leadership at all levels, from class leaders to being bishops or moderators.

### Ordained ministry

Why should women not be ordained if God calls them to ordained ministry? I don't believe God is so sexist that she only calls men. Many women may have been called to ordained ministry, but prevented from responding to it by the sinful world of stereotypes. They may have been blocked, first, by their own socialization, thus believing that it's impossible; second, by other women who thought they were crazy; and third, by their ministers who felt ashamed of the idea that a woman can play such a role, etc.

What I'm saying is not the reversal of the process where men assume that they have a direct line to God whenever they feel moved to serve their Creator. Women should be allowed to exercise their ministry according to their gifts and commitment to serve.

Do women have a special and different kind of ministry from that of men? We all as individuals have our own special and different kind of ministry. But once we say the speciality and difference should be based on race, sex, or class, then it becomes unacceptable. In as much as I have condemned racial discrimination I should condemn gender discrimination.

## Feminist theology

Theology has always been regarded as a man's terrain. As women we have come to realize that everyone can do theology in spite of the fact that some may have to go to formal institutions to study theology. As a black woman who

162

experiences oppression because of my blackness as well, I think it is important for there to be black feminist theologians just as much as there should be black theology. I believe that should be done contextually. So if people are poor they should theologize about their situation and ask if it is God's will that they should be in that situation.

Therefore as black women we need to theologize on our situation: Where is God in our lives; at home; at work? What does it mean to be fully human in the image of God? How are we being called to serve God? Generally the majority of women are subjected to threefold oppression: as women; as workers/ peasants; and as blacks. Therefore black reality of oppression differs from that of white women. They see the God they worship through similar eyes as women, but different eyes as blacks and whites in South Africa and as the privileged and the underprivileged.

As women we have always been made to feel that the Bible talks about courageous, good, and strong men on the one hand and weak and sinful women on the other, because the Scriptures were being interpreted by men for women and by whites for blacks!

*Black and white feminist theology*

Because of the apartheid structure of our society that led to inequalities in the privileges enjoyed between blacks and whites in South Africa, white feminist theologians are more privileged than black women.

Regardless of race, women theologians should come together as sisters to share their problems and to theologize together. This is also important for one another's support. However, white feminist theologians should be wary of using their privileged positions to articulate the frustrations of black feminists. A sisterly way to do it would be to accompany black women by empowering them to play their meaningful role in Church and society. This I am saying because the extent of the oppression felt by white women in the Church differs drastically from the pain felt by black women. White women theologians should be prepared *to listen* to the fears and frustrations of black women. Listening may be regarded as retrogressive by some of them, but I think it is important if we are to travel the journey together and on a par with one another.

## Black feminist theology

Black feminist theology can contribute a lot to the liberation struggle, because black women are in the majority in churches; therefore if black women are empowered to develop and serve God to the fullest of their abilities, they will develop enough skills and self-confidence to make a meaningful contribution to society.

## Social analysis

There is a definite relationship between racism, classism, and sexism. To me, these are all forms of discrimination used to keep power in one section, e.g., white women may use racism to maintain their own power base; black men keep their power base through sexism; the privileged class use classism to maintain their base. Most black women are subjected to all three forms of oppression.

As a black woman who is a teacher under the present dispensation I can never be a leader in a white school because I am black and also because I am a woman. A classic case is that of black domestic workers who have no status or recognition in our society and yet they keep the economy afloat by ensuring that other people go out to work.

Therefore, sexism is gender apartheid, and like all other forms of discrimination it should really be outlawed. Although some people argue that because sexism is a result of socialization and culture, therefore attitudes and stereotypes should be tolerated, with the hope that one day people will change. We, as women, are working hard to ensure that the new South African constitution brings a better deal for women. South Africans should regard sexism with as much seriousness as racism, so that they should support the idea of outlawing it in the new constitution, e.g., many women have been deprived of promotions or job opportunities because of their biological differences. That is unfair, unjust, and evil. Many a woman has been deprived of proper housing, business deals, etc., because she is a minor according to the South African legislation. The South African constitution has actually legitimated gender discrimination. It is time a new constitution gave women a fair deal.

As a woman I should be able to take a person or people/organizations to court, if I feel deprived of my rightful role as a result of gender discrimination.

If we leave this to goodwill we will never get fair treatment because sexism is also a power struggle. People do not relinquish power without pressure. So the male species will not open up the privileges that it has been enjoying simply because they are men. Pressure has to be brought to bear to ensure that the wrongs of the past are corrected.

## African culture

African culture, especially as interpreted today, prevents women from playing leadership roles in our society and Church. African culture has undergone metamorphosis. It has been influenced to an extent by Western culture. In traditional African culture women were regarded as weaker than men, so that the man walks ahead of a woman when they are walking together, to protect the woman.

One hears of powerful women in African history, but their importance is played down in the same manner in which women in the Bible are played down. In African religious tradition a woman should be regarded with respect, if ancestors used her to communicate with people.

Nonetheless there are lots of African cultural practices that need revision if we are to maintain our important cultural heritages. I do not mind a cultural practice if it does not contribute to the belittling of women. Once people exploit, discriminate against, and deprive women of their God-given status, in the name of culture, I begin to have problems as a Christian woman. I begin to have problems once men and husbands sexually abuse women in the name of culture. Our societies have allowed men greater freedom to do anything

165

simply because of their sex. Time has come for this freedom not to be enjoyed at the expense and suffering of women.

African men sing "Viva!" when people talk about racial and class exploitation, but they can hang you if you dare talk about sexism. They say African culture legitimates it and, if they are Christians, sections of the Bible seal it for them.

Those who have attempted to find out what the position of women was in African traditional societies before the influence of Western culture argue that women enjoyed a very special status. They were respected and allowed to play a meaningful role in their societies. For example, women played an important economic role by participating in farming. They were farmers of the community, even if the division of labor was along sexist lines.

Therefore, I believe it is very un-African to regard women as useless children who are not capable of participating in any meaningful nation-building process. Traditionally, African women had tremendous power. It is Western culture with its new economic power relations that has brought with it new power relations that are gender-based.

I also need to mention that it is extremely un-African to lift a finger to a woman. Today people beat up their wives under the guise of African culture.

Culture is dynamic anyway. How can we Africans pretend that we live in a society that has not been affected by other cultures and other realities? Africans have a lot to teach people of other cultures, just as much as we have something to gain from them.

How would I think the situation of rural black women could be improved in society and in the Church? Through education that takes into consideration the realities experienced by rural African women. Unless the Church and society take seriously the health, education, and general poverty problems that rural women experience, they can never be improved. Once this is done, then women should be made conscious of the fact that the development and improvement of their communities also depend on them. So long as rural women are made invisible by the Church and society, their situation cannot improve. Projects on rural development should be promoted in rural areas and women should be empowered to participate in these. Also, income-generating programs, cooperatives, skills training, and literacy programs should be embarked upon with rural women. It is difficult, for instance, to get into health programs if women are illiterate. The improvement of rural women will lead to a general improvement of living conditions in these areas because women will be taking their development into their own hands.

## Conclusion

As things are, the future looks bleak. I feel we will go through a period of pain, darkness, resistance, and schisms if the struggle against sexism is taken seriously by the churches. There will be lots of casualties; both men and women who will be ostracized, humiliated, ridiculed and harassed before the sun shines. Just as South Africa went through such periods in the 1950's, 60's, 70's, and 80's, where there were lots of casualties, so will the sexist struggle. Just as a number of blacks joined in the humiliation of political activists thinking that liberation was never to come, so will other women join in the persecution of those men and women who stand against dehumanization of women.

As a Christian, I live with the hope that one day truth will prevail. There are times when I want to give up, but the pain that Christ went through gives me the strength to go on preaching the good news of a liberating God.

❖    ❖    ❖

□ *In the introduction, I mentioned the importance of women gaining access to theological education. Without it, feminist theology could not have developed. Millions of women in the countries of the Third World are still deprived of the most rudimentary education and basic literacy. They struggle to get more access to education, but even the privileged few who struggle on behalf of their less privileged sisters often have to overcome tremendous obstacles in order to become educated and gain access to higher theological education. However, even where such education is obtained, theologically trained women are not always welcomed by their churches, since it is difficult for women in a male-dominated Church to find their gifts and talents rightly used. In an unpublished paper on theological education, Bette Ekeya described her experience in the Roman Catholic Church in Kenya in the following words:*

> *In this country it is near impossible for a woman, particularly a lay single woman, to gain recognition in the church on the basis of an acquired theological expertise. It is impossible for a woman to win ecclesiastical sponsorship to enter theological universities with the understanding that a service in the church would be given such a one. It is difficult for religious sisters who have the backing of their religious vows and communities, it is futile for women without such backing or matrimonial integrity to even try. One of the prerequisites for such a sponsorship is the recommendation of the bishop. I do not know of any single lay woman who has been sponsored by any bishop to undertake theological studies in preparation for service in the church.*
>
> *A young woman may be enterprising enough to seek such studies by her own efforts, and she may indeed equip herself with all the knowledge and courage needed and may even be offered some job in the field of the lay apostolate, but the going will be uphill from the outset. She will be thwarted, misunderstood and suspected at every turn. Should she show a certain competence, creativity and vision in her work, she will be accused of insubordination, incompetence and presumption and will be told in no uncertain terms, that she has no right to presume on her position and assume powers*

*she was not given. She will be spied upon so much so that each social contact she makes, particularly with men, will be noted as a mark against her. Should she make the fatal error of becoming too familiar with the priests with whom she must inevitably come into contact within the course of her work, she will be accused of corrupting the clergy and the church. In the end she will be dismissed as "too dangerous for the church of God" to have around. The vocation to be a single lay woman within the church is non-existent. The reasons for this are connected with the way sexuality, particularly female sexuality, has been understood by the exclusively celibate men who have assigned themselves the task of determining how women should behave in order to be acceptable within the church as part of the congregation they, the celibate men, have to minister to.*

*In the two extracts in chapter 15, two women from very different cultures speak of their experience of education. In the first extract, the well-known African woman theologian Mercy Amba Oduyoye describes the wider context of her educational background and work taken from her chapter on "The Empowering Spirit of Religion," in Susan Brooks Thistlethwaite and Mary Potter Engel, eds.,* Lift Every Voice: Constructing Christian Theologies from the Underside, *San Francisco: HarperCollins, 1990, p. 245.*

*The second extract is based on a brief interview held in 1990 with Roina Fa'atauva'a, who was then the first Western Samoan woman to be accepted in the Bachelor Theology program at the Pacific Theological College in Fiji. (See Tessa Mackenzie, "Roina Pioneers Theological Education for Samoan Women," in* Pacific Journal of Theology, *series II, no. 4, 1990, pp. 38-40. Women's situation in Indian theological colleges is described by Prasanna K. Samuel, "Women in Theological Education",* The Asia Journal of Theology, *vol. 2/1, 1988, pp. 79-82.)*

*Mercy Amba Oduyoye originally trained and worked as a school teacher. She received her higher education at the University of Ghana (B.A., Religious Studies) and the University of Cambridge, England, where she obtained a M.A. in Theology in 1965. From 1967 to 1973 she worked as Youth Education*

*Secretary for the World Council of Churches in Geneva, and from 1974 to 1986 she taught in the Department of Religious Studies at the University of Ibadan in Nigeria. She was Visiting Professor at Union Theological Seminary in New York for a year, and then, in 1987, she became Deputy General Secretary of the World Council of Churches. Oduyoye was also a member of the WCC Commission on Faith and Order 1976-87, and the first woman and the first African to serve as President of the World Student Christian Federation. She has said that her own special mission is "to call attention to missiology and to African women's potential for contributing to the theological enterprise."* (Quoted in Deane William Ferm, Profiles in Liberation: 36 Portraits of Third World Theologians, *Mystic, Connecticut: Twenty-Third Publications, 1988, p. 55, where more details can be found about her life and thought on pp. 53–8.)*

## 15  MERCY AMBA ODUYOYE AND ROINA FA'ATAUVA'A

# The Struggle about Women's Theological Education

"AN AFRICAN WOMAN'S VOICE"—
by Mercy Amba Oduyoye

I am first and foremost an Akan, a member of a matrilineal society that speaks the language of Akan, found in Ghana and the Ivory Coast. I was raised to believe in the centrality of woman to the human community. Having been brought up in the Church and having worked with churches and taught theology, my worldview has been shaped by a utopia that is Christocentric. But this does not mean that I am blind to all else. In fact, it is as an African that I am Christian and I have no conflict with that, only periodic depression with regard to how little the Church in Africa concerns itself with social issues.

I have had problems with how the Church, academia, and the patriarchal society into which I married assign roles to women. My definition of personhood and identity as an Akan has led me several times into conflicts with role-expectations of people around me. My crosscultural experience of twenty years has fueled my commitment to the promotion of the visibility of women in Church, academy, and society.

I have also developed and nursed a deep passion for relevant education. In Africa we continue to educate for unemployment, rural exodus, and brain-drain. It hurts me to see how many young lives we are inadvertently plotting to throw into the streets to struggle for their survival. Miseducation happens not only at the level of the economy—it seems to be an all-round disaster area. My experience of teaching in certificate-oriented institutions that do very little to nourish creativity has been painful, so my working life has been divided between formal and informal education. I continue to advocate variety in educational opportunities, as education relates directly to the meaning and value of being human. It is as critical to me as the meaning of being a woman.

In Africa, poor quality and lack of vision in creating alternatives can be partly attributed to the lack of resources. This lack of resources, the result of the exploitation of the continent, has been a major influence on theology. The bondage of Africa's human, material, and spiritual resources propels me to seek a theological approach that is contextual. The injustice experienced by young people and women is part of the larger challenge of global inequities.

My involvement in practical social work is very limited. I have tried to contribute through writing and speaking that challenges people to be critical and committed to effecting humanizing changes in their environment. I began this "ministry" with a study of alternatives in youth education and employment. I produced cartoons relating to these situations to help young people to analyze their communities and to see how they are placed and may be placed.

At the university I revised a traditional dogmatic Christian theology course into one that looked at contemporary theology in relation to society and to Africa in particular. Liberation theology of Latin America and black theology of the USA and South Africa enabled me to move my classes toward women's perspectives on Christian theology. I took every opportunity to speak, preach, or conduct Bible study, in order to challenge people to take another look at their community and see if the Spirit of Christ does not convince them to challenge the structures of death around them.

I have arrived at a point where I no longer wish to be patient with sexism, racism, and injustices against the dignity that rightly belongs to beings made in the image of God. These labels are losing their force, but the realities they point to, the burden and the evil we are naming, continue. Those who live under them feel their iron weight. I may not be classified materially poor in my own community, but as long as I am a woman and black and refuse to accept any condition or attitude toward me that makes me feel less than accepted and included, I stand with all who are trampled upon and with all who want to struggle to see the end of inhumanity in the human community.

"A SAMOAN WOMAN'S VOICE"

"My presence in this college is a gate for other women from my country and my church," says Roina Fa'atauva'a, a second-year student at the Pacific Theological College (PTC). Roina is the first Samoan woman to gain entry to theological education. The path for Roina has not been an easy one, but instead a long struggle.

**Struggle with tradition**

The struggle began with herself, for when it was first suggested to her that she study theology, she could not see herself in this role. She and her family had always thought in the traditional way that ministry in the Church is a man's job.

At that time she was working for an airline and had no intention of doing anything else. But when she thought about the idea of studying theology she realized that she had talents suitable for ministry, and she agreed to be put forward.

The struggle against the traditional way of thinking has had a wide front. She has met opposition from the Church, from other women, and from the students with whom she has studied. "I don't blame them all," says Roina, "after all, I had the same understanding: it's not a woman's world."

During these two years at the Pacific Theological College she has seen much change and acceptance of herself as a serious student of theology. Now her home church, the Methodist Church of Samoa, is supporting her financially with a scholarship that she feels brings her to the door of being accepted.

## Obstacles to entering Pacific Theological College

The struggle to gain admission to PTC was a series of battles for Roina. When she first arrived in Fiji to study she found herself at the Deaconess College, for this was where the Methodist Church of Samoa had sent her. For Roina this was very frustrating. There is no deaconess order in her church, so she felt that this would lead nowhere.

She therefore sought to enrol at PTC to do a diploma, but was told this could not be done. She then thought of enrolling to do full-time Bachelor of Divinity studies, but again the answer was no. The college said that she needed a background in theological education and to have attended a theological college prior to entering PTC.

Roina went to see the Principal of PTC to explain that for her this was not possible. Women are not accepted at theological colleges in Samoa, because there is no separation between theological education and ordained ministry. "If you send me home, there is no hope," Roina added.

Eventually, PTC offered Roina a place on the condition that she pass examinations at the end of the first semester. However, Roina then discovered another barrier. Students entering PTC require the sponsorship of a church organization, and at this stage the Church withdrew its sponsorship and financial backing. Roina appealed to the women of her Church, and eventually, after much discussion, they agreed to sponsor her—although without finance. By this time Roina felt utterly rejected. She was in a position where she felt her identity was lost. "Who am I? Where do I stand?" was her cry. In the end, it was left to her family to support her through the first year at PTC.

### The challenge of theological studies

Once she had embarked on her studies at PTC, Roina began the struggle to make up for her lack of preliminary theological education. She admits that her biblical knowledge was minimal; even though her childhood had been spent on the campuses of theological colleges, she had not been exposed to the normal Sunday school and youth education of someone growing up in a congregation.

At first she felt lost because of the use of theological language in the lectures. She had to ask around a lot and read a great deal. It was a challenge, but she persevered and passed the necessary examinations. Now at the end of her second year, Roina is enjoying her studies and appreciates being able to learn so much. She pays tribute to the faculty members of PTC who have been supportive throughout her studies.

Roina sees the need for people to understand that theological studies do not necessarily have to lead to ordained ministry. It is her wish that other women could see the value of doing theological studies. She realizes how much women are missing out because of lack of opportunities—and also because of lack of interest.

Through all her tears, prayers, hardship, and struggles, Roina has not been aiming for ordained ministry for herself, and still does not see clearly whether this is where God is calling her. But she says, "It is my dream to see women ordained. At least I have made the way through for women of my country to come to theological college, and I sure hope more women will follow."

*Since the publication of this interview Roina Fa'atauva'a has obtained her B.D., and has written a B.D. thesis on the role of Samoan women in church and society. This provides the basis* for her article on *"Samoan Women: Caught in Culture Change"* in Pacific Journal of Theology, *series II, no. 7, 1992, pp. 15-27. This number has been described as "a truly historic document in South Pacific church history" because it features for the first time theological reflections and personal narratives by theologically trained Pacific women from different nationalities. It also contains what may be considered the first printed articulation of a Pacific women's theology (see the article by the Tongan sister Keiti Ann Kanongata'a, "A Pacific Women's Theology of Birthing and Liberation", op. cit., pp. 3-11).*

❖   ❖   ❖

☐ *Part Two of this Reader has included the voices of women from different countries and continents speaking about their oppression, their pain, their struggle against the patriarchal institutions in both society and the churches. These are women of courage who speak out, who challenge established norms and institutions, and who fight for a recognition of the full humanity of their sex, inspired by the vision and spirit of their Christian faith. The social and cultural neglect and denigration of women runs very deep, as is evident from international population trends and statistics. In a widely quoted article in* The New York Review *(December 20, 1990) entitled "More than 100 Million Women Are Missing," Amartya Sen pointed out that, contrary to the generally held belief that women make up half the world's population, the sex ratio of women to men can be as low as 0:94, or even lower. While women outnumber men substantially in Europe, the USA, and Japan—where women, in spite of various types of bias against them, suffer little discrimination in basic nutrition and health care—women in South Asia, West Asia, North Africa, and China suffer many disadvantages. Taking into account several factors, Sen calculated an overall shortfall of women of about 11%, and thus, estimated that over 100 million women are missing as a result of their neglect and low social esteem. In many Third World countries the position of women has suffered a further deterioration. Thus the oppression of women is a systemic problem and because of structural violence, this is difficult to eradicate quickly. A gigantic process of social transformation is required, demanding a change of structures, consciousness, beliefs, and practices.*

*More women are now being empowered by new insight to speak out about the oppression of their sisters. Women also take part in the ongoing process of theological reflection for transformation and renewal. Like their brothers, they seek to work for justice, peace, and the integrity of creation. At the conclusion of an Asian women's regional conference on this theme, the participants published a letter addressed to the women of the world; this expressed their experience of oppression and hope for change. It is reproduced here (chapter 16) from* The Asia Journal of Theology, *vol. 2/1, 1988, pp. 138-9.*

*(The same issue also contains another declaration from a different women's conference on the theme of "Militarization and Its Effects on Women in Asia," pp. 136-7.)*

## 16 ASIAN WOMEN'S CONSULTATION ON JUSTICE, PEACE, AND INTEGRITY OF CREATION

# Letter Addressed to the Women of the World

Dear Sisters,

We, the forty women who have been meeting together in an Asian Regional Consultation on Justice, Peace, and Integrity of Creation (Bangkok, December 1-7, 1986) from seventeen countries, greet you, knowing that the life stories we have heard must be shared with you.

We have listened to the voices of the women of Asia, who have expressed their concern about oppression and exploitation which continue to confront Asian women.

In most countries of the world, women still remain the most deprived, the consistently ignored, and the least consulted (if at all), so that they are without equal rights and opportunities and remain largely exploited in the Third World.

We heard about Siti, whose health has been affected by working with chemicals in a TNC that often flouts international safety standards.

We heard about Zareena, in whose country the resurgence of fundamentalism and communalism have manifested themselves in legislation discriminatory to women.

We heard about Shanti, who told us of the arbitrary arrests,

177

detentions, and extra-judicial killings that have come as an aftermath of the ethnic riots in her country.

And about Miriam Dugay and Pulsara Liyanage, who are languishing in jails as political prisoners.

We heard from Salome about the use of the islands of the Pacific for nuclear testing and waste dumping and of the resultant birth defects now becoming common.

We heard about Moana and the Maori people's struggle for land and cultural rights denied since colonization.

We heard about the abuse of Gowri's body by a health and family planning policy that has taken away her right to informed choices.

And we met Lek, whose exploitation has been institutionalized by the sex tourism industry.

We heard of the denial of rights to Young-Ja by a military authoritarian government and the increasing sex-specific forms of torture used in her country.

We heard from Akiko about the increasing pollution of the environment of her country by a policy of runaway industrialization.

We heard about Marita, a migrant woman worker who is underpaid and overworked, and works in substandard conditions.

We were empowered by stories of movements of hope as women increasingly organize for change, in spite of opposition and even repression, and to hear of new feminist approaches and understanding of life. We were encouraged by our attempts to develop new strategies for the protection of the environment.

We expressed our concern that in all our countries:

(1) the little money and resources that are allowed to be channeled into food, health care, education, and other basics are grossly inadequate;

(2) expenditures for defense are wholly disproportionate to real requirements and are being diverted from urgent social needs;

(3) such military expenditures are directly responsible for widening the gap between rich and poor both within and between countries.

We share with you this moment of power and we call on you

to continue efforts to mobilize women to participate with all progressive forces and movements for change in global solidarity. We urge you to join us in our struggle to make our region a zone of peace, friendship, and cooperation.

It was suggested that an Asian Women's Human Rights Commission be set up to mobilize action and to be alert in support of women in the movements. This will remain only an idea without your involvement.

❖     ❖     ❖

# PART THREE

# The Bible as a Source of Empowerment for Women

□ *The Bible is a central source of inspiration for doing theology in the Third World. From within their experience of oppression and pain, women are rereading the Bible with new eyes. Reflecting on the stories, parables, and figures of both the Hebrew Bible and the New Testament, they find much material to empower them to take on their struggle for liberation; to seek justice and peace, and to build new communities of hope and resistance. Such women are discovering the Bible in a non-biblical world. This is a world where they have to face issues raised by people whose lives are shaped by different religious and cultural insights and experiences, and not by the biblical vision.*

*In a book entitled* New Eyes for Reading: Biblical and Theological Reflections by Women from the Third World *(eds. John S. Pobee and Bärbel von Wartenberg-Potter, Geneva: WCC Publications, 1986), the editors point out that women rereading the Bible with a sharpened consciousness challenge us in three ways:*

- *They clearly indicate the context from which they write and they reflect on God's word from within their own situations, however much these may vary from one Third World country to another.*

- *They express the theological and spiritual discoveries that they have made and show that feminist approaches to the Bible and Christian traditions are not the prerogative of Western women alone.*

- *The spiritual insights of women can greatly enrich the churches. Women's reflections on the Bible are part of an ongoing ecumenical dialogue that has to grow worldwide. Up to now, women who raise critical questions are in a minority, but the number of female theology students is growing rapidly and women need to assume leadership positions in greater numbers in more churches.*

*Women not only read and study the Bible, but they use it as a resource for workshops, dramatizations, role-play, paintings and collages, liturgies and worship, as well as a basis for commitment to action. The following extracts can only give a glimpse of the richness of biblical reflections undertaken by Third World women. A marvelous resource for more material created by women from South and North, from both the Third and First Worlds, is the book of Bible study outlines and resource materials edited by Wendy S. Robins,* Through the Eyes of a Woman: Bible Studies on the Experience of Women *(London: World YWCA, 1986). It links biblical passages and reflections to the experiences of refugees and migrants, women's work, their bodies, health and environment, justice and peace and, central to them all, the theme of being created in God's image.*

*Part Three brings together material from very different sources. It opens with a personal account of the deep influence that the Bible had on Rigoberta Menchú's struggle for justice in Guatemala (chapter 17), and it ends with a women's homily from Asia inspired by one of Jesus' sayings in the New Testament (chapter 23). In between is an essay on rereading the Bible by the Mexican scholar Elsa Tamez (chapter 18); four biblical reflections from women's groups in different countries (chapter 19); followed by an African contribution on "Women as Living Stones" (chapter 20); a Central American woman's encounter with Jesus and the Samaritan woman (chapter 21); and another contribution on nonviolence and the Bible written by a Christian Palestinian woman (chapter 22).*

❖     ❖     ❖

*□ The attention of the whole world was drawn to the Indian woman Rigoberta Menchú from Guatemala when she received the Nobel Peace Prize in 1992 in recognition of her struggle for justice and peace among her people. Quite a few years earlier Rigoberta had told her story in the book* I, Rigoberta Menchú: An Indian Woman in Guatemala *(edited and introduced by Elisabeth Burgos-Debray, London: Verso, 1984), from which the brief extract in chapter 17 is taken (pp. 131–3). In it she explains that the Bible became the main weapon in her community's struggle against oppression and that the many wonderful stories of the Bible were used as texts through which to educate people in her village.*

## 17   RIGOBERTA MENCHÚ

# The Bible and Self-Defense: The Examples of Judith, Moses, and David

We began to study the Bible as our main text. Many relationships in the Bible are like those we have with our ancestors, our ancestors whose lives were very much like our own. The important thing for us is that we started to identify that reality with our own. That's how we began studying the Bible. It's not something you memorize, it's not just to be talked about and prayed about, and nothing more. It also helped to change the image we had, as Catholics and Christians: that God is up there and that God has a great kingdom for us the poor, yet never thinking of our own reality as a reality that we were actually living. But by studying the Scriptures, we did. Take Exodus for example, that's one we studied and analyzed.

It talks a lot about the life of Moses who tried to lead his people from oppression, and did all he could to free his people. We compare the Moses of those days with ourselves, the "Moses" of today. Exodus is about the life of a man, the life of Moses.

We began looking for texts that represented each one of us, and tried to relate them to our Indian culture. We took the example of Moses for the men, and we have the example of Judith, who was a very famous woman in her time and appears in the Bible. She fought very hard for her people and made many attacks against the king they then had, until she finally had his head. She held her victory in her hand, the head of the king. This gave us a vision, a stronger idea of how we Christians must defend ourselves. It made us think that a people could not be victorious without a just war. We Indians do not dream of great riches, we want only enough to live on. There is also the story of David, a little shepherd boy who appears in the Bible, who was able to defeat the king of those days, King Goliath. This story is the example for the children. This is how we look for stories and psalms that teach us how to defend ourselves from our enemies. I remember taking examples from all the texts that helped the community to understand their situation better. It's not only now that there are great kings, powerful men, people who hold power in their hands. Our ancestors suffered under them too. This is how we identify with the lives of our ancestors who were conquered by a great desire for power—our ancestors were murdered and tortured because they were Indians. We began studying more deeply, and came to a conclusion: that being a Christian means thinking of our brothers around us, and that every one of our Indian race has the right to eat. This reflects what God himself said: that on this earth we have a right to what we need. The Bible was our principal text for study as Christians and it showed us what the role of a Christian is. I became a catechist as a little girl and studied the Bible, hymns, the Scriptures, but only very superficially. One of the things Catholic Action put in our heads is that everything is sinful. But we came round to asking ourselves: "If everything is sinful, why is it that the landowner kills humble peasants who don't even harm the natural world? Why do they take our lives?" When I first became a catechist, I thought that there was a God and that we had to serve him. I thought God was up there and that he had a kingdom for the poor. But we realized that it is not God's will that we should live in suffering, that God did not give us that destiny, but that men on earth have imposed this suffering, poverty, misery, and discrimination on us. We even got the idea of using our own everyday weapons, as the only solution left to us.

I am a Christian and I participate in this struggle as a Christian. For me, as a Christian, there is one important thing. That is the life of Christ. Throughout his life Christ was humble. History tells us he was born in a little hut. He was persecuted and had to form a band of men so that his seed would not disappear. They were his disciples, his apostles. In those days, there was no other way of defending himself or Christ would have used it against his oppressors, against his enemies. He even gave his life. But Christ did not die, because generations and generations have followed him. And that's exactly what we understood when our first catechists fell. They're dead, but our people keep their memory alive through our struggle against the government, against an enemy who oppresses us. We don't need very much advice, or theories, or documents: life has been our teacher. For my part, the horrors I have suffered are enough for me. And I've also felt in the deepest part of me what discrimination is, what exploitation is. It is the story of my life. In my work I've often gone hungry. If I tried to recount the number of times I've gone hungry in my life, it would take a very long time. When you understand this, when you see your own reality, a hatred grows inside you for those oppressors that make the people suffer so. As I said, and I say it again, it is not fate that makes us poor. It's not because we don't work, as the rich say. They say: "Indians are poor because they don't work, because they're always asleep." But I know from experience that we're outside ready for work at three in the morning. It was this that made us decide to fight. This is what motivated me, and also motivated many others. Above all, the mothers and fathers. They remember their children. They remember the ones they would like to have with them now but who died of malnutrition, or intoxication in the *fincas*, or had to be given away because they had no way of looking after them. It has a long history. And it's precisely when we look at the lives of Christians in the past that we see what our role as Christians should be today. I must say, however, that I think even religions are manipulated by the system, by those same governments you find everywhere. They use them through their ideas or through their methods. I mean, it's clear that a priest never works in the *fincas*, picking cotton or coffee. He wouldn't know what picking cotton was. Many priests don't even know what cotton is. But our reality teaches us that, as Christians, we must create a Church of the poor, that we don't need a Church imposed from outside that knows nothing of hunger. We recognize that the system has wanted to impose on us: to divide us and keep the poor dormant. So we take some things and not others. As far as sins go, it seems to me that the concept of the Catholic religion, or any other more conservative religion than Catholicism, is that God loves the poor and has a wonderful paradise in heaven for the poor, so the poor must accept the life they have on earth. But as Christians, we have understood that being a Christian means refusing to accept all the injustices that are committed against our people, refusing to accept the discrimination committed against a humble people who barely know what eating meat is, but who are treated worse than horses. We've learned all this by watching what has happened in our lives. This awakening of the Indians didn't come, of ·course, from one day to the next, because Catholic Action and other religions and the system itself have all tried to keep us where we were. But I think that unless a religion springs from within the people themselves, it is a weapon of the system. So, naturally, it wasn't at all difficult for our community to understand all this and the reasons for us to defend ourselves, because this is the reality we live.

As I was saying, for us the Bible is our main weapon. It has shown us the way. Perhaps those who call themselves Christians but who are really only Christians in theory, won't understand why we give the Bible the meaning we do. But that's because they haven't lived as we have. And also perhaps because they can't analyze it. I can assure you that any one of my community, even though he's illiterate and has to have it read to him and translated into his language, can learn many lessons from it, because he has no difficulty understanding what reality is and what the difference is between the paradise up above, in heaven, and the reality of our people here on earth. We do this because we feel it is the duty of Christians to create the Kingdom of God on earth among our brothers. This Kingdom will exist only when we all have enough to eat, when our children, brothers, parents don't have to die from hunger and malnutrition. That will be the "Glory," a Kingdom for we who have never known it. I'm only talking about the Catholic Church in general terms because, in fact, many priests came to our region and were anti-communists, but nevertheless understood that the people weren't communists but hungry; not communists, but exploited by the system. And they joined our people's struggle too, they opted for the life we Indians live. Of course many priests call themselves Christians when they're only defending their own petty interests and they keep themselves apart from the people so as not to endanger these interests. All the better for us, because we know very well that we don't need a king in a palace, but a brother who lives with us. We don't need a leader to show us where God is, to say whether he exists or not, because, through our own conception of God, we know there is a God and that, as the father of us all, he does not wish even one of his children to die, or be unhappy, or have no joy in life. We believe that, when we started using the Bible, when we began studying it in terms of our reality, it was because we found in it a document to guide us. It's not that the document itself brings about the change, it's more that each one of us learns to understand his reality and wants to devote himself to others. More than anything else, it was a form of learning for us. Perhaps if we'd had other means to learn, things would have been different. But we understood that any element in nature can change man when he is ready for change. We believe the Bible is a necessary weapon for our people. Today I can say that it is a struggle that cannot be stopped. Neither the governments nor imperialism can stop it because it is a struggle of hunger and poverty. Neither the government nor imperialism can say: "Don't be hungry," when we are all dying of hunger.

To learn about self-defense, as I was saying, we studied the Bible. We began fashioning our own weapons. Our weapons were very simple. And at the same time, they weren't so simple when we all started using them, when the whole village was armed.

*Rigoberta Menchú goes on to describe the armed struggle of her people in some detail and returns to the Bible toward the end of her story where she says: "We all come to important conclusions by studying the Bible. . . . We discovered that the Bible has been used as a way of making us accept our situation, and not to bring enlightenment to the poor. The work of revolutionary Christians is above all to condemn and denounce the injustices committed against the people" (p. 245). She believes that "together we can build the people's Church, a true Church," but she also affirms that "the only road open to me is our struggle, the just war. The Bible taught me that" (p. 246).*

❖　　❖　　❖

*The Bible as a Source of Empowerment for Women*

☐ *The Bible plays a central role in Latin American liberation theology. Christian feminists in that continent have drawn much strength from the many stories about women in the Bible, as have Christian feminists elsewhere. The Methodist theologian Elsa Tamez from Mexico, author of the book* The Bible of the Oppressed *(Maryknoll, NY: Orbis Books, 1982), describes at some length in chapter 18 women's rediscovery of the Bible from the Latin American perspective of the poor. It is taken from the book* With Passion and Compassion *(eds. Virginia Fabella and Mercy Amba Oduyoye, Maryknoll, NY: Orbis Books, 1988, pp. 173-80), where other biblical reflections can also be found. (See Teresa Okure, "Women in the Bible," pp. 47-59, and Ana Maria Tepedino, "Feminist Theology as the Fruit of Passion and Compassion," pp. 165-72.) Elsa Tamez comes from a Presbyterian background in Mexico, and is now active in the Methodist Church in Costa Rica. For more information on her see D. W. Ferm,* Profiles in Liberation: 36 Portraits of Third World Theologians, *Mystic, Connecticut: Twenty-Third Publications, 1988, pp. 189-93.*

❖   ❖   ❖

# 18  ELSA TAMEZ

# Women's Rereading of the Bible

## The rediscovery of the Bible

Not long ago, when the Latin American poor burst on the scene of church life in Latin America, the consciousness of a large number of people was stirred. The Bible took on new meaning. That book — read by many, but until now assimilated through a safe, unidimensional interpretation controlled by a predominantly unchallenged way of thinking — became the simple text that speaks of a loving, just, liberating God who accompanies the poor in their suffering and their struggle through human history. This is not the only new development on our continent. On the contrary, it appears as one more breakthrough in a fast-growing movement in Latin America, a movement propelled mainly by the strong yearning of the poor for life. For multiple reasons and in many ways, the poor are today stronger than ever in their commitment. This is why we, in Latin America, speak of a new way of being Church, of doing theology, of reading the Bible.

A reading of the Scripture that truly liberates responds to the situation that has motivated the reading. It seems that, in a context of hunger, unemployment, repression, and war, creativity more than abounds in theology, hermeneutics, liturgy, and the pastoral field. At least, this has been our experience. Both Catholic and Protestant grassroots communities provide clear examples of the ways in which the Bible has been and still is being rediscovered. The study, discussion, and meditation based on the word has become an integral part of the meetings of the Catholic grassroots Christian communities. Everybody studies and discusses the Bible from the point of view of liberation. In the progressive Protestant communities, where the Bible has always been fundamental to the liturgy, hermeneutic keys have changed and the Bible has come to be read from the perspective of the poor. In both communities the Bible has been rediscovered.

Characteristically, their readings are strongly linked to the daily life of the members of these Christian communities. There is an unquestionable bridge between the life of the people of God in the Old Testament and that of Jesus' followers in the New Testament.

This reading of the word from the point of view of the poor has been consolidated and has become so evident that Holy Scripture is regarded as a threatening or dangerous book by some sectors of society that do not share a preferential option for the poor. These sectors might be either religious or secular, such as the government (particularly in countries where the National Security Doctrine is actively enforced). Some religious circles have even decided to avoid biblical discussions. Do they fear the Bible? The ancient book of Christianity has indeed become new and defiant when it is read from the perspective of the poor.

### "However . . ." say the women

Despite this situation, women with a certain degree of female consciousness have started to raise some questions about the Bible. It is not that they don't feel included in the main liberation experiences of the Bible: the exodus and the historical role of Jesus. It is that women find clear, explicit cases of the marginalization or segregation of women in several passages of both the Old and the New Testaments. There are, then, differences between reading the Bible from the point of view of the poor and reading it from a woman's perspective. The poor find that the word reaffirms in a clear and direct way that God is with them in their fight for life. Women who live in poverty, however, even when they are aware that the strength of the Holy Spirit is on their side, do not know how to confront the texts that openly segregate them. These texts sound strange and surprising to someone who is not familiar with the culture of the biblical world and believes in a just and liberating God.

This concrete problem has not been regarded as such until recently. First, the discovery of the Bible as "historical memory of the poor" was greeted with great enthusiasm by both men and women. This discovery implied that it was necessary to discuss a significant number of biblical texts essential to the history of salvation from a new perspective, starting with those texts where the liberation of the oppressed is most apparent (Exodus, the Prophets, the Gospels). Up until now texts that segregate women have been disregarded and subordinated because the main criterion has been to experience God as a God of life who has a preferential option for the oppressed, including women. Second, only in recent years has a feminine consciousness gained some strength in the theological and ecclesiastical worlds. There have, of course, always been women who have openly questioned the Church and theology. This is happening to an increasing degree in our days, especially with the upsurge of liberation theology and the proliferation of grassroots Christian communities where women are the majority and their participation is key.

For several reasons this problem of the marginalization, or segregation, of women is harder to solve than it appears to be. One of the reasons is that our society is extremely sexist—a phenomenon that can be detected at both a tacit and an explicit level. Nor are grassroots Christian communities free from this sexist ideology, which has deep historico-cultural roots that are hard to pull out in a single tug. To the extent that there is an easy correspondence between two cultures that marginalize women, it becomes even harder to discuss the biblical texts that reaffirm women's marginality.

Furthermore, it is a well-known fact that throughout history this correspondence of two patriarchal sexist societies has resulted in their mutual consolidation. On the one hand, old-time antiwomen customs of Hebrew culture have been declared sacred; on the other hand, certain texts have consequently been held up as biblical principles to prove that women's marginalization is natural in daily life. It is in this sense that the Hebrew–Jewish lifestyle presented by the Bible is perpetuated precisely because "thus is written the word of God." This explains why the Bible has been used to reinforce the position of inferiority in which society and culture have placed women for centuries. Today this attitude is not so apparent as in the past, but in some churches it still manifests itself, albeit in disguise.

Something different takes place in grassroots Christian communities. They react in different ways to difficult biblical texts. Sometimes they disregard antiwomen texts, at other times they juggle them to come out with a positive side or they soften the oppressive nature of the content. On other occasions they wisely simplify the problem by stating that those were other times, that reality should be different today, that God is a God of life and therefore he cannot favor discrimination against women.

Having experienced all of these attitudes in the context of different religious communities I have never taken this problem seriously. In truth, the problem would not be serious if everybody considered the Bible for what it really is: a testimony of a Judeo-Christian people with a particular culture, for whom holy revelation works always in favor of those who have least. Women would then feel included among the oppressed and they would contextualize those texts that segregate them. I believe this is what happens in many communities.

However, I have come to think that the problem is serious. Its seriousness comes, first, from the effects that these antiwomen biblical readings have produced on so many women and men who have internalized, as sacred natural law, the inferiority of women. Second, there is an inherent difficulty in interpreting texts that not only legitimate, but also legislate, the marginalization of women. Third, and this is mainly for Protestants, the problem is the principle of biblical authority as it is traditionally perceived. These are three difficulties that women are consciously confronting. Let us look at them in detail.

## Myths, texts, and biblical authority

After working with some biblical texts, like the famous narration in Genesis 3, it is easy to perceive that between the text and its current interpretation is a long series of ideologizing (or mythologizing) readings of this narration that are more harmful to women than the actual texts are.

Genesis 3 and the second account about creation have been the basis for creating a mythical framework that legitimizes women's inferiority and their submission to men. Myths— ideologies that distort reality—have been created based on these texts, not so much because of information contained in the story per se, but because of the conditions imposed by a society structured around men as its center; and by a particular way of reading the story, which places emphasis on its peripheral aspects; and by a storytelling technique that employs literal description and repetition as literary devices.

There are also other texts in which the example of a patriarchal culture has been brought in for a specific purpose. However, on many occasions, the readers of these texts have elevated the example to the category of divine law. The result is thus a legitimation and legislation, as if it were holy, of an order unfavorable to women.

Women are called, therefore, to deny the authority of those readings that harm them. It is here, then, that the collaboration of women experts in the Bible or of male exegetes with feminist perspectives is needed to reinterpret the texts, using a new hermeneutic approach.

Thus it would finally be possible for women to do a liberation-oriented reading of a text that for centuries had been used against them. However, on occasion there will be no other way to interpret the text except as a putdown of women. Its exegesis will show only the patriarchal ideology of the author, the commentator, the culture, and the historic moment in which the text was elaborated. This is the other Bible-related problem that women confront.

The tendency of some First World radical feminists to reject the Bible is, it seems to me, an exaggerated reaction. I think that by assigning too much importance to these peripheral texts, many leave aside the central message, which is profoundly liberating. From my point of view, it is precisely the gospel's spirit of justice and freedom that neutralizes antifemale texts. A reading of the Bible that attempts to be faithful to the word of the Lord will achieve that goal best when it is done in a way that reflects the liberating meaning of the gospel, even when sometimes fidelity to the gospel forces the reader to distance herself or himself from the text. Therefore, a time has come to acknowledge that those biblical texts that reflect patriarchal culture and proclaim women's inferiority and their submission to men are not normative; neither are those texts that legitimize slavery normative. The rationale behind this statement is essentially the same as that offered by the Scriptures: the proclamation of the gospel of Jesus calls us to life and announces the coming of the kingdom of justice.

German theologian Elisabeth Schüssler Fiorenza, who lives in the United States, proposes a new hermeneutic approach. She tries to reconstruct the beginnings of Christianity from a feminist perspective. Using this method she finds very interesting situations that explain women's active participation in the beginnings of the Church. She also discovers contradictions in some of St. Paul's writings, which eventually were used to promote the submission of women. From an exegetical point of view, this is one of the best and newest approaches to the Bible. We must admit that, for Third World women, this is an important contribution regarding the analysis of the text from a woman's point of view. However, it is likely that in some communities, mainly Protestant, it will be hard to accept the idea of questioning a biblical author, not to mention an apostle, as is the case with Paul.

This presents us with the third problem: the classic formulation of the doctrine of biblical authority. I shall refer here to Protestant churches because I know them a bit better.

Women with a certain degree of female consciousness, who move in conservative sectors, at times confront the difficulties of the principle implied in the idea of inspiration, namely, being without error, or God's word in a literal sense. I stress that they confront it *at times*, because, according to my experience, a curious phenomenon takes place in real life: there is a mismatch between belief in the traditionally formulated principle of biblical authority and daily-life practice. Women in both traditional and grassroots Protestant churches have achieved an important degree of participation in the liturgy and other areas and—except in the case of extremely conservative churches—this has not been a problem even though it is clear to these institutions that St. Paul called for "women to keep silent" in church. The issue is not even under discussion; in practice there is a tacit acceptance of women's participation and an increasing recurrence of texts that suggest the active participation of women. However, in some more traditional churches, when a woman becomes dangerously active or threatening to those in powerful positions, aid is found in the classic Pauline texts to demand women's submission to men. It is in moments like these that some women do not know how to respond. This is because they either lack the proper hermeneutic tools or have a mistaken interpretation of the principle of biblical authority.

On the other hand, when at meetings of Christian women there is an attempt to study texts such as Ephesians 5.22-4 or 1 Corinthians 14.34, the discussion frequently winds up on a dead-end street. The conflict arises because women, although not in accord with the texts nor practicing such behavior in everyday life, concede at the same time that the Bible has all the authority of the word of God. Thus they find themselves trapped within a framework of literal translations, forgetting that the word of God is much more than that.

This situation tells us that it is about time to reformulate the principle of biblical authority, from the point of departure of our Latin American reality. From a woman's perspective it is time to look for new hermeneutic criteria, patterns that not only will help us to handle patriarchal texts, but also will illuminate our rereading of the whole Bible from a feminine perspective, even texts that do not explicitly refer to women. I shall discuss now some matters that come from my own experience.

### Guides toward reading the Bible from a Latin American woman's perspective

*Gaining distance and coming closer*

To counteract myth-laden readings of biblical texts and to avoid the risk of repeating the interpretations of other readers, I believe in the importance of gaining distance from the text, mainly from those parts that have been frequently read and therefore have become overly familiar to our ears. When I say "gaining distance" I mean picking up the book and ignoring the interpretations that almost automatically come to mind even before reading the actual text. To distance oneself means to be new to the text (to be a stranger, a first-time visitor to the text), to be amazed by everything, especially by those details that repeated readings have made seem so logical and natural. It is necessary to take up the Bible as a new book, a book that has never been heard or read before. This demands a conscious effort that implies reading the texts a thousand times and very carefully.

This way of reading is going to be conditioned by or embedded in the life experience of the Latin American reader. Her or his experiences must be very consciously taken into account at the time of the reading. It is this experience, in the end, that will facilitate the distancing of oneself from the all-too-familiar interpretation of the common suppositions in the text, and will help to uncover keys to a liberation-oriented reading. This is the process of coming closer to daily life, which implies the experiences of pain, joy, hope, hunger, celebration, and struggle. It is clear from this process of gaining distance and coming closer that in Latin America the Bible is not read as an intellectual or academic exercise; it is read with the goal of giving meaning to our lives today. In the confusing situation we find ourselves, we want to discern God's will and how it is present in our history. We think that the written word offers us criteria for discerning. Already this is a way of reformulating the principle of biblical authority.

The process I call "gaining distance" and "coming closer" is not only geared to finding a woman's perspective. Every Latin American reading of the Bible needs to shake off rote readings that cloud the text. We must approach it with questions coming from life. However, considering that a reading of the Scriptures from a woman's angle is very new for us, considering that it is mandatory to discern between "macho" cultures and the gospel of life, the process of gaining distance from "macho" readings and texts and coming closer to the experience of Latin American women gains relevance for all women.

## *The reading of the Bible with the poor as a point of departure*

Every liberation reading from the perspective of Latin American women must be understood within the framework that arises from the situation of the poor. In a context of misery, malnutrition, repression, torture, Indian genocide, and war—in other words, in a context of death—there is no greater priority than framing and articulating the readings according to these situations. The poor (men, women, blacks, Indians) comprise the large majority, and it is because of their discontent that repression and mass killings generally take place. They are in a privileged place, hermeneutically speaking, because we conceive of the God of life as one who has a preferential option for the poor. Besides, the mystery of God's reign is with them because it has been revealed to them (Matt. 11.25). Therefore, a reading from a woman's perspective has to go through this world of the poor. This will be a guarantee that it has a core theme of liberation, and it will shed light on other faces of the poor, such as blacks and native peoples. This kind of reading will also give us methods to develop specific approaches to salvation in each of their situations.

Besides, this reading key, which has as a synonymous parallel "God is on the side of the oppressed," is the key to cancel and disallow those—really very few in number—antiwomen texts that promote the submission of women to men and affirm the inferiority of certain human beings because of their gender.

It should be remembered that a reading of the Bible from the perspective of the poor is a hermeneutic key offered by the Scriptures themselves, mainly through "events that create meaning" such as the exodus and the historical praxis of Jesus. Much has been said about this, and it is not my aim to discuss it more extensively here.

### *A clear feminist consciousness*

To read the Bible from a woman's perspective, we must read it with women's eyes, that is to say, conscious of the existence of individuals who are cast aside because of their sex. This procedure includes not only women. Men who feel identified with this specific struggle might also be able to read the Bible from this approach. This simple step is fundamental to achieve a reading that attempts to include other oppressed sectors besides the poor. It is a stamp that will distinguish this reading from others that consider the oppressed in general.

This approach, as noted above, is recent in Latin America. Therefore, even we women are not entirely conscious of it yet. For this reason, our reading does not come out spontaneously, and a conscious effort is needed to discover new women-liberating aspects, or even elements in the text that other perspectives would not bring to light.

Women, as victims of sexist oppression, will obviously perceive with less difficulty those aspects that directly affect them. Their experiences, their bodies, their social upbringing, their suffering and specific struggles give them keys (insights) to this reading.

Some liberation theologians agree that to the degree women actively engage themselves as readers of Scriptures and participants in other theological activities they offer important contributions to exegesis, hermeneutics, and theology.

It must remain clear that when I speak of reading the Bible from a woman's perspective, I am not referring specifically to texts that mention female subjects, but to the whole Bible. It is here where an enriching contribution from a perspective long absent until now can be made.

The novelty of such readings comes from reflection on the experiences of women. Women, for example, as a result of their experiences of oppression, can pose new "ideological suspicions" not only to the culture that reads the text, but also to the heart of the text itself by reason of its being a product of a patriarchal culture. Furthermore, their "ideological suspicions" are also applied to biblical tools, such as dictionaries, commentaries, and concordances, tools that are regarded as objective because they are scientific, but that are undoubtedly susceptible to being biased by sexism. This fact has been proved true by female exegetic scholars.

If to the oppression women endure we add the fact that they live a particular experience as women—in the sense that they are closer to vital processes, and have a unique stance in their view of the world—we shall see new contributions reflected in their readings (in recent years much has been discussed about women's identity).

In conclusion, the "gaining distance" from and "coming closer" to the Bible, the retrieval of liberation keys from the perspective of the poor, and a feminist consciousness are three basic skills indispensable to reading the Bible from a Latin American woman's perspective.

❖ ❖ ❖

## The Bible as a Source of Empowerment for Women

☐ *Biblical reflections can be undertaken in many different contexts. In chapter 19, different Gospel passages have been chosen to show how a collective group of women (and in one example, one individual) can draw a sense of affirmation and spiritual empowerment from reflecting on biblical passages and examining their bearing on women's lives. These passages are Matthew 15.21-8; Luke 1.26-55 (two extracts), and Mark 16.1-11. The source of each reflection is indicated with each passage.*

*The first passage is based on Matthew and comes from the report of the Programme on Women and Rural Development of the World Council of Churches. It is taken from Ranjini Rebera, ed.,* We Cannot Dream Alone *(Geneva: WCC Publications, 1990, pp. 72-6). In the second passage, which is based on Luke, Marie Assaad of the Egyptian Coptic Church reflects on Mary, the mother of Jesus. (See Marie Assaad in John S. Pobee and Bärbel von Wartenberg-Potter, eds.,* New Eyes for Reading: Biblical and Theological Reflections by Women from the Third World, *Geneva: WCC Publications, 1986, pp. 25-7.) This is followed by a third text, this time, a collective reflection on the "Magnificat," again taken from the Programme on Women report. (See above R. Ribera,* We Cannot Dream Alone.*) The fourth passage (Mark 16.1-11) reflects on the Easter story where Mary Magdala, Mary the mother of James, and Salome are on their way to Jesus' tomb, and wonder who would roll away the stone for them from the entrance to the tomb, so that they could anoint Jesus' body. Relating to this story today, women ask: "What is this stone, this obstacle on the path of women? And who has the power to remove the stone?"*

*The image of rolling a stone or obstacles away has been used elsewhere, for example in Mercy Amba Oduyoye's description of the churches' work for women,* Who Will Roll the Stone Away? The Ecumenical Decade of the Churches in Solidarity with Women *(Geneva: WCC Publications, 1990). The fourth text is a biblical reflection presented by Christian women from Pakistan on moving the stone from the tomb, and the hope that we today can draw on the experience of the three biblical women who "went to anoint a dead body and instead found a living God" (published both in Urdu and English, this version is taken from* In God's Image, *June 1989, pp. 28-9).*

201

# 19

# Reflections on Biblical Texts

**Text: Matthew 15.21-8**
**Theme: The empowering of women**

We have spent much time reflecting on, analyzing, and reading the stories of women involved in many aspects of development. Some of the stories are personal because we know the women telling the stories. Some of the projects are new to us, but the stories identify with our own stories or ones we know from other women. The story in Matthew's Gospel is one of a woman who felt that she could relate to the popular healer, Jesus, on a one-to-one basis. She felt she could say what was on her mind. She then did the unthinkable—she talked back at Jesus.

This story has always been in the Bible, but how many women have spent time studying the story and the role of the woman in it? There is much that makes this woman a remarkable figure.

The woman came from somewhere near the cities of Tyre and Sidon and this made her a non-Jew, a Canaanite woman. To Jews, therefore, she was a second-class person. She was also a woman, and women had no standing in Jewish society. This led to a double discrimination. Her purpose, however, was simple. Her daughter had been very sick and was said to be possessed by evil spirits. In the first century, possession by a demon was an accepted label for conditions such as epilepsy or even mental disorders. Only the mother, who was closely involved with her sick daughter, knew the trauma, the anguish, and the need for healing for her child. This gave her the selfless courage needed to face Jesus. The story points out many interesting facts:

- At the first confrontation Jesus is silent. To us, this is out of character for Jesus, who went about ministering to people's needs. One wonders if Jesus was reacting in a traditionally male manner by being silent in the face of confrontation.
- The disciples attempted to send her away by giving Jesus negative advice: "Send her away! She is following us and making all this noise." A typical reference to women who become too insistent and forceful even today.
- When Jesus finally speaks to the woman, he seems to be on the defensive: "I have been sent only to the lost sheep of the people of Israel." It is hard to know what Jesus meant by this statement. He could have reverted to his Jewish traditions by stating his mission within the context of the Jewish race. The woman was an outsider in the situation.
- The commitment of the woman to gain healing for her daughter and her tenacity in the face of opposition gives her the wisdom to use other means. She appeals to the compassionate side of Jesus' nature: "Lord help me!"
- Jesus continues to speak as an elitist Jew: "It isn't right to take the children's food and throw it to the dogs."
- The woman does not give in. Her resourcefulness leads her into the realm of debate: "Yes, Lord, that's true but even the dogs eat the leftovers that fall from the master's table." Her argument is strong and forceful and she has a valid point. Jesus may belong to a superior race, but even dogs have rights and will not be denied scraps from the table.
- Jesus seems to capitulate. The woman's commitment, forcefulness, and intelligence seem to have triumphed. Jesus sums up: "What you want will be done for you." Her daughter is healed.

The story has implications for women involved in development work:

(1) As leaders, facilitators, catalysts, animators in development, we have nothing to lose as we challenge superiors, people in authority and power structures that hold us in bondage. The woman in the story demonstrates through her selfless courage that she had nothing to lose and everything to gain if she could only get Jesus' attention and his help in healing her daughter.

(2) Women need to be aware of their strengths and use them to their advantage. The Canaanite woman knew she was good with words and turned her strength into an advantage when she debated with Jesus.

(3) Women need to be able to handle conflict and not run away from situations that seem oppressive. They need to develop the skills to stand up to men when they use masculinity as a form of oppression.

(4) Through standing firm in the face of discrimination, women can educate men and force them into making choices. By challenging Jesus to recognize her need, the woman learned that Jesus' message was to non-Jews as well as to the Jews.

Discussion starters

(1) How do we motivate women to be courageous in the face of conflict?

(2) What forces of discrimination are evident in your community/group/organization? How can they be confronted and eradicated?

(3) How do women handle power and is power a male prerogative alone?

**Text: Luke 1.26-45**
**Theme: Reversing the natural order**

Every time I reflect on Luke 1.26-45, I realize how much it reverses all that we take as the natural order of this world and how God is still asking us today to reverse this order.

Here we learn about Mary, young and unknown, a woman in the patriarchal Jewish society, the poorest of the poor.

Why was she so highly favored? Why did the angel Gabriel greet her in this manner? Isn't this a reversal of the natural order of this society?

Gabriel assured her that the Lord was with her. How often are we told that when we work with God, God will be with us! Is God truly with us? Don't we often waver in our faith? Even Mary was disturbed with this greeting. Why is she specially chosen? "I am a humble and weak woman. I have always been ignored. How can I suddenly get so much attention? And from whom—from Yahweh, the almighty, all-present, all-compassionate."

In effect Mary is told: "Although you are weak and have rarely received any attention; although you are used to work and toil in silence and nobody takes much note of what you say or do; although you feel you have so far only obeyed orders and listened to others; although you are not among the powerful and prominent, you have God's favor. Therefore, do not be afraid. Listen, and believe. God will give you a son."

"But how? I am not married. I am a virgin." Here we note the second reversal of the natural human order.

Everything is possible with God. "The Holy Spirit will come upon you," answered the angel, "and the power of the most high will cover you with its shadow."

What a task and responsibility! And what overwhelming news! She will conceive and have a baby. How will Joseph react to this news? Will he suspect her? Will he reject her? Will the world condemn her? How can she face the hostile world? Won't she be too weak to face all this alone? Won't people gossip about her? Won't she be shunned by all, especially the women in her neighborhood?

Yet, because she was used to listening and obeying, Mary did not argue or object. She said: "Let what you have said be done unto me."

Mary must have spent sleepless nights pondering over this visitation and its significance. "Why me?" she must have asked herself several times. "How will I cope?"

At dawn a still small voice must have told her: "Do not be afraid, Mary. Obey and I shall be with you, step by step."

It is with this deep conviction that the way will be shown her, step by step, that Mary decided to leave her home and travel alone from Nazareth to a town in the hill country of Judah, to Zechariah's home (not Elizabeth's, mind you).

Elizabeth's greetings affirms Mary's faith. With this show of solidarity from another woman, Mary's weakness and lingering doubts disappear. She is not suffering from hallucinations. This indeed is God's work. Not only is she chosen for a particularly difficult role, but she will be sustained at every step. The Holy

Spirit is surely with her. How could she doubt? How could a child leap in a womb at the sound of a greeting? Is this natural? Here again is another reversal of the natural order. Yet, as Gabriel said, nothing is impossible with God.

Elizabeth was a modest, quiet wife, who had gone through years of grief because she had not fulfilled her greatest role as a woman and as a wife. She could not be a mother, and within Jewish tradition her existence had little meaning. She is getting old and her life has been futile. Yet Elizabeth, a woman, is filled with the Holy Spirit and declares, after the angel Gabriel: "Of all women, you are the most blessed, and blessed is the fruit of your womb. Why should I be honored with a visit from the Mother of my Lord?"

Yes, blessed is she who believes that the promise made her by the Lord will be fulfilled. What reassurance! What a gift! How significant this was for Mary! How often do we need reassurance when we are challenged, or required to face difficult situations, or to carry heavy responsibilities! Is this what we mean by building solidarity among women?

With this assurance Mary feels liberated. She is liberated from her fears and misgivings, from her feelings of weakness and of inadequacy. She is liberated from what she was taught as a woman. Suddenly she sees the significance of Gabriel's message. She realizes what it actually means to be empowered by the Holy Spirit and how such power can reverse all so-called natural human order.

Then Mary, like Hannah before her, is filled with joy and gratitude and breaks out in a hymn of praise to God, her Savior.

A humble young woman who suddenly discovers herself and what God can make of her, Mary offers the greatest song ever sung: the Magnificat. The song that is filled with the assurance that with God nothing is impossible. God can use us to reverse the state of affairs in our world of disorder, hunger and death, injustice, militarism, nuclear destruction. God can make us agents of shalom. God can commission us to prepare for a world where the lion will lie with the lamb and the rich will be accountable to the poor.

In this text God's option is not only for the poor, but also for women who are often the poorest of the poor.

*The Bible as a Source of Empowerment for Women*

**Text: Luke 1.26-55**
**Theme: The Magnificat**

This Bible reading was presented as a dramatic reading followed by a period of silence. During the silence participants used the single lighted candle in the centre of the room as a point of focus.

Participants then went into small groups and shared their own reflections on Mary's response to God's call, her song, and her role in the liberation process of humanity.

The reflections that are presented sum up the discussion that followed.

### (1) *Mary as a figure of empowerment and hope*

- Power in humble people who receive God. The Holy Spirit enters their lives and gives them courage to demand justice.
- Mary, an image of one asking for justice.
- Mary's decision to take risks and be responsible for the consequences of such a decision.

This passage gives us strength to break the Good News to women who are poor, especially rural women. Identifying with Mary gives us strength to face problems and a willingness to be at risk. Women are able to see God's revelation and spontaneously express praise. In using a woman (Mary) as the source through whom God worked to liberate the human race, the potential for ordinary situations to be used by God in the process of liberation is confirmed. Mary, through her song of liberation, reverses the material order of the world and confirms God's options for women and for the poor in the world.

### (2) *Mary as a figure of compassion*

To Coptic Orthodox women in Egypt, Mary is especially present with the sad and the afflicted. She is a source of consolation to mothers who identify with her troubles as a refugee who fled to Egypt to save the life of her baby and as a mother who saw her son unjustly murdered.

## (3) *Mary Mother of God (Theotokos)*

The mothers of the disappeared daughters and sons in Argentina have taught us that motherhood has a new value—a new strength that goes beyond physical motherhood. It led women to fight for justice for everyone, not only for their children or for other women. Their concept of motherhood stretched beyond the personal into the caring for all people who are victims of injustice.

## (4) *Women—builders of solidarity*

In their humility and solidarity in spite of age and class differences, Mary and her cousin Elizabeth affirm each other and give us a model for networking and strengthening each other. In her need to share her experiences, Mary turns to another woman—Elizabeth—who extends to her the caring understanding Mary must have needed at this time. Elizabeth was able to listen and to give Mary confidence as she responded to God's call. This affirmation and solidarity between these two women is a model to all women trying to establish a relationship between women. Once again, God worked through ordinary people and ordinary situations.

## (5) *Women—creators of new images*

Women need to create new images of Mary through new insights and interpretations of the life of Mary and her role in the liberation of human beings. Paintings, images, and interpretations of Mary still exist that reinforce her weakness as a woman, and as a consequence the weak state of women everywhere. These images lead women to accept unjust systems because of their own lowly positions. Emphasis on the virginity of Mary is used as a tool to oppress women and have control over fertility. Virginity is upheld as a prerequisite to purity and a model for all unmarried women. Women need to be sensitive to this kind of bondage and work together in creating new images that will liberate them to see Mary as a catalyst in the liberation of all women.

**Text: Mark 16.1-11**
**Theme: Who will move the stone?**

An ecumenical group of women (from various churches here in Pakistan) met in the Pastoral Institute, Multan, from March 31 through April 3, 1989, to reflect on the reality of Pakistani women in this country. Each participant presented a paper dealing with one aspect of this problem. St. Paul's first Letter to the Corinthians, with special emphasis on chapter 11, was used as a way of focusing on the interplay of religion, culture, and the situation of women. The tone of the meeting was set by reflection on the story of the women at the tomb, Mark 16.1-11.

In faithfulness and love, the women went to anoint Jesus' dead body. As they walked, they became distracted because of the problem of how they would remove the stone in front of the tomb, thus forgetting their original purpose for a few moments. Despite this, they continued the journey and found the stone rolled back from the tomb. (In our own struggles, help often comes unexpectedly.) The women showed their special charism through their undemanding love that accepted Jesus as he was, without trying to change him. They remained faithful to the end and beyond the end. Love and faithfulness were shown in culturally appropriate ways as the women waited until the end of the Sabbath before going to anoint Jesus' body. At the same time, they moved out of their cultural boundaries because of love. Normally, a woman anointed another woman's body while a man did the same service for another man. In this case, the women on their own initiative undertook this final service of love and respect for Jesus while the men, his friends, were in hiding.

Overcoming their fears, the women continued to go forward and found a calling far greater than they first envisioned. They went to mourn a loved one, but instead were called to be the first apostles and sent out to preach and pronounce the resurrection message. As we look for ways to recognize the dignity of women, we must, like the women at the tomb, name the stones that block our way and discover ways of removing them. We have hope to go forward in faithful memory of our sisters, those brave women at the tomb. For they went to anoint a dead body and instead found a living God.

## Naming the stones

### (1) Misinterpretation of culture

A number of cultural practices are neither good nor bad in themselves but what counts is how they are interpreted for women, e.g., a woman's style of clothing is not important—what is important is the interpretation put on it. When we say that *purdah* preserves a woman's reputation (protects her), what are we saying about woman? We must look at who is making the interpretation of culture. Are we taking woman's dignity seriously or are we denying it? Who interprets the culture? We must not leave it to the men alone.

Jesus does not destroy culture, but he does say, "The Sabbath was made for people, not people made for the Sabbath."

### (2) The image of women

We cannot give a general definition of what a Pakistani woman is—there are too many different types and classes (rich-poor, educated-uneducated, etc.). The single denominator for all Pakistani women is that they are second-class citizens. One reason for their subordination is the image of women held by some men and, unfortunately, by some women themselves. Generally, the image of women is that they are weak, incapable of making good decisions, stupid, etc. Women internalize all of this and pass it on to their children; e.g., in our culture it is generally thought, "To give education to a daughter is watering a neighbor's plant." Similarly, if a man is gentle or understanding, he is sarcastically asked, "Are you wearing bangles?" (Are you a woman?)

(3) Misinterpretation of Scripture

In Corinthians there are clear passages that suppress women and, although we can understand the reasons and the context in which they were written, the question we raise is: Why are these passages emphasized in the Church? Why is there stress on Genesis 2, where Eve is created from Adam's rib, rather than on the Genesis 1 version of creation, "God created humanity in his own image; male and female he created them"? Why do we concentrate on oppressive passages in the epistles rather than on the liberative example of Jesus in the Gospels? One of the particular problems in our community is the literal and legalistic way in which Scripture is understood and the unwillingness to see the spirit of the Scriptures rather than the letter of the law.

(4) Manipulation of love

For Christian women especially, love is a unique value. We see our charism as love, but it has been manipulated to oppress us as women. For the sake of love, we put up with repression in religious orders. For the sake of love, we become timid and cowards, sacrificing our lives for love. We need to find the image of love in Jesus, who sacrificed—but was never annihilated as a person.

(5) Inequalities and double standards

In almost every aspect of life, women face the dual handicap of inequality and double standards:

- in the workplace, women are paid less for their work;
- in the area of morality and sexual ethics, women bear blame and responsibility to the extent that rape is considered to be the same act as adultery and the punishment is the same.

(6) Men's insecurity

Most people recognize that women are insecure, but we need to recognize the fact that men are insecure also. The growing participation of women in the Church, society, and the home can be perceived as a threat by many of our male partners during this time of transition.

## (7) Structure and power

When we talk about women's equality, we are talking about changing the power structures. We note that the passages in Corinthians that deal with women's role in the Church are talking about power as well as law. All too often, the church institution is, in fact, a power structure. When women seek to fulfill their ministries in the Church, the status quo concept of the diaconate must be removed.

## (8) Sexist language

Much of the language that we use in church liturgies and documents exclude women. At the baptism ceremony, the child is defined as the son or daughter of the father only. The same applies to most registrations and documents. In our liturgies, we confess our sins to our brothers, but often with no mention of sisters. The symbols used emphasize the maleness of God, ignoring the female aspects.

## *Who will remove the stone?*

We quickly realized that the stone removers are ourselves. We can begin to remove the stone by:

- continuing in the struggle and in solidarity with all women, by linking with and supporting other groups;
- being involved in women's education — starting study groups at the grassroots level;
- finding new ways to interpret Scripture — sharing lifegiving interpretations for women rather than oppressive ones;
- encouraging women to learn social analysis and become agents for constructive change;
- encouraging them to become involved in political issues;
- enabling women to discover and demand recognition of their self-worth and dignity;

- developing forms and symbols that truly express women's humanity and harmony with creation;
- conscientizing men into an awareness of women's rights to be equal.

The vision that enables us to go forward in the struggle is that of women giving birth to life in pain and blood and nurturing that life with their own bodies. It is also the vision of Jesus, who gave birth to new life on the cross in pain and blood and who still nurtures that life with his own body.

❖  ❖  ❖

□ *At the end of the last chapter, an ecumenical women's group from Pakistan reflected on the need to remove the weight of dead stones—all the many obstacles on women's path to liberation and to full equality in church and society. They finished their reflections by realizing that women must remove these obstacles themselves and become inspired and empowered by Jesus teaching in the Bible.*

*In this chapter, Grace Eneme, a Presbyterian from Cameroon, considers the distinction between dead and living stones that is part of the traditional heritage of her African people. The truly living stones are people sustained by the power of Christ and the Spirit. What does this mean for women in the Protestant Church of Africa?*

*Chapter 20 appeared originally in the collection edited by John S. Pobee and Bärbel von Wartenberg-Potter,* New Eyes for Reading. Biblical and Theological Reflections from the Third World *(Geneva: WCC Publications, 1986, pp. 28–32). At the time of writing this contribution Grace Eneme was working for the member churches of the Federation of Protestant Churches and Missions in Cameroon and was also a member of the WCC Central Committee.*

## 20   GRACE ENEME

# Women as Living Stones

The image of "living stones" brings different images to different people, depending on their cultural backgrounds. I shall try to limit myself to my culture, trusting that the reflection will speak to others who share the same cultural heritage with me and to others who share my faith in Jesus Christ.

Among the Bakossi people in the forest region of the south-west province in Cameroon, stones are classified into two main groups: living stones and dead stones. Living stones are stones that are movable, portable, and usable. These include tripod stones, grinding stones, building stones, and many others. Dead stones are stones that are embedded in the bottom of the river, boulders and great rocks. These were hardly used till dynamite was introduced in the country.

Of the living stones, tripod stones for cooking have great significance to the Bakossi women. These stones serve a vital purpose in the life of the family and the community. Around them people meet for family discussions. Here is where moral instruction takes place and folk tales are told, a place of warmth and a refuge for strangers.

When a man takes a bride, one of the ceremonies that integrates her into the family is the laying of the tripod stones. The first stone is pitched by the bride and her husband, signifying oneness in building up their home.

The second stone is pitched by the bride and the eldest woman in the family, signifying her acceptance and integration into the family and village community. It also symbolizes her active participation in family affairs, mutual respect, and sharing with others.

The third stone is pitched by the bride and her chaperon (sister or aunt). It symbolizes a bridge of contact for the two families, the husband's and the wife's. By that stone the bride is assured solidarity by her family members in both good and bad times.

From that moment on the stones assume their functions and the wife feels integrated in the family. Is the image of tripod stones the same as the image of living stones? Certainly not, but there is some similarity between them.

The image of living stones as presented to us by Peter signifies the Church as a community of believers whose main function is service and witness. The community is compared to a building, having Christ as the foundation stone and Christians as stones in the edifice. As each stone is important in erecting the walls, so is each Christian in the community of believers. The appeal to build up Christ's Church is an open invitation to all, male and female, young and old.

As the tripod stones integrate the bride into the family, so does Christ, the foundation stone, integrate each Christian into the family of God. Christ's family is bigger than any human family. It includes people of all races and colors, and it is bound together by his Spirit.

The call for integration into the family of God explains the universality of the Christian Church. Never mind the denominational labels we carry. They are a mark of human sinfulness. How to put away our labels remains a problem in Christ's Church, because each denomination struggles to keep its identity and tries hard to build up its empire—often neglecting its functions in the society where it has been called to serve as living stones. This struggle hinders Christians from being open to one another or having meaningful supportive fellowship with one another.

Worse still is the oppression of women in Christ's Church. Some church structures have laid down principles that are against women's development. They are happy to see women do menial jobs in the Church and would like to keep them at that level. For others, the worth of women's organizations is measured by their economic importance and what they contribute to the general upkeep of the Church and in supporting pastors.

Any program aimed at developing women to know their worth and their place in Church and society is often met with resistance from church leaders. Usually, the small group of women who campaign for such programs are named "revolutionaries," and are sometimes ostracized by church leaders.

It is even more pathetic to see women themselves teaming up with pastors to discredit the so-called "revolutionary" women. Yes, we are a people groping in darkness. We need light, but that light must come with great healing power. For decades we have been taught to be subordinate "little angels," and all the way through those social tapes play back to us.

In the family we are subordinate.

In the church we are subordinate.

In the offices, despite the laws and decrees made by the state to ensure equality, we are subordinate. No man would admit that a woman is equal to him, in spite of her qualifications. Christ alone assures us that we are not subordinate.

Christ was the only rabbi who did not discriminate against the women of his time. Since Christians have assumed the rights of Israel we share the rights that Christ gave the Jewish women. As he allowed Susanna, Joanna, and others to minister with him, so he has given us the full right and privilege to work with him. Since he is the Living Stone, our attachment to him makes us become living stones with him. While many Christians are dead stones, embedded in their old ways while they fight for power and riches, we are called to be living stones and the pillars of that Church that is being crushed by evil. This brings to my mind Father Balasuriya's theory "power + greed = evil." This evil has wholly permeated our churches. If there is hope for the Church, it lies in the women—who are being "rejected," but remain the "cornerstones" of the churches.

All church women ought to unite and be in solidarity with one another for effective service in the world. We must congratulate our American sisters who have succeeded in creating an association of church women through which they can speak with one voice and witness to the world through corporate action.

We need a common voice and cooperative action to liberate our sisters who are exploited, be it by church structures, political systems, or tradition.

It is most disheartening to see that women constitute a majority in most churches, yet in decisionmaking bodies they are only a decorative minority. In my church there are 17,000 women as against 6,000 men, according to the 1981 census.

In the African Protestant Church women constitute 85% of the membership. They are very active, contributing to the building of chapels and the maintenance of churches. They pay for the training of pastors. But in leadership, decisionmaking, and the management of funds, they have no part. Quite often, the funds they provide are misappropriated by the elders and pastors.

In all these, it is evident that the rebuilding of Christ's Church is in our hands. We have powers that we are unaware of! There is no great man in the world who did not pass through the nurturing hands of a woman, from birth right through to the grave. We have the gift of intuition and the capacity for prompt action. Christ was aware of this: that was why he made women his first evangelists after his resurrection. His words "go and tell" mean that we should go and tell the broken Church and the broken society what God is, what he has done for us, and what he is capable of doing.

To prepare ourselves for this task, we must first of all know Christ. "Find out for yourself how good the Lord is, happy are those who find safety in him."

Knowing Christ is not a matter of theory. We have to experience it and allow that experience to become the basis of our existence. Only then would we know our worth and proper value, and our obligations to Church and society.

As a bride constitutes a bridge of contact between her family and the husband's family, so are Christians a bridge between the world and God.

Peter reminds us that we are a royal priesthood, meaning that every Christian is a priest. This statement is too difficult for us to understand. The tendency is to look at our spiritual leaders as all in all. And there is no doubt that some leaders enjoy being all to their flock.

What Peter is telling us is completely different. He is saying that our eyes should change direction. Instead of looking at the priest we should look at ourselves. As priests we are a bridge between God and our family, between God and our community, between God and our place of work, between God and our Church. In short, we are a liaison between God and all life conditions through our prayers of intercession and our service. We have to offer all our daily tasks with all their drudgery to God in our sacrifice of worship and praise. As we do this, we dedicate ourselves to God and he gives us strength to move forward. We are not allowed to be static. Each new experience must bring us closer to God and the lives of those we are called to serve.

Building stones have one enduring quality. They can resist intense heat, rain, snow, frost—most of the normal climatic changes.

As women on the move in a changing society how do we see ourselves in the ministry? How far are we ready to go with Christ? Are we ready to take insults and shame? Nasty comments from friends and church leaders? Are we ready to be misunderstood, even when we are on the right path? Are we ready to spend sleepless nights, sometimes in tears, under the pressure of the discriminations we suffer and the concerns we cherish?

As living stones we have to resist it all through the power of the Holy Spirit. Looking up to Christ, our hope, our liberator, our captain, the road we must take.

Sisters, power has been given to us by God.
By the world's standards it can never be given to us.
We have to struggle for it and grab it. So gird up your loins.
Christ our liberator is our captain.

❖    ❖    ❖

☐ *Women in the Third World, like women everywhere, draw their strength from different experiences, images, and stories in order to find encouragement and sustenance for the struggles of their life. While the African, Grace Eneme, appeals to the image of women as "living stones," Raquel Rodríguez from Central America explores the gospel story of Jesus and the Samaritan woman found in John, chapter 4. In reflecting on the meaning of this story for women, Rodríguez emphasizes the need to open our eyes, to learn to see anew, so that we understand our situation in a fresh way, which can transform much that we have taken for granted. We have to abandon many traditional attitudes and ideas about women in order to find the message of the full life proclaimed by Jesus to the Samaritan woman.*

*Raquel Rodríguez comes originally from Puerto Rico but now lives in Costa Rica. Ordained as a Lutheran pastor, she works as a researcher in the Department of Ecumenical Research and focuses on women's struggles in Latin America. Her chapter was first published in* The Power We Celebrate *edited by Musimbi R. A. Kanyoro and Wendy S. Robins (Geneva: WCC Publications, 1992, pp. 53-61).*

## 21  RAQUEL RODRÍGUEZ

# Open Our Eyes

It is not only good, but also "right and proper," for Christians to seek strength, power, and understanding in the biblical message, to look to it for the enlightenment that helps us to "open our eyes" and truly enables us to open ourselves to understand and, with one another, to reflect on the task that has been entrusted to us.

Our problem, as women, basically is not that of total blindness in regard to the situation that confronts us on all sides. None of us—or perhaps it would be better to say very, very few of us—suffer from that malady. Our problem is like that of the Samaritan women (John 4.1-29, 39). Like her, we have not opened our eyes *enough*. We see only part of what is in front of us, what is most obvious, most tangible, that which affects us most directly. We have to open our eyes, or help each other to open our eyes, to a deeper reality, to see what lies beyond what we can see with the naked eye. Opening our eyes in this way allows us to be agents of change, transforming our reality, in the same way as the woman in the passage was able to transform her reality.

Let us approach this passage to discover the sources of light it can provide for the task of opening our eyes.

### Jesus and the Samaritan woman

First, we encounter two characters in the story.

According to the Gospel account, Jesus is on his way to Galilee and has to pass through the region of Samaria. He comes upon a well, a source of spring water, which tradition says is the well of Jacob. Jesus is tired and sits down by the well to wait for his disciples, who have gone in search of food. There he meets a woman who has come to draw water, and their dialogue begins.

Up to this point the passage does not seem strange or shocking when read in the context of our reality today. However, in its historical context, in the social and religious context of that time, it is practically a scandal. We are called to open our eyes to an underlying reality different from our own.

Let us examine those elements that convert this simple encounter into something scandalous.

Jesus is a Jewish man. She is a Samaritan woman. These two peoples, who had the same origin, were in conflict. The Jews considered themselves superior to the Samaritans because the latter group had fallen into the hands of the Assyrians. The Samaritans despised the Jews because they had destroyed their most important temple in the city of Gazirin (128 B.C.E.). Of course, the two peoples had not been worshipping Yahweh in the same temple. Each group had its own sacred mountain. Yet they shared a common origin: the patriarchs, Moses, and the Law. Also, both were awaiting the Messiah who had been promised to them. The prophet par excellence of the Samaritans was Hosea, who portrayed the problem of religious syncretism using the image of the prostitute wife.

Besides the ethno-religious problem, we are confronted by an act that was seen as scandalous in that society: a man speaking to a woman in public, a woman who, as we learn later in the text, doesn't have the best reputation in her community.

### Opening our eyes to Jesus' message

What reality does Jesus want to open our eyes to with this act that was so scandalous in the context of that time? I believe that he wants to open our eyes to the message of inclusiveness. None of us would want to believe that we have exclusive rights to the message of the life of the reign of God. In so doing we would exclude those who we think should not be allowed to hear that message. The message of life of God's reign is universal in the fullest sense of the word. We have not been called to predetermine to whom the message ought to be directed. Ethnic, ethical, and sexual characteristics (or any other ones) are not what God takes into account when pouring out his love and grace on us.

This passage and others like it open our eyes to the reality that social, ethnic, religious, ethical, and sexist prejudices cannot be allowed to keep us from announcing the message of life, which has also been announced to us as women and which social constraints have tried to diminish or take away from us altogether.

To open our eyes to this Gospel reality, Jesus breaks through the traditional social barriers. He embodies the human condition in his state of dependency, in his desire to satisfy a basic human need: thirst. That he possessed two attributes that in that context would make him superior (being a man and a Jew encountering a woman and a Samaritan) does not take away from the fact that his thirst was a quality common to every human being. To be in this situation of lacking something so vital shows that we are all, as human beings, equal before God.

Putting himself in a dependent position vis-à-vis the Samaritan woman, who could help him to quench his thirst, is a concrete expression of the breaking of barriers imposed by society.

The passage continues, recounting the dialogue between this woman and Jesus. He asks her for water. She is amazed that a man and a Jew is asking her for water. From there a dialogue ensues in which it would seem that each one of them is talking about something different.

Perhaps we would be able to understand this dialogue better if we were to open our eyes to what this well, and water itself, meant for both Jews and Samaritans.

Water, as we all know, is indispensable for life. We can survive without eating for long periods, but without water we wouldn't be able to survive much more than three days. In desert areas, sources of water are not abundant. Each spring or well is of great importance to the people who depend on it. Water is synonymous with life.

But, in addition, this particular well has a religious and historical connotation. It is the well of Jacob, the patriarch of both peoples. It represents a common historical tradition and a link with the God of life who protected them and brought them to the promised land. The well represents life in many different dimensions.

The Samaritan woman talks about the life that this well and its water represent for her and her people. In a way she mocks Jesus when he says that now, after having asked her for water, he is offering *her* water, although he has no container with which to draw it from the well. In contrast with the woman, Jesus is speaking of a new dimension of life, also symbolized by the water. She has her eyes opened to life according to her tradition, her faith, and her history. Jesus invites her to open her eyes to another reality of life.

Jesus wants the woman to open her eyes to a possibility that until now neither her tradition, her society, nor her religion—all symbolized in the water in the well of Jacob—has given her. He uses the concept of water with all that it represents for the woman.

The woman is not blind; she can see and talk about the water. But she cannot see beyond the water that is right in front of her, the water that quenches physical thirst. She still has not opened her eyes to all the conditioning that this well, with its historical background of social and religious traditions, signifies for her.

Nevertheless, as soon as the woman opens her eyes to Jesus' announcement of a new possibility for a life that would allow her to realize herself as a human being, she is ready to leave behind all that would tie her to a life of death. Here is a real and lasting new way, no longer that of a life not fully realized. This is why she asks where she must go to obtain this "water." In so doing, she leaves behind and breaks with the well of Jacob and all the conditioning given by her tradition.

The passage also opens our eyes to see that if we want to pass from a life conditioned and devalued by historical events on to a life fully realized, this cannot happen in a vacuum. Taking such a step implies a break with the past that first has to be mediated by our recognition of the concrete reality that must be faced before we can make that break. Opening our eyes to the reality, recognizing it, gives us the power to take that step. For this reason the dialogue between Jesus and the Samaritan woman changes abruptly, and we might ask why Jesus involved himself in this woman's private life at that precise moment.

Exegetes have made exhaustive studies of this passage. It seems to me that we can understand this part of the dialogue better if we understand that, as a result of the Syrian occupation, Samaritans worshiped five different gods, one of whom was Yahweh. This woman's five husbands (and the implication that the man she is with now is not really her husband) could symbolize the situation of religious syncretism that existed. Jesus wants to open the woman's eyes to the reality that, in the same way that she comes to the well to satisfy her thirst, her list of "husbands" symbolizes her search for a way to satisfy her desire for a full life. But none of the husbands has been able to accomplish this. It is this concrete reality with which she must break. It is not enough to say that she would no longer go to the well. She must also break with all that the well represents.

**Opening our eyes to the true God in love and service**

Immediately, the dialogue between Jesus and the Samaritan woman takes another turn. When Jesus speaks to her about her past life, without her having mentioned it, she recognizes him as a prophet: one she cannot accept because he is Jewish. Although until this point she has been opening her eyes to the deeper realities, here the conditioning of her historical and religious traditions returns to cloud her vision. She returns to her concept of the relationship between herself and God as an act of religious ritual. She has not really understood the image that is evoked by the "spring of life-giving water."

Jesus wants her to open her eyes to her need to break with her conception of encountering God as well. He opens her eyes to the reality that it is no longer ritual, but true worship that allows one to encounter the true God. He wants her to see that this comes out of a concrete relationship with others in love and service, because it is in that context that God can truly be found. That is what it is to worship in Spirit and in Truth or, as one modern version of the Bible says, to worship in an authentic way, in keeping with the Spirit of God. Love and service will come to be substituted for the old relationship with God, which was based on sacrifice, humiliation, and religious ritual. The relationship and the encounter with the God of life are to be found in this Spirit of life, in the struggle to achieve that life for ourselves and for others. Thus, the woman is being called to a life of full realization. To be able to participate in the new life she will have to break from the former relationship and begin a new relationship with God. That new relationship is to be seen in her announcing, and facilitating the new possibility of life for other people around her.

Even with all the clues that the Samaritan woman has been given by Jesus, she resists opening her eyes fully to the reality that is "right in front of her eyes." Perhaps the conditioning that she has experienced over so many years keeps her from opening her eyes completely to the reality that Jesus is "he who would come." But Jesus believes that now is the time to help her open her eyes completely. He gives her that last little push and reveals himself to her as the Messiah. He says, "I am he, I who am talking with you."

We could say from the way in which the dialogue has been going that it is quite likely that the woman had known for some while that she was speaking to the Messiah, but wanted to be on the safe side and preferred that he should say it first. She has just opened her eyes, but it's possible that she is afraid that because she is a woman, and a Samaritan, he will not confirm her great revelation. She still has not broken totally with the barriers of her tradition and her society.

Jesus, by revealing himself openly, allows her to break with these last barriers. As a result, she leaves her water jug cast aside to go and tell her people about the reality to which her eyes have been opened. The water jug symbolizes her relationship to the well, and the well her relationship with her tradition. The woman has just broken away from all that to embrace the possibility of full life in the reign of God announced to her by Jesus. That she communicates the message to her people by asking them "Could he be the Messiah?" doesn't mean that she still isn't sure of the truth. Rather she hopes each of them will take the opportunity to open his or her eyes to the revelation of the Messiah. She wants to help those women and men to have the same opportunity that she has had.

### Our relationship with the Samaritan woman

Now, after discovering this message through which Jesus opens the Samaritan woman's eyes, you may be asking yourselves, "What does all this have to do with us?" A great deal, I believe.

We have been called to open our eyes to the very concrete realities that are to be found all around us. For many of us this may be one of the first opportunities offered to us really to open our eyes.

Our cultures and our traditions have reduced our opportunity to live full lives as human beings. Our possibilities for living a full life have been limited by a patriarchal concept of society in which women are discriminated against because of their gender. We are women, therefore we are inferior. Church structures have not been exceptions in this discrimination.

But many of us come from countries where entire populations are also denied the possibility of living a full life. These are people overwhelmed by extreme poverty, incorrectly referred to as "on the road to development," because the process is not taking them forward but backward, and many of our people are in a worse situation now than they were twenty years ago.

Many of us also come from countries that are highly militarized, where the threat of death is constant and inescapable for each person who lives there. With death lying in wait, when we are looking down the barrel of a gun, how can we think that there could be a possibility of opening our eyes to an abundant life?

We all come from countries where, in one way or another, the problem of external debt makes it difficult, and in some cases impossible, to think of possibilities for abundant life. Because this debt was created and promoted by the international economic system, there is no escape from its outcome.

In addition to this, we have all felt the effects of the degradation of our environment, which was created by God for the benefit of all humanity. We continue to feel the effects of this apparently limitless destruction, and those effects make us realize that the chances for a full life in a contaminated environment grow less every day.

All these situations mean that we live in societies in which violence is the most common way of relating to one another. Our societies are characterized by asymmetries: marked differences within the society on the basis of race, class, gender, or some other distinction. Violence is exerted against those persons who are part of the group considered inferior. Some of us come from the Third World and see how whole populations are discriminated against. We feel the violence inflicted in so many ways on all our people. But, as women, we recognize that those who are most under attack in this system are women and children. With so much violence in the world, and with new manifestations of violence occurring all the time, the possibilities for abundant life are very few, not to say almost nonexistent. Faced with these realities, we are called together to open our eyes.

Our responsibility is very great, because, since we have

received the grace of the love of God, we are committed to being proclaimers of the message of the full life of God's reign. Jesus Christ reveals to us the message of the full life as he did to the Samaritan woman. Ours is the responsibility to run as she ran, to proclaim the message, so that others may have the opportunity to quench their thirst for a life with real possibilities.

It is our responsibility to let all humanity know that this message of full life is universal and excludes no one because she or he is "different." It is a message that breaks through the barriers of asymmetry and announces the possibility of full life for each person, whether man or woman, old or young, black or white, native or non-native, able-bodied or disabled, rich or very poor, marginalized or socially acceptable. We do not hold the power to decide who has the right to live a full life and who only has the right to survive.

But it is very difficult to proclaim a message of abundant life when all around us the only thing being proclaimed is death. To be able to proclaim life we have to be able to know our concrete reality so that we can break with that reality and proclaim that we can now begin to drink the water that truly satisfies our thirst.

To break with that concrete reality is not easy. It is not enough to leave behind the water jug as the Samaritan woman did. It is not enough to say that we no longer accept poverty or the external debt or militarism or the destruction of the environment, nor to say that we want the violence against women and children to end, nor to say that discrimination against women must end. These by themselves would not put an end to the problems. It would be closing our eyes to reality.

Neither can we be content with the easy traditional responses: the poor are poor because they are lazy; women bring violence upon themselves by provoking men; corrupt governments steal the money that comes into poor countries and leave them in debt; the ecological situation can be solved by planting a tree. We need first to open our eyes to concrete situations, look for the root causes that have given rise to these situations of injustice and death, and then direct our energies to the search for solutions that may be able to turn these situations around.

If we do not complete this task, then the same thing that

Jesus described to the Samaritan woman will happen to us: we will have to keep returning to the well to satisfy our thirst, because easy answers—or just wishing the problems didn't exist—will not be sufficient to reverse the process of death.

We have acquired a responsibility because we have received the grace and love of God. Our responsibility is similar to that which the Samaritan woman acquired when her eyes were opened and the message of the full life of God's reign was revealed to her. She ran to bring the message to her people.

It is time to begin the process of opening our eyes. It has been revealed to us that the way we can give thanks to God for such infinite grace is not by means of rituals, but by love, through serving others in concrete form. "The time is coming, in fact it is already here" when we are asked for proof of our gratitude to God. It is time to worship God "in an authentic way, in keeping with the Spirit of God." We can begin to do this by serving our sisters and brothers around the world, by opening our eyes to the situations that prevent the coming of the reign of life, by denouncing those situations and by searching for concrete solutions that can help to overcome injustice and death.

It will be the responsibility of each of us to leave behind the water jug that ties us to whatever social, historical, or religious traditions keep us from being agents of transformation in our society. In encounters with the situations experienced by other women and other peoples and cultures, we will have a unique opportunity to open our eyes to the concrete reality of our universe and to search together for solutions to our problems.

This is the well of the encounter of the Samaritan woman with Jesus. Jesus Christ makes himself present here and calls us to open our eyes. We come with the water jug in our hands and all that it represents. In this encounter with Jesus Christ, it will be our responsibility to leave the water jug and go out to proclaim the new possibilities for life.

❖    ❖    ❖

□ *Christian women's struggle in Latin America is in many ways quite different from that of Palestinian Christian women active in the Intifada, the organized uprising for liberation from Israeli occupation, which began in 1987. In May 1990 Palestinian and Western Christians came together for a conference whose papers,* Faith and the Intifada: Palestinian Christian Voices, *were edited by Naim S. Ateek, Marc H. Ellis and Rosemary Radford Ruether (Maryknoll, NY: Orbis Books, 1992). They contain several contributions by Palestinian Christian women describing their work in the Intifada and in the churches. These include the text of chapter 22 by Jean Zaru (pp. 126-9 of original). Here, she does not discuss any biblical text in detail, but reflects in a more general way on the inspiration of the gospel for nonviolent action. Her discussion indicates how it is not always easy to draw the line between violence and nonviolence, or to be certain which is the right course of action to adopt in a situation of extreme oppression.*


## 22   JEAN ZARU

# The Intifada, Nonviolence, and the Bible

As a Christian Palestinian woman, native of the Holy Land, I have been confronted all my life with social, economic, political, and religious structures of injustice that violated my dignity and self-esteem. The Church, as well as my mother, taught me not to resist, for this is not Christian and is not in favor of peace, the way they understood it. Even now, I remember very vividly that the only time my mother ever hit me and was really angry with me (as a child of eight) was when I did not listen to her and climbed the fig tree in our backyard and picked figs. She claimed this made my grandmother angry, and that I should not make her angry. I thought I had a right to the tree, to my father's and grandfather's property, just as my grandmother had. I could not understand why I could not have some of our figs. Peace for my mother meant submission and relinquishment of rights. I have come to see that this results in doing violence to ourselves and others.

The rebel in me started searching, agonizing, and asking questions. I kept asking myself, if we say there is something of God in every person, why is it often so difficult to see that presence of God in others? Why is there so much evil and suffering in our world? For many years I struggled with this Christian truth, that we are made in the image and likeness of God. I was happy to learn that the belief in the divinity seems to be part of all religions. "The kingdom of God is within you," said Jesus. "You are the temple of God," wrote St. Paul. "He who knows himself knows God," said the Prophet Mohammed, and this is echoed by many Sufis.

This recognition of our shared brotherhood and sisterhood convinced me that it must lead to the disappearance of injustice, exploitation, oppression, and everything that comes from false beliefs that justify ourselves and degrade others. So, acknowledgment of our true selves is revolutionary. It must lead to great changes and to peace. Thus the search for peace and for the recognition of true reality are identical.

All along, as Palestinians and as women, we were told to be peaceful. This was understood to mean being passive, being nice, allowing ourselves to be walked over. The Israelis talked to us about a "peace" that was achieved by pounding the opposition into submission, a "peace" maintained by crushing protest against injustice, a "peace" for the rulers at the expense of and through the misery of the ruled.

In December 1987 our Intifada started. With it we created an atmosphere of nonviolent action—notice I say "action"—by which we hoped to resolve our problems of occupation and oppression and to promote peace. We started by affirming one another. All of us felt empowered. We had a sense of our own inner power and worth, young and old, men and women, rich and poor. This affirmation and morale building helped us to think clearly and gave us the confidence to take creative action.

We started sharing feelings, information, and experiences with others, and this helped to break down the sense of isolation we had been experiencing. This was done through Al-Kuds radio, demonstrations, worship services in mosques and churches, leaflets, funerals, strikes, films, fasts, sit-ins, and many other activities in the community. We helped reveal the violence of the Israeli army, and the world realized that the power of our Intifada is moral.

This is a true revolution that has united us as a people, while the violence of the Israeli authorities has divided them and isolated them. Our Intifada is based on respect, education, nonviolent struggle, and the faith and courage of the oppressed. We are all telling each other that we can do it, that we all count, and that everyone is part of the solution to the conflict. We have overcome fear. Our self-esteem is high, and we feel optimistic and more competent, in spite of the suffering and death. The Israeli government thinks that by using more oppressive measures against us, we will give up our struggle and submit. But the Intifada has taught us not to relinquish the power to make our own decisions about how we want our lives to be. The Intifada contradicts the idea that our situation is hopeless and that we are helpless in solving it. We are not helpless, and it is not hopeless. Isn't this also the message of the resurrection?

We live daily as persons and as communities in the midst of violence. We often find ourselves willingly or unwillingly participating in social organizations that practice and embody violence. We may deliberately act in violent or nonviolent ways to promote justice. Can we say to those who have opted for violence against injustice that we would rather see you die than defend yourselves? Who will throw the first stone to condemn them? Who is morally superior? There are many Palestinians who sacrificed their lives so we may have life with dignity and freedom. Isn't this Jesus' message?

As we opt for violence or nonviolence in our revolution, we know that the liberty to choose is not always there. I believe the division between the pacifist and the non-pacifist is not an absolute one. The pacifist and the non-pacifist, both committed to the struggle for a just future, should regard one another as allies on most issues. The conflict is not between them, but between those who support the oppressive structures of the status quo and those on the side of liberation. As Christians, the gospel compels us not to support the oppressive structures. Such an alternative is not possible for us today.

One peculiar strength of nonviolence comes from the dual nature of its approach—the offering of respect and concern, on the one hand, and of defiance and stubborn noncooperation with injustice, on the other. Put into a feminist perspective, nonviolence is the merging of our uncompromising rage at patriarchy's brutal destructiveness with a refusal to adopt its ways, a refusal to give in to despair or hate. To rage against, yet refuse to destroy, is a true revolution, not just a shuffle of death-wielding power.

No matter what our situation, life presents a succession of choices between life and death. Many of these choices may be subtle, and sometimes we scarcely take notice of them. But there is always, among the range of options available, one that is suitable to our present spiritual resources and practical circumstances, one that affirms truth. The Intifada is that right path for us today.

I once visited the Jalazone refugee camp after three weeks of curfew. The people there had been punished by having their electricity cut off and their supply of gas curtailed. Women told us how determined they were to find a way to bake their own bread. They collected wood and rubbish and made a communal fire, which was kept alight by burning old shoes and rags. When the soldiers came to put the fire out and throw away the dough, the women resisted, shouting, "Go tell your leaders that no matter what you do, we will not allow our children to starve. We will find a way to bake bread, and all your efforts to destroy our spirit are not going to succeed. What God has created, no one can destroy."

I visit the refugee camps often because the YWCA has many projects there. We ask women whose houses were demolished, who have no work or security, and whose husbands, fathers, or brothers are in jail, "How do you manage?" They say such things as, "God who created us will not forget us. Sometimes we wake up in the morning to find food supplies at our doorstep.

On Easter Day, some young people tried to share eggs with their poorer neighbors. Every house they knocked at to offer a gift of eggs referred them to a more needy person, for they said, 'Thanks be to God, we are not starving.'" Their faith challenged me and reminded me of what Jesus told us: "Your God will feed you; see how God feeds the birds and clothes the flowers; therefore, be not anxious." Jesus taught us not to worry, but to seek first and find God's Kingdom and to align ourselves to its righteousness (Matt. 6.25-33).

We are seeking God's Kingdom, God's will where peace will prevail. Searching for this peace is often a cause for strife. Jesus himself foresaw this. "Do not think that I have come to bring peace to earth. I have not come to bring peace, but a sword!" Where can we find peace? Many people, including women, think that they can find peace by running away from the world, by doing nothing about it. The churches have become a refuge for tired folk. But this is not the message of the Gospels, for God loved the world, so we should be in the world that God loved and loves. The world is full of strife, and it is our duty as Christians to bring peace. We cannot bring peace only by proclaiming it. We should work. Wherever injustice and wrong exist, we should be there to say, this is not the will of God, this should be changed. But, we cannot fulfill this duty if we are not at peace with ourselves. The saddest thing in our time is that Christians have found it so difficult to live at peace with one another, locally and internationally.

There are many Christians whose theology brings to me, as a Palestinian and a woman, strife and confusion. These Christians are part of the structures of injustice we are facing. An example of this is the phenomenon of Christian fundamentalism in the West. Many of these Western Christians give blind support to Israel. They never question what Israel is doing, because they see the Jews as the "chosen people" and Israel as a "fulfillment of prophecy." Interpretations such as these affect us directly as Palestinians.

For the last two years, our people have been bleeding. Daily we are reminded of life and death, of the crucifixion. We feel the words of Jesus, who said, "Weep for yourselves and your children" (Luke 23.27-31). We often pray as Jesus did that the bitter cup of death may be taken away. We often shout with a loud voice, God, why have you forsaken us? But, until we surrender to God as Jesus did, and until we reach that stage where we can forgive those who have offended us, we will not have peace, and we will not have liberation.

❖    ❖    ❖

□ *The last text included in Part Three (chapter 23) is a homily put together by Asian women and preached at the Harvard Divinity School Noon Worship on February 19, 1986, by Noda Kesaya, Kim Hee Sang, Paula K. R. Arai and Kwok Pui-lan. The latter published the text in* The Asia Journal of Theology, *vol. 1/1, 1987, pp. 90–5.*

## 23  KWOK PUI-LAN

# Worshipping with Asian Women: A Homily on Jesus Healing the Daughter of a Canaanite Woman

The Gospel of Matthew tells us the story of Jesus healing the daughter of a Canaanite woman; it says:

> And Jesus went away from there and withdrew to the district of Tyre and Sidon. And behold, a Canaanite woman from that region came out and cried, "Have mercy on me, O Lord, Son of David; my daughter is severely possessed by a demon." But he did not answer her a word. And his disciples came and begged him, saying, "Send her away, for she is crying after us." He answered, "I was sent only to the lost sheep of the house of Israel." But she came and knelt before him, saying, "Lord, help me." And he answered, "It is not fair to take the children's bread and throw it to the dogs." She said, "Yes, Lord, yet even the dogs eat the crumbs that fall from their master's table." Then Jesus answered her, "O woman, great is your faith! Be it done for you as you desire." And her daughter was healed instantly (Matt. 15.21–8).

We have heard this story many times, but we have seldom asked the identity of this Canaanite woman. Yes, who is this Canaanite woman?

- She is the woman down on the dirty road of Calcutta.
- She is the mother of a political prisoner in Seoul.
- She is the old garment factory worker in Hong Kong.
- She is the mother whose daughter is a prostitute in Jakarta, Taipei, or Chiang Mai.
- She is also this survivor from Hiroshima:

*I would be a witness for Hiroshima (Voice A)*

I wish, as a survivor,
To be a real human being;
Besides, as a poor mother,
Fearing a day when the blue sky
Above the red-cheeked children
And those thousands with promising futures
May be smashed to atoms all of a sudden,
Endangering their bright futures
And now, to be repeated at the nations' cost.

I resolved to shed tears supposed to be shed on dead bodies,
Afresh for those people living now,
Declaring against all war, first of all.
Even if I should perchance be punished under a disgraceful
    name—
From a mother's protest against death for her own son's
    sake,
I should never dare to hide myself, never!
Because the day was too much impressed on my retina,
The hellish day of that fatal blaze.

It was August sixth in 1945,
At an early hour of the day;
Men and women were to start their daily work,
When unexpectedly
The city and all were blown away;
Blistered hideously, each and all;
The seven rivers were filled with naked corpses.

237

Supposing there is a tale of the inferno
Which a man caught a glimpse of once,
And happened to warn me of its horror
To be called back by the lord of the inferno,
The moment he tells of it to someone else,
I would go wherever it is, as a witness of the Hiroshima
 Tragedy,
That I might proclaim its misery;
I would sing for my life
"No more wars on the earth!"

Sadako Kurihara, Japan[1]

She is this woman who prays to the divine mother in Sri Lanka:

*Grant the grace to break our sorrows (Voice B)*

Gracious mother we call to thee
Look in mercy on our distress.
All these hill-land homes he grips
The demon of poverty and grief.
Many without homes dwell on the streets.
There's not much left, life's ebbing out.
O Goddess, who grantest all requests,
This much alone we ask of thee:
Give them just one small spark of joy
To lighten however dimly darkened lives.

Not long ago, they fell of thee,
A child cried "mother" in its hunger;
Your name you heard that cry you answered
And fed that child, O Divine Mother.
Hearest thou not this pitiful crying
Echoing through these valleys and hills?
Babies sucking at breasts without milk.
Thousands of little ones calling thy name;
Come now as their mother and save them
At thy feet we humbly pray.

The yoke of poverty thou canst break
And bring an end to all distress.
See thy children small and ill-fed

238

Roaming streets and begging for food;
Rummaging for castout meals in garbage
Looking for some morsel to satisfy
A hunger which draws its claws on them
Till they die emaciated nothings.
Thou art light who destroys all sorrow,
Canst thou not see this piteous sight?

Because the women tirelessly toil
Their daily labor offer forth.
The hills are covered with a carpet
Of green and fertile strands of tea.
Their daily work they view as worship
A sacrifice given to the land.
In exchange for this their offering
Wealth comes in from all o'er the world;
But thy slaves experience no reward.
Mother, to them their labor bless!

Kurinji Thennavan, Sri Lanka[2]

This woman is the poorest among the poor,
the oppressed among the oppressed,
she is at every corner of Asia,
and she fills the Third World.

*Woman, you have to pray (Voice C)*

Well, the problem is not I did not pray,
But I've prayed too much.
People say I am mad, I am insane,
They say I believe in miracles.

*I heard a rumour that a Canaanite woman has begged Jesus
and her daughter was healed. Perhaps you could
do the same (Voice A)*

Who? Jesus? Who is this Jesus?
Is this the same Jesus that the rich worship?
In the name of whom, the powerful nations "convert"
    the world?
Is it not true the disciples of Jesus chase the Canaanite
    woman away?

Asian women have met another Jesus.
They have found the Messiah among the *Minjung*.
There, at the corner of the street, in the prison cell,
in the vast exploited land, and in the people who never
    lose hope.
The Canaanite woman must have found the same poor,
lowly and ragged Jesus.

We have found the Messiah in the hope of the Hiroshima
    people:

### *Eternal green (Voice B)*

In the delta of Hiroshima
Whirl round, green leaves
In the memory of fire and death.
May these, our prayers, live long!
Eternal green!
Eternal green!
Flourish ever fresh and green
In the delta of Hiroshima.

Tamiki Hara, Japan[3]

in the courage of this Philippine woman:

### *Who am I (Voice C)*

I am a woman
  I am alive
    I am struggling
      I am hoping.

I am created in the image of God
just like all other people in the world
I am a person with worth and dignity.
I am a thinking person, a feeling person, a doing person.
I am the small *I am* that stands before the big I AM.

I am a worker who is constantly challenged and faced
    with the needs of the Church and society in Asia
    and in the global community.

I am angered by the structures and powers that create
    all forms of oppression, exploitation, and
    degradation.
I am a witness of the moans, tears, banners, and
    clenched fists of my people.
I can hear their liberating songs, their hopeful
    prayers, and decisive march toward justice and
    freedom.

I believe that all of us—women and men,
    young and old, Christian and non-Christian are
    called upon to do responsible action;
    to be concerned
    to be involved
    NOW!

I am hoping
  I am struggling
    I am alive
      I am Filipino
        I am a woman.

Elizabeth Tapia, the Philippines[4]

in the bonding of Third World women:

*Today I hold Alice Walker's hands\* (Voice C)*

Today I hold Alice Walker's hands.
They are small,
but from these small hands,
come such powerful poems,
the ghosts cry and gods scream.

Ten thousand miles away,
she flew to see us.
Immersed in the sea of yellow faces,
happily she sang:
Colorful people, people of color,
Tra-la-la-la-la.

241

Across the ocean I came,
to see people like her,
fierce fighters for justice,
yet a mother,
in search for the mothers' gardens.

Today we have met,
a moment is eternity.
Witness a new force,
a new bonding forming.
We are sisters, black, brown and yellow,
Tra-la-la-la-la.

Kwok Pui-lan, Hong Kong[5]

* For Alice Walker, the African-American writer poet, who visited China and wrote a poem "Song" for us.

PART FOUR

# Challenging Traditional
# Theological Thinking

☐ *The chapters in Parts One to Three challenge the traditional way of doing theology, though each from a different perspective. Each relates the process of theological reflection—whether in the form of questions, analysis, or insight—to a specific context of Third World women's experience. We now turn to several well-established topics central to theology and also much debated in Western feminist theology. Who is God? What language, symbol, and metaphor are most appropriate when referring to God's presence and power in our lives? Who is Jesus for Latin American, African, and Asian women? And who is Mary for women in the Third World? If space permitted, each of these questions could be documented by a whole series of essays, but we have to restrict our selection to just one or two in each area.*

*Women in today's world are seeking and seeing God anew. Their new vision has important implications for what it means to be created in the image of God as both female and male, and also for our understanding of the Trinity and the work of the Holy Spirit.*

❖     ❖     ❖

□ *In chapter 24, I have selected two brief passages (pp. 65-7 and 72-6 in the original) by the Indonesian writer-theologian Marianne Katoppo, whose pioneering book* Compassionate and Free *was published in 1979 (Geneva: WCC Publications 1979; Maryknoll, NY: Orbis Books 1980). Katoppo touches briefly on the understanding of the Holy Spirit, and on the oppressive aspect of a Trinity understood as all-male. The possible openings for a feminist trinitarian theology, especially in terms of integrating the masculine and feminine, are also discussed elsewhere by María Clara Bingemer (see her chapter "Reflections on the Trinity," in Elsa Tamez, ed.,* Through Her Eyes: Women's Theology from Latin America, *Maryknoll, NY: Orbis Books, 1989, pp. 56—80). Katoppo draws on biblical and Asian sources in her reflections on God and the Spirit. Her thinking is not only grounded in a wide experience of Christian ecumenism, but also in the rich world of Asian religious pluralism.*

## 24   MARIANNE KATOPPO

# The Concept of God and the Spirit from the Feminist Perspective

A professor at a theological seminary in Indonesia once said to me in all seriousness: "Well, you can't deny it—God is male: just look at the way he is referred to as 'he' throughout the Bible, with all the masculine forms of the verbs and nouns!"

Of course I could have answered that, if you look at things that way, you could also argue that God was Jewish, although a bit later in the stage of revelation, "he" also adopted a Greek garb and expressed "himself" in a Hellenistic fashion—and whereas the people "he" had revealed "himself" to were originally the Chosen People (i.e., the Jews), presently they came to include the Greeks. All *men*, of course, since after the Babylonian exile Jews had started to give thanks to the Lord for having created them as Jewish *men*, not gentiles, slaves, or women; and the Aristotelean concept of the human being was rather similar, only he thought of *Greeks* for *Hebrews*.

In the Indonesian language we don't have such a problem with pronouns, as "Dia" means both "he" and "she." Neither do we have such a fierce dichotomy as is evident in the West. My preoccupation with pronouns really started when I had to theologize in English, Dutch, and German (in Swedish, God is "he," but *människa*—"human being"—is always "she"!), and I heartily sympathize with my Western sisters. Language is, after all, where theology begins.

Anyway, my answer to the professor went like this. I asked him about the original meaning of *rechamim*, which is used for God's mercy, compassion (e.g., Exod. 34). He admitted that it literally means "movements of the *womb*" (*rechem*).

Neither of us knew of any males who possessed wombs, so my professor was persuaded there might be a touch of the feminine here. This was, in my opinion, a Great Leap Forward, because browsing through Hebrew lexicons and the like, I found that some male theologians will perform the most extraordinary contortions exegetically in order to avoid relating *rechamim* to the feminine aspect of God.

I also asked how women could have been created in God's image if God was so decidedly male. And I pointed to the case of the Holy Spirit. The Third Person started out in Hebrew as the feminine *Ruach*, but was then effectively neutered by the Greek translators of the Septuagint, then made masculine by Latin. Therefore, we are now blessed with an all-male Trinity. (We will return to the Spirit later.)

Thirdly, I asked whether there were no legitimate reasons for the old Hebrews to refer consistently to God as "he"—and did they *really* do that?

We must learn to read the Bible again. Over and against the masculine imagery—which does dominate the text—there are also feminine images that tend to be conveniently overlooked. We accept that the texts that have come to us are "the products of a society driven to choose male metaphors by virtue of patriarchal structures predicated upon sexual inequality," as Paul D. Hanson says.[1] We may still live in a society of patriarchal structures, but we flatter ourselves that there is no more sexual inequality.

In that context, one wonders why the name of God, Yahweh, which is a verb, not a noun, is still consistently translated as "Lord." This has been happening for centuries. To quote Dr Hanson again, it is "a conspiracy spanning three millennia." It is a fact that frequently the original texts make no indication of gender—this has been supplied gratuitously by translators.

As James White pointed out, though anthropomorphisms abound in Scripture, usually even the faint suggestion of female anatomy for God troubles us.[2] Thus, in the prologue to John's Gospel, translators shy away from an exact rendition of the last verse (1.18), which says literally: "God's only begotten, he who is in the Father's *breast* [Greek: *kolpos*]." The New English Bible discreetly puts it as: "He who is nearest to the Father's *heart*."

When God is called "Father," this is not to be taken in an ontic sense, i.e., it does not necessarily limit God to being male. "Father" is intended to express the loving concern of God who takes care of us. Here the category "father" is a symbol of divine fecundity and creativity.

The excessive emphasis on the maleness of God is seen by some as a reaction against the fertility goddesses of the Canaanite religious system. Although the dominant metaphor in this cult was feminine, it reduced woman to a sex object, as is amply illustrated by the fertility plaques with their exaggerated representations of the breasts and genitalia. This is something that we will have to bear in mind constantly in our search for a whole image of God.

Again, Asians may look at the other religions. In the meta-cosmic soteriologies of Asia, such as Hinduism, it is unthinkable to dichotomize male and female to the extent the Christian West has done, any more than it is possible to dichotomize life and death.

# Challenging Traditional Theological Thinking

## The oppression of an all-male Trinity

The Borobudur is a world-famous temple in central Java. Built in the seventh century A.D. it is a Shiva-Buddhist shrine. Although it is structured in the form of a *stupa*, adorned with statues of the Lord Buddha and reliefs of his life, it is also replete with *lingams*, which are symbols of the Lord Shiva.

In high school, during cultural history classes, the teacher explained offhandedly that the *lingam* was a phallic symbol. We dutifully copied down this information in our notebooks, without having the slightest idea what the symbol stood for, as none of us knew either Sanskrit or Latin.

Actually, every *lingam* stands on a base called the *yoni*, which symbolizes the female organ. The whole thing was a fertility symbol, and whoever was responsible for building the Borobudur was sufficiently cognizant of the facts of life not to ascribe fertility to one sex only.

In the primal (or cosmic) religions of Asia, people have worshipped their ancestors—not just a male father. In the cult of the Rice Mother, who is still venerated throughout the Indonesian archipelago, people also worship her spouse.[3]

I find Hinduism most interesting. The *Sakti*, the feminine aspect of the deity, is by no means subordinate or inferior to the deity; she *is* the Deity.

Durga is also the goddess of death. The oldest temple in Bali is perched on a steep promontory hundreds of meters over the Indonesian Ocean, of which she is believed to be the queen. Durga's statue, which must be over a thousand years old, is almost worn smooth. How can people worship a goddess of death with such devotion? Because she is also the goddess of life, activity, energy, power. Life and death are one.

Forcing people to relate to an all-male Trinity is oppression. In the context of Asian cosmic religion and meta-cosmic soteriologies, it is also ridiculous.

## The Holy Spirit

In the tradition of the ecclesiastical West, the Holy Spirit is "he." As I have already pointed out, this is a result of the fact that the feminine *Ruach* of the Hebrew was first effectively neutered by the good fathers of the Septuagint, then made masculine for good measure by the Latin.

Is it coincidence that the symbol for the Holy Spirit is the dove? In Greek, this word is *peristerà*, which means "Bird of Ishtar," the virgin goddess who we discussed earlier.

Is it so far-fetched to think that the battle between Yahweh (supposedly male) and Ishtar (definitely female) still seems to be going on?[4]

Somewhere along the line, it was apparently decreed that the Trinity should be all male. Hence the adoration of the Virgin Mary as "daughter of the Father, mother of Jesus, *spouse* of the Holy Spirit." A perfect example of the way some men would like to see women: always as daughter/mother/spouse, never as a human being in her own right. And Mary, the virgin in the primal sense of the word, becomes the dutifully domesticated symbol of that which she is *not*.

In view of the quality and the function of the Spirit as God who creates, who comforts, "the Giver of Life" (as the Nicene Creed says), it is not surprising that the Gnostic writings, such as the Gospel of the Hebrews and the Acts of Thomas, called the Holy Spirit explicitly "*Mother* of Jesus, *Mother* of all creatures."

Of course, these writings are not canonical. As a matter of fact, they may be considered heretical. This is a symptom that is often cited in history, more especially church history. Whoever begged to differ was usually in for a sorry fate—like the Montanists, who gave great prominence to the Spirit, and who ordained women. We all know what terrible and perverted creatures they were from the writings that have come down to us. Not *their* writings, to be sure, but the treatises that good and true Christians wrote against the Montanists' horrible heresies.

In this connection, one wonders how Luther or Calvin would have fared, if the only source we had of their lives and teachings was the official Vatican version of the time.

This insistence that the three persons are all male has led to some complications.

In one Pakistani language, the word for Spirit is feminine.

However, thanks to the Nicene Creed calling the Spirit Lord, as the English liturgical texts also do, this language had to be changed: the natural idiom ceased to exist, and in its place the people got "translationese," or perhaps it would be more accurate to say here "religionese." How wonderful. More than ever, Christians will have an awareness of being a people that has been set apart, if even their language is unintelligible except to a select few.

The Spirit, who goes where She wills, is the first of the Three Persons to be reified (made to be a thing). The whole *filioque* controversy should make this clear.

From God, the Spirit became a thing. Eventually, She was regarded as "the monopolistic possession of the Judaeo-Christian tradition imprisoned within the steel and concrete structures of western dogma and a permanent Atlantic Charter."[5]

The best illustration I ever saw of this point was in Taizé's Church of the Reconciliation, to which we were taken during the 1978 Bossey Graduate School of Ecumenical Studies.

Kneeling in a church that was so dark that I had an atavistic sense of being back in the womb, I saw something white moving in the flickering lights of the altar. When I went up after the service to have a closer look, I realized it was a white dove in a cage—put there to symbolize the Holy Spirit, as I was told.

I went out of the church much saddened by what we do to the Spirit in the darkness of our minds and the narrowness of our thinking.

Is it heresy to say that the Spirit sings to us in the *Bhagavad Gita*, the Song of God, or dances for us in Lord Shiva's dance, or speaks to us in the words of the Enlightened One? If so, why is it all right to send small children out into the garden early in the morning to look for Easter eggs—a custom connected with a forgotten spring goddess called Ostara? How is it possible that the Christmas tree has become such an established symbol of Christianity that political parties (for example, the now dissolved Parkindo, Indonesian Christian Party) have used it as their emblem? There are very few people in Europe today who remember that the origin of the Christmas tree was in the heathen legend of Odin, Father of the Gods, who vowed to destroy the world when the last leaf had fallen. As the fir tree does not shed its leaves, the world was saved. Boniface was able—and allowed—to transform this piece of pagan practice into a ritual that Christians all over the world go through now every year, no doubt to the great delight of manufacturers of Christmas cards and other trimmings.

The very essence of the Spirit is "boundless freedom." It follows that to put any limits on the Spirit's activity is to negate that freedom. This doesn't mean that there are no discernible signs to recognize the Spirit's continuing work.

As Stanley Samartha says, the Spirit means life (vitality, creativity, growth), not death. Order (meaning, significance, truth), not chaos. Community (sharing, fellowship, bearing one another's burden), not separation. Wherever these marks are found, there one should sense the work of the Spirit.

❖     ❖     ❖

□ *More than ten years after Marianne Katoppo's pioneering publication, the Korean woman theologian, Chung Hyun Kyung, has produced another, more substantial work on Asian women's theology. Katoppo's work was very much just her own — one Asian woman's theology; whereas, Chung can base herself on a whole generation of Asian women thinkers and workers. Her book* Struggle to be the Sun Again *(Maryknoll, NY: Orbis Books, 1990; London: SCM, 1991) covers historical, social, and theological perspectives. What does it mean to be fully human? Who is Jesus or Mary for Asian women? What are the characteristics of Asian women's spirituality? What contribution does Asian women's theology make to a new understanding of theology and a new theological methodology?*

*These questions are discussed in great detail in her book, which is written with passionate commitment and stirring personal concern. Chapter 25 reproduces a section of this book (pp. 47–51 in the original) that discusses different images of God. When reflecting on the statement "To be human is to be created in the image of God", we discover images that convey not only a larger vision of the divine, but that also lead us to a deeper understanding of ourselves.*

## 25   CHUNG HYUN KYUNG

# To Be Human Is to Be Created in God's Image

In their search for full humanity, Asian women receive strength through biblical teachings. However, for Asian women good news from the Bible is not a free gift to accept without suspicion since the Bible carries so many oppressive messages for women.

251

Out of the many contradictory teachings in the Bible, Asian women use most frequently the teaching from Genesis that contains the message that men and women are created equally in God's image (Gen. 1.27, 28). "In God's Image" is an important biblical phrase Asian women have adopted to define their perspectives on humanity. Human beings—men and women—were created in God's image. Who we are as humans is defined by who God is. This may appear to be quite Barthian or neo-orthodox, and perhaps that influence has affected Asian women's language, but the key to their anthropology is really not theology. It is in fact the other way round. The key to their theology is anthropology, that is, Asian women's experience of suffering and hope. God is defined by their experience. To understand Asian women's perspectives on humanity, therefore, it is important to note a transformation in their thinking about God.

### God as both female and male

Many Asian women think God has both female and male qualities in the God-self. It is natural for Asian women to think of the Godhead as male and female because there are many male gods and female goddesses in Asian religious cultures. Padma Gallup from India claims that Western Christianity lost the inclusive quality of the Godhead who has both male and female sides because it was "wrapped in layers of ponderous patriarchy, Zoroastrian dualism, Greek philosophy, and the ethics of the marketplace and morality of the dominant male of the Puritan tradition."[1] Gallup also proposes that Asian feminist theology should draw its sources from "its own millennia-old culture, and all the living faiths of its neighbors."[2] She gains insights from Hindu religion and culture in order to understand *Imago Dei* from an Asian women's perspective. For Gallup, the Hindu image of *Arthanaressvara* (the deity in which the masculine *Sivam* (absolute good or love) and the feminine *Sakti* (absolute power) form a whole in which neither can function without the other) is a positive model for the *Imago Dei* for Asian women. Gallup thinks that "a concept of the Godhead that holds the masculine and feminine in equivalence could possibly engender non-dualistic, non-competitive modes of thought and action."[3]

Many Asian women believe that an inclusive image of God who has both male and female sides promotes equality and harmony between men and women: a "partnership of equals."[4] However, they also are concerned about the way harmony and complementarity are used against women in Asia. Virginia Fabella warns Asian women that the emphasis on complementarity and harmony should not be achieved at the expense of women's equality. She explains how many Asian churches are using complementarity for men's convenience in order to perpetuate stereotypical feminine roles for women. Fabella claims that for liberated women, "complementarity is acceptable only if it respects equality."[5] In sum, Asian women's yearning for and rediscovery of a Godhead that contains both male and female qualities is the same yearning for full humanity in which both males and females are fully respected as equal partners.

## God as community

Asian women view God not as an individual, but as a community. When she interprets Genesis 1.26, Elizabeth Dominguez from the Philippines claims: "To be in the image of God is to be in community. It is not simply a man or a woman who can reflect God, but it is the community in relationship."[6] In a genuine community everyone is a "steward" to one another. "All the parts are for one another and all the parts have their role."[7] This community is characterized by "interdependence," "harmony," and "mutual growth."[8]

The image of God as "the community in relationship" empowers Asian women to get out of their individualism. It also encourages them to honor their responsibility and rights as a part of the community. Interdependence, harmony, and mutual growth are impossible when there is no balance of power. Monopolized power destroys community by destroying mutuality. Therefore, in this image of God as the community in relationship, there is no place for only one, solitary, all-powerful God who sits on top of the hierarchical power pyramid and dominates all other living beings. Where there is no mutual relationship, there is no human experience of God. Asian women emphasize the importance of community in their theologies because only in community can humanity reflect God and fulfill the image of God in which we were created for mutual relationship.

### God as creator in nature and in history

Asian women believe God is also "creator of this beautiful universe in all its splendour and variety."[9] They experience this creator God in their own "creativity as a woman who gives birth, as a cook, gardener, communicator, as a writer, as a creator of the environment, atmosphere, life."[10] The creator God draws people out of their own captivity and invites them to be a co-creator with God. When Asian women touch their own creativity and create their own healing, they touch the life source—God. They create babies, food, and gardens. They also create history. God is not a prime mover who just started the universe and then sat back out of the universe after creation. God's creation is a continuous, ongoing process. This creator God walks with us in our own creation of history. This is the "God of history who is with the oppressed people in their struggle for justice."[11]

When women get out of their oppression and create alternative structures that are life-giving for them, they meet their God through the process of liberation. They know the God of history takes sides with the oppressed as witnessed in Exodus, Jesus' life, and the many unbeatable people's movements in Asia. With their trust in this God, Asian women draw strength for their struggle for justice. In their faith, Asian women know they are invited as God's partner to the covenant of "justice, peace and the integrity of creation."[12]

### God as life-giving spirit

The emerging generation of Asian women theologians emphasize God as a life-giving spirit they can encounter *within* themselves and *in* everything that fosters life. This move is the manifesto of their shift in the theological paradigm, which is different from that of the older generation. Until recently, Asian theologies have been heavily based on the neo-orthodox theology

254

from the West. Neo-orthodox theology promotes a transcendent, absolute other God, and Christian revelatory truth over other religious truth. The younger generation of Asian women theologians lift up the immanence of God in their theologies. They are longing for an image of God that is all-embracing: God as life-giving spirit who is present everywhere and moves everywhere opens the door for a new understanding of the divine. Indian dancer/musician/poet Susan Joseph confesses that her image of the spirit is a bird. She says:

> The holy spirit was my bird. My encounter with the Spirit moved my image of God into a more inclusive, unrestrictive image.[13]

Lee Sun Ai resonates with this inclusive, unrestrictive image of God, when she writes:

God is movement
God is the angry surf
God is like mother
God is like father
God is like friends
God is power of being
God is power of living
God is power of giving birth[14]

When women see God as an all-inclusive reality in everything (especially within themselves), they begin to trust their personal power. Astrid Lobo, an Indian scientist and active lay reader in the Catholic Church, confesses that her growing confidence in herself as a person is directly related to her new image of God. She contends:

> As a woman it is important for me that I am in God, and God is in me. No longer do I see God as a rescuer. I see her more as power and strength within me.[15]

While drawing new insights from Hinduism, the universality of God, Lobo discovers God within herself as the "Supreme Center." The more she looks within herself for the source of strength, the more she begins to trust her own power. She stops begging for God to rescue her as a helpless victim. Lobo shares this new understanding further:

> I no longer see the victim-rescuer game as healthy, so I have learnt to shed the needless dependence on God. I am increasingly aware of the resources God has given me. I feel strongly the need to develop and create as my response to God's love shown in my creation.[16]

## God as mother and woman

Many Asian women think God as a life-giving power can be naturally personified as mother and woman because woman gives birth to her children and her family members by nurturing them. In many Asian women's writings, God is portrayed as mother and woman. Some Asian women claim that women are more sensitive to fostering life than men because of women's experience of giving birth and nurturing others. A group of Asian women emphasized the point by reflecting on the event of Moses' birth and killing of male infants in Exodus:

> Every woman is close to life and loves her child. Woman is life and love. The killing of the male baby is ironic of the two edged sword that patriarchy has in itself, namely, in male power is also death.[17]

God as mother and woman challenges the old concept that emphasized, along with other attributes, God as immutable and unchangeable. Woman's body grows and changes radically through menstruation and pregnancy compared to the male body. God as mother is more approachable and personable. When Asian women begin to imagine God as woman and mother, they also begin to accept their own bodies and their own womanhood in its fullness. The female God accepts us as we are more than the patriarchal male God. This female God is a vulnerable God who is willing to be changed and transformed in her interaction with Asian women in their everyday life experiences. This God is a God who talks to Asian women, listens to their story, and weeps with them. This God is a God who struggles with Asian women in their claims of power in this world, a God who is growing, changing, and walking with them.

Asian women's trust in this God enables them to trust themselves and to hope in the midst of their hopelessness. The power of God evokes in Asian women a different kind of power, which has been lost in patriarchal religion and society:

> The power that fosters life rather than death
> the power of working together,
> the power of experiencing one's true feelings,
> the power of acclaiming others and
> enabling them to realize their full
> potential as human beings.[18]

With this new power, Asian women struggle to be persons with power for self-determination. They dream of a new world where woman is not the moon that has to change according to the sun. Rather they want to become the sun that shines in its own light out of its burning core of life, fostering life on the earth.

> Originally, woman was the Sun.
> She was an authentic person.
> But now woman is the moon.
> She lives by depending on another
> and she shines by reflecting
> another's light.
> Her face has a sickly pallor.

> We must now regain our hidden sun.
> "Reveal our hidden sun!
> Rediscover our natural gifts!"
> This is the ceaseless cry
> Which forces itself into our hearts;
> it is our irrepressible
> and unquenchable desire.
> It is our final,
> complete,
> and only instinct
> through which
> our various
> separate instincts
> are unified.[19]

In Asian women's perspective, knowledge of self leads to a knowledge of God. In their suffering, Asian women meet God, who in turn discloses that they were created in the divine image, full and equal participants in the community with men. To know the self is to know God for Christian Asian women.

❖　　❖　　❖

□ *If you wish to follow up Chung Hyun Kyung's reflections on Jesus Christ, you need to turn to chapter 9, "Who is Jesus for Asian Women?", in her book* Struggle to be the Sun Again *(Maryknoll, NY: Orbis Books, 1990; London: SCM, 1991, pp. 53–73). There she discusses the traditional images of Jesus as Suffering Servant, Lord and Immanuel (God-with-us), and contrasts those with newly emerging images of Jesus as Liberator, Revolutionary, and Political Martyr; as Mother, Woman and Shaman, as Worker and Grain.*

*In chapter 26 we reproduce a moving poem by an Indian woman from the last section of chapter 4 in* Struggle to be the Sun Again *(pp. 72–3), followed by a chapter on Christology from an African perspective. If you want to explore a Latin American perspective on Christ, I refer you to Nellie Ritchie's chapter entitled "Women and Christology" (in Elsa Tamez, ed.,* Through Her Eyes: Women's Theology from Latin America, *Maryknoll, NY: Orbis Books, 1989, pp. 81–95). Ritchie looks at Jesus from within the context of Latin American liberation theology and enters into dialogue with passages about Jesus from Luke's Gospel. She explores themes on Jesus as the Christ of life, the Christ of grace, the liberator Christ, and the Christ of the Kingdom.*

# 26   ANONYMOUS POEM

## "God as Food for the Hungry"

Every noon at twelve
In the blazing heat
God comes to me
in the form of
Two hundred grams of gruel.

I know Him in every grain
I taste Him in every lick.
I commune with Him as I gulp
For He keeps me alive, with
Two hundred grams of gruel.

I wait till next noon
and now know he'd come:
I can hope to live one day more
For you made God to come to me as
Two hundred grams of gruel.

I know now that God loves me—
Not until you made it possible.
Now I know what you're speaking about
For God so loves this world
That He gives His beloved Son
Every noon through You.

❖    ❖    ❖

□ *Chapter 27 gives yet another perspective from an African woman. Teresa M. Hinga, a lecturer at Kenyatta University, discusses "Jesus Christ and the Liberation of Women in Africa" in Mercy Amba Oduyoye's and Musimbi R. A. Kanyoro's book* The Will to Arise: Woman, Tradition and the Church in Africa *(Maryknoll, NY: Orbis Books, 1992, pp. 183-94). The image of Christ presented by missionaries is full of ambivalence because Christ is experienced both as conqueror and liberator. She contrasts these images with alternative ones in contemporary African Christianity, where Christ is presented as personal friend and savior, as an embodiment of the Spirit, and as an iconoclastic prophet, a "Black Messiah." What implications these images have for African women's search for liberation is a question that Christian women in Africa need to address.*

## 27   TERESA M. HINGA

# Jesus Christ and the Liberation of Women in Africa

In the emergent and emerging theologies of liberation, both in the West but particularly in the Third World, the question of Christology has gained significant proportions. Theologians are trying to analyze and articulate the implications of Christianity and belief in Christ for their particular and often quite personal situations. A central question has been: Who is Christ? And what does belief in him mean, particularly for those who find themselves caught up in conditions of oppression?

This essay atttempts a reflection, however preliminary, on the implications of belief in Christ in the context of African women's search for liberation. It seeks to point out the ambivalence apparent in prevailing Christologies, and the need for the evolution of an African feminist Christology—or, at least, the need to create pointers in the right direction.

In recognition of the fact that feminism in Africa is a relatively novel extension of feminism in the West, and also of the fact that Western feminist theologians have reflected to a considerable depth, though without seeming to reach an unequivocal consensus, on the relationship between Christology and women, it is useful to reflect on what kind of ideas they have come up with so far.

A broad sweep of the Western feminist theologians' literature on the issue of Christology reveals that there are at least two perspectives. On the one hand, there is what may be referred to as the radical feminist view, which is probably best epitomized in the works of Mary Daly. On the whole, this view holds that cultural and social institutions, including religion, are so irredeemably warped by patriarchy that they can hardly be considered as allies of women as they try to liberate themselves. On the contrary, patriarchal culture and other social institutions help to engender their oppression and subjugation. This goes both for religion and received theology articulated largely by people who are perceived to be sexist and "misogynist" in their approach.

On the less extreme side of Western feminist theological discourse lie the thoughts of those who, for want of better terminology, I would call "reformist." These represent the view that social institutions are not distorted beyond repair. It is felt that aspects of culture and religion are salvageable, and that theology can help women in their struggle for emancipation and justice. In this category fall feminist theologians like Rosemary Ruether, Elisabeth Moltmann, Phyllis Trible, and Elisabeth Schüssler Fiorenza, among others.

## Christology and African women: the ambivalence of the encounter

In general, the above two perspectives reflect Western women's views concerning Jesus Christ and their specific context of a search for emancipation. At best, they reveal a certain ambivalence in their encounter with Christ. To what extent could these views be said to be universal? Could the same be said of the encounter between Christ and African women?

To be able to answer these questions, it is important to take into account the realization among contemporary theologians that Christ encounters people in various contexts. He has also been presented and appropriated in a variety of images or "faces" as Bonino prefers to call them. It would seem that in Africa, also, more than one image of Christ has been presented to and appropriated by Africans, including women, with, as I shall endeavor to show, mixed results.

Going back to history, we recall that during the period of colonial and imperial expansionism, the prevailing image of Christ was that of Christ the conqueror. Jesus was the warrior King, in whose name and banner (the cross) new territories, both physical and spiritual, would be fought for, annexed, and subjugated. An imperial Christianity thus had an imperial Christ to match. The Christ of the missionaries was a conquering Christ. Conversely, winning Africa for Christ was a major motivating factor in missionary zeal. Africa was the booty to be looted for Christ. What were the implications of this perception of Christ for the Africans?

The conquest of Africa often implied an erasing of most of what Africans held dear. The missionaries, in the name of Christ, sought to create a spiritual and cultural *tabula rasa* upon which they could inscribe a new culture, a new spirituality. This attempt at "erasing" was not all that successful, and, instead of creating a clean slate, the missionaries more often than not managed to create an identity crisis in the African minds—a sense of gross alienation. This is the kind of alienation and confusion that is lamented, for example, in Ngugi wa Thiongo's *The River Between*, or Chinua Achebe's *Things Fall Apart*.[1]

The cultural and spiritual imperialism[2] of the missionary endeavor has had some dire consequences. In dealing with some of what they deemed to be obstacles in their battle for Africa on behalf of Christ, in their zeal the missionaries often did not pause to reflect adequately on the consequences for the persons they sought to convert. Many examples can be given here, but I will highlight only two.

In treating the issue of polygamy, for example, the missionaries acted in a manner that was largely detrimental to the welfare of the women concerned.[3] Often, the polygamist would be asked to abandon all but one of his wives as a condition for baptism. The policy of "disciplining" polygamists in this way undoubtedly brought untold pain to women and children thus discarded.

Another example that I give, because it comes from a culture I know well, is the issue of female circumcision encountered by missionaries in Kenya. Again, in their unilateral decision to stamp out what they considered to be a barbaric African custom, they ended up causing the women involved to suffer tremendously. Many a Protestant father was forced to sign, on pain of excommunication, that they would not circumcise their daughters. Meanwhile, their daughters continued to be exposed to a barrage of derision and ridicule for failing to undergo the rite that culturally defined them as women.[4] Many uncircumcised Protestant girls could not withstand the psychological torture, abuse, and social ostracization that was poured upon them, and they were secretly circumcised anyway.

No doubt, however, many missionaries would not have agreed with the above interpretation of their actions. This is because at the overt and conscious level, they expressed the desire to liberate the Africans from what they perceived to be the clutches of the devil. They were ostensibly motivated by the zeal to save Africa from the evils of slave trade, and to redeem her people from the state of savagery and apparent godlessness. They thought that by so doing, they would be implementing the gospel of Christ the liberator—for they would be "proclaiming liberty to captives" and opening the prison for them that are bound.[5]

Thus missionaries with a lot of commendable zeal were in the forefront, for example, of the movement for the abolition of the slave trade, the freeing of captured slaves, and their rehabilitation.[6]

When the missionaries ventured into the African interior, they established mission stations that often functioned as centers of refuge or, in the view of the missionaries, "centers of Christianity and civilization." It is illuminating in this context to note that at least initially, the people who were attracted to the mission were the socially disadvantaged. Thus the White Fathers, for example, established their missions as orphanages, in which ransomed slave children could be taught self-reliance and "be brought up in the faith, away from the dangers of heathen environment."[7] In the same vein, another author observes that the people who were often attracted to the mission stations in Kikuyuland were from poor families. These people saw the mission community as a possible avenue for social and economic mobility and, for a time, sending children to school was an admission of poverty![8]

Moreover, the missionaries used education as a strategy for proselytization. This was welcomed by Africans as a means of social mobility, especially when education came to be correlated with a high economic status in the new secular sector.[9]

It was probably the perception of the emancipatory impulses within missionary Christianity, at this point, that led to the positive response given to Christianity by many Africans. We read in history books of mass conversions, and of the spectacular phenomenon in Uganda where within seven years of missionary work, there were African Christians ready to die for their new found faith.[10]

It is apparent that women also perceived these emancipatory impulses of the new religion and responded accordingly. Among the "refugees" who took shelter in mission stations were women, some of whom were trying to break away from unsatisfactory marriages or harsh parental control. Thus it has been noted that a major component of the adherents to the AIM mission among the Kamba of Kenya were girls who revolted against parental control and fled to the missions.

It could be said, then, that these two images of Christ, that of Christ the conqueror who seemed to legitimize the subjugation of whole races, and Christ the liberator, glimpses of whom could sometimes be seen in some of the charity work that missionaries were doing for Africans, found expression in missionary praxis. The Christ of the missionary enterprise was, therefore, an ambivalent one. His encounter with Africans, including women, had ambiguous results, an ambiguity that many an African writer has not failed to notice and to highlight.

## Some alternative images of Christ in Africa
## and their implications for women

While the above is a description of the Christology that found expression in missionary praxis, it cannot be said to be coterminous with Christ as expressed through missionary teaching. In their presentation of Christian doctrine, for example, the missionaries often made reference to the Bible as the authoritative source of the doctrine.

Consequently, the Africans gained access to the various "images" of Christ enshrined in the New Testament. Through the Bible, Africans caught glimpses of who Christ was, and what loyalty to him implied for his followers. They appropriated one or several of these images of Christ and made them their own, despite the distortions apparent in missionary praxis. By way of illustration and conclusion, I will discuss here three quite "common" perceptions of Christ as understood by Africans, and their implications for women.

Firstly, there is the very popular conception of Jesus Christ as the personal savior and personal friend of those who believe in him. Quite contrary to the view that Christ demands their subjugation—whether politically, socially, or culturally—many Africans have come to perceive that Jesus desires to accept them as they are, and to meet their needs at a very personal level. They have come to accept Jesus as the friend of the lonely and healer of those who are sick, whether spiritually or physically.

To some cynics, the view that Jesus is a personal friend, savior, or healer, smacks of an unwarranted "privatization" of the person of Jesus to fit a highly subjective context. To others, a confession of Christ as "personal" savior is an indication of Pharisaism and gross pretentiousness on the side of those who make such claims. However, I would suggest that, while not ruling out the possibility of some Pharisaism, the image of Jesus as a personal friend has been one of the most popular among women, precisely because they need such a personal friend most. (Thus, the image of Christ who helps them to bear their griefs, loneliness, and suffering is a welcome one indeed.)

Secondly, another popular image of Christ is that which seems to blend Christology with pneumatology. Jesus is seen as the embodiment of the Spirit, the power of God, and the dispenser of the same to those who follow him. This image of Christ is particularly popular in the so-called independent churches. In our search for a feminist Christology, it may be pertinent to note that, by and large, the patrons of these movements are women, among other marginalized peoples. It is also noteworthy that, in these movements, where the power of the Spirit (of Christ) is accentuated, women are peculiarly articulate and much less inhibited and muted than in established churches. In this "pneumatic Christology," then, Christ becomes the voice of the voiceless, the power of the powerless. Women, as victims of oppression and muteness in society, would no doubt find this image of Christ useful in their quest.

A third face of Christ, also derived from the New Testament, is the conception of Christ as an iconoclastic prophet. Jesus stands out in Scripture as a critic of the status quo, particularly when it engenders social injustices and marginalization of some in society. This is the kind of Christ whose "function" of "iconoclasm" is thought by many participants in the African independent churches to be "incarnated" in their founder members whom they sometimes hail as "Black Messiahs." These prophetic leaders in Africa have emerged in continuity with the prophetic role of Christ as the champion of the cause of the voiceless, and the vindicator of the marginalized in society.

In conclusion, I would suggest that in the African women's quest for a relevant Christology, aspects of the above three images of Christ would form some of the defining characteristics of the Christ whom women confess.[11] For Christ to become meaningful in the context of women's search for emancipation, he would need to be a concrete and personal figure who engenders hope in the oppressed by taking their (women's) side, to give them confidence and courage to persevere.

Secondly, Christ would also need to be on the side of the powerless by giving them power and a voice to speak for themselves.[12]

Thirdly, the Christ whom women look for is one who is actively concerned with the lot of victims of social injustice and the dismantling of unjust social structures. Christ would, therefore, be expected to be on the side of women as they fight for the dismantling of sexism in society, a sexism that has oppressed them through the ages.

It goes without saying that, along with formulating a relevant Christology, women would also need to be on the alert, and to be critical of any "versions" of Christology that would be inimical to their cause. They would have to reject, like others before them, any Christology that smacks of sexism, or that functions to entrench lopsided gender relations. Only in so doing would African women be able confidently to confess Christ as their liberator, as a partisan in their search for emancipation.

❖   ❖   ❖

□ *Another discussion of African Christology is found in Elizabeth Amoah's and Mercy Amba Oduyoye's "The Christ for African Women," in Virginia Fabella and Mercy Amba Oduyoye, eds.,* With Passion and Compassion: Third World Women Doing Theology *(Maryknoll, NY: Orbis Books, 1988, pp. 35-46), where the authors contrast what African men and women say about Christ. They also consider what kind of Christ can be a Christ for African women—a Christ whom they can worship, honor, and depend upon, but also a Christ who liberates and is the friend, teacher, and true "Child of Women" because in Christ "the fullness of all that we know of perfect womanhood is revealed." The authors come to the conclusion that an "African woman perceives and accepts Christ as a woman and as an African" (p. 44). The same volume includes a chapter on "The Christ-Event from the Viewpoint of African Women" (pp. 22-34) by two authors from the Cameroon (Thérèse Souga and Louise Tappa) who present a Catholic and a Protestant perspective on Christology.*

*Also in the same book, Virginia Fabella from the Philippines reflects on "A Common Methodology for Diverse Christologies" (pp. 108-21), where she highlights common themes and differences among Asian women's approaches to Jesus Christ. She emphasizes that the Asian focus is not so much on "who" Jesus is, but "where" and "what" Jesus Christ is for Asian women. Christological controversies are of less interest than the emphasis on Jesus as a truly liberating figure for both man and woman. Jesus' maleness is accidental to the liberation process and does not disturb women struggling toward full humanity for all.*

*Another model for women is Mary, seen as a fully liberated human being whose acts of courage are celebrated in her song of praise, the Magnificat (see chapter 19 in this Reader for reflections on Mary and the Magnificat).*

*Chung Hyun Kyung, in her book* Struggle to be the Sun Again, *devotes a whole chapter to the question "Who is Mary for Today's Asian Woman?" (pp. 74-84). Mary is both a model for full womanhood and of the fully liberated human being. As a virgin, she is a self-defining woman; as mother, she is giver of life to God and new humanity; as sister, she is a woman in solidarity with other women and with the oppressed. But Mary is also a model of true discipleship and co-redeemer for human salvation.*

*For a Filipino approach to Mary, see the reflections by Sr. Hilda Buhay, "Who is Mary?", in Sr. Mary John Mananzan, ed.,* Women and Religion *(Manila: Institute of Women's Studies, St. Scholastica's College, 1992, pp. 55-9).*

*Some of these new approaches to Mary are incorporated in a joint ecumenical paper on Mariology that Asian Christian women produced at a conference in Singapore in 1987. It is reproduced in chapter 28 from* In God's Image *(December 1988, pp. 6-8), but it is also found in* Asian Women Doing Theology: Report from the Singapore Conference, November 20-29, 1987 *(Hong Kong: Asian Women's Resource Center for Culture and Theology, 1989). This conference brought together thirty-two women from sixteen countries in Asia and the Pacific region — that is to say, Australia and Aotearoa, which is the Maori name for New Zealand. A theological debate is taking place there between* Pakeha *women, the descendants of white European settlers, and* Maori *women; this is reflected in some documents of the Singapore report. Half of its material is devoted to the contextualization of Asian women's theology within a socio-political and cultural situation of oppression; the other half contains papers on Jesus, the Holy Spirit, the Church, and on spirituality and worship. (This report can be obtained from the Asian Women's Resource Center for Culture and Theology, now at 35 ChungChongno 2-Ga, Sodaemun-Ku, ChungChongno P. O. Box 16, Seoul, 120-650, Korea.)*

❖    ❖    ❖

# Summary Statement on Feminist Mariology

The task of feminist Mariology is twofold:

(1) We must name, and liberate ourselves from, the destructive effects of 2,000 years of male interpretation of Mary.

(2) We must return to the Scriptures as women within our own cultural contexts, to rediscover the Mary who is liberated and liberator.

The Magnificat emerges as the most powerful focus of our reflection on Mary. Mary announces the reversal of the present order. We must take this challenge seriously. The first reversal must be to rescue Mariology from the control of Catholic male celibates, and hear the voices of women, both Protestant and Catholic, as we observe the mother of Jesus. Mary is also the mother of *all* and *all* Christian traditions, so it is the combined task of women of all traditions to redefine her. In both Catholic and Protestant traditions, women have been, and are still, oppressed. In the Catholic Church, Mary's exaltation has been used to reinforce women's oppression, while in the Protestant Churches the rejection of Mary has oppressed women. It is, therefore, urgent that all Christian women take up the task.

The beginning of Mary's story in the Gospels is the announcement that she will be the mother of the Messiah. It is on this that the doctrine of the virgin birth rests. This doctrine and its interpretation emerged from male fear of female sexuality, and have had destructive effects on women. However, we should understand that the real meaning of the virgin birth is that the human male is excluded from this event. The end of patriarchy is announced. There is an even clearer message for

271

the Churches when we remember that Mary's response to the angel's message reverses the disbelief of the priest, Zechariah, in the announcement story which balances this one (Luke 1).

The glorification of a narrowed understanding of virginity in the Catholic tradition is reinforced by the concept of Mary's perpetual virginity. No other woman can be both virgin and mother simultaneously — so all women are offered an impossible model, and thus convinced of our lack of worth. The idea of Mary's perpetual virginity has also given us Mary, Joseph and Jesus as the example of the "ideal family." In this family, the two adults have no sexual relationship, and there is only one child, who is not the son of Mary's husband. It is not surprising then that Catholics have inherited a marked sexual neurosis.

Mary's faith, shown in the annunciation story, has been used to promote female obedience to a male God, a male priesthood, and all men, as God's representatives. We see, instead, that she who responds, "Thy will be done," is the mother who teaches her son the same response. These are also his words in the garden of Gethsemane. We learn from this that Mary's servanthood is the same as the servanthood of Jesus.

The nature of the servanthood is spelled out in Mary's next words, as Luke records them — the words of the Magnificat. This young woman, who is to be the mother of the Messiah, claims the right to announce what *kind* of Messiah her son will be. It is *Mary* who will describe Jesus, not Jesus, or a male Church, who will describe Mary. This young woman, who belongs to an oppressed people, sings of revolution in the words of Hannah, another woman of Israel. Her words are addressed to an older woman, Elizabeth, who, like Hannah, has become pregnant after years of infertility. This song, the Magnificat, announces a complete change in the present, patriarchal order. This means moral, social, political, economic, and cultural reversals. The woman who sings this song is a liberated woman, standing in the line of the strong women of Israel.

We must also remember that the song is Mary's response to Elizabeth's greeting. There is great encouragement for women in the support and solidarity that women give to one another — especially that given by older women to younger women.

With the singer of the Magnificat as his mother, it should not surprise us that Jesus' first words in Luke's account of his public ministry are also a mandate for radical change. Predictably, however, the Church has forgotten that Mary is the first to announce this change. Understanding this is basic to our response to everything else about Mary. She is the woman who survives and returns from exile. She is the one who pushes her son into responding to the needs of hospitality at Cana. She is present in support of Jesus' ministry, which she inspires and initiates, from its beginning to its end. Jesus' words in Luke 11.27-8, "Rather, happy are they who hear the word of God and obey it," therefore mean not that Jesus is rejecting the claims of his mother and brothers, but that he is acknowledging that it was from his mother, in his family, that he himself learned to hear and obey the word of God.

The Church's tradition has excluded old women and widows from honor in what it has said about Mary. She is venerated as virgin and mother, as lady and queen. However, the young woman who sings of revolution *does* age. The woman who stands, with other women, at the foot of the cross, and who is present with the community at Pentecost, is an older woman, a woman of wisdom and strength, who suffers, with God, the loss of her son—the consequence of commitment to live for change. It is she who, with the Spirit, gave birth to the Messiah, who makes it possible for the Spirit to give birth to the Church. So, in the home of Mary, mother of John Mark, Mary becomes the mother of the new community.

It is time for us to claim and celebrate the presence of the Spirit in old women. We need them. At the same time we claim a place for Mary in a new kind of church structure—a place that really reflects a community based not on hierarchical domination, but on just relationships.

## Mary as one of the bases of feminist theology

Each of us, within our own culture, has found different strengths in the process of reclaiming and redefining Mary. We can look at Mary the mother and see her womb as the place of the action of the Holy Spirit—a place of struggle and suffering which brings new life. The struggle of mothers in the Asia/Pacific context, who struggle with and for their children, to give birth to a new and just reality. Mary is the mother of suffering, of those who suffer.

If we recognize that Mary is a woman of the poor, we must also challenge the lie that depicts her as jeweled and elaborately dressed. Because the good news of the Magnificat is bad news for the rich, we reject Mary's hijacking by a wealthy Church — for the consolation of the rich. This simply reinforces the oppression of the poor. If we understand the virgin birth as the beginning of a new order, in which patriarchy can no longer be the basis of human life, we must hear the angel's greeting, "Hail, full of grace," as addressed to all of us. We too must participate in changing oppressive relationships and cultural symbols — overcoming patterns of domination and subordination between north and south, rich and poor, male and female, black and white.

The Magnificat is the rallying point for ecumenism, as Christians join together working to liberate the poor and all victims of injustice. It is the liberation song of women, who are, with their children, the poorest of the poor. However, in the context of the indigenous struggles of Aotearoa* and Australia, it is necessary for women of the dominant group to remember that while we are oppressed by patriarchy, we also benefit from institutionalized racism, so our sisterhood is not one of equality. So while we too sing the Magnificat in our countries, we must learn the response of relinquishing power as indigenous women take control of their own lives.

We acknowledge that in Asia and the Pacific the need for economic and political liberation is often used to trivialize women's struggle. However, the struggle of indigenous women is a fight for a people's survival. If feminist theology is concerned only with sexism, and not with the liberation of the whole human race, it too is oppressive. We see feminist Mariology as a liberation theology that gives hope of humanization to all the world.

Our task now is to describe Mary as Asian/Pacific women. This will mean addressing Christology, ecclesiology, sacramental theology, worship, language, music, and symbols from the perspective of suffering women. Our liberation starts within each of us. Let us begin.

* The Maori name for New Zealand.

□ *Following this statement on feminist Mariology from the Singapore conference are some reflections on Mary from a Latin American perspective. They consist of two extracts from Ivone Gebara's and María Clara Bingemer's book* Mary, Mother of God, Mother of the Poor *(Maryknoll, NY: Orbis Books, 1989, pp. 28–31, 91–3). The two authors set their reflections on Mary within the larger context of liberation theology. After outlining a new anthropological perspective (which includes feminism together with several other dimensions) and a new hermeneutics for Marian theology, they examine Mary in the New Testament and discuss the new meaning of Marian dogmas arising from the poor and the spirit of our age. This is followed by traditions of devotion to Mary in Latin America, concluding with those in contemporary base Christian communities and with a discussion of the Magnificat as "Song of Mary, Song of the People."*

*In chapter 29 Ivone Gebara and María Clara Bingemer discuss personal factors conditioning their interpretation of Mary, and then present some assumptions on which their rereading of Marian dogmas is based.*

# 29  IVONE GEBARA AND MARÍA CLARA BINGEMER

# Mary—Mother of God, Mother of the Poor

The written text should always generate within us a suspicion—or better, questions—about what has not been written, and what has been lost or omitted by choice. A written text is always selective. The author or authors choose some events they believe to be important, and they interpret them, while leaving aside others that from another perspective might be regarded as the most important. That being the case, the full history of the people of the Bible is much more than what has been written. For instance, St. John ends his Gospel by saying of Jesus, "There are still many other things that Jesus did, yet if they were written about in detail, I doubt there would be room enough in the entire world to hold the books to record them" (John 21.25).

The purpose of all we have been saying is related to the texts that speak about Mary. As we know, there are very few of them in the New Testament tradition, but on the basis of these few texts and various traditions that have arisen in the midst of the people, each period in history seems to build an image of Mary and her activity in history both past and present. So we cannot say that the only truth about the life of Mary is in the little bit that the New Testament texts tell us. The fact that something is not written does not mean that it did not happen.

The announcing of the Good News of the Kingdom, if it *is* actually good news for humankind, must of necessity involve the participation of men and women—even if the texts written by men and from a patriarchal viewpoint leave out the active participation of women and, in our specific case, that of Mary. That is the reason why we must take up a critical stance toward texts, interpretations, and data, a stance that can open space for us to reconstruct and recover the history of the past, and thereby grasp the revelation of the God of life in the lives of women as well.

Besides these preliminary observations, which we regard as essential clarifications, there are today, as in the past, many aspects of a personal nature that leave their imprint on our interpretation of the texts and our stance toward theological reflection. We recall simply a few that we regard as especially important for this Mariological endeavor and that are connected with the lives of the authors of this essay. That is what the next section is about.

## Personal factors conditioning a hermeneutic

We are both Latin American women striving to reflect on Mary and attempting an essay in Marian theology: women living on a continent marked by oppression, marked by the suffering and daily death of thousands of people, especially children, a continent marked by the scourge of hunger and by violence expressed in various ways; two women with different stories who, despite the privileges that come from being intellectuals, feel and suffer with the oppressed women of the Third World and with them seek to say a word about liberation. The word we have to say, the word that engages us in this struggle, is a theological word. It is with profound humility and even with a certain trepidation that we dare to pronounce a theological word, especially because of the marvelous mystery enclosed in it. The theological word is not "scientific" in the ordinary sense of the term and is not subject to rigid laws. The theological word is a vital word, referring to the deep meaning of our activities, of our life and our death. It is connected to the life and death of whole peoples, of the great human masses and, in our case, to the great masses of Latin America, the overwhelming majority of whom are poor, enjoy no adequate quality of life, and lack respect, bread, love, and *justice*.

Our starting point for reading the reality in which we live and hence for reading sacred Scripture, the Christian tradition and the theology produced in the Christian West, is a stance from which we reject the oppression produced by the capitalist system under which the bulk of the Latin American population lives. That stance conditions our "doing theology," and our reading of the Bible, turning it into a reading aimed at establishing justice on our continent and in our world. It is a committed reading, on the side of the poor and oppressed.

We have become more and more aware of the suffering and struggle of the women of our continent, especially of the poorest, those who are ranked third or fourth in the cruel categorization of the class system in which we live. Not all of them are saints; they are not pure, but they are people who beget and sustain life in the midst of the trash produced by what is supposed to be "civilization." We have paid attention to their problems, especially to their religious experience and the questions they raise. We have paid attention to the insights that emerge from their reflection on life and on God. All this has led us to take on as our mission the theological task of explaining and developing the faith, but doing so from a woman's slant. Hence our reading of the Bible is tinted with our subjective/objective problems and the problems of the poor women with whom we have received the grace of sharing experience and the grace of getting to know them. Many things we have seen in the Bible, in the life of Mary, in the life of the people symbolized by Mary, take their inspiration from this common ground of the life of women of Latin America and from the lives of all the oppressed of our continent.

The aim of our biblical and theological reading is to open up space in society and in the churches so that the various religious experiences of women can be expressed from what they actually experience and intuit. Our intention in this reading is not necessarily to put women in a privileged position, but we do always bring out the way religious reality is experienced by women, since it is two women who are doing the thinking—with our differing life experiences, our different "states of life" (one lay, the other religious), and therefore with our different theological and literary styles.

Having established these initial points about our hermeneutics, we now begin to go through the New Testament in order to rediscover the countenance of Mary speaking to us and to our age. For our hermeneutics is dialogical, entering into conversation with the texts, a conversation charged with life and seeking paths for this life, in which men and women alike are called to proclaim the Good News of God's Kingdom.

In this sense, the aim of our hermeneutics is not simply to understand the texts of the past and the story they tell as an example; our aim is also to understand and reactivate the past for the sake of today's liberation struggles. The Spirit of God is in us, and the Spirit's creativity, liberty, justice, and love are forever.

☐ *After explaining their hermeneutics for a Marian theology, the two authors examine in detail the New Testament facts on Mary, and then go on to discuss some assumptions for re-reading Marian dogmas.*

## Some assumptions for rereading

First, an *anthropological assumption.* We are going to try to read these dogmas in fidelity to the anthropology guiding this outline of Marian theology. This anthropology seeks to take into account the recent progress of human and social sciences, which are attempting to overcome the anthropological vices that have most characterized and distorted the West. Among these we have singled out male-centrism, dualism, idealism, and one-dimensionalism, and we are making every effort to do our Marian theology, with its rereading of dogmas, on the basis of an anthropology that is human-centered, unifying, realist, and pluri-dimensional. We are aware of the difficulty inherent in such an effort, since many of these dogmas were proclaimed during periods of history that had other anthropological visions. Nevertheless, we regard as worthwhile the theological effort to go beyond debilitated and out-of-date formulations and expressions in order to rescue the very heart of the mystery that continues to make dogma valid within the Church.

Second, the *properly theological assumption.* Since we began our theological effort by making the idea of the Kingdom of God the unifying factor of Christian theology in its various aspects, and examined our biblical texts from that standpoint, we intend to remain faithful to that central assumption now with regard to tradition and dogma. In rereading the Marian dogmas that the Church has proclaimed throughout so many centuries of Christianity, it will be our ongoing challenge to recognize the potential of these dogmas for announcing the coming of the Kingdom of God; we shall also seek to discern the signs contained in those dogmas that can help set the Kingdom in motion.

Third, the *feminist assumption.* Talking about Mary means talking about woman—specifically a woman who was born and lived in Palestine 2,000 years ago. Christian faith venerates the mystery of *this* particular woman and theology reflects on that mystery. Devotion to the one whom Christian faith calls "Our Lady" basically resides and is expressed in the theological facts proclaimed by Marian dogmas: Mary was Mother of God, virgin, immaculate, and was assumed into heaven. The people of God preserves the memory of these facts in its devotion. Marian theology strives to reflect on the common thread running through and connecting these facts and giving them their substance. The mystery of Mary leads back to the greater mystery, the mystery of God, and it opens a unique and original perspective for viewing this mystery: the feminist perspective. The tradition of faith has concentrated on the feminine in Mary, the Mother of Jesus. It has viewed all women's potentialities as realized in her. She is Our Lady because she is virgin, mother, wife, companion, widow, queen, wisdom, tabernacle of God, and so forth.[1] Moreover, the very fact that it is two women who are here pondering this mystery, trying to develop it, opens up space and possibilities in this reflection, not for the traditional perspective already mentioned, but for the kind we have already advocated in an earlier chapter. To recognize in Marian dogmas the traces of the feminine as revealed by God, the theological face of the feminine element of God, God's face as seen from a feminist perspective, is something that we will be constantly striving to keep in mind here.[2]

Finally, the *pastoral assumption*. At first glance, Marian dogmas look like statements characterized by theological inflation and doxological enthusiasm. In them the Marian mystery contemplated in the light of God's plan and paschal glory is exalted. Nevertheless, we cannot forget that this mystery is just as much a mystery of poverty and anonymity. The exaltation that understandably comes out in dogma cannot slide toward the mythological and hide what is essential in God's salvation, that is, making God's glory shine on what is regarded as insignificant, degrading, or marginal.[3] Marian dogmas, which exalt Mary, immaculately conceived, assumed into heaven, virgin and mother, must reflect a knowledge that in exalting her they exalt precisely her poverty, her dispossession, and her simplicity. This is the only key for understanding the mystery of God's incarnation in human history, of which Jesus and Mary are the protagonists. This is, moreover, the only key for understanding the mystery of the Church as a community of salvation, holy and sinful, striving amid the most diverse kinds of limitations and problems to be a sign of the Kingdom in the midst of the world. Further, this is the only condition that will enable the Church, which sees the symbol or figure of itself in Mary, to be in Latin America today the Church of the poor, those whom Mary declared liberated, fed, and exalted in the song of the Magnificat.

❖    ❖    ❖

## Feminist Theology

☐ *In doing theology, Third World women wrestle with questions about God, Christology, Mariology, and those of spirituality. Another vital topic concerns the role of community, of the Church, and especially, of women's participation in the life of the Church.*

*Betty Govinden has represented the Church of the Province of Southern Africa at many national and international meetings. Her reflections on women in the Church in chapter 30· are closely linked to the experience of apartheid, yet they also explore wider concerns affecting women's liberation everywhere. Doing theology in a communal context, whether in Southern Africa or in other parts of the world, and seeking a renewed humanity in community—a truly united family of God—leads once again to the heart of the Christian story, to crucifixion and resurrection. This story can help women and men to find wholeness by surmounting the divisions created by the diversity of gender, race, culture, language, and tradition.*

*The struggle against apartheid in society and Church raises for the South African writer deep spiritual questions about our journey to and silence before God. It thus provides an appropriate linking chapter to Part Five of this Reader that deals with "A Newly Emerging Spirituality." Betty Govinden's chapter, reproduced here in abbreviated form, is found in full in Denise Ackermann, Jonathan A. Draper, and Emma Mashinini, eds.,* Women Hold Up Half the Sky, *Pietermaritzburg: Cluster Publications, 1991, pp. 274-97.*

❖    ❖    ❖

# No Time for Silence: Women, Church, and Liberation in Southern Africa

## Introduction

Over the years I have come to accept that the Church cannot change its traditions, structures, and theology overnight; I have grown to realize that there is much wisdom in the Anglican processes of "gradualism," "restraint," and "reception," the spirit of which goes against the grain of manipulation, coercion, and unholy haste.

Yet these processes do not take place automatically and naturally: there must, I believe, be responsible openness, a willingness to probe questions systematically and consistently, to wrestle with them, under the guidance of the Holy Spirit, in order to discern new understandings. It saddens me when the virtues of "the stature of waiting" are cited in a formulaic way as a solution to controversy and deadlock, particularly when the waiting has not been active, interactive, and creative. I have been greatly encouraged by church leaders who have felt the pain and anguish of women's exclusion in different ways in the life of the Church. Others have shown me that perspectives on women in the Church cannot be approached in a one-dimensional or simplistic way. As I began to formulate my own thinking on the subject, and began to take a position in what is, undoubtedly, controversial terrain, I have reserved a deep respect for those whose views have differed from mine, especially where these views have been held, after intense searching, on conscientious grounds. At the same time I have been saddened by the ill-conceived and uncritical opinions that have been expressed by persons, often in positions of influence and authority, on aspects of women's ministry in the Church. It has also been disappointing when concerns of women are totally ignored; when a noncommittal silence is maintained; or when there is a tendency to make those who do speak up appear ill-informed, short-sighted, or anarchic. In this essay I should like to consider a few links between women, the Church, and liberation, in order to prompt further discussion in the churches' quest "towards a united Christian witness in a changing South Africa."

## A global movement

> ... There is a cry everywhere, everywhere in the world, a woman's cry is being uttered. The cry may be different, but there is still a certain unity (*African Literature Today* 15).

These words are from Mariama Bâ, a writer in West Africa.

One of the most important features of the closing years of the twentieth century is the increased focus worldwide on the role of women in all spheres of society. From different contexts women are rising up, to speak of their experiences and tell their stories. After years of invisibility and silence, women are gaining confidence and discovering their voices. Despite their diverse experiences, women across the world are becoming increasingly aware of discrimination and oppression in all forms and guises.

Such feminist thinking, in fact, is being articulated in various kinds of contexts and situations. From the educated, middle-class to the homeless, poor, and unemployed, women are "making statements," through their words, or their very lives. Oppression and alienation take various forms, and are mainly related to physical and material conditions of living, but may also include the intellectual, spiritual, cultural, or social. Some have the psychological space, training, and facility in theory and language to reflect on their experiences, while others may be involved in practical action. Much can be gained by an openness to feminist issues, whether these are emerging from academic disciplines such as sociology, history, psychology, religion, and literature—to name a few—or from experience in day-to-day situations. An important bridge that must certainly be strengthened is the one between academic and activist sectors, although the division between the two is not always mutually exclusive. If there is to be any real sharing of resources and mutual interdependence, all the diverse and even contradictory experiences that women are exposed to should be reflected upon and critically considered.

While there are differences in social and economic conditions that make many reject the notion of universal femininity, there is also much that unites women everywhere. The starting points may be different and the discussions may take divergent routes, but there is much traversing of common ground. Such dialogue does help to define positions, clarify terminology, and point to possibilities for the future. The other point that needs to be stressed is that feminist studies are evolving, and are not unimpeachable. They should not be seen as a complete and discrete corpus of thinking, nor as blueprinted guidelines for action. There are many differences in perception and formulation, as well as of strategy. The wide diversity is often forgotten, as may be gauged from the kind of flippant and stereotyped criticisms that are usually made of feminism.

It is important to note that all spheres of experience and study are coming under close scrutiny in the modern secular context. Religion is being challenged on many fronts, and must engage in rigorous introspection in order to give a credible witness of the very "faith confessed." I believe that a critical analysis of *all religions* in relation to the attitudes to women is necessary. There is need to explore and expose attitudes to women that are discriminatory, especially when those attitudes are undergirded by religious beliefs and time-honored "tradition," interlinked with cultural values. In South Africa it is imperative to explore women's issues from many vantage points, as part of our work to build a "new South Africa."

### Women under apartheid

Any movement, in secular or church contexts, concerned with revolutionary emancipation in South Africa must be committed to a complete change in society. Such transformation would include dismantling patriarchy in a deliberate and systematic way. All movements concerned with liberation are beginning to see that the national question in South Africa needs to be reformulated to ensure that the struggle becomes a gender-conscious one. The hope that gender discrimination will simply go away once forms of racial exploitation are removed is a delusory one. There must be systematic engagement with all laws, practices, and ideological apparatuses that uphold patriarchy. Apartheid has so affected our means of articulating perceptions of domination, subjugation, exploitation, and repression that we cannot see the way gender discrimination has been sedimented into the fabric of our society.

What is the nature of women's oppression in South Africa and how can the Church be more aware of its mission in this area of its life?

Amid the many scenarios of "opposition-politics" in this country, the Church has been in the forefront of criticism of apartheid; I have been personally "conscientized" by the Church's trenchant and consistent condemnation of racism. After many years of grappling with the nature of this destructive canker in the fabric of our society, the Church experienced a new freedom and strength when it named apartheid as heresy. I believe it came to this position through years of wrestling with the precise nature of the evil of apartheid.

While the Church continues to speak against apartheid fearlessly, and works for its uprooting and eradication, it needs to articulate more distinctly and unequivocally the particular injustices that women have experienced under the apartheid regime, and to become more critical of its own response to such oppression, and of the way it creates "the alternative community" for men and women.

Unraveling gender relations in our apartheid-ridden society is quite a complicated business. While there is great diversity and complexity of women's experience with respect to race and class, it is revealing to consider the plight of women in relation to apartheid and patriarchy. I believe that a Church Commission on Women and Gender in Southern Africa should be set up to study the various feminist and gender-sensitive issues that confront the Church in its engagement with the state, to explore the way in which colonialism, apartheid, capitalism, and reformist politics are all underlined by a patriarchal ideology.

Patriarchy is not peculiar to South Africa, but, colluding with apartheid, has deliberately undermined black women. While we have had much sound analysis of the oppressions of racism and the economy, sexism in our apartheid context has not been adequately addressed. What we need, as Mamphela Ramphele has suggested, is a thorough-going "integrated analysis of power relations."

Patriarchy is upheld by a network of laws, and public and private structures including the family, religious, and educational structures. Women in all South African communities have been either the victims of traditional patriarchal customs or of the legacy of colonialism and slavery. If we glanced only at the period of institutionalized racism, we will uncover many historical factors affecting the lives of the black working-class women, who make up the majority of women in South Africa.

In precolonial days, in spite of gendered relations in the traditional society, there was coherent communal and family life, and women, particularly the aged, enjoyed security. With the evolution of a capitalist economy from a feudal and rural one significant changes in gender relations in rural areas were experienced. As the African rural economy weakened, black men were forced to migrate to industrial areas; this coincided with the growth of the mining industry and its demand for cheap labor. As a result of the consequent influx control and pass laws, most women remained in the rural areas, where the stable indigenous societies began to dissolve.

The brunt of repressive laws aiming to control the African population was, in effect, borne by the women. Many were removed to poverty-stricken rural areas, and later, bantustans, and denied access to employment, housing, and other facilities in the urban areas. The universal phenomenon of the "feminization of poverty," resulting from industrialization and urbanization, had its own particular expression in Southern Africa.

A large number of women were and continue to be the sole supporters of their households. Nearly a third of all African households in the metropolitan areas, and nearly two-thirds in the bantustans, are headed by women. Women, confined to narrow and depleted worlds here, have been responsible for the maintenance of the household. They indirectly bolstered the capitalist industries by providing domestic support systems for their husbands. The (extended) family even in its threatened existence provided the only haven in a hostile world. It was therefore not a feature of "resistance politics" to turn inward and criticize patriarchal family relationships. The tentacles of apartheid have been long and surreptitious.

### Women fight back

Much of the resistance of women against apartheid has been subsumed within the broad national liberation struggle, with women developing into a major radicalizing force, growing in militancy both inside and outside the country. Black women, together with women from other "population groups," have devised survival strategies and organizational initiatives in response to apartheid's dismal conditions.

With wage employment of African women growing significantly since the early 1960s, the possibility of large-scale trade-union organization among them became brighter. The 1970s saw the decade of mass action against apartheid with black women being active in the politics of mass mobilization. Women were in the forefront of organized boycotts against rising prices in the urban townships in rent, electricity, transport, and consumer goods. Women have played key roles in community struggles against forced removals.

It is encouraging that the liberation movements are beginning to realize the important need to focus on women's liberation in a distinct way. All groupings are being urged to collect information specifically related to gender in order to formulate and implement detailed and specific policy. A statement recently issued by the National Executive Committee of the African National Congress acknowledges the need to address the emancipation of women in its own right within the ANC and society as a whole. Various papers presented at the Malibongwe Conference, Amsterdam, 1990, show evidence of critical introspection within the national liberation movement with regard to women's experience. The experiences of women in neighboring Southern African states who played active roles in national liberation wars have also influenced the view that a concerted effort must be made to guarantee women's liberation within the national initiative.

A positive move has been the work of the South African Council of Churches' Women's Desk in organizing a conference on women and the new constitution. This ecumenical venture was part of the *Decade of Churches in Solidarity with Women*, and considered women's oppression in South Africa in relation to a host of injustices and prejudices that women face in all walks of life. But how many churches have really taken "the Decade" seriously?

## The Church and women

The Church is a sign and hope of the "alternative society" in Southern Africa. When the world around has caused alienation and separation, the Church is encouraged to be a model of what society should be. What sort of affirming atmosphere do women encounter in the Church, when so much in the society denies them a sense of their intrinsic worth and dignity as persons? Is it right to believe that, unlike the "world," there are other types of criteria by which dignity and worth are measured in the Church? Is not a false dichotomy being created between the world and the Church?

When women, exposed to discrimination in different forms in the society at large, approach the Church, what do they see? The Church is male in structure, in all visible activities. In its deliberations on the life of the Church, and in decisionmaking — at regional councils, diocesan, episcopal, and provincial synods — there are more male representatives and delegates than women. This is a reflection of the fact that lay leadership, as well as the three levels of ordained ministry, are dominated by men.

Is the Church really in touch with women's deepest needs? Is it encouraging autonomy and a sense of dignity among women? Is it providing much-needed nurturance and affirmation?

Women, with the variety of experiences that they are exposed to, may be either aggressive or passive, traditional or modern, confident or bewildered, and the Church must provide a spiritual home for such a mix of persons. A deepening contemplative spirituality, in the quest for peace of mind and spirit and the quest for identity, is an important ministry that the Church can provide to women in Southern Africa. The longing that women have for homecoming, to their Holy Mother the Church, to a place where there is love and acceptance and growth into full humanity, should not go unheeded.

Another argument that is frequently used against developing the ministry of women in the Church is that it will divert attention from the struggle against apartheid. It is feared that addressing the question of women's ordination, for instance, may threaten the unity that the Churches enjoy in their solidarity against apartheid. There is fear of creating divisions in the liberation struggle; this has sometimes led to watering down women's specific concerns, or to a plea for the "priority" of the liberation struggle. The charge is made that the Church has to devote its energies to fighting apartheid; that the debate over women's ordination and other ministries is an entirely different issue, and far too complex and difficult, anyway, to handle in a short space of time. A priest once said to me that there are so many areas of concern in our society, that when people come to the Church seeking comfort and sustenance they are distressed to find that Church spending its time discussing the ordination of women.

The Church is guilty of double standards. In many ways, alongside its valiant fight against apartheid—in its statements, ministries, justice and reconciliation work, and solidarity campaigns—the Church has continued its normal "church" life, appointing bishops, priests, archdeacons, and canons. Many of those appointed to these church positions are chosen because of their ministry in our present political crises—the Church, in affirming them and their ministry, sends out an important signal to the Southern African world.

We try to redress the imbalances created by apartheid, for instance in the clergy appointments we make. As we proceed with all this we speak of the church family going about its normal activities and duties. Yet one of the fears expressed about permitting the ordination of women to the priesthood is that initially there will be mainly white women who may come forward. There are misgivings expressed about the possibility of white women priests being appointed in black congregations of men and women. At present we appoint white male priests to black congregations and black male priests to white congregations and consider this as an important move forward in bridging the racial divide. And the irony is that in most of our congregations, both black and white, the majority of parishioners are *women*.

Have we not, perhaps, restricted the movement of the holy "wind of thought," and assumed that the Holy Spirit can deal with just one situation at a time? Surely there is room in the heart of Christ for all the world's pain and suffering, for all its just causes and "priorities"? How often in the Church and in this land do we—women and men, young and old, black and white—build barriers by separating our hurts and pain into various categories and hierarchies, clinging to our own suffering, and setting ourselves apart from the pain of others.

The point that is often forgotten is that the ministry of women is not there for itself, but for the enhancement of the Church's mission to a broken and divided land. The view that feminism and feminist theology is a bourgeois, Western import in Africa, that it is out of tune with the needs and aspirations of African women, should be critically examined.

I believe that this criticism is another strategy that may be used to deflate women who are traversing strange and uncharted territory, such as feminist theology. The condemnatory and arrogant posture that may be adopted tends to belittle women, confused and perplexed as they are in the process of assimilating and acting on quite revolutionary thinking. It stifles the enthusiasm of white women, who are sensitive to the history of colonialist domination, and who do not want to seem to perpetuate such domination. White men and women in the Church in South Africa, because of the guilt over imperialism and colonialism, in society and Church, often overcompensate in conceding to "black perceptions," without realizing this attitude still suggests patronage.

Also, the "Western tag" confuses black women, who are wary of further cooption by anything "too Western." While such criticism could well turn out to be a necessary and well-meaning caution, the emotive nature of the subject could actually prevent further objective questioning. This ploy was used at a conference on women's ministry that was arranged in my diocese. There was also censure from some bishops from Africa when Mercy Oduyoye (of the WCC) gave her impressions of the ministry of women in Africa at the 1988 Lambeth Conference. The bishops charged that she was no longer "African" but "Western."

Feminism may indeed be seen as another colonial imposition and the danger of the specter of "Western feminism" remains real. There are aspects of Western theories that offer a monolithic image of women and define the middle-class First World woman's status and needs as universally female. This is patently inappropriate to Africa. We need a particular expression of our own ideas, and these should not be a mere modification of a Western model.

The need to be vigilant in this connection is important. Africa has been the ground of many liberal Western ideas—ideas that did not get to the crux of servitude and oppression. In South Africa, in particular, apartheid has made us suspicious of alignments around other causes. Amid the commonality there is also much diversity of women's experience in Southern Africa. The condition of being female may be a defining characteristic of any women's grouping, cutting across differences of class and race. Yet the painful separation created by apartheid is soon experienced. We begin to realize that we are sisters of two worlds, even in the same Church. The differences between white and black women are indeed entrenched by the divisive system of apartheid in its many manifestations.

A corrective approach in South Africa would thus involve a consciousness of gender-related issues, combined with that of race, class, culture, and politics—all within a critique of inhibiting structures within the Church. We face the challenge in the coming years of forging a South African feminist liberation theology, critically and firmly based within the experience of the history of black struggle in our situation, combining the insights of women in our different cultures and traditions, together with ongoing reflection on our own diverse experiences, in both Church and society, in order to create a viable, autonomous movement.

The argument that is often used in the Church is that "black culture" does not allow us to accelerate any movement for women to take on leadership roles. Yet can it not be argued that because of our particular mix of apartheid history, of oppression, and resistance, together with the impingement of modern, secular values—some of it undoubtedly Western in origin—in tension with inherited traditions of customs and beliefs, we are evolving a particular South African culture that makes it inevitable and imperative that we consider the women's question in Church and society in a deliberate way? This "culture" is by no means uniform and monolithic, but the gender question is common to all contexts, albeit with diverse manifestations.

A "*Kairos* Document" for women would draw on the diversity of women's experience in Southern Africa, with liberation, women, and the Church as its unifying theme. Many mistakes are bound to occur, as we push at the frontiers of our life here, but we must not be daunted by the task that lies ahead.

### Liberation, women, and the Church

Is it not time—the *Kairos*—to spell out the gospel, the real Good News, so long kept secret, to all women on earth?

Liberation theologies focus on the experience of oppression in relation to race, gender, and class. They constitute a radical reinterpretation of the Christian gospel, and underline their opposition to all forms of domination, based on prejudice and power. Liberation theologies emerge from material, concrete, social contexts. Liberation theology properly understood and implemented does not ignore feminism, nor does it isolate it, but it enables the integration of feminist concerns as part of the political and cultural struggle for liberation. The challenge is that women and men hear the gospel as existential truth—it speaks to day-to-day experience. This process has already begun, and needs to continue even more vigorously.

When confronted with feminist demands, many speak of "not going overboard," of "maintaining a balance," so that women's concerns do not become "a priority." But if we take seriously the "commitment to the epistemological privilege of the poor and oppressed," then there should be no question of including women's issues as well in an agenda that is confronting injustice in all its manifestations.

There are many in the Church who protest that they are not feminists. "We are sympathetic to women's needs," they will say, "but we are not feminists." This attitude is the result of stereotyping the contemporary women's movement as being new-fangled, subversive, and "worldly," and the tendency to despise anything that appears to emerge out of a secular humanism.

We have to accept that the impetus to criticize the Church may come from a secular context or from the very heart of the Christian gospel (the terms "secular" and "Church" are used in this essay in their traditional senses—I accept that these old distinctions between the two terms are limiting). We must resist the temptation to assume that God's revelation of justice and liberation only operates in a solely Christian milieu. Although the points of departure and the motivation may be different in secular and church situations, we have to find the points of intersection and interaction. We cannot circumscribe and confine the action of God. Such an attitude is the result of a rather narrow reading of the Christian faith, and of a facile and dangerous distinction between the secular and sacred: the Church has long rejected such dualism.

The Church is being prompted in its ministry and mission toward "wholeness" in all aspects of life in church and society; it is constrained to reappraise the entire Christian tradition, in different ways, and certainly one of the challenges to the Church is emerging from feminists' insights (see Coakley in Furlong).[1]

I believe that feminist theology should not be seen as an imposition on "straight," traditional theology, or a deviation from it. Throughout the history of the Church there have been challenges to its authority and doctrines from various quarters, with Martin Luther typifying the most important "paradigm shift" (although he himself did not acknowledge the existence of discrimination against women). What feminist liberation theologians are demanding is, in a sense, not new, as the rebirth of images is central to Christianity, and entirely consonant with the spirit of a dynamic, creative, and exploratory faith.

I agree with Phyllis Trible that in many ways there is a depatriarchizing principle at work in the Bible. Depatriarchizing is not a process of imposing one's own values and beliefs on Holy Scripture, but a dynamic process within Scripture itself.[2] In *God and the Rhetoric of Sexuality*, Trible explores this deconstructive principle at work in the Bible:

> Moving across cultures and centuries, then, the Bible informed a feminist perspective, and correspondingly, a feminist perspective enlightened the Bible. Shaped by a rhetorical-critical methodology, this interaction resulted in new interpretations of old texts; moreover, it uncovered neglected traditions to reveal countervoices within a patriarchal document.[3]

It is part of the work of feminist critical thinking in theology and in literature to retrieve these suppressed and "neglected themes and counterliterature." Women (and men) are learning to study the Scriptures with love, thoroughness, and expectancy, and are now being open to the revelation of hidden meanings and meanings glossed over in relation to understanding women's place in the tradition of faith. The directions that theology takes are not a matter of chance. They emerge as a result of dialogue between an inherited theological tradition and new questions confronting that tradition. They come from deeper reflection of the Scriptures, but may also emerge from secular sources and the movements of world history, from new prevailing philosophical frameworks. We in the Church need to be alert to the bursting of the wineskins, to make room for fresh insights.

We have long accepted the principle of "doing theology" in a communal context. But is our "community of interpreters" still a community of men? Are we ignoring the growing numbers of women who are exploring their faith? Women are asking questions about the relationship between sexuality and society, repression and civilization, and are caught up in a process of self-discovery, and the Church, as part of its mission and evangelism, has to consider this changing cultural context more astutely. It cannot dismiss it as being subversive.

Are feminist liberation theologians' claims in keeping with the fundamental tenets of the Christian faith?

While there are different expressions of feminist theology, it is worth highlighting that essentially it is concerned with liberation. Ironically, feminist theology is not readily seen as liberation theology in Southern Africa; even proponents of "black theology" and "*Kairos* theology," while in agreement with the values of feminist liberation theology, do not spell out the diverse injustices that have been experienced by women solely on the basis of their gender, nor do they analyze the way gender and race differences have been conflated in different ways.

Liberation in all forms is at the core of the Christian gospel.

Feminist theology is not heretical in calling for a new understanding of the relationship between God and the world, a new way of interpreting what "salvation" means. This is consonant with the "prophetic" tradition where God vindicates the oppressed, and with the Church's aim to criticize the dominant systems of power as well as the effect of ideology on thinking and action. We have always said that our theology must be practical. In Stewart Sutherland's words, theology is the "articulation of the possible."

Christians believe that all those forces of alienation that have acted to dismember the universe are once again integrated in the cross, which encompasses the universe. This is at the heart of feminist liberation theology. It is not about the ascendancy of women over men, but a movement toward equality in grace, in which men and women are finally reconciled in a renewed humanity.

Does the Church in Southern Africa want anything less?

## Conclusion

As we try to create a truly united family of God, in word and deed, in different ways in this country, in both Church and society, we experience hurt and wounding. The story of the crucifixion is that healing and wholeness is achieved through a difficult and painful "way of sorrows." The suffering may be the result of the selfishness of others, or caused by a God-pain implanted within us: a deep longing, in fact, for the healing of the sad divisions of our human family. As we are vulnerable to each other, and open up the wounds of our divisions, we will come to a new sacrificial unity in Christ.

But the story of the crucifixion also reminds us that we must resist making too many claims for ourselves, our suffering, our hurts, our causes, and our ability and wisdom to have all the answers to the Church's and the world's ills. We tend to assume that in some way we are more authentic because we are more oppressed; we do still cling to the victim-image. As we surmount the divisions created by the diversity of gender, race, culture and language, history, and tradition, we have to find creative ways of celebrating our many differences, so that the whole spectrum of human existence is enriched.

As we discover many answers to our questions, we must also allow ourselves to be interrogated by Holy Scripture. While Phyllis Trible sees the Bible as being itself on a pilgrimage through the years, Rowan Williams, writing of Christian spirituality through the centuries, gives another angle to the deconstructive principle at work in and through Scripture when he says:

> The questioning involved here is not our interrogating the data, but its interrogation of us. It is the intractable strangeness of the ground of belief that must constantly be allowed to challenge the fixed assumptions of religiosity; it is a given, whose question to each succeeding age is fundamentally one and the same. And the greatness of the great Christian saints lies in their readiness to be questioned, judged, stripped naked and left speechless by that which lies at the centre of their faith.[4]

This treading on the holy ground of the word must be done by all in humility and honesty and integrity.

The paradoxical challenge to all women is that as we find ourselves, we will lose ourselves. We must be wary that, in all our anxious and vexed attempts to uncover truth and fight for justice, to demystify the ideologies that we have been heirs and heiresses to, and find our voices, we have *no time for silence* — a

silence before God. In all our journeying and the achievements
of human thinking and reason, we only begin to enter into an
ever-greater mystery—the mystery of God.

we had been silent for so long
speaking a language of
half
truths
that told us who we were
and who we could
become
the icons
became
idols
as we closed our eyes
and clasped our palms in veneration
hallowed
and blessed them
made them food
for our bodies our souls
now
we are reading the Scriptures
for ourselves
sounding out the dark hollow words
that rebirth us
renaming ourselves
and renaming
GOD
in the stained
glass
we see the blood and water
we are speechless
with a new
silence

Can we not trust Christ in faith to be faithful . . . ?

PART FIVE
# A Newly Emerging Spirituality

☐ *Newly emerging forms of spirituality are part of the themes suggested for exploration by the Women's Commission of the Ecumenical Association of Third World Theologians. The theme has been taken up with much enthusiasm by Asian women who live in a religiously plural world and encounter the rich spiritual traditions of Asia. This experience is not shared to the same extent by Latin American or African women who feel challenged in quite a different way by the indigenous traditions of their own continents.*

*For this reason several of the following chapters come from Asian women; however, they are of much wider relevance than for Asian women alone. The Philippine Benedictine sister, Mary John Mananzan, Dean of St. Scholastica's College, Manila, and Sun Ai Lee Park, a Korean woman minister and editor of the feminist theological journal* In God's Image, *contributed a fine chapter on "Emerging Spirituality of Asian Women" to the book edited by Virginia Fabella and Mercy Amba Oduyoye,* With Passion and Compassion: Third World Women Doing Theology *(Maryknoll, NY: Orbis Books, 1988, pp. 77-88). Another chapter on the same theme is found in Chung Hyun Kyung's book* Struggle to be the Sun Again *(London: SCM, 1991, pp. 85-98).*

*At the 1987 Asian Women's Singapore conference, from which a statement on Mariology has already been quoted in chapter 28, a whole section was given over to the newly emerging spirituality among women. A few extracts on spirituality are quoted here from the summary statement of that conference on spirituality (see pp. 311-12 of the report):*

*What is Asian women's spirituality? Spirituality is faith experience based on convictions and beliefs which motivate our thought processes and behaviour patterns in our relationships with God and neighbor. Spirituality is the integral wholeness of a person concretizing his/her faith through daily life experience. Asian women's spirituality is the awakening of the Asian woman's soul to her concrete historical reality—poverty, oppression, and suffering. It is a response and commitment of a soul infused by the Spirit, to the challenge for human dignity, freedom, and a new life of love.*

*Traditional spirituality was individualistic and removed from the world. It had to do with the interior life of perfection to attain salvation—it was passive and totally unconcerned with reality. Whereas contemporary spirituality is integral, it is outgoing, community-orientated, active, holistic, and all embracing. Contemporary spirituality irrupts into history through the concrete life of the poor, and integrates persons at every level—in families, in neighbourhoods, in communities, and in the larger society—in mutual love and service. Contemporary spirituality seeks justice and peace for all oppressed and exploited peoples. It is a new spirituality born from reality . . .*

*To break patriarchal structures, spirituality needs to be creative and flexible, so that we can move towards a new heaven and a new earth. To be spiritual is not to be easily discouraged by the many events, failures and shortcomings of the established order, which hinder our commitment and action. We need to look ahead in a spirit of faith, and to be continuously aware of the challenges of an unjust world. We need to be aware of the situations, and realities that limit us, and be prepared to persevere on the path of justice and the restoration of freedom.*

*The greatest response to this challenge is to discover women's strength, both spiritual and biological. Women can endure suffering in silence and in love. Therefore, the discovery of our own physical and spiritual strength will empower and enable women to struggle for the well being and survival of all, for social justice, human rights, and peace in faith. To struggle against the injustices done to the minorities, and ethnic groups, and oppressed peoples—the Dalits and Tribals in India, the Aborigines in Australia, the Maoris in Aotearoa, the Korean and Burakus in Japan. It will strengthen women to struggle against sexism, and against the crimes committed—as in India, bride burning, sati, female infanticide, female foeticide, and dowry deaths. Spiritual strength will enable women in Pakistan to eradicate evil traditional practices like the tattooing of women's faces, and to safeguard the rights and privileges of young girls who are sexually exploited by rich men and hence deprived of marriage.*

*All over the world women are awakening and are getting organized. They have understood that spirituality is the driving force that enables them to cope with the pressure of everyday life. They are involved in socio-cultural analysis to eradicate social evils perpetuated by society against women. Christian women are appropriating the message of the Bible for themselves without the mediation of men. Asian women have many experiences which they share. This sharing encourages and empowers them to reach out to millions of women who are in need of help. Asian women's spirituality emerges from our common experience associated with the creative process, in partnership with the God of life, to co-create, sustain, and nurture life. This creative process also involves care and concern for others . . .*

*We Christian women are doubly responsible to authenticate our spirituality in this confused world. The spirit of God pervades us, enabling us to quench our thirst through the living water which we receive from our faith in Christ (Jn. 10.14). We believe in Christ. Christ is our strength, and we yearn for God's presence with us in spirit.*

*The coming of the Spirit as described in the Acts of the Apostles is the great pentecostal advent that has inspired and sustained Christian life through generations. Christian women today, with their new experiences, questions, dreams, and visions, often turn to this biblical story for fresh insights and empowerment. In their belief and hope that the divine Spirit will make all things new, they searchingly ask how the Spirit is present among contemporary women. How do women experience the life, power, and transformative dynamic of the Spirit in their actions and reflections?*

❖     ❖     ❖

*□ Chapter 31 is a collectively produced biblical reflection on the pentecostal story from one of the workshops held in connection with the evaluation conference on the Program of Women and Rural Development organized by the WCC, already referred to in chapter 19. The text is taken from Ranjini Rebera, ed.,* We Cannot Dream Alone, *Geneva: WCC Publications, 1990, pp. 76-9. It expresses the deeply held belief that the gift of the Holy Spirit enables women to be fruitful in both a spiritual and practical sense, to be filled with strength and power, with the new empowerment needed to overcome the numerous difficulties of their personal and community life, so that society and Church will be transformed.*

## 31  WORKSHOP REFLECTION

# From Barrenness to Fullness of Life: The Spirit as Enabler

---

*Biblical reflection on Acts 2.1-6, 4.32-5*

During our opening worship at the commencement of the workshop we saw the barrenness of the situations in which we find many of the women with whom and for whom we have worked in development, as well as our own feelings of barrenness from time to time. We saw also that barrenness does not necessarily refer only to the inability of women to bear sons for patriarchs, but also to unproductivity, the incapability of producing results and bearing fruits, resulting in dullness — and sometimes even stupidity. We also saw the different ways in which we become barren: for some it is biological, for some it is imposed by a system, for others it is self-imposed — the refusal to bear fruit.

Through the stories of Sarah, Hagar, Abraham and Isaac,

Rebecca, and her slave girls we established the present condition of our own barrenness as well as the barrenness of the people we are trying to work with in the processes of development. It is from this state of barrenness that we wish to help our rural sisters to emerge as empowered women within an empowered community.

To start with, it is imperative that we have a vision of a different kind of life toward which we are to help our people grow. In ecumenical terms we call this God's mission (*missio Dei*) and indeed that mission is the goal of the ecumenical movement, "that they shall be one" and "at the appointed time, all things in heaven and all things on earth shall be united." This was also the hope of the Israelites—the hope for the shalom community. This was also Jesus' main message—the establishment of the Kingdom of God on earth. John describes this message even further in the Gospel of John as fullness of life, where there will be community, security, freedom, and abundance—a wide open space (*yasha*) (John 10.7-16). This is the heaven that we have been taught to long for and work toward.

But how does one move from barrenness to this fullness of life, to this shalom, to the reign of God? How do we move from a state of emptiness and unfulfillment to a state of abundance and meaning? We are told in the story in Genesis that from a void and from chaos God created the universe and established order. We come to realize that our moment of revelation is an awakening to an awareness of our needs. This form of social analysis is similar to the account of the two who walked with a stranger on the Emmaus road, as recorded in Luke 24.13-17. We are told that "their eyes were opened and their hearts burned within them" as they realized that they had just walked and shared a meal with Jesus, the resurrected One. Once we have recognized that moment of revelation, then we move on to the building of consciousness-raising through the variety of programs being evolved for development.

However, no matter how well planned and organized our projects may be, with detailed feasibility studies, guidelines, monitoring of funds and programs, assessments, and reports, unless the presence of the Holy Spirit is evident, the vision of a new community will not come to fruition. It is the Spirit that makes possible the moment of seeing visions of a different kind of lifestyle. It is the Spirit that brings about that moment of awakening and gives the perseverance to struggle on and the wisdom to know when we have reached the end of our own resources. It is God's way of being present in our work.

The Old Testament bears evidence to the work of the Spirit as an Enabler. People were given:

- skill (Exod. 31.3),
- insightful wisdom (Isa. 11.12),
- unusual ability and intelligence (Exod. 35.34),
- uprightness (Ps. 143.10),
- loyalty (1 Chron. 12.18),
- commitment (Exod. 35.21).

In the book of Numbers (11.24-5) we see how the Spirit moved from Moses to the seventy elected leaders. When the leaders were empowered by the Spirit of God, Joshua comes to Moses and tells him "Stop them, sir!" referring to two people who were using their powers in the camp. And Moses replies: "Are you concerned about my interests? I wish that the Lord would give the Spirit to all people and make all of them shout like prophets!" (Num. 11.29). This same Spirit moves today to recreate people and communities.

In the account of the Pentecost in the New Testament, the *wind* signifies "the meaning of freedom as well as power, accomplishing things beyond the capacity or calculation of those who work solely by control or organization" (Acts 2.1-2).

But what really is this Spirit? We have seen it used to condemn, to ridicule, to divide, to destroy. Samuel Ryan suggests that it is "seeing and acting from God's point of view" or seeing things and doing things God's way and not according to the way of the world with its mass media, culture, and political ideologies. God's way was spelled out most eloquently in our study of the Magnificat (Luke 1) which portrays the image of God as the Savior "who will lift up the lowly, feed the hungry, and show mercy to those who honor God, who brings down the mighty and sends away empty those who are proud . . ."[1]

Therefore, it is now evident that first, the Spirit brings about the empowerment that we have set out as our main task and agenda. It transforms and brings about that which is new and unthinkable. It turns dreams into reality.

Secondly, the Spirit brings about community and creates community—*koinonia*. *Koinonia* is a gift from God, and Jesus prepared his disciples for living in community at the time of Pentecost by instructing them to stay together and not to scatter until they had received the power of God through the coming of the Holy Spirit (Acts 2.1-6). This same Spirit still builds community. It is as we work together that the risen Christ will help us to understand each other, listen to each other, and build each other up. Through *koinonia* our ability to communicate will supersede the many different languages we speak as human beings, just as the events at Pentecost contrasted with the chaos that emerged in the Old Testament story of the Tower of Babel.

However, the real test of the presence and power of the Spirit was not confined to the one place in which the events of Pentecost took place. The emerging community spread throughout the whole region, forming more and more caring-sharing communities (Acts 4.32-5). The Spirit continues to gather us in communion, creates understanding, bridges differences and distances, and creates deeply feeling and committed communities even today. This community, then, is the manifestation of the Kingdom of God on earth.

The work of the Spirit through community is not confined to the spiritual alone. It encompasses the ideals of self-sufficiency and self-reliance through involvement in the economic and physical needs of the community. The early Church experienced this work of the Spirit for a brief time and throughout history the same experience has emerged from time to time.

There are signs today that the Spirit is still at work in creating and recreating community. In fact, wherever we witness the creation of order out of chaos and fullness out of emptiness, we can identify the work of the Spirit of God. The many examples of success, both individual and communal, that we read about in case studies bear witness to the work of this same Spirit. Communities that have evolved in this manner we now acknowledge as the *emerging Church.* These are the communities that are faithful, or trying to be faithful, in doing the will of God—those who are seeing, acting, and living from God's point of view.

That is why, in the end, we can affirm the words of Jesus: "Behold, I make all things new!" (Rev. 21.5).

❖   ❖   ❖

□ *Three categories of people, the blacks, the Amerindians, and women, are presenting new challenges to Church and society in Latin America as the theology of liberation comes of age. These groups have been oppressed for centuries by their color, race, and sex. They are bringing into theology new issues, a new method, and a new language. In chapter 32, María Clara Bingemer develops the contribution of women to theology, doubly oppressed as they have been by their socioeconomic situation and by their sex. As a woman theologian, she emphasizes some feminine insights of modern theology, particularly in the context of Latin American theology of liberation. These insights express a concretely lived spirituality amid the struggles of life. Bingemer is a well-known Catholic lay theologian from Brazil. She is professor of theology at the Pontifical Catholic University of Rio de Janeiro and the Santa Ursula University. She has also acted as regional coordinator of the Ecumenical Association of Third World Theologians (EATWOT) for Latin America. Her essay was published in LADOC (Latin American Documentation), vol. 20/6, 1990, pp. 7–15.*

## 32  MARÍA CLARA BINGEMER

# Women in the Future of the Theology of Liberation

It is audit time in Latin America. The theology of liberation is coming up to its twentieth birthday. It is time to look back to the past in order to be able to recognize the present and, having recognized it, to be able to desire and construct the future. It is time to ask some questions. After these twenty years of laborious construction and slow consolidation, what does the theology of liberation look like? What is its future?

To answer these questions we have to look at the faces of those who have the leading roles in this theology, those without whom the theologians themselves, and even Latin American theology, would not exist—the poor and oppressed.

Today, however, the faces of these poor and oppressed look different. Three types in particular are emerging, attracting attention, and presenting new challenges to Church and society—the blacks, the Amerindians, and women. These groups, oppressed for centuries by their color, race, and sex, are now essential for an evaluation of the theology of liberation, and for any attempt to glimpse its future, because they bring into theology new issues, a new method, and a new language.

Women in particular are the focus of this essay. Their state of double oppression—by their socioeconomic situation and by their sex—calls for the attention of society and the Church. Their presence in the development of Latin American theology has recently been felt with increasing weight and frequency. Their ideas and their language have already been recognized as among the most serious and solid products of Latin American theology. This presence enjoyed by women in the theology of liberation enables us to hope for a bright and joyful future. The mouths and hearts of these once silent and invisible workers for God's reign now speak a message that says, "Rejoice!" The half of humankind that thought of itself as absent from theology's discourse—and in particular from the theology of liberation—has now made itself present and is speaking.

## Women as practitioners and subjects of theology

One of the fundamental features of the Latin American theological venture known as the theology of liberation is that it is a collective theological enterprise. The theologian of liberation no longer regards herself as someone who thinks, writes, and speaks in isolation out of her individual experience, her reading, done on her own, or her own insightful reasoning. She sees herself as the spokeswoman for the great mass of oppressed persons who have recently awoken from centuries of the most bitter oppression of all kinds, and who are now standing up and rediscovering themselves as responsible and active initiators. They are eager to rewrite history, from their own point of view. They want to reinterpret the liberating message of God's covenant with the people and Jesus Christ's liberating act in terms of their own situation of captivity, turning that message into a source of strength and strategy in their struggle.

Theology comes into this process as an ally and the theologian as a spokesperson. Sharing in the faith-lives of these oppressed persons, the theologian finds her raw material. She then returns it to them in the form of a worked-out, systematic argument. The oppressed have helped to bring this theology to birth and, along with her, they too are creators and theologians.

Having the word of God and the gospel of Jesus as their only wealth, the women of the Latin American poor are taking over the leadership of the majority of the Bible groups and basic ecclesial communities. They are giving the church a new look and a new vigor. Women's future in the theology of liberation is thus the future of the liberation of all human beings, men and women, who call out for the God of life, who brings liberation — socioeconomic, political, cultural, racial, ethnic, sexual — from every type of death.

## Theological method

Women's entry into the domain of theology brings with it a new way, a new method of conceiving and expressing a 2000-year-old theology. Entering into the domain of theological reflection with their specific and different bodiliness, open to ever-new and innovative messages, available for invasion and creative fecundation, destined to be host and protector of life, women are revolutionizing the rigor and system of theological method. Their present irruption into the rational male theological world of the past is as disconcerting and new as that of the woman who, with her presence and her perfume, in John's Gospel (12.1-8) invaded the meal taking place within the very strict social and ritual norms of Judaism. Breaching expectations and regulations and following the impulse of the desire that overflowed from her heart, the woman filled the space with a new scent, which none could avoid breathing in.

The presence of women in theology brings with it this same air of the new and unexpected. The female way of doing theology is finding its place and gaining ground. The courage to pour out the perfume at someone else's party is followed by the moment at which the perfume poured out struggles and collides with the ancient scents that have traditionally formed the environment. The present theological field is made up of this plurality of scents, sometimes apparently incompatible, and often in conflict.

## Born of desire

The future of the female way of doing theology is therefore inseparably linked with desire. The cold circumspection of purely scientific inquiry must give way to a new sort of systematics springing from the impulse of desire that dwells at the deepest level of human existence. It combines sensitivity and rationality, gratuitousness and effectiveness, experience and reflection, desire and rigor. "God is love" (1 John 4.8). If this is so, in the beginning God can only be the object of desire—not of necessity nor of rationality. Theology—which seeks to be reflection and talk about God and God's word—must therefore be moved and permeated in its entirety by the flame of desire. At a particular point in its articulation, reason, science, and systematic rigor have their role and their place but they can never suffocate desire, never tame the divine pathos that, from all eternity, has broken silence and become a loving word, kindling an irresistible desire in the hearts of women and men. Theology is called humbly to bear witness to, and give an account of, this burning desire. Born of desire, theology exists as theology only if it is upheld and supported by desire.

## Women and the Bible

Women and the poor in Latin America rediscovered the Bible at the same time. Women were present when the poor who had been kept out of the way, outside the word of God, discovered once again the book that was theirs, the book that spoke of their struggles, their hopes, their desires, and their covenant of love with a compassionate and loving God. They felt deeply

311

involved and identified with the great accounts of liberation contained in Scripture. Jesus' treatment of women as described by the gospels proclaimed to them the Good News about a reign of the discipleship of equals. On the other hand, in their reading of the Bible they came up against the problem of the clear marginalization of women in various passages of Scripture in both Old and New Testaments. This drew the attention of women who were becoming aware of their situation, particularly women theologians specializing in Holy Scripture.

The work of these new biblical scholars revealed something new—there is a difference between reading the Bible from the point of view of the poor and reading it from a woman's point of view. Whereas a poor man may find himself affirmed and defended by the word of the living God throughout the Holy Scriptures, the poor woman, in contrast, does not know as a woman how to deal with the texts that seem to marginalize her and treat her as an inferior human being. This problem is all the greater in that the poor communities where this explosion of biblical renewal is taking place are particularly marked by patriarchal and male-supremacist ideologies. In this context, reading biblical texts that seem to reaffirm female segregation may help to confirm women still further in the oppression that crushes them—and this time with the very authority of the word of God.

Because of this, Latin American women biblical scholars are working particularly with women from poor communities for a deeper understanding of the nature of biblical texts. They present the text as the testimony of a people, a faith-community within which divine revelation is transmitted as a saving word that always supports the lowest and oppressed people—including women. This spirit of the revealed text relativizes the anti-feminism of a patriarchal culture that may have given a negative tone to some parts of the Bible.

In addition, they are attempting to recover the origins of Christianity from a woman's perspective. In so doing, they bring to light and emphasize the women who appear as builders of the history of salvation. A traditional interpretation often forgets them or relegates them to a secondary plane. Examples are the Egyptian midwives of Exodus 1, the subversives Tamara and Agar who felt completely free to question the Jewish law, and the whole legion of women in the Gospels and the Acts of the Apostles who played an active part in the early stages of the Church.

## Mary of Nazareth, traveling companion

Speaking about women from a Christian point of view inevitably means speaking about Mary of Nazareth, the mother of Jesus venerated by Christianity from the beginning as the perfect woman. Mary was, and continues to be, presented to women as the model to be imitated and inwardly assimilated. However, traditional Mariology has often presented an image of Mary that, instead of promoting and liberating women, has confirmed and confined them in their ancient oppression. Submissive and passive, entirely absorbed in domestic activities, idealized and exalted for her individualistic virtues, Mary of Nazareth was a source of perplexity rather than inspiration for those involved in the struggle.

The theology of liberation set out to recover the figure of Mary in its liberating and prophetic potential. Stressing above all the text of the Magnificat (Luke 1.46-55), this theology gives to the poor women of Latin America, to the women who lead the basic ecclesial communities, a Mary whose face is no longer only that of Our Lady, glorious Queen of Heaven, but also and primarily an elder sister and traveling companion. In Latin America this prophetic and liberating Mary takes on many loving faces: the Morenita of Guadalupe who appeared to the Amerindian Juan Diego in Mexico, the black Aparecida who allowed herself to be found in the waters of the River Paraiba in Brazil, Nicaragua's Purisima, Cuba's Virgin of Charity, and so on. In all these, Mary the valiant and prophetic daughter of Sion, committed to justice, faithful to her God and people, inspires and strengthens women's unity and struggle, redeeming and ennobling them in their own eyes.

*Feminist Theology*

## The threefold God in a female perspective

### God

For some time now theology has begun to see the need to conceive and speak of God in the feminine: to believe in, invoke and proclaim God in the feminine. It is no longer adequate to reflect on the Divine Mystery that creates, saves, and sanctifies us as identified primarily with one of the two sexes. Rather, the Divine Mystery should integrate and harmonize the two sexes without suppressing their enriching differences, while at the same time it transcends them. To achieve this, theology has to go beyond traditional theological concepts that see a woman as God's image only in her rational soul and not in her sexed female body. It has to go beyond seeing God as andromorphic, conceived and understood in male terms as identifying the divine party (God) in the covenant as male and the human party (Israel, the Church) as female.

### Christ

Christology, developed from a woman's viewpoint, has sought to be a way into this new conception of God. The form this has taken in Latin America has been the key that the liberation approach has used throughout its study of the Gospels—an analysis of Jesus' egalitarian behavior as revealed by his encounters and relations with women. One of the clearest ways in which Jesus broke with tradition has to do with women. His behavior toward the women marginalized by Jewish society was not only new, but even shocking, surprising even his own disciples (John 4.27). Women were singled out as beneficiaries of his miracles (Luke 8.2; Mark 1.29-31; 5.25-34; 7.24-30) and leading recipients of the Good News he brought.

### Redeemed bodiliness

As well as breaking the taboo that marginalized women, Jesus redeemed their bodiliness which had been humiliated and proscribed by Jewish Law. In curing the woman with the hemorrhage who was thus impure to the Jews, he exposed

himself to the risk of making himself impure by touching her
(Matt. 9.20-2). In allowing his feet to be touched, kissed, and
anointed by a known public sinner, he provoked his Pharisee
host to cast doubt on his prophetic status (Luke 7.36-50). Jesus
also allowed women to question and influence him. His
encounters with them changed not only them, but him too. The
Gospels show us Jesus learning from women and giving way to
their requests. He did so with his mother Mary when he
advanced his "hour" in Cana (John 2.1ff.). He did so with the
Canaanite woman, who "dragged out of him" the miracle she
wanted with much pleading, and so set in train the process
of the proclamation of the Good News to the gentiles (Matt.
15.21-8; Mark 7.24-30).

*The Trinity*

Nevertheless, it is not so much in Christology as in the doctrine
of the Trinity, in the mystery of the communion of the three
divine persons, the unquestionable center of the Christian faith,
that the main breakthrough to a concept of God in women's
terms is being sought. To say that God is Father, Son, and
Holy Spirit is not, and cannot be, in any way equivalent to
saying that the divine community is composed of three persons
identified as male. Women theologians in Latin America today
seek to recover the word "rahamin" (womb) to refer to God's
love as the biblical root of the experience of God. Countless Old
Testament texts, especially in the prophets, refer to God by
this part of the female body. Thus in theology—feminist or
not—God the Father is being called also Mother, or Maternal
Father or Paternal Mother. This divine female womb, pregnant
with gestation and birth, identified with the Father, appears
also in the incarnate Son. In the Gospels Jesus is driven to cry
out his frustrated maternal desire to gather under his wings the
scattered and rebellious "chickens of Jerusalem" (Luke 13.34).
It appears in the Spirit, the divine "ruach," who in the labor of
creation "hatches" the cosmos that will burst forth from the
primitive chaos. The Spirit is sent like a loving mother to
console the children left orphaned by Jesus' departure (John
14.18, 26) and to teach them patiently to pronounce the Father's
name, Abba (Rom. 8.15).

## The womb of God

A rich future is in store for the theology of liberation in the female dimension of God. The poor, discovering themselves as active makers of history and organizers of liberation, are experiencing God as the God of life embodying the very fullness of life and the only source from which to derive hope in the situation of death that is their everyday experience. God's female maternal womb, fertile, in labor and compassionate, enables this liberation to come about with force and firmness, but also with creativity and gentleness, without violence. Once God is experienced, not only as Father, Lord, strong warrior, but also as a Mother protecting and loving, struggle is tempered with festivity. Permanent and gentle firmness ensures the ability to be strong without losing tenderness. An uncompromising resistance can be carried on without excessive tension and sterile strain—even with joy.

God's compassion, as flowing from female and maternal organs, takes on itself the hurts and wounds of all the oppressed. A woman who does theology is called to bear witness to this God with her body, her actions, her life.

## Eucharist celebrated and symbolized by the female body

The liturgy has a predominant place at the base of the Latin American Church and in a special way in the basic ecclesial communities. The women of poor communities find a privileged space in the liturgy in which to express their work and their struggles—in the unions, the mothers' clubs, the neighborhood associations, the community gardens and canteens, and in the various other forms of popular community organization. The Eucharist, celebrated where women are active participants, is both the subversive memory of the Lord's death and resurrection, and the agape of the New Testament Church (Luke 2.46).

## Woman's body, eucharistically given

There is another dimension of the Eucharist in which women find themselves. This is the strict significance of the sacrament as the transubstantiation and real presence of the body and blood of the Lord which is given to the faithful as food. Feeding others with one's own body is the supreme way God chose to be definitively and sensibly present in the midst of the people. The bread that we break and eat refers us back to the greater mystery of Jesus' incarnation, death, and resurrection. It is his person given as food; it is his very life made bodily a source of life for Christians. It is women who possess in their bodiliness the physical possibility of performing the divine eucharistic action. In the whole process of gestation, childbirth, protection, and nourishing of a new life, the sacrament of the Eucharist, the divine act, happens anew.

Throughout Latin America, in the rural areas and the poor districts on the edges of cities, there are millions of women conceiving, bearing, and suckling new children of the common people. Sometimes they do it with difficulty, pain, and suffering, sometimes with the last trickle of life left in them. The female body, which multiplies in other lives, which gives itself as food and nourishes with its flesh and blood the lives it has conceived, is the same body that wastes away and dies tilling the earth, working in factories and homes, stirring pots and sweeping floors, spinning thread and washing clothes, organizing and chairing meetings, leading struggles, and starting the singing at liturgical celebrations. Woman's body, eucharistically given to the struggle for liberation, is really and physically distributed, eaten, and drunk by those who will—as men and women of tomorrow—continue the same struggle. Breaking the bread and distributing it, having communion in the body and blood of the Lord, means for women today reproducing in the community the divine act of surrender and love so that the people may grow and victory may come.

Women who do theology in Latin America and who share the same sacramental vocation, the same eucharistic destiny with their sisters from the poorest environments, are called to open a new path, a possible future so that this sacramental act may become more present, recognized, and believed in Latin American's journey toward liberation.

□ *For Latin American women, spirituality cannot be divorced from their daily struggles and concrete actions arising out of the need to fight economic and political oppressions. It is a struggle for justice, for liberation, for national identity, and for building new communities. It is a struggle for new life. For some women this means participation in revolutionary activities—as, for example, for the women in Nicaragua. In chapter 33 Luz Beatriz Arellano, a Roman Catholic sister from Nicaragua, reflects on women's spirituality in the revolutionary process; in the course of this reflection, she touches on many theological themes—the understanding of God, of Jesus, of the transformative power of crucifixion and resurrection, of new relations to community, and of Mary, the mother of Jesus. Her insights remain relevant even though the political situation in Nicaragua has changed since this chapter was written, adding poignancy to her words: "In the future there will be new challenges that we cannot yet envision" (p. 338). The text is taken from Virginia Fabella and Mercy Amba Oduyoye, eds.,* With Passion and Compassion: Third World Women Doing Theology *(Maryknoll, NY: Orbis Books, 1988, pp. 135-50).*

## 33   LUZ BEATRIZ ARELLANO

# Women's Experience of God in Emerging Spirituality

Speaking about the living experience of God in the new spirituality of Nicaraguan women means speaking of a faith incarnate in the revolutionary process that the people of God are experiencing in Nicaragua. The new spirituality springs very much from these concrete experiences of building the new society. It is our lot to live in a time that is a privileged theological locus in which is incarnate, and from which springs, a new spirituality. This newness arises more from an everyday practice than from any theoretical reflection. Faith here enters into history and becomes incarnate in the process of the daily life of the people's journey. Thus it arises out of their struggles and their hopes.

The commitment of women to the people as a whole is very deep, so much so that we could say that this involvement of women is a characteristic feature of this new process in which the Nicaraguan people are engaged. The ongoing striving for freedom, for sovereignty, the challenge of attaining it fully and holding onto it, is also part of an ongoing dynamic. Nevertheless, it should be pointed out that living a new spirituality continues to be a challenge for many women. We can speak only of an ongoing movement of women to live and incarnate their faith in a way that is consistent with what we are experiencing.

Thus my presentation will approach the topic by way of three steps: first, I shall describe how a new experience of God emerged during the liberation struggle in Nicaragua; second, I shall speak about some traits of the spirituality of women in the present Nicaraguan revolutionary process; finally, I shall point to some challenges connected with deepening the experiences and spirituality of women in Nicaragua.

## The experience of the liberation struggle: God present in faces of the poor

Our first experience of God was that of allowing ourselves to feel the impact of the situation of suffering and oppression that our people were undergoing. From that moment on, we began to discover God present in the suffering, oppressed, and outcast countenance of our poorest brothers and sisters. What struck many women, and also many men, in Nicaragua at this point was discovering the situation of children, children in the street who were working from the time they were little; finding out that many women died in childbirth and that many children died because they had no way of getting proper attention; and

319

finally discovering the situation of young people in our country who had no future because they were suffering brutal repression at the hands of Somoza's Guards.

Another aspect that left a deep impression on us was the situation of men and women in the countryside who had to work very hard simply to live, and sometimes in conditions that were worse than those of animals. Personally, I was struck one day to find how a Christian lady with a lot of money was treating peasants, both men and women. When a peasant woman asked if she could buy a pound of pork loin, the woman answered, "How outrageous! You want to buy the best kind of meat and you don't have enough to pay for it. You should be happy if we sell you the bones." It pained me to see that, and I wondered, "How can we say God is love in a situation like this?" And I realized that this situation would remain unchanged unless we struggled to change it.

### God present in our history: the God of life

Thus in this new experience of God we were not only discovering the Lord in our poorest, most oppressed, most outcast brother or sister, but also finding that God was asking us to work and to do all in our power so that this situation would not continue. We have gone from an experience of oppression, marginalization, and suffering to a realm of hope that is impelling us toward change, toward transformation. From that time onward, we have begun to discover the Lord present in our own history, inviting us to live and refashion this history of oppression into a history of liberation.

Even in the 1960s many men and women did not see this situation of poverty as something natural, and they began to ask questions such as, "What is our role as Christian men and women in this subjugated, dependent, oppressed society where life is impossible?" In a very natural way, we began to search and we tried to uncover the roots of these problems. We began to confront this situation with the word of the Lord. This helped us to find specific approaches to solutions and changes. We were also discovering that God was different from what we had been taught. We were discovering God as the God of life, closer to us, as one who journeys with us through history.

I recall that it was women who most insisted on discovering God as God of life. I believe that women were better able to make this discovery and translate it into life more easily because of their calling to motherhood, among other reasons, since that is a calling to life and peace. Being essentially bearers and sustainers of life, women find a new meaning in the discovery of God as God of life, and they themselves become stronger and more conscious as defenders and bearers of life, not only in the biological sense but in all its dimensions, the fullness of life to which Jesus calls us as his followers: "I came so they might have life and have it in abundance" (John 10.10). From this angle, Nicaraguan women walk beside their people in creating new life, in giving a meaning to life, taking part in and actively defending a project in history, one that is liberating and is generating new rights to justice.

In this journey, women discover feminine elements in God: care and concern for children, even those who are not their own, defense of life, love, affection, and empathy for suffering. Such characteristics—more feminine, if you will—of a God found to be closer to us and more tenderhearted, led to a rediscovery of God as mother, not just as father, not just as protector, but as one who is immensely concerned for the poor and for the least, for those who have been left unattended, and it gave us a deep hope and a deep sense of having found something new.

At the same time, women encounter the hope of a whole people, where the emphasis is especially focused on what is small and weak, on the poor as protagonists in a history of life. This new, creative, and committed spirituality enables us to overcome all obstacles and even to accept our present life with aggression on all sides, because all those who are guided by the Spirit are children of God (Rom. 8.14).

### A new image of Jesus

Out of their participation in the suffering of our people, while also battling through their own struggle, women discover a new image of Jesus—a Jesus who is brother and sister, in solidarity on the journey toward liberation, the people's journey, and their own journey; a Jesus who is a *compañero* (colleague, fellow revolutionary) in building the new society.

Jesus' face is present in all the men and women who endure weariness and give their life for others. Jesus is identified as God, man and woman, standing in firm solidarity with the struggle. This is a God who is sensitive to suffering, a God who goes along with the people incarnate in history. The discovery of, and faith in, a God who is in pilgrimage with the people,

> the God of the poor,
> the human and simple God,
> the God who is sweating out in the street,
> the God with the gnarled face*

identified with the cause of justice, is a discovery that gives meaning to their struggle and makes everyday life bearable in the midst of oppression—and today in the midst of the aggression, shortages, and unceasing threats caused by the war the United States is financing against the people of Nicaragua.

### A new relation with the community

As we discovered the God of life and Jesus as *compañero*, we also were discovering that the Church must be a community, one that not only questions itself, but also takes on responsibility for the poorest and the least. In this sense, we began to focus more on the Kingdom than on the Church—that is, we began to see that Jesus' basic message was announcing the Kingdom.

We began to ask ourselves: How are we going to announce the Kingdom as Good News, to announce the Good News of Jesus with deeds and not simply with words? And the more we reflected on it, the more we began to take on small tasks aimed at transforming society. That is, it was our experience that the love between us women, the love that is the Lord's basic command, had to be not only affective but effective as well. All of this meant that we were experiencing the Lord out of our own painful experience.

*from Misa Campesina *of Carlos Mejia Godoy.*

322

From the beginning, women have been outstanding in their involvement in this process. Right away, we women discovered that no one was going to liberate us from outside. We discovered that the Lord was really present within us, and this impelled us to change our own situation.

Hence when the first basic ecclesial communities were organized in the 1960s, there were more women than men involved. A new dimension of spirituality came to the fore: the "pious" woman, praying a novena, calling on the Lord, became a committed woman, reading the Bible in terms of her own situation and in terms of a new responsibility within history. In this manner we began to experience that there was much more space for women in the life of the Church.

This kind of commitment led to a change in the relationship between women and their community. Women gradually overcame the hierarchical relationship of men over women. Galatians 3.28 is becoming something real, since women are finding that they are protagonists in history, history-making subjects liberating themselves and liberating their people. The community takes on solidarity with the pain and suffering of mothers. Thus women find the space in which they can denounce the situation of pain and suffering, and also announce, out of their own practice, the new spirituality, that is arising out of concrete life experiences. Their combative spirit commands the respect of others. Thus their sense of community is deepened. It is in community that women find their true place; it is when the community comes together that people pray for the situation of the country, for the men and women who are defending their homeland, for peace and justice. The community is also the place for celebrating those small victories that represent the hope for something new, that which is becoming new.

## Woman's dignity as image of God

We have also discovered another important aspect for women, that of human dignity. Reading and practicing the word of God in relation to the real situation, as their involvement in action became more prominent with each passing day, women discovered their own dignity. In the community they now began to speak of women's rights, of women's dignity as human persons, and they began to discover that they were cast aside and mistreated in their own houses; they began to realize that if they wanted a different future for themselves and their children, they had to struggle. In this sense, reading the word of God from woman's perspective played a very important role in developing the consciousness of both men and women. I recall how some of the passages that people in the communities — especially women — most enjoyed reading were in Genesis, the passages about the creation of man and woman. I also recall the joy with which women discovered that they were equal, that they had been created in the image of God just as much as men. That was the starting point for demanding their own rights and their own opportunities. They encouraged other women to form new groups and to encourage their husbands to go to the meetings and to urge their children and everybody else to discover this reality of the dignity of the children of God as a new experience of God in a Church that was beginning to be changed under the impulse of the word of the Lord. This made the women of Nicaragua more and more aware that their new role was not that of simply "taking care of their house and going to pray in church"; their role was to be history-making subjects of their own liberation, and hence to take part in the struggles to transform their country. Later on, we were to find that women of all ages played a very active, dynamic role in the people's liberation struggle because they had found this liberating dimension in the word of the Lord.

This new women's spirituality that enables them to bear suffering in struggle and still to maintain strong hope finds expression in this poem by Michele Najlis, a Nicaraguan who has been active in the struggle since she was thirteen, and who is a Christian and a revolutionary:

> They pursued us in the night,
> they surrounded us,
> and left us no defense but our hands
> linked to millions of hands linked together.
> They made us spit up blood,
> they scourged us;
> they filled our bodies with electric shocks
> and they filled our mouths with lime;

324

they put us in with beasts all night long,
they threw us in timeless dungeons,
they ripped out our nails;
with our blood they covered even their rooftops,
even their own faces,
but our hands
are still linked to millions of hands linked together.


## Women in the liberation struggle

Understanding that women's liberation would be incomplete unless there was pressure for the liberation of all the people, the women in the basic ecclesial communities became involved in the struggle against the dictatorship. They were particularly involved in the first women's organizations in Nicaragua, the Association of Nicaraguan Women to Deal with National Issues (AMPRONAC). After that, women participated, for example, in marches to denounce the murder and crimes being committed. At one point, they took part in a very important action in the church in Las Palmas to denounce the fact that more than a thousand peasants had disappeared from the countryside. Women went to the streets shouting the slogan, "Donde estan nuestros hermanos campesinos—que contesten los asesinos." ("Where are our peasant brothers and sisters? Let the murderers answer!") They were also involved in occupying the United Nations building in Nicaragua to protest against the large number of political prisoners then being held. Women were very creative: they not only took part in marches and protest actions, but also served as couriers between organizations or persons involved in underground work, and later they also supported the organizations involved in direct struggle, became involved in the underground, and so forth. Women were really quite conscious that their faith impelled them to do this, and that it was impossible to be a good Christian and not take part in this struggle.

Women arrived at this point of participating in AMPRONAC and other activities related to the struggle as the fruit of a powerful experience of God. We reasoned that if God is the God of life, and life was being repressed and destroyed in every way, we had to struggle to make life possible in Nicaragua. This arrival point was also the starting point from which women experienced solidarity: it is precisely by being organized that women discover that a new force is coming into being. This solidarity among women to defend life was likewise an experience of solidarity to defend the life of the people as a whole.

## *An ecumenical spirituality*

The new spirituality of Nicaraguan women that I am trying to reflect is a truly ecumenical spirituality, a spirituality shared not only with Christians who belong to the various churches but also between Christians and non-Christians. The struggle for women's rights and dignity—although women in Christian communities discover it through their Bible discussions—is also a broader expression of values found in the struggle for women's liberation, values that are at once Christian and human, with no need to attach any religious term. An excellent example of this spirit, of a Church without borders, is found in the letter of Idania Fernandez, a young Nicaraguan woman who became aware of the situation of her country in a group called Metanoia, one of the church youth groups that I served as adviser. She wrote this letter on International Women's Day in 1979, a few weeks before she was killed in the liberation struggle. The letter reads:

My dearest little daughter:

Right now we are living through moments that are extremely important for humankind: today in Nicaragua, soon throughout Latin America, and some day it will take place on every continent around the world.

The revolution demands our all from each one of us, and our own level of consciousness impels us to make demands on ourselves as individuals, and to put every possible effort into being useful to the revolutionary process.

My greatest desire is that the day will soon come when you will be able to live in a free society where you will be able to fulfill yourself as a true human being, where people will be brothers and sisters rather than enemies.

### A Newly Emerging Spirituality

I would like to walk arm in arm with you through the streets, and see happy smiles on all the children, and see the parks and rivers. I would like to smile for joy, see our people growing like happy children, see them become the new person, honest and conscious of their responsibilities to all humankind.

You will have to learn to appreciate this whole paradise of peace and freedom you are going to be able to enjoy. I say that because our most wonderful people have spilt their precious blood for this cause, and they have done so with love, out of love for the people, for freedom, and for peace, for the sake of future generations, for children like you, so you will not have to experience the repression, humiliation, hunger, and misery in which so many men, women, and children have lived in our beautiful Nicaragua.

I am telling you all this in case it happens that they don't tell you, or I don't make it to tell you. That is possible because we are all well aware of where we are going and who the enemy is, and we feel at ease if we know that we die as true revolutionaries in the full sense of the word. For we have known how to take our place in our historic context, and we have known how to take on our responsibility and our duty. That is our greatest satisfaction as revolutionaries, as human beings, and as mothers.

"Mother" does not mean being the woman who gives birth to and cares for a child; to be a mother is to feel in your own flesh the suffering of all the children, all the men, and all the young people who die, as though they had come from your own womb.

My greatest wish is that one day you become a true woman with pure feelings and a great love for humanity. And that you know how to defend justice whenever it is being violated and that you defend it against whomever and whatever.

To do that, to know what it is to be a true human being, get to know, read about, and assimilate the great figures of our revolution and of all revolutions in other countries. Take the best of each one as an example and put it into practice so that you will be better each day. I know you can do it, and are going to do it. This gives me a great sense of peace.

I don't want to leave you words, promises, or moral

327

platitudes. What I give you is an attitude toward life, my own attitude (although I'm aware that it is still not the best) and that of all my Sandinista brothers and sisters. I am sure you will be able to assimilate this attitude.

Okay, kid. If I have the privilege of seeing you again (which is also quite possible), we will have long talks about life and revolution, and we will go hand in hand to carry out the tasks the revolutionary process entrusts to us, and we will sing with a guitar and we will be together to play, to work, and to get to know each other better, and learn from one another.

> When I recall your beautiful face
> Beautiful like flowers and like freedom,
> I work even harder in the struggle,
> Joining your smile to our situation.
> I remember you every day.
> I always picture you as you are.
> Always love our people and humankind.

With all the love that is in your mother, Idania.
Ever on to Victory! Free Country or Death!

## Women's spirituality in the revolutionary process

Nicaraguan women are outstanding in their tremendous dedication to work and their yearning for study, training, and self-improvement, and that is how they press for recognition of their dignity as women. In this revolutionary process, Nicaraguan women feel spurred on by great feelings of gratitude, and also by an awareness of their responsibility in the historic moment that our country is experiencing.

Accepting the presence of the Spirit who creates life, who gives life and makes everything new, along with the challenges posed by the Spirit, is one of the first steps that enables us to speak of the characteristics of a new spirituality in today's Nicaragua. Both personal conversion, which since 1979 is expressed in the establishment of more just structures for the benefit of the poor (which includes the bulk of our people), as well as the formation of a new woman and a new man are ongoing dimensions of this spirituality.

Since victory, women continue to be quite active. We see women present in the reconstruction process. Women were massively present in the literacy campaign, and were very ready to go out to the countryside and teach reading and writing to their brothers and sisters who have been deprived of education for such a long time. We see women present in all aspects of rebuilding the country: in activities relating to health, in guard duty, standing guard to defend life. Women are participating in a very strong and intense way in this deep experience of the Nicaraguan people as they move from slavery to freedom: a deeply paschal experience.

Women's lives are changing. The revolution has disrupted traditional cultural patterns through which the traditional image of women had been created. In our traditionally macho society, woman was idealized as the reverse side of the exploitation she suffered as victim: besides her sexual image, her idealized image was one of motherhood, which gave her back, or tried to give her back, as a mother, what had been taken from her as human person and as woman: her dignity, her participation, and the chance to be not just one who reproduces human life, but also one who creates new life and transforms her own society and her own culture. From this traditional perspective, in addition to being doubly exploited, as women and as members of the popular classes women were reduced to reproducing male cultural patterns and even male interests.

The fact that they are following Jesus, who stands in solidarity with the struggles of the poor masses and with the struggles of women, means that Christian women at this momentous period in Nicaraguan and Central American history have a deep feeling of responsibility. They feel the pull of "the freedom of the children of God" (Rom. 8.21); they feel that they must be linked in solidarity with their sons and daughters, with their husbands, brothers, and all those companions in struggle who are on the warfront, defending their country's peace.

One woman who exemplified this commitment to defending life was Mary Barreda, who together with her husband was murdered by the contras (Nicaraguan rebels) after they were kidnapped during the coffee harvest in 1982. As a woman who played leadership roles in the liberation of the people, she could not stand back, but decided she had to engage in practice alongside the least and the poorest. At that moment, such a practice alongside the people meant going out to harvest coffee, knowing that her contribution would become foreign exchange that would contribute to changing the life of the people. Before going out with the harvest brigade, she wrote the following letter to members of her basic ecclesial community in one of the poorest neighborhoods of Estelí:

To my dear brothers and sisters in Omar Torrijos neighborhood:

You can't imagine how much Don Ramón and I have been waiting for this moment. From the time we began to share our lives with one another, you have been a part of us, and we love your streets, your houses, your children and, indeed, everything about you. As far as I am concerned, the best gift the Lord was going to give me would be sharing this moment with you. I was also thinking that I had to give you a good present, but I couldn't come up with anything. But suddenly I've been given the chance to give you a good gift, although it means I won't be with you physically, and that is a chance to go harvest coffee these next ten days. That is why I am writing this brief note, to tell you that this is my gift for all of you: the little I shall be able to harvest will be translated, or rather, converted, into health care, clothing, shelter, roads, education, food, etc. That is why I am going to harvest coffee with all the love and enthusiasm I am capable of, and you can be assured that in every coffee bean I harvest, each one of your faces, those of your children, and even those of people I don't know, will be present. Because of this love I have toward you, I know that the Lord will multiply what we harvest.

I want to ask you that you also make a gift to the Lord this Christmas, in a smile, in taking better care of your wives, husbands, and children.

Wherever I may be, I am thinking about you at this moment while Don Ramón is reading you these few lines.

Greetings to all and a big hug. I love you very much.

Mary

## A Newly Emerging Spirituality

*Martyrdom to defend life and for the sake of justice*

Mary Barreda's example shows that their commitment of themselves leads women in the direction of martyrdom. There is an aspect of martyrdom in the lives of Nicaraguan women, an aspect they share with the population as a whole, and especially with young people who fall in battle. Obviously men are more present in the war, but women are also called to experience and suffer this double dimension of martyrdom. There is the martyrdom of seeing their children fall for the sake of the liberation and defense of their country and in order to bring about a more just society, in which a new life for new men and new women may become possible. They may also give up their own lives. Many women go to the warfronts to defend life. They are there to encourage their children, their own and those of others, the children of the people whom they have adopted spiritually as their own. They fortify the *compañeros* who are there in the name of peace and justice, bearing the weight of the aggression on the front line. They do this out of love for their children and their companions in struggle, for "there is no limit to love's forebearance, to its trust, its hope, its power to endure" (1 Cor. 13.8).

The danger of running into the contras is real, and the risk of losing one's life is real. The Spirit, however, does not remain static but, rather, impels us forward, makes us move along, since "it was for liberty that Christ freed us. So stand firm, and do not take on yourselves the yoke of slavery a second time!" (Gal. 5.1).

The constant striving for full freedom and for peace as the fruit of justice energizes women to take on full solidarity with our people's struggle for liberation. Endowed with this readiness to suffer and hope along with their sons and daughters, and along with their male and female companions in struggle, women find in the Spirit, who is love, strength to transcend themselves and surrender their lives to support those who are building the new homeland.

Love is the fruit of the Spirit. "There is no greater love than this: to lay down one's life for one's friends" (John 15.13). This has been what Nicaraguan women have understood. The love of mothers has become so strong that it can lead to their giving their lives for their children, as events have shown: on July 31, 1985, eight Nicaraguan mothers were murdered by the contras, after being raped and later barbarously hacked to pieces, as they were on their way to Molocucu to visit their children.

Women find in Jesus the example of the freedom of giving one's life for others, and the example of a life placed at the service of others with utter gratuity.

In addition to facing the possibility of martyrdom, Nicaraguan women, along with the people as a whole, are impelled prophetically and emphatically to denounce to the whole world the increasing aggression our people are suffering. Another characteristic of Nicaraguan women who have heeded the Spirit at this dawn of our history is sensitivity to the present situation of Nicaragua and responding adequately to this historical moment.

Heeding the Spirit not only leads women to act boldly. Action springs from prayer. Women pray and fast for the peace that they yearn for so that life may grow and flourish as a sign of God's reign.

Impelled by the Spirit along this journey, women experience their limits, and the different dangers from the enemy, all aimed at destroying life. Instead of allowing themselves to be trapped by fear, however, they live this situation in a dialectic of boldness, rashness, and weakness that becomes strength. Their weakness comes not from being women, but from being human beings who know that the life of their people is continually threatened and under attack. Thus women are not arrogant in their boldness. Their boldness leads them to move forward, transcend themselves, take on new things they have never undertaken before, but they are weak in the face of death-dealing attacks. Nevertheless, they do not become paralyzed, but march forward and believe with hope in a world that is new, just, and human: the promise of the Spirit emerging, like wheat in the midst of weeds.

*Two realities: crucifixion and resurrection,*
*death and life*

Because of the war of aggression that our people are undergoing, crucifixion and death, resurrection and life are two realities present in all dimensions of life. In death, the mystery of life is already present: many die consciously surrendering their lives to defend an effort to build something within history, convinced of the new life gestating today in Nicaragua. Nicaraguan women feel the stimulus and strength of the Spirit, and out of their faith they actively accompany all those men and women who are defending life along the different warfronts. "God did not give us a Spirit of cowardice, but one of strength, of love, and good judgment" (2 Tim. 1.7).

The incarnation of this new spirituality transcends what is individual and commits us to struggle for the life of the whole body of the people and for all of life. Resurrection is already present in crucifixion. The road toward the building of the Kingdom by way of the rise of the new society entails pain, death, and suffering, but it also means the hope of greater life, justice, peace, and love incarnate in history. Both aspects, crucifixion and resurrection, are part of the process of passing from death to life "through the body of Christ" (Rom. 7.4).

*Joy is paschal*

Out of the daily suffering of poor women and out of the lives surrendered in the struggle against the causes of this situation of death, people are living a renewed paschal experience. The experience of death, war, abduction, rape, and abandonment enables them to experience more profoundly the meaning of the Lord's resurrection. Joy is thus the result of the hope that the historic project of life will overcome the situation of death and war that the people are suffering. Hope in the resurrection in no way means escape from present reality but, rather, it means a deeper involvement in the struggle against death. Joy comes from faith, from the hope that death is not the last word. That is why we can already celebrate the joy of resurrection in the midst of war. The following words from the Message of the National Conference of Religious of Nicaragua, after the revolutionary victory, are apt:

God has passed through Nicaragua acting with a powerful and liberating arm. These are some of the signs of his marvelous presence that have been, and continue to be, found in the midst of our struggling people: the hunger for justice in the poor and oppressed, courage, the presence of women, exemplary unity, hospitality and companionship, the responsibility with which each person has taken on tasks in reconstruction, and finally generosity in victory and a joy pregnant with hope that leads the whole population to dream of a tomorrow when things will be better for all and not just for a few.

Joy accompanies the people's journey; we can always celebrate it when life overcomes death, when justice overcomes injustice, when women find their place in society as men have. The signs are already there, we can already celebrate: joy is paschal; resurrection is already something real that we can talk about and celebrate.

## Conflict in society and Church: incorporated into the new spirituality

The twofold experience of crucifixion and resurrection, the presence of suffering along with hope, conflict between the project of death and the project of life—here is no reason for Nicaraguan women to drop back, here is nothing that should discourage them. On the contrary, experiencing conflict energizes both women and men to move ahead in the struggle for a more just society that may be a sign of God's reign which is "a matter of . . . justice, peace, and the joy that is given by the Holy Spirit" (Rom. 14.17).

Similarly, conflict within the Church, which reflects social contradictions, does not hold Christians back, even though many Christian women find it painful that their pastors do not accompany the people in their anguish and suffering, their joy and hope, rooted in biblical reflection and aimed at a liberating practice to defend life and peace. Indeed, even though in the short run this conflict is preventing Christian commitment to the revolutionary process from growing in a massive way, in the long run it opens up the hope that the Church will truly be born of the people and of the Spirit. Thus it is possible that among the communities may emerge a spirituality that will overcome class-based contradictions and the male clerical ideology that presently prevails in the Church.

## Challenges facing the new spirituality of Nicaraguan women

We still have a great deal to discover. The process we are involved in is very dynamic, on the move. We are obviously sharing a new experience of God under the guidance of the Spirit, in a history-making process that is generating life for both men and women. We believe it is significant that this new spirituality reflects the attitude that many men and women have taken toward the historic change that runs right through the new society. There are signs that lead us to see this new spirituality as the ability of men and women to take new and bold steps, despite the risk and the uncertainty caused by the constant threat under which people must live, steps toward transforming our history as a sign of life taking flesh in history.

This new spirituality emerges from the new historic situation that characterizes the lives of women in a society that is both in transformation and under threat. Such a spirituality is marked by the signs of gratuity and hope, as experience of grace encountered in history. However, we cannot say that this experience is yet finished or complete, and hence we can only speak of new characteristics. The conflictive situation within our churches is one of the very factors that most hinder people from becoming conscious and developing new ways of living their faith.

Rereading the Bible in connection with our own situation has certainly been a key factor leading to a transformed consciousness among Nicaraguan Christians, especially women. However, we continue to be challenged by the possibility of rereading the Bible from the viewpoint of women, with women's eyes, with women's feelings, so as to rediscover or continually rediscover, from our own perspective, a new face of God, a more human and closer image of Jesus.

We also recognize that a challenge we women face is the fact that emphasizing motherhood, being a mother, can be dangerous, since it can limit us to our biological functions. Praising mothers can serve as the best disguise for a male ideology. Sometimes we feel we are trying to strike a balance between the just claims of mothers and the male lauding of motherhood. Thus, avoiding male deception is another great challenge.

One thing is clear: it is impossible to come to a definitive conclusion about the new women's spirituality. Nicaragua is changing. In the future there will be new challenges that we cannot yet envision. With the challenges already put to us, we are struggling on our long journey through the desert toward the promised land of peace, of justice, of equality, of liberation, for both women and men.

We women note another challenge in the fact that in Nicaragua today there is more room for women in the life of the revolutionary society than within the Church itself. Institutionally, the Church continues to be male and clerical. Hence there arise questions of how to translate the new spirituality of Nicaraguan Christian women within the Church, not only within basic ecclesial communities, but within the whole ecclesiastical institution.

Finally, we could bring all these challenges together by asking ourselves how we can move from being a people that is sociologically Christian to being a people that is really believing, that deeply lives out its experience of God, that does not center its faith on a body of doctrines, rituals, rules, and "spiritual exercises" from a Eurocentric, male, and clerical culture, a people whose practice is liberating, whose experience is that of encountering the Lord in the experience of the least, the most humiliated, the most impoverished brothers and sisters, so as to be able, out of that situation, to announce and embody the joyful and exhilarating Good News of Jesus, of the coming of the Kingdom of justice, peace, and fullness of life.

In striving toward and seeking to embody this new spirituality that we have tried to uncover in this presentation, and in meeting the challenges that lie in store for us, we lift our gaze

toward Mary, the mother of Jesus, and we contemplate her as
the new woman, the liberated woman, prophetess of the God of
the poor, who in anticipation sang of the liberating exploits of
God on behalf of the poor, who surrendered her womb and her
whole life to the realization of God's liberating plan in history.
In her, Nicaraguan women see the model for their own
commitment to history and their new spirituality.

I would like to conclude with the text of a simple, popular
Nicaraguan Marian hymn* that expresses all the affection and
commitment present in this new image of Mary as embodied in
the life of our Nicaraguan people:

Mary virgin bird,
Joyful virgin bird,
you with the aching feathers,
you with the thorns and roses.
Little bird in the cotton fields,
bird in the coffee groves,
brown-skinned virgin bird,
black bird in the canefield.

We pray to you through your son,
the beloved one from your womb,
the worker, the peasant,
the humble one, the exploited one.
We pray to you through your people.
Virgin bird, when you fly,
don't let your flight be stained,
little bird of peace.

Virgin bird, seed,
Mary of the corn that has been resown,
Mary, bird and mother
of my tortured brother;
Mary, bird out in the sun,
selling fried food on the corner,
little bird up all night,
little bird on militia duty.

* *Spanish lyrics and music by Carlos Mejia Godoy, poet and composer.*

337

*Pajarita huasiruca*
Virgin bird of maize,
brash little birdie,
border-guarding bird,
little bird from the Segovias,
little bird from San Juan,
little bird from Subtiava,
little bird from Ayapal.

Mary virgin bird,
little bird from Monimbo,
birdie Nicaragua,
bird of Revolution,
freedom-loving birdie,
little bird without borders,
necessary bird,
little guerrilla bird.

Bird with a mature womb,
bitter and sweet beak;
there won't be cages in the future,
little bird of insurrection.
The hope of your wings,
will penetrate all the pain,
birdie Guatemala,
birdie El Salvador.

## A Newly Emerging Spirituality

□ *Chung Hyun Kyung has described the characteristics of Asian women's spirituality as concrete and total, creative and flexible, prophetic and historical, community orientated, pro-life, ecumenical and all-embracing, as well as cosmic and creation-centered. She writes, "Asian women are undertaking a critique of culture and religion. They participate in the interfaith dialogue 'sorting out what are the really liberating elements and what are the oppressive elements in them'. Through this sharp cultural and religious analysis, Asian women are looking for either alternatives or a new synthesis of religio-cultural understanding where women's lives are honored. In this sense Asian women's theology is one of the most important manifestations of their emerging spirituality"* (Struggle to be the Sun Again, *Maryknoll, NY: Orbis Books, 1990, p. 98*).

*In an article that describes her spiritual transformation through educational and social work in the Philippines, Sr. Mary John Mananzan characterizes the newly emerging spirituality of women as showing four trends: it is liberational, integral, feminist, and oriental. Some extracts of this article are reprinted in chapter 34. These tell how she underwent a "baptism of fire" in the Philippines when returning there after traditional academic training in the West. The full text of Sr. Mary John Mananzan's chapter is found in Marc H. Ellis and Otto Maduro, eds.,* The Future of Liberation Theology: Essays in Honor of Gustavo Gutiérrez, *Maryknoll, NY: Orbis Books, 1989, pp. 420–32.*

❖　　❖　　❖

# Theological Perspectives of a Religious Woman Today—Four Trends of the Emerging Spirituality

To be a Christian today in a land where injustice and oppression abide is a challenge. To be a religious woman in such a situation is doubly so. It calls for a radical rethinking of the meaning of being a Christian and of the imperative of religious commitment. It precipitates a spiritual crisis. It demands a consequent revision of one's way of life—a true conversion, a *metanoia*.

This essay will not be a theoretical speculation of what could be the challenges of being a religious woman today, but is a sharing of actual experiences and ongoing reflection on them. Some of these reflections have already been put in writing, so I will quote extensively from my own writing.

## Societal context and personal commitment

One of the most valuable insights of liberation theology is the contextualization of theological reflection and the necessity of the analysis of society as its starting point. It is likewise the characteristic of this way of theologizing to regard one's involvement in the process of societal liberation as the substance of its reflection. This first section will therefore be devoted to these two important points.

### Characteristics of Philippine society

I am a religious woman living in a Third World country, the Philippines. My country is known as the only Christian country in the Far East, having been Christianized by the Spanish colonization in the sixteenth century. It remained a Spanish colony for roughly three and a half centuries, and then fell into the hands of the United States in 1898, becoming its colony for the next fifty years. It was occupied by the Japanese for three years during the Second World War. It became independent in 1946 and was put under martial law in 1972, suffering twenty years of one-man rule, which ended in the famous Edsa Event of February 1986.

But this event, impressive as it was, did not end the misery of the people. There was a change in the head of the nation, but there was no change in the class of those who rule. The oppressive political machinery and its armed component remain. The orientation of the country's economic development model continues. In other words, there was no social revolution. Thus the fundamental problems of the people still prevail—namely, the grossly inequitable distribution of resources (2% of its 56 million inhabitants owning and controlling 75% of its land and capital); and the foreign control of its economy through transnational corporations and through the debt link to the IMF and World Bank. US interventions into its economic and political life have in fact become more overt. These core problems have been responsible for the massive poverty existing in the land, causing 75% of the population to live below the poverty line with dire consequences such as malnutrition, brain-damaged children, unemployment and underemployment, brain and muscle drain, chronic insurgency, and intensifying militarization that has cost so many Filipino lives.

*Baptism of fire*

It was the same situation of crisis, oppression, and injustice that made me respond to a telephone brigade in 1975 asking nuns, seminarians, and priests to come to the rescue of 600 striking workers in a wine factory, La Tondeña. It was the first strike attempted after the strike ban issued following the declaration of martial law in September 1972.

I had just come from a six-year study leave in Germany and Rome, and I was teaching contemporary philosophy in the Jesuit Loyola University. I joined a group called "Interfaith

Theological Circle," which aimed at evolving a "Filipino theology" in the air-conditioned library of the university. Needless to say, we came under critique for doing "intellectual gymnastics" in spite of producing what appeared to us as extremely erudite papers on the subject. After a period of defensiveness, we realized that it was indeed futile to evolve such a theology without getting involved in the struggle of the people. This was what made me respond to the invitation of the Tondeña workers. There I had my first encounter with military brutality and experienced helplessness before the reality of force and institutional violence. That was where we established the "Friends of the Workers."

The Tondeña strike inspired 100 more strikes in a period of three months as we went from one factory to the other, gaining valuable learning experiences from people, getting an insight into the root causes of their problems. Helping workers immersed us in the problems of slum dwellers, for the workers lived in slums. We joined human barricades to stop demolitions. We formed composite groups that spearheaded rallies and marches. We were recruited into negotiating teams to face the military in mass actions. And inevitably we got involved in the fate of political detainees who were arrested in marches, rallies, and pickets, and snatched from their houses in midnight raids.

### The anguish of awareness

This initiation into the struggles of the people shook the framework of my Christian and religious existence. I quote at length an article I wrote at the time describing this experience:

> Social awareness can mean real anguish. Exposures even on a minor scale to the miseries of our people and a serious reflection on these experiences can confront us with facts that would question our former values. And yet it takes time to adopt and synthesize a new set of values one is beginning to perceive. One is back to zero, during this period. One is barren. One stops giving talks or writing articles, because one feels empty, one needs to be reeducated. This awareness gives one a sense of urgency that may seem fantastic to those who either do not see or who confine social consciousness to

community assemblies. Here is where one can make a mistake in strategy, become overzealous, and turn off people. But there is indeed a constriction of the heart, which one feels when one talks with persons who see no further than the four protective walls of their houses or convents. Here is where awareness can cause real loneliness. All of a sudden one is on a different plane when talking with one's family, one's closest friends and colleagues. Not to be able to share values can be a painful form of isolation and the slow, painstaking trial and error attempts to share these new values and new imperatives without turning people off can bring one to a point of helplessness and frustration further aggravated by one's clearer and closer perception of the magnitude of the problem and the uncertainty, tasks, and corresponding magnitude of the proposed solutions. To confront in others time and time again one's own prejudice, one's own blind spots, one's own doubts, is to relive time and time again one's own metanoia without the sense of relief at the thought that the decision and choice lies within one's power. But perhaps the greatest anguish is the yawning gap between one's insight and one's generosity. Insight brings with it imperatives to action that may mean crucial decisions, and to perceive and yet not to have the courage or moral energy to act is a real agony. To conscientize is truly a serious business, because the price of awareness is anguish.[1]

To take stock of things and understand what was happening to themselves, thirty priests and sisters initiated an alternative retreat, which they called *Hakbang* (step forward). These were five days of sharing in-depth experiences of how they got involved, a sharing of anxieties, doubts, apprehensions, fears, hopes, engaging in an analysis both of the society and the Church, and formulating visions for both a transformed society and a renewed Church. Every day was climaxed by a creative liturgy that recapitulated the sharing during the day. This alternative retreat was repeated for other groups. The result was a leveling of consciousness, a greater clarity of vision, a renewed courage born out of common experiences of personal liberation, and a greater motivation to go forward.

## Commitment to women's concerns

The feminist movement is new in the Philippines. Although concerned with prostitution in the Philippines, I did not get involved in the feminist movement until 1978 when I was invited to a World Council of Churches conference in Venice on human rights and women. When I returned to the Philippines I cofounded with three other women the *Filipina*, which can be considered the first organization of women with a conscious and expressly feminist orientation. With another woman I established the Center for Women Resources. This latter took the initiative in 1984 to call a conference of all women's organizations that mushroomed at the time. In this conference, the federation of women's organizations, GABRIELA, was born. It is now the most extensive federation of women in the Philippines, counting 100 member organizations and about forty thousand individual members. In 1986 I was elected its national chairperson and in 1987 re-elected for a period of two years.

GABRIELA has clearly defined the orientation of the women's movement in a Third World country like the Philippines. It sees women's liberation within the context of the economic, political, and cultural transformation of society. This is the necessary, though not sufficient, condition of women's liberation. There is no total human liberation without the liberation of women in society. And this is not an automatic consequence of either economic development or political revolution. In other words, the women's movement is an essential aspect of the very process of societal liberation.

## The cost of commitment

In the preceding pages, the anguish of awareness has been shared. This is preliminary to the cost of commitment. In the thirteen years that I have been involved in the struggle of the poor and the oppressed in the Philippines, I have witnessed the tremendous cost of commitment of persons I knew and worked with, ranging from black propaganda, disappearances, arbitrary arrests, torture, political detention, and rape, to massacre, assassinations, and "salvaging."

I have been labeled a "communist" subversive, and have been served a subpoena for speaking at a rally on the oil price hike, which was considered "agitation for rebellion." Not only is one harassed by the military and by the conservative press, one is likewise subject to the suspicions of church officials who feel "disturbed" and "threatened." There is also the alienation of former friends and relatives who cannot understand one's commitment and involvement.

**Theological reflection**

With a group of theologically trained persons called THRUST and a wider interdisciplinary group called FIDES, theological reflection on the continuous struggle is being undertaken. Lately, the group has published its first volume, *Religion and Society—Towards a Theology of Struggle*. I would like to discuss this work by sharing our efforts and insights in three ongoing endeavors: reflecting on a theology of struggle, developing a feminist theology of liberation in Asia, and evolving a new spirituality. [Editorial note: only part of the last two reflections has been reproduced in what follows.]

*Developing an Asian feminist theology*

As a religious woman, my commitment to the oppressed, which started with political militancy, developed into a commitment for the struggle of women against gender oppression. Again, being a religious woman brought my attention to the religious roots of women's oppression. Together with Asian women coming from different religious and cultural backgrounds, we came to the insight that all religions have oppressive as well as liberating elements, which could serve for or against women; so far, more of the oppressive factors have been used to rationalize and justify the continued subordination of women.

The starting point of this Asian effort at theologizing from the women's perspective is the particular struggle of Asian women.

# Feminist Theology

## The emerging spirituality

Involvement in human struggles brings one to a spiritual crisis. I have described the anguish that comes with initial awareness and the costly consequences of commitment. One goes into a kind of dark night of the soul (*noche oscura*) and, when one emerges, one experiences a shake-up in one's spirituality, which may result either in "giving up one's faith" (some of my friends have chosen this option), or undergoing a real *metanoia*.

The emerging spirituality, in my experience, shows four trends. It is a spirituality that is liberational, integral, feminist, and oriental.

During the *Hakbang* or alternative retreat of the religious and priests mentioned in the beginning of this essay, each one shared their journey to commitment. The remarkable consensus was that each one experienced an inner liberation. Christ, the fully liberated person, became the inspiration. The involvement with oppressed persons helps one toward better self-knowledge and self-acceptance, which becomes the basis of an inner liberation that manifests itself in a growing freedom from fear, from idols, and from bitterness and resentment. Freedom from fear does not consist of not feeling fear, but in the ability to distinguish between groundless fear and substantiated fear, and to act in spite of such a substantiated fear. One becomes less worried about what the "anonymous they" might be thinking or criticizing. Besides being free from this "negative idol," one also experiences a freedom from legalism and from sacralizing law or from being enslaved to positive idols that one had put on pedestals during one's life. Although acknowledging the bitterness and resentment in one's negative experiences, one begins to transcend them into a creative and positive resolution of one's problems.

There is also a remarkable simplifying of one's faith and one's practices. There is an integration of the vertical and horizontal dimensions of one's religious life. To elaborate:

> It is understandable that one's spirituality will be influenced by this new thrust, or else there will be a painful dichotomy. One's life of prayer will be "invaded" by the anguish of people. The psalms take on a relevance in confrontation with

new pharaohs and a new Egypt or the need for a new Exodus and a new Promised Land. Liturgy will have to echo the crying aspirations of the oppressed as much as the joy of every step toward their liberation. The asceticism of the religious committed to justice need not be contrived. It will be imposed on her by the difficult situations that will inevitably arise; the demands of people that cannot be put on a rigidly controlled timetable or calendar; in the expected persecution from the rich and powerful whose vested interests will be endangered; and in the misunderstandings of friends and loved ones who would be threatened by one's radicality.[2]

The feminist perspective to spirituality developed as women started to reflect on their experiences as women, both personal and social, as well as on their common struggle against their manifold oppression. This spirituality is nourished by their growing understanding of their self-image which has been obscured by the roles that have been assigned to them by a patriarchal society. This in turn influences their interpersonal relationships and touches the collective consciousness that is growing among them as they struggle against exploitation and discrimination. It is shaped by the victories, small or big, which they have achieved in their struggle. Women's emerging spirituality is therefore not just a vertical relationship with God, but an integral one. It is shaped not only by prayer, but by relational experience and struggle, personal, interpersonal, and societal.

The release of creative energy and the new insights in the women's struggle have likewise affected a new focus and new expressions of spirituality. It is creation-centered rather than sin- and redemption-centered. It is holistic rather than dualistic. It is risk rather than security. It is a spirituality that is joyful rather than austere, active rather than passive, expansive rather than limiting. It celebrates more than it fasts; it lets go rather than holds back. It is an Easter rather than a Good Friday spirituality. It is vibrant, liberating, and colorful.

The holistic aspect that feminist influence has exerted on spirituality has likewise given rise to a phenomenon newly observed among activists in the Philippines, and that is the reclaiming of the contemplative heritage of Asia's great religions. More and more social activists in the Philippines are taking up the practice of Zen, which they undertake with great enthusiasm. Ruben Habito explains that the term "spirituality" equates with the Greek *pneuma* (spirit), which in turn equates with the Hebrew *ruach*, the breath of God. Throughout the Old and New Testaments, the breath of God plays a key role in all the events of salvation history from creation to the incarnation. Habito then shows the relationship between Zen practice and social militancy:

> Paying attention to one's breathing in Zen is seen not simply as a physical exercise that keeps one concentrated on one point, but as the very abandonment of one's total being to this Breath of God, here and now. It is letting one's whole self be possessed by the Spirit of God, to be vivified, guided, inspired, and fulfilled in it.
>
> And as one is "overshadowed" by the Spirit, one's whole being is offered for God's dynamic liberating action in history, to preach the good news to the poor. To proclaim release to the captives. To set at liberty those who are oppressed.[3]

In another way of expressing this, Sister Elaine MacInnes writes of the socially significant effect of Zen practice:

> Our dissipated energies gradually become more unified and we start to gain some control over our superactive mind. Tensions are released, nerves are relaxed, and physical health generally improves. Emotions are sensitized. We begin to experience a kind of inner balance and gradually dryness, rigidity, hang-ups, prejudice, egoism melt and give way to compassion, serenity, egolessness, and social concern.[4]

The koan method presents the Zen student with "riddles," which the intellect repels but are grasped by the self-nature in an intuitive response. The student soon comes to see that everyday life is a koan, which invites response. As Sister Elaine further writes: "When we see someone thirsty, we give a drink. When we are confronted with injustice, we cannot remain unmoved."[5]

This recourse to oriental mysticism for social activists closes the full circle of action/contemplation/action.

## Conclusion

Being a religious woman today is more difficult, less simple, more demanding, but definitely more challenging. When I hear a young woman answer the question "Why do you want to enter the convent?" with "Because I want to have peace and quiet," I just smile.

The religious life has come a long way from the *fuga mundi* principle of the early days of monasticism. Religious women who were particularly the objects of enclosure laws of canon law (because they were not only *religious* but *women*) have emerged from this constraint and have become involved in the burning issues of society, and in some cases have been at the forefront of militant causes.

Personally, I find being a religious woman today in a Third World country a dangerous, but challenging and meaningful, existence. It forces one to go back to the original meaning of the core of the Christian message. Impelled by a sense of urgency because of the lived experience of suffering and oppression, religious women are inspired to a consequent living out of this Christian imperative in the concrete struggles of their world. This in turn gives them an experiential insight into the meaning of the paradox of committed freedom. The religious woman committed to justice becomes truly convinced that to seek her life is to lose it and to lose her life is to gain it, not only for herself but for others—for those who will perhaps see the fulfillment of her vision of a better world, something she will probably not see in her own lifetime.

❖     ❖     ❖

☐ *The Asian religions possess great spiritual resources for the renewal of faith in the contemporary world. Christian women in Asia have begun to discover this heritage and have entered into dialogue with some of their sisters. The first Asian women's consultation on interfaith dialogue was held in Kuala Lumpur in 1989 (see the report* Faith Renewed, *Hong Kong: Asian Women's Resource Center for Culture and Theology). Feminism and interfaith dialogue are beginning to have an impact on each other, although this has not been much noted yet in official circles—where the spokesmen of dialogue tend to be mostly male religious leaders of traditional religious institutions. For other sources on women and dialogue, consult Diana L. Eck and Devaki Jain, eds.,* Speaking of Faith: Cross-cultural Perspectives on Women, Religion and Social Change *(New Delhi: Kali for Women; and London: Women's Press, 1986);* Virginia Ramey Mollenkott, ed., Women of Faith in Dialogue *(New York: Crossroad, 1988); Maura O'Neill,* Women Speaking, Women Listening: Women in Interreligious Dialogue *(Maryknoll, NY: Orbis Books, 1990).*

*The importance of interfaith dialogue has already been touched upon in chapter 6 where Kwok Pui-lan wrote on "The Future of Feminist Theology." Chapter 35, written by Aruna Gnanadason from India, looks at Asian spirituality primarily from the Indian perspective of divine female power or* shakti. *It is taken from the journal* In God's Image *(December 1989, pp. 15-18).*

❖     ❖     ❖

# 35  ARUNA GNANADASON

# Women and Spirituality in Asia

Shakti means power, force, the feminine energy, for she represents the primal creative principle underlying the cosmos. She is the energizing force of all divinity, of every being and every thing. The whole universe is the manifestation of Shakti, a Shakta or follower of Shakti-worship, regards her as the Supreme Reality. The ritual side of the Shakta philosophy consists of the worship of the different forms of this Universal Energy personified as a goddess. Shakti is known by the general name *devi*, from the Sanskrit root *div* "to shine." She is the Shining One, who is given different names in different places and in different appearances, as the Symbol of the life-giving powers of the universe.

India is the only country where the goddess is still widely worshipped today, in a tradition that dates to the Harappan culture of 3000 BC and earlier. Mother-goddess and fertility cults in which female divinities predominate appear to have constituted the indigenous religious beliefs of the prehistoric period. A prehistoric megalith is still worshipped at the shrine of the Earth Mother, Bolhai, in Madhya Pradesh, Central India. The Goddess is represented by a smooth, oval, red-costed stone. The capstone is about seven feet long, and rings like a bell when struck, or when rubbed with another stone in a ritual still practised. The whole surface has been fashioned without metal tools as a representation of the Earth Mother who is "the personified abstraction of cosmic life." She is the first creation, and conceived of as the Great Mother.

"Shakti" means more than *power*, as we understand it. It is more than mere economic, political, social, and cultural power—it is not the power to dominate or oppress. Shakti is a spiritual energy, a feminine force, which is the essence of the great religious traditions of Asia. It is an energy that is at the source of all things—*purusha* (human) and *prakriti* (nature). It is the foundation of Asia's spirituality, which makes sacramental the relationship between humanity and the rest of creation.

And yet, in spite of the presence of this strong spiritual power that is the essence of Asian womanhood, the reality of the lives Asian woman live is not even a small reflection of this power. The majority of Asian women in fact live a life of total powerlessness caught in the grip of poverty and deprivation, denied basic social, political, religious, and economic rights. Twice and thrice oppressed Asian women sell their labor and sexuality to a system that is dependent on exploitation and abuse of large sections of the society, in which women are the worst sufferers.

Where is Shakti in a woman who would be willing to sell her daughter or herself in prostitution so that she can feed her children? Where is Shakti in a woman who would be harassed by the military, tortured, and raped in a jail for her political beliefs? Where is Shakti in a woman who watches helplessly her husband, her son, her brother shot dead by the bullet of an armyman *or* the bullet of a freedomfighter? Where is Shakti in a woman who drains her labor for low and unequal wages and sometimes faces sexual harassment in a sweat-shop of the capitalist or in the fields, who submits to degrading medical technologies or is coerced into aborting a female fetus or into inhuman control of her reproductive rights? Where is Shakti in a woman who can be advertised to sell goods or who is forced into becoming a mail-order bride?

Shakti, the Great Mother, has been submerged under the onslaught of patriarchal religions. Swami Vivekananda, one of the greatest religious/philosophical leaders India has ever known, and who lived in the late nineteenth century, had predicted that the hope for all creation lies in "the resurgence of the Mother into the consciousness of the world's population, after patriarchal religions had forced her into concealment in the unconscious."

Shakti, the Great Mother, has also been submerged under the kind of economic, political, social, cultural, and religious directions the world has taken. It is a direction built on a particular development model that is Eurocentric and androcentric in orientation; and that can flourish *only* on the exploitation of human labor and of the earth and its resources. It is a model that has become the universal for all nations. It is based on one European system of "knowledge" which has undermined the experience and indigenous knowledge of women, of the poor, of the outcast, of the people who live in close affinity with nature. It is built on a "scientific temper" that has no place for feelings, the emotions, for a spiritual dimension. This scientific/technological monster is slowly destroying the earth and all its peoples, the forests, the waters, the air, even space. We now live in this "modern" age of denuded forests, of floods and droughts, of acid rain, and the greenhouse effect, of pollution and new, strange, and dangerous viruses, of nuclear leaks and dead fish in the rivers, of plenty in the midst of poverty, of wasteful expenditure in the midst of external debt and its vice-like grip, of exotic food habits and the habit of chewing the deadly beetlenut leaf to ward off hunger. We now live in the "modern" age! Shakti has no place here.

## A new spirituality

But from the midst of all these symbols of death there is a fresh burst of new life. Oppressed people struggle to break out of the chains that bind them. The human spirit cannot be suppressed forever. As Asian women participate in this process of struggle, they give birth to a spirituality that is particularly women's and specifically Asian. The Great Mother breaks out of all that has bound her and frees, creates anew, and liberates all creation "which has been groaning as a woman in travail." Shakti emerges triumphant.

What is this Asian women's spirituality? Mary John Mananzan and Sun Ai Park describe it this way:

In Christian theology and practice, an old understanding of spirituality would more or less describe it as theology applied to daily life—to one's personal life of prayer and asceticism, to be more precise. There is, however, an emerging understanding of spirituality as the inner core made up of all the experiences and encounters one has had in one's life and out of which come the motivations, inspirations, and commitment that make one live and decide in a particular way. One might say, it is the shape in which the Holy Spirit has molded herself into one's life.

Gustavo Gutiérrez expresses the holistic nature of spirituality in a rather pointed way: "When one is concerned with one's own stomach, it is materialism, but when one is concerned with other people's stomachs it is spirituality." Both are concerned with the stomach, but one is called materialism and the other spirituality. Christian spirituality deals with this fine distinction, which can be summed up as the unity of self and others, the material and the spiritual, love and justice, community and individuals, religions and politics, peace and struggle toward holistic salvation.

Women's struggle is part and parcel of the historical struggle for the holistic salvation of all humanity. Women can make a unique contribution toward this goal based on their spirituality, which is formulated throughout their concrete pro-life way of living and experiencing. All the disastrous dimension of patriarchal culture is typically exemplified in its demeaning, ignoring, and despising the very spirituality of women that is oriented toward and sustaining life in love. The spirituality affirming womanhood, reaching out for liberation of all women and all humanity, is emerging in all parts of the world, and Asia is not exempt.

Thus it is a spirituality that emerges out of the "han" (accumulated anger, as Korean theologians would call it) of the exploited and powerless women of Asia. In the words of the Korean *Minjung* theologian Hyun Young-Hak:

Han is a sense of unresolved resentment against injustice suffered, a sense of helplessness because of the overwhelming odds against, a feeling of total abandonment ("Why hast thou forsaken me?"), a feeling of acute pain, of sorrow in one's guts and bowels making the whole body writhe and wriggle, and an obstinate urge to take "revenge" and to right the wrong, all these constitute "han".

Asian women, who normally have never been given the public space to give expression to their pent-up anger, develop a sense of deep resignation and submissiveness to their lot. The releasing or the Han of Han-pu-ri (a ritual in a popular women-centered religion Shamanism in Korea) is an expression of the emerging spirituality of Asian women:

> Han-pu-ri became one of the few spaces where poor Korean women played their spiritual role without being dominated by male-centered religious authorities, Han-ridden women got together and tried to release their accumulated Han through Han-pu-ri (a ritual dance).

There are three important steps in Han-pu-ri. The first step is *speaking and hearing*. The shaman (priest, more often priestess) gives the Han-ridden persons or ghosts the chance to break their silence. The shaman enables the persons or ghosts to let their Han out publicly. The shaman makes the community hear the Han-ridden stories. The second step is *naming*. The shaman enables the Han-ridden persons or ghosts (or their communities) to name the source of their oppression. The third step is *changing* the unjust situation by action so that Han-ridden persons or ghosts can have peace.

## Some characteristics of the re-emergence of Shakti

The rebirth of Shakti has led Asian women to have a "hermeneutics of suspicion" of traditional spiritualities, of traditional interpretations of scriptures and even of traditional understandings and analysis of society. It has led to a critique of models of development and patterns of life. It has therefore liberated Asian women from narrow definitions of what women's freedom and power may mean. It is *not* individualistic or based on the wresting of small concessions or benefits within existing unjust structures. It has made women conscious of their responsibility to all of humanity—particularly the most oppressed—and to all of creation. It is in this re-emergence of Shakti, or spiritual energy, that Asian women find God.

**This discovery is based on:**

## (1) An affirmation of a new community in Christ

Asian feminists are growing in consciousness of the need to affirm the community dimension of Asian society. This cornerstone of Asian society must only be nurtured and strengthened. The search is for a communal social ethic built on what Rosemary Radford Ruether calls "communal personhood." Women find their dignity, their selfhood, and reclaim their right to define what their womanhood is, what their femininity means—all *in community*.

Motherhood has played a crucial role in the new emerging spirituality in Asia. Mary John and Sun Ai write:

> The experience of motherhood must be incorporated in the process of marching toward a new society, which feminist women and men envision. The nature of this new society is feminist. Feminism promotes the equality of all human beings, and the ideology is derived from the experience of women giving birth, and nurturing their children and family to the extent of denying themselves in the highest spirituality of love. The women do this in order to give life and to provide for others so that all may live. Here the self and the community are one.

However, it is this same noble quality of selfgiving of Asian women that has been used to keep them in a position of subservience. Mary John and Sun Ai continue:

> However, there can be a danger of condoning the traditional self-effacing masochism of women reinforced in the glorification of motherhood, keeping them in the depth of despair and resignation. This is so if motherhood is used for exploitation, by an individual man, of one or more women where nothing is questioned and no meaning is given. However, when conscientized women and men act and live out this supreme spirituality toward the goal of a new heaven and new earth in concrete models, it is liberational.

Therefore, the search for a community of people where all will find space for creativity and fulfillment, a community that will live in real peace with justice, a community that will be ever alert to its responsibility to give birth to new life by challenging forces of death—this is the most important characteristic of Asian women's spirituality.

## (2) Asian women will be critically involved in liberation struggles

Asian women are seeking feminist alternatives to the destructive and anti-life attitudes that now abound. In this process they provide a critique of the development model followed by their countries and the mounting pressures on the poor to sustain the burden of this so called "progress." Feminists also provide a critique of existing political ideologies and their indifference to cultural questions such as caste, race, and gender. The feminist liberation paradigm offers to the movements of people a critique in terms of leadership, decisionmaking processes, their hierarchy of patriarchal relationships, and also their very "masculine" methodologies and strategies. Thus it is a critical involvement in liberation struggles of the people. The emerging Shakti not only attempts to provide new answers—it raises new questions too.

## (3) Celebration of plurality

Asian women of all faiths together are engaged in a common spiritual search for a new society. They transcend with ease narrow divisions of faith, caste, cultural identity, and ideology to reflect and act on issues of importance. The increasing religious fundamentalism in all religions makes women conscious that religion can in fact be used against them, because the first victims of fundamentalism *are* women—restrictions of time, space, and movement are quickly imposed on them. In almost all Asian countries, women are the most affected by attempts by the majority religious community to exert "uniformity" on all identities *and* by the inevitable paranoiac attempts by the minority religious groups to preserve their identity at all costs. The attempts by the past President of Pakistan at "Islamization"; or the uproar caused by fundamentalists to a poor woman's (Shah Bano) attempts in India to seek refuge in the Supreme Court against the unjust Muslim law that denies her the right to maintenance from her estranged husband, or Malaysia's context of worsening communal relations—all point to the need for women to play a more courageous reconciling and anti-communalist role. In the midst of all the prevailing suspicion and even hatred, women have begun to celebrate their plurality.

In spite of all these abuses of religion and in spite of the fact that all religions have gone through a process of patriarchalization, women seek the liberative strands in their faiths. From the great religious traditions of Asia, women draw out a spirituality that empowers, a spirituality that can support women in their struggle for a new world order. And through their fervent prayers and by their participation in the liberation struggles of their people, they discover the meaning of the spirituality that can sustain them through their pain, their tears, their hopes for a new world.

## (4) Popular religiousness

More recently Asian women are drawing strength from the popular religions of the people. These ancient religious traditions are the religion of the poor and marginalized. They often contain within them elements of protest that can become a force for social change. It is interesting that in many of them women have played an important role—they are in essence women's liberation-centered. Reference is already made in this presentation to Shamanism from Korea. Passion (the recital of the Passion and death of Jesus) and Samahen de Tres Personas Unos Divos (the Association of Three-Persons-One-God) in the Philippines are pre-Christian cults that later appropriated Christian symbols. These cults express the aspiration of the people for justice and liberation.

India has a tradition of female worship before pre-Aryan patriarchal culture penetrated the Indian scene:

Evidence of Feminine ultimacy is widely prevalent in India whether venerated as Nature or the life-force, as Mother or Virgin, as Great Goddess, or as the Ultimate Reality. As well as the goddess figurines discovered at the various archaeological sites such as Harappa and Mohenjo-daro, the Atharva Veda, which mirrors the way of life and thought of the indigenous peoples, shows that pre-Vedic, non-Aryan religion and belief were to a great extent Female-oriented.

Folk religions today are mostly women-centered. Almost every village deity in South India is a female form. Worship of the Mother goddess and fertility goddesses center on the restoration of the soil and its nourishment for the production of food for the people of the earth, establishing a principle that lays emphasis on humanity's responsibility to the earth.

Asian women recognize that religiousness can become oppressive and escapist, but there is a realization that these traditional popular religions cannot be ignored—they have to be appropriated to become a force in the transformation of society.

In this process, attempts are made to go to folk sources— poetry, music, stories, myths (many of which have been lost, as they belong to the oral tradition)—to derive from them the wealth of meaning and spiritual power they provide. Dalit and tribal literature in India is a case in point. Shakti is also known as *Svatantrya*, meaning independence and freedom—she is the source of liberation for enslaved peoples.

### Shakti—a spirituality of empowerment

The life experience of voiceless, faceless, powerless women of Asia who search for their organized power is essentially a spirituality. Women's attempts to break through the culture of silence and to transform their pain into political power is a deeply spiritual experience. Women's attempts to draw out their suppressed creativity, their songs, and their stories of struggle and liberation are deeply spiritual.

It is a spirituality that would say "yes" to life and "no" to forces of death. It is life affirming, nurturing, creating spirituality—in the bleeding of blood, the cleansing and preparing for new life month after month have drawn new power that will no longer control and stifle their creativity, but will be symbolic of the longing for a new and transformed Asia. In sisterhood, in communal selfhood, in solidarity with all other oppressed people, in the simplicity of the lifestyle of the women's movement, and in their commitment to heal a wounded creation and wounded world, women are expressing an Asian feminist spirituality. Shakti, the feminine energy force, our liberator God, has re-emerged in splendour—to her we turn for a new vision of a new world order.

*□ The notion of the Spirit is linked with that of power, with a life-giving dynamic—an experience of empowerment, strength, and vital energy. It is also connected with the idea of healing, of being made whole and healthy. In many religions, such experiences of healing and wholeness are seen as a divine gift bestowed on humans by a superhuman power or Supreme Spirit that is referred to by many different names.*

*In chapter 36, Mercy Amba Oduyoye from Ghana describes traditional African experiences of prayer and ritual linked to the spiritual empowerment of women. Charismatic churches in Africa frequently draw on indigenous ideas and blend these with Christian beliefs and practices. Oduyoye looks at women's prayers, the power derived from singing and other aspects of ritual and spiritual life that provide women with sources of strength, and give them great spiritual potency recognized by the community. The chapter is reprinted from Susan Brooks Thistlethwaite and Mary Potter Engel, eds.,* Lift Every Voice. Constructing Christian Theologies from the Underside *(San Francisco: HarperCollins, 1990, pp. 246–58).*

## 36 MERCY AMBA ODUYOYE

# The Empowering Spirit of Religion

The Christianity of the rank and file is not necessarily that of the priestly class, though it is the face of the Church that the world sees. People of the Church who are ordinarily in daily converse with one another are the carriers of religion. How they live and what they live by is what constitutes Christianity for the observer. If Christians read their Bibles, pray with the African Instituted Churches (AIC—churches in the charismatic tradition in western Africa) as well as the Roman Catholic priest, they reinforce the notion of openness of the spirit that moves all Christians. It is the popular beliefs and practices passed on from mothers to their children that build up a person's spirituality.

The religious lives of women in Africa are yet to be studied in any detail. General observation of the high proportion of women compared to men who practice distinctive types of spirituality suggests this as an important arena for investigation. Given that women of Africa visit shrines, diviners, holy persons, and traditional doctors, some preliminary questions are: Why do women follow religio-cultural rites and rituals that are sometimes physically risky? Why this keen awareness of a necessity to stay close to the mysterious forces behind creation? What makes women so vulnerable to the spiritual dimensions of life? The all-women cults in West Africa will also yield material for further understanding of spirituality. It is not enough to keep saying women are religious. One should also ask why they are and what benefit they derive from it.

This chapter explores spirituality (understood here as the energy by which one lives and which links one's worldview to one's style of life) in the lives of African women. It observes women at prayer in two religious traditions, the primal religions of Africa and Christianity, examining prayers and praise uttered by a Ghanaian woman, Afua Kuma, and moving into an exploration of songs as carriers of spirituality. The ways in which integration of this traditional spirituality takes place in the lives of Christian women are illustrated with examples from Malawi. I have concluded with my reflections on the significance of these prayers and songs for a distinctively African women's spirituality.

### The power of a woman's prayer

A woman sat in an extended family meeting astonished at the lack of caring in the handling of the matter at hand. It all sounded to her most "untraditional." Another woman was being scolded in the presence of younger members of the family. Present at the meeting was a maternal uncle's son who, according to custom, was not a member of his father's family and therefore should not be at the meeting to witness the debating of what was a serious threat to the unity of the family.

When the astonished woman could not hold on to herself any longer she left the meeting room, which had belonged to the previous head of family who had passed away a decade or so ago. She put both hands on her head and cried out *"Nana ee bohwe woegyir"* ("Grandfather come and see/supervise what is going on here, now that you are gone"). It was the turn of the men sitting as judges in the hall of meeting to be distraught. "What is she doing, is she calling our uncle to come and punish us?" A cry of distress directed to the ancestors is bound to have repercussions if injustice is being done to a member of the family.

My reading of this situation and others like it is that women's alacrity and initiative in matters of religion arise out of the fact that they are usually the first or the most directly affected by catastrophe. In direct appeal to spiritual powers and praise of God, women are first to be moved by the Spirit. It is in formal liturgy that women are pushed to the margins, usually by all-male performers of religious ritual.

In African religions the formal incantations that accompany sacrifice, and in Christianity the recitation of prayers in sacramental rites, are usually denied to women. The leaders of organized religion, like their brothers in politics, hesitate to empower women to perform. In Africa it is in African Instituted Churches, founded and led by African women and men, that this men's monopoly is beginning to break down. In the AIC, women are on a par with men in the matter of singing and praying. In the original languages, prayers from these churches do not make a gender differentiation. It is only when they have been "reduced" into English by "collectors" that the women are blotted out by the generic use of *man*. Let us see what a feminist consciousness reveals from these AIC prayers.

## AIC-designated "Spiritual Churches"

Rosemary N. Edet, a retired schoolteacher studying to become a Presbyterian minister, has had many encounters with the AIC. She describes the practices of the Christ Army Church founded by Elijah Garrick Braide in 1915 as a movement away from the Anglican Church of Bakan in Nigeria. Like several new Christian movements of the late nineteenth and early twentieth centuries elsewhere in Africa, it was born out of opposition to the racism and ethnocentrism of Euro-Americans on the continent. Edet finds its distinctiveness in the seriousness with which Acts 2.17 is appropriated: "Your sons and daughters shall prophesy." This has freed women from the imposed understandings of themselves as clients of a male priesthood. Not only that, they have appropriated the role of diviners, by prophesying in the context of worship.

In this church the healing ministry is in the hands of a prophetess called "Mother," and it is her ministry that draws members to the church. Through her ministrations people are able to have the causes of their many afflictions identified and remedies proposed. The system of healing she practices lends itself to the suspicion that "powers not altogether Christian" are being used. But then, I ask, who can fathom the deep roots of human spirituality amid a religiously pluralist people? The fact is that prayer-healing is a central aspect of the life of AIC, resorted to by both women and men. It has established itself as a gift of the Holy Spirit, given to women and men alike.

Elizabeth Amoah contends that to get at "the vital aspects of women's experience of God" in Africa, one would have to take into account all the living religions in Africa. She contends further that cutting across all religions is the fact that women are more demonstrative of their spirituality and more ready to confess their dependence on the movement of the Spirit. Writing on women in the AIC-designated "Spiritual Churches," Amoah says: "Women in these churches are very much convinced that true spirituality can be attained and sustained through vigorous fasting, praying and reflecting on the word of God. This they claim is the true way by which God grants them the Spirit and the power to do the tasks ahead of them."[1] They rely on God for the Spirit that empowers them. That women's spiritual powers are often calumnized as of the devil is nothing new. But women survive, strengthened by the sayings of Jesus: "By their fruits you shall know them"; "How can Satan cast out Satan?" These women add, "And by what spirit do men perform comparable deeds?"

Spirit-directed women appropriate the healing power of Jesus for the benefit of those who come to them. Women who face marital problems, tensions associated with barrenness, or trading problems, consult these Spirit-directed women, who make new songs and pray effectively for every occasion. Like Edet, Amoah observes that "many people are attracted to them because they want to know what the future has for them."[2] The effectiveness of the Spirit-directed life of the AIC and the efficacy of their prayers is acknowledged by many in Africa.

An Anglican laywoman and a Yoruba, Bisi Sowunmi, challenged a group of Nigerian theologians with the question, "Where is theology in Nigeria?" In her piece she refers to the "indigenous appellations of God" as "profound and inspiring" and points to their use in the AIC, "where prayers are more meaningful, deep and efficacious." The importance attached to names in Africa is such that the AIC are digging into extra-biblical materials and spirituality for more names for God, using Akan sources that give people confidence.

## One woman's spirituality

With this we are ready for Afua Kuma, a charismatic leader in the AIC, whose prayers are resplendent with potent names of God. Sowunmi asks Nigerian theologians whether they have considered using imagery from the IFA corpus of divination poems. Afua does not have to resort to a collected version of an African corpus. She lives in the midst of it and can tap directly into it. She "uses the language of African customs and proverbs, and African traditions of worship and chieftaincy to praise the name of Jesus."[3] Her prayers are distinguished by the fact that even petitions are made implicit in praise. Her appellations for Jesus range from human titles of royalty and warriors to that of friend and mother, the highest praise a woman gives a man. She calls on Jesus as a strong presence in nature, mountains, rocks, pythons, or in dependable human creations like unsinkable boats. Even modern professionals like doctors, lawyers, teachers, police, and soldiers become image-bearers of the Christ figure. Jesus is "The Big Tree which enables the vine to see the heavens while shedding drops of water from its leaves to nurture the undergrowth."[4] It is Jesus, the savior of the poor, who supports the poor, and makes them into respected persons. Creepers and climbers all enjoy the mothering care of Jesus.

Between the trickster tradition of Akan folktales and the "wonder-workers" of the Bible, Afua Kuma has built up for herself and those with whom she prays a powerful image of "Jesus, the wonder-worker" while holding on to the wise and intimate friend image. In times of difficulty a woman affirms "Jesus is the rock in times of trouble. He helps the poor very often (always)." With such a one for a friend, life's battles are won hands down. Afua Kuma's prayers are in the spirit of this "Efik woman's Thanksgiving":

Jesus is my true friend
He saved my soul from death
He gave me everlasting life
He is worthy to be praised
O glorify Jesus Christ

*Mmrane* in Twi and *oriki* in Yoruba mean praise-names of one's forebearers often associated with one's own name. These are less formal than the family and official histories of great deeds of generations. Recitation of *mmrane* provides one with courage and confidence to face the task at hand, heightens the will to live, and to do so honorably and creatively. What Afua Kuma offers us is the *Mmrane of Jesus Christ*. Believers who hear this walk confidently in the power of those praise-names. Their spirits are lifted, their faith established, and their hope is strengthened. With all this, their strength is renewed for the tasks of life before them.

A spirituality that derives directly from one's personal experience of Jesus is sometimes questioned by the official clan priests, who see themselves as mediators of grace through prayer and sacrament. It is therefore no surprise that by the time one gets to the fourteenth page of Afua Kuma's *Mmrane* of Jesus, one meets the question:

You and I have got Jesus
What a precious find
What about these priests?

Read in the original Twi language, the question *"Na Asofo yie?"* sounds like "and these priests, where do they come in?" It seems to be a characteristic of Jewish and Christian traditions for the priests to try to appropriate women's independent expression of spirituality and sanctify it by priestly presence (see 1 Sam. 1.1-19). Afua's *Mmrane* of Jesus turns toward the end to a gospel call. To share the source of one's strength is the sign of a life rooted in faith:

Come, all you people, to Jesus
And you too will shine.

This is followed by the interruption, "It is Jesus who has made the priests into shiney ones," which is evidence of priestly cooptation of women's spirituality. The priests have inserted themselves into the chant.

The attempts of the priestly investigators to coopt Afua's vivid Christology is evidence of the genuine power derived from her spirituality which is expressed in the following:

We have come to earth to tire ourselves out
In Jesus we find rest.

and

Jesus is the pod which explodes to scatter the beans
That make the sterile beget twins.

## The potent prayer of women

The way women pray, says Annie Nachisale of Malawi, has not changed very much. All Christian women have done is to pray through Jesus rather than through their grandmothers and great-grandmothers who have gone before them.[5] In her country, she says, women have more concern for serving God. "If God is sparing the world, it is because of the prayers of women." Whether traditional women or Christian, when women gather to pray, they pray first for the whole world, then for their leaders and their families, and only finally for themselves. The hearts of women in Africa meet in prayer. All women believe that because *they* are, that's why *we* are. Standing together is strength for women, and there are several women's praying groups in Malawi.

African women pray in times of sickness and health, for rain and for well-being of the community, and in thanksgiving. Prayers for children and appearances at every available shrine in order to secure them and keep them healthy are the prime essence of women's spirituality. Like men, they believe that life is meaningless unless one bears children. When the children are sick, women do not sleep, they pray the whole night as they nurse the sick child:

Lord, you gave me this child as a gift.
Let the child grow, so that it might also
serve you and I might rejoice together
with you. Please Lord, spare the child.

When a child is dead, women do not stop praying. They continue:

Lord, we do thank you that you gave us a child that
it may make us happy in our friend's family. It is
a sorrow to see that it has pleased you to take what
is yours. We pray, "Help the mourners, remove their
sorrow and tears from their eyes in the name of Jesus."

When there is sickness in the village, a communal prayer is offered under the leadership of the village prophetess, who prays:

*aa Nkazikunkholo*, children are finishing in the
village. Let the children cry and make noise in our
houses. When the moon is shining, let the children
sing and dance outside our house. Please
grandmother, hear our prayer. God have mercy on us.
Let the children grow.

Priestess and the people then pray:

Yes, yes, yes, *Mthini, yes, yes, yes, Maseko.*

Mthini and Maseko are names of respect for the clan's ancestor spirit. It is an honor to appease the spirit by praising it.

When her husband dies, in her grief a woman laments "my husband, you have abandoned me."[6] The dirges sung by women are full of praise for the dead and regrets for the parting. They weep because "what death holds on to, a human being cannot snatch," while they sing "human beings would indeed be worth nothing if there was no death." Death is both welcomed and abhorred. It is, however, accepted as inevitable after every known cure has failed.

In a culture in which men don't cry, it is not easy to ascertain the nature of men's grief and in what way it is verbalized. Men wear all the symbolic trappings of mourning. But women's protest against the separation and the disruption that death causes to the community is always loud and clear.

Women are a rearguard of prayer and ritual performances at all of life's many war fronts. In Africa rain is one such front. In Malawi when there is no rain in the country, a woman functions as a prophetess with priestesses. They come together under a big tree, bringing with them a plate of flour, some beer, and perhaps an animal they have sacrificed. The prophetess, with her assistant priestesses, kneels down under the tree, calling on the ancestor spirit:

| | |
|---|---|
| Prophetess: | *A Sofiva, a Nkazikunkholo, a Phalaro!!!* |
| Priestesses: | *Sorry, Sorry, Sorry . . . ry!* |
| Prophetess: | The country is dry, we have drought, we need rain. Please convey our plea to God. We your children will die of hunger. |
| Priestesses: | Sorry, Sorry, Sorry . . . ry! |
| Prophetess: | *A Nkazikunkholo*, do you want all of us dead with hunger? Who is going to continue the clan's name? Give us rain. |

Within a short time clouds start forming and later the rains fall—sometimes even before they have finished praying. Women derive strength from the knowledge that God hears and answers the prayers of sincere believers who are dedicated to the welfare of the whole community.

Women who operate entirely in the African religion are energized by the prayer, songs, and rituals of their traditions.

They are both "clients" and "professionals," appropriating the strength emanating from the spirit-dimension to support them in the arduous duties of mothering the people. They develop a self-image of servants whose service is their source of honor and dignity. They are who they are because they make the community what it is. It is a spirituality of self-giving and a sense of justice and fair play. It is a spirituality founded on sharing all that is life-giving. As a Kenyan song says:

Great love I found there
Among women and children
A bean fell to the ground —
We split it among ourselves.

This is a spirit of *harambee* (cooperation and sharing that characterize self-help groups of urban or rural women in Africa) that women strain themselves to promote. This concern for wholeness in women's spirituality flows among Christian and Moslem women too, for it is embodied in traditional African womanness.

I do not wish to minimize the intensity of the spiritual contribution of women in the mainline churches of Africa that are more Westernized. I call attention to the AIC because that is where the spirituality of women has found a wider range of expression. What we find in the AIC, however, could be said to apply to all Christian women, especially when they pray outside a formal church gathering.

The thanskgiving prayers of African Christians reflect the petitionary prayers of both the African religion and the AIC. However, since giving thanks under all circumstances is a demand of Christianity, there is added a petition "Let us not give thanks in sorrow." Women, like men, are nurtured in this spirituality and in that strength they confront the vicissitudes of life in Africa with unshakeable faith.

In the AIC Jesus is the main recipient of prayer, although there are invocations of the Holy Spirit and thanksgivings to God. In these prayers Jesus seems much closer and is often addressed as an intermediary. An awareness of the complexity of Christian God-talk and the frailty of human vocabulary as compared with feeling and "certainty" is evident in these pages.

370

We yearn to make affirmations of God for which we have no vocabulary. The poetry and rhythm in song become an effective carrier of deep spiritual affirmations.

## The power from singing

To explore the spirituality of a community, one must take into account all facets of its worship life, e.g., prayer and singing, as well as its ethical life. As in the prayers, so in the songs of African spirituality one is unable to completely isolate the women's word. I am therefore depending on the popularity of these songs and the numerical preponderance of women in these assemblies to highlight them as words that give women the nourishment they need for struggle in the battle of life. Men and women alike are immersed in this spiritual exercise, but, judging from the enthusiasm and dedication of women singers in churches, one can say singing is mainly a women's avenue for ministry in African Christianity.

The songs are mainly prayer and praise and express the theology that corresponds to the African people's spirituality. They are based on a belief in the lively presence of God/Jesus. Some call on God to come, see, or hear. They expect God to enter our human experience, know how it feels in order to make the appropriate response. The experiences brought before God are many and varied, but they are all very real, daily needs of human life in the community of the living, expressed to the "God of Grace who saves us from the death of children, and from sudden deaths, protects us when we journey and brings us home safely." Prayer is a "telling it to God," as expressed in this lyric by a woman cantor:

> Jesus, when we touch anything it breaks.
> When we pull it snaps.
> You who still the sea, control the elements.
> Aid our efforts, direct our ways.[7]

A few of these African songs have been included in the African versions of the Western hymn books brought in by missionaries. One finds in these additional hymns a strong belief in God who heals both physical and spiritual diseases.

371

Lyrics are often woven around the stories of Naaman, The Ten Lepers of the gospel, and Bartimaeus. Jesus is the wonderful "compassionate healer in whose words people find comfort." The story of Hannah and Peninnah gets woven into lyrics that warn against gloating over other people's misfortune. Hannah, more so than the other mother-figures of the Bible, has captured the imagination of African women because of her polygynous marriage, a marriage that seemed to become intolerable to her. The themes of struggle, empowerment, and defeat of the oppressor are sounded in the prayers and songs in the name of Jesus, who is the reward for all who struggle for liberation.

### The faith of Africa

The spirituality of African Christianity as it comes to us in prayer and song is a faith founded mainly on three affirmations. First, Satan is real and strong, but God is ultimate reality, and Satan cannot stand before God.[8] Second, all that brings pain can be conquered by God if we can tell it out. Third, all that breaks community can be healed by God. African spirituality seeks fullness of life here and now, even as it hopes we shall have it in the other dimension of life. It has modified the eschatological interpretation of salvation with the cosmological one favored by traditional African religions. Shalom before God here on earth is as much God's will as the everlasting shalom before God in the hereafter.

Hymns from the Christ Apostolic Church in Nigeria express many of these concerns, using imagery also found in the Fanti *Compositions on Deliverance*. Jesus is the healer, the leader of the army, who goes ahead of us, but who is also behind. Such affirmations have become the theme of all choruses to hymns sung in the AIC. The power of Jesus is "super power"; all other powers are empty. The empty powers may be religio-political (Ogboni) or mystical (Osho witchcraft). Deliverance by Jesus is sure, and those who experience it call to all "those who know the goodness of Jesus, to join me and praise him."

Formalized "abuses," a test of language skills (mainly analogies) intended to defeat the opponent without resorting to physical combat, have found their way into Christian choruses as a source of power against evil. This battle of words is traditionally a device used by women. Men resort to wrestling.

Satan you cannot be a match to God.
Look at your feet, your hands, your face.
Look at you, coming to compare yourself to God.

The phrase "look at you" alone is expected to reduce the enemy to nothing. That God is "super power" becomes the source of strength to those who sing the chorus for, while singing, they actually in their own mind's eye see the downfall of Satan. Confidence is re-established as they sing, "Only Jesus can save, the Diviner cannot save." The centrality of Scripture is modified by the same affirmation that "only Jesus can save." Direct access to Jesus enhances the self-esteem of people who most of the time in the world have little to feed their self-worth. Thus empowered, they send out the mission call: "*Adasamina, monso nhwe na munnhu se Yehowa ye*" ("Mortal ones [human beings] taste and see that YHWH is good").

Battles in the physical world are first won on the spiritual level, for the confidence that God is able to lead one out of misery enables the believers to rest secure. Assured of a God who never fails, they sing "Magnify the Lord, the Lord is able." Sometimes this confidence is established by observations from the natural order put in place by God, much in the style of the biblical psalms. The God who has done all this will never be thwarted by any other power. Therefore believers can depend on God to be faithful, just as the laws on which the universe is founded are dependable:

None can stop the rain from falling in the rainy
season, or quench the sun. None can take the light
of the sun away nor prevent it from shining
through the dry season: Nobody!

In this way Christians pray for rain, but do not claim to be rainmakers. God is in control and in the hands of such a One, one cannot but rejoice and live a life of praise and thanksgiving.

Praise, hardly heard in African religions except in praise-names of God and in daily individual outbursts, has become a major expression of the spirituality of the AIC. People bring every individual success before the community to celebrate in song and dance. "Come join me to lift up my sorrow."

> God has done a lot for me,
> my legs dance, my heart should rejoice,
> my mouth should sing the glory of God.

In praise, they worship Christ as the "King who does not allow the waves of life to overwhelm" them.

Those who join in celebration of victories won for others by God then turn to God in prayer. The God of AIC, more so than in the Western churches of Africa, is a "miracle-working God." Even the charismatic movement in some Roman Catholic churches in Africa exhibits this characteristic. At a healing Mass, people strive to get drops of holy water from the bishop's palm branches. They open bottles of olive oil, cologne, and water to receive the power that flows from the prayers and blessings of the bishop and take them home to use, convinced of their potency and efficacy. Faith in the efficacy of the words and actions of a cultic functionary pervades this Christianity, as it does African religions.

The power of God is very real and immediate. One can conclude that, apart from family tradition and inertia, the young people who sing these songs today do so because they derive strength from knowing that "it is not too much for God to do." Such is the affirmation that empowers people to make their own efforts. "While there is sun, and the rain has not stopped falling, we shall never lack, we shall get our share," also means getting on with the farming. For it is in getting on with your assignment as a human being that you stand on the side of God, and from that place then you can sing, "weeds shall not grow in our mouths," i.e., we shall not starve; and "our clothes shall not turn to rags." The spirituality of African religions in indigenous prayers and songs is a spirituality that empowers one to combat the powers that threaten to reduce human beings to nothing. This trust in the generosity and unearned grace of God is acknowledged in calling God "*Okyeso Nyame*"—God who leaves no one out of the distribution of good things.[9] To depend on such a God is sure security.

## Conclusion

We have been focusing on the spirituality of African Christian women who have tapped deeply into the primal religious sources of their own communities. This is possible because Africans never saw the God of the Christian religion as different from the God they had known in their pre-Christian religions. Praying and singing in their own language, they have been able to retain this source of spiritual nourishment. In matters of religion African women have not been as completely subverted as in other aspects of life. Women's cults and women-founded Christian congregations are common developments. It is from this active involvement that we can observe the spirituality of African women.

African women have drawn on traditional sources and on the teachings of Western Christianity as passed on to them through Western missionaries and their collaborators. The examples from Malawi illustrate how African Christian women have integrated the various sources of spirituality and how they have derived strength from their religious life. African women believe in prayer as a form of "potent-speech" which once uttered releases power into the human community and reverberates throughout the cosmos.[10]

Together with fasting, ritual meals and objects, symbols and signs, African women live a life that is in every sense sacramental. Nothing is common; all occurrences may be seen as portents. This deep sense of the spirit-dimension of life is a source of strength for women. But much of what empowers African women may be described as a spirituality of sacrifice. Commitment to community well-being, beginning with the immediate family and expanding to the wider community, gives women a sense of participation in life-giving and life-protecting processes. Women's absence from overt displays of power and authority does not seem to affect women's sense of self-worth. After all, the spiritual powers most potent and instrumental in life are not seen to be physically present. African women's strength lies in the belief that the spirit-world is on the side of those who protect life and combat all that carries death in its wake.

In the spiritual dimension of life there is justice, for all are accounted and treated as the children of God. No human being has a God-given power to exploit or oppress others, for none of these things are hidden from God. God is the protector of the handicapped. God drives flies off the tailless animal. With the assurance of God as the final arbiter, African women do not hesitate to say what they see as inimical to the good of the community. African women are not bashful in resorting to the spirit-world for protection, comfort, strength in times of stress, and healing in times of sickness. They do not hesitate to call down the wrath of the spirit-world on all who would trample on their humanity and on the sense of community.

Society recognizes the potency of women's spirituality and has all sorts of devices to ensure that these powers are always used for the good of the community. The widespread accusation of witchcraft against women is evidence of the acknowledgement of this power, and women confess to being witches when they feel they have used these powers against others or solely for their individual advancement. African women believe in and operate in the context of human links to the spiritual world, and it is this that empowers them to cope with, combat, and control the harshly oppressive physical, economic, psychological, and political conditions of their continent.

❖     ❖     ❖

## A Newly Emerging Spirituality

□ *Mercy Amba Oduyoye reflected on the empowering spirit of religion from the background of her African experience; whereas Aruna Gnandason based her discussion on Hindu insights. Other women look for spiritual resources in Chinese and Japanese traditions. To quote examples, Jane C. N. Chui from Hong Kong wrote an article entitled "From the Goddess of the Chinese Folk Religion to See the Necessity of Developing the Goddess Tradition in Christianity"* (In God's Image, *June 1989, pp. 23-6), and Naomi P. F. Southard has looked at Chinese Buddhism and Korean shamanism for spiritual resources (and also at the goddess in the ancient Near East — a section that has been omitted in the extract in chapter 37).*

*Part One of this Reader included contributions from womanist and mujerista theology in the USA that draw attention to the voices of black and Hispanic women. Women of Asian origin who feel similarly marginalized in the USA have also begun to organize themselves into groups, so that they can express their own distinct theological vision. Yet Asian-American women neither share a common language, nor a single expression with which to describe themselves. However, it is important to give Asian-American women a voice in this Reader, alongside those voices from other parts of the Third World. Naomi P. F. Southard from the National Federation of Asian-American United Methodists published an article in the* The Asia Journal of Theology *(vol. 3/2, 1989, pp. 624–38), part of which is reproduced in chapter 37 with reference to Kuan Yin and also to the figure of the shaman. For a general introduction to the issues discussed by Asian American women, see the article by Naomi P. F. Southard and Rita Nakashima Brock, "The Other Half of the Basket: Asian American Women and the Search for a Theological Home" to which the following chapter refers.*

❖　　❖　　❖

# 37 NAOMI P. F. SOUTHARD

# Recovery and Rediscovered Images: Spiritual Resources for Asian American Women

In an article for the *Journal of Feminist Studies in Religion*,[1] Rita Nakashima Brock and I discuss the context and some of the major issues in Asian American women's theology,[2] the barriers to the development of those themes, and "unexpected paths," or possible sources for healing and reflection. This essay is an attempt to identify some spiritual resources for Asian American women—symbols and images for empowerment and healing that will hopefully aid in the development of communal and personal transformation.

One of the primary motivations for this essay is that Asian American women have not yet been able to "build a theological home," due to isolation and marginalization within both the Church and ethnic communities: accordingly, Asian American women have few, if any, common symbols or images that empower their ministries and their lives. It is my hope that this community will be strengthened by spiritual resources that address the marginalization that is particular to Asian American Christian women. An outgrowth of this strengthened community might be the foundation of a theological home—a place for further reflection in dialogue with the communities in which we work and live, somewhere to develop a clear prophetic voice.

## The context

Asian American women describe a sense of loneliness and fragmented identity that is common to most persons of multinational heritage—they are familiar with several languages and cultures and, as a result, have developed plural loyalties (some might term this pejoratively, "divided loyalties"). Additionally, Asian American women are subordinated, while we identify ourselves with minority communities that struggle for justice and economic independence, at the same time we also recognize that we live "in the belly of the beast"; i.e., for most of us, our ministry is within a majority religious institution which supports (and occasionally calls to accountability) the exploitive power and dominion of the USA and the West. As much as we struggle against exploitive power, we know that we are enmeshed in it as well. The challenge to Asian American women is to identify and articulate the theological vision that is born of this context, so that the Good News may be heard anew.

In response to this understanding of our situation, Asian American women speak about particular theological themes: the significance of relationship/connectedness, an ever-widening circle that becomes community. The foundation of this community is suffering—when persons can embrace each other's suffering, they are in community; similarly we experience oneness with God, as God in Christ is our co-sufferer.

Asian American women also mentioned some areas that need to be further explored as possible sources for healing in light of the universality of suffering. These sources included two images of spiritual power: "the goddess" and shamanism.

Theological reflection on the co-suffering of God and humanity and an extended vocabulary of images of spiritual power will be vital companions to our personal spiritual journeys and ministries. Therefore, I will suggest some possible resources, in the forms of symbols and images, that relate to the themes identified above:

> The suffering community: recovery and rediscovered images
> (a) God as co-sufferer: Jesus Christ and Kuan Yin
> (b) The shaman.

## The suffering community:
## recovery and rediscovered images

Asian American women are generally very inclusive in their definitions of suffering—the ravages of war, colonialism, disease, poverty, racism, and personal trials all figure prominently in our reflections. There is particular interest in the specific experiences of women's suffering. One of the most striking and apt metaphors for the suffering of women and minorities (under a patriarchal system) is provided by mental health professional Anne Wilson Schaef in her *When Society Becomes an Addict*.[3]

In our present context, potentially liberating symbols have been rendered less effective through their enmeshment in a patriarchal system. While Christian Scripture and tradition have no lack of powerfully spiritual and spiritually powerful women, much of their history has been forgotten, obscured or interpreted in such a way as to render them ineffective as models for *all* Christian women. The problem does not lie with the wisdom and strength we see, for example, in Ruth, Esther, Julian of Norwich, or Mother Teresa. Rather, the problem lies with the patriarchal system's impact on the development of the Christian Church and spirituality. Despite the teachings of Jesus (and the book of Acts) that affirmed the equality of women and men before God, and the early Church's encouragement of women such as Dorcas and Tabitha in positions of leadership, women returned to the downward spiral of subordination beginning in the fourth century.

The traditions and customs of women's subordination continue into our own times, and have had a detrimental impact on women's spirituality. Men have dominated the research, teaching and writing on this subject; unfortunately, these men, virtually all of them participants in the patriarchal system, functioned on the assumption that "the male system is the only reality" and are

> largely ignorant of the existence of a feminine approach to the spiritual life that might be quite different from their own. Male spiritual directors, retreat directors and preachers habitually propose for women a combination of masculine spiritual practice and the ideal of the "eternal feminine" which, in Jungian terms, is more a projection of the male "anima" than a real ideal for women.[4]

In this way, spiritually powerful women have been rendered invisible. Further, women became co-dependent with male-dominated spirituality because:

> ... ministers/priests and women identified religious with domestic values. For example, obedience to God became synonymous with domestic virtues of humility and selfless devotion, which were cited as evidence that women were naturally more religious than men.[5]

Male-dominated Christianity has been able to restrict most women throughout our history to these values because of the suppression of alternative values or symbols. For Asian American women to recover from the patriarchal system, we need to embrace a spirituality with images and symbols powerful enough to accompany us through the difficult passage. The process of rediscovery leads us to reexamine orthodox views and explore relevant non-Christian sources. The patriarchal distortions of Jesus and the cultural domination of the West and Christianity make the development of rediscovered images such as Kuan Yin and the goddess absolutely necessary for a whole and healing faith experience.

### (a) God as co-sufferer: Jesus Christ and Kuan Yin

Christian tradition affirms several very different images of Jesus Christ/God, which may be experienced in considerable tension. One image is of Jesus the co-sufferer, lamb of God, who "never said a mumblin' word" in the face of the enemies, who embraced and absorbed all the pain of full humanity. In the Hebrew Scriptures, we find this image associated with the suffering servant. This image of Jesus who liberated through the "weakness" of saying "yes" to death can be identified with the revolutionary who rejected the patriarchal values of control and domination. The suffering servant becomes identified with this image of Jesus that has sometimes been anachronistically called a "feminist":

> Fundamentally, Jesus renews the prophetic vision whereby the Word of God does not validate the existing social and

religious hierarchy but speaks on behalf of the marginalized and despised groups of society. . . . This reversal of social order doesn't just turn hierarchy upside down, it aims at a new reality in which hierarchy and dominance are overcome as principles of social relations.[6]

This is Rosemary Radford Ruether's Christology of Jesus the liberator—of oppressed people, of women. She asserts that theoretically speaking, "the maleness of Jesus has no ultimate significance" (1983, p. 137) for he is here to overturn oppressions, including those of gender.

An image of God the co-sufferer that is perhaps more in harmony with liberation aspirations and Asian American women's viewpoint is offered by Christin Lore Weber in *Woman Christ*.[7] In accordance with traditional Christian theology, Weber describes the incarnation as the means by which God identifies with humanity and our suffering. Like God, who descends from heaven to be incarnated as a human being, Weber explores the spiritual power that is released in descending/suffering/ebbing/death:

> Ebbing has been called weakness, but perhaps we will discover in it a new kind of power. Perhaps there is power in all that we have associated with the ebb side of the cycle: silence, waiting, emptiness, darkness, receptivity, detachment, aloneness and death.[8]

It is because of Jesus and our own *descent* into incarnation that we are able to be truly related in community to one another—related in our mutual incarnation of the Word, related in our common experience of suffering:

> Incarnational consciousness demands descent to the body: my personal body, the body of my community, my earth, this cosmos. Not only do I need to unlock the Word and Image hidden in me, personally, and embody it; I need to be available for descent into that body of the community.[9]

Similarly, there is remarkable harmony between the understandings of the compassionate Jesus Christ and the compassionate Kuan Yin.

Like Weber, Asian American women speak fervently about Jesus Christ, emphasizing a specific aspect of the incarnation — his suffering with humanity in its pain. This emphasis on suffering is not surprising to find among persons who have contact with Buddhist- and Hindu-influenced cultures. The centrality of the teachings about human suffering and compassion in Asian religions is remarkably relevant to Asian American Christian women's theology. In the Mahayana (Buddhist) tradition, relatedness/connectedness to others is understood as *self*-empowerment: "cultivating certain forms of relatedness and compassionate involvement offer insights into ways of deriving personal strength from the experience of living."[10] Buddhas embody this value of relatedness, in that Buddhahood, in large part, comes from "cultivating a close, compassionate relationship with other beings . . . and though they [Buddhas] are powerful and active, their sense of 'self' is not organized around a conception of dominance."[11] This understanding of the great depth of spiritual power that is released through relatedness and co-suffering correlates almost identically with the theology expressed by Asian American women.

A parallel to the "meek and mild" Jesus, one of the most widely known (and beloved) Buddhist symbols of compassion is Kuan Yin (Kwannon).[12] Kuan Yin is revered primarily in China, Japan, Korea, Singapore, and Vietnam, as a goddess by common folk and as a celestial bodhisattva by scholars. Hers is the suffering of the bodhisattva who has delayed entering Nirvana's final peace as long as there are other sentient beings caught in the cycle of rebirth. Kuan Yin may provide Asian American women with a female icon that incorporates some of our most deeply felt beliefs about relatedness, community, and suffering.

Her iconography, significance, and rites of worship throughout East Asia are rich and complex. Kuan Yin, whose name means "She-who-hears-the-cries-of-the World," may be seen as an embodiment of complete and unconditional compassion:

She could be relied upon to behave like a fondly indulgent parent, provided only that one's wish was not evil in itself. No special degree of piety or strict conduct was required of the petitioners beyond firm belief in Kuan Yin's power to aid. . . . Kuan Yin is unique . . . in being utterly free from pride or vengefulness and reluctant to punish even those to whom a severe lesson would be salutary. The cursing of the withered fig tree and the whipping of the temple money-changers which so disfigure the otherwise beautiful gospel stories are without counterparts among the exploits attributed to Kuan Yin.[13]

Kuan Yin also appears as a wisdom figure (thus enhancing her appeal to scholars) and, according to the Sanskrit version of the Heart Sutra, it was Kuan Yin (Avalokita) who was able to discern in the teachings of the Buddha new and more profound meanings.

In the mystical traditions of Kuan Yin, she often appears in a vision to persons in need (not unlike the Virgin's appearance at Lourdes, for example). Her function as an icon, the subject of supplication and meditation, make her "available" to those who call upon her:

> Kuan Yin is regarded by some as a mental creation and by others as being hardly distinguishable from a goddess . . . there is no question of the one view being right, the other wrong. She is both an abstraction and a goddess; how one sees her depends upon one's expectation and attitude of mind.[14]

Kuan Yin offers us a companion to Jesus Christ, as the all-loving compassionate one who suffers for the benefit of others. She may also be compared to the Virgin Mary, especially as she is venerated in the Roman Catholic popular traditions. The centrality of sacrificial compassion and intimate relationship from the Buddhist-Hindu context offers us an opportunity to identify ourselves physically and psychologically with the image of an Asian female, and theologically with values that are reflected both in Asian culture and Christian faith.

The feminist critique of self-sacrificial suffering in both Christianity and Buddhism has centered on the problem that women have too often sacrificed for the wrong reasons—because of a patriarchal system that forced women to suffer unwillingly, or that told them they had to sacrifice in order to overcome their "unacceptable" female (created) nature. Women must not allow themselves to fall into the trap of suffering because they have accepted the patriarchal dictum that it is "their lot" to suffer; Buddhism and Christianity do not advocate sacrificial suffering as an antidote for being unworthy: rather such action should be a result of love. One should not attempt to develop sacrificial compassion until "one has reached some psychologically effective sense that [Bodhisattvas] have already gloriously fulfilled one's own needs [for love]. In other words, one is operating out of a sense of fulness . . . to repay in kind what one has already received in plenty."[15] Further, suffering is not the goal of faithful living—neither for Christians who celebrate their redemption, nor for Buddhists who seek transcendence. Christians and Buddhists both affirm the virtue of *compassion*, a kind of "wise suffering," in which we may consciously seek a difficult path (which some might call suffering) because we believe in the possibilities of radical transformation. Another possible source of spiritual nurture is "the goddess" of the ancient Near East and West, who offers us a parallel to the commonly depicted maleness of Yahweh (although female symbols of Yahweh do exist), and God the Father of the Trinity; in this case, the goddess gives us the opportunity to identify ourselves physically and psychologically with a female deity, and theologically with values that have predated and informed our Christian faith.

### (b) The shaman

Perhaps one of the primary reasons for Asian American women's interest in the shaman is the knowledge that this has been an important role for women in the midst of Asian patriarchal societies. While there are several kinds of shamans whose roles have changed over time and place in Korea, Japan, and other parts of Asia, there are some consistent features that serve to define this role. There are two main recurring types of shamans:

(1) Those chosen usually by heredity who function as a kind of "family priest" in Korea, or those in Japan who held official positions in the imperial court of Japan, and

(2) In Korea and Japan, professional shamans, who evidence spirit possession, experience training, and rites of initiation.

In our consideration of East Asian shamanism, Ichiro Hori's *Folk Religion in Japan: Continuity and Change*[16] includes historical detail regarding the specific role of Japanese shamans in particular geographical areas. For example, he refers to Japanese shamanic queens attested to by Chinese documents describing the period AD 233–97, and influences on early Shinto-related shamans by the entrance of Buddhism in Japan. Hori also describes some of the difficult tasks taken on by shamans: professional mediums who worked complementarily with Shinto or Buddhist priests, dancers, or singers who communicated with spirits, deities, and the dead, seers who "practiced divination and fortune telling through trance; prayers for the recovery of the sick and of new buildings, wells, stones and hearths; performers of memorial services for ancestors, and perhaps prostitutes."[17] One of the factors influencing historical development of shamans and their role was "supposedly based on the transition from the ancient matrilineal to the patrilineal society strongly influenced by China."[18]

However, one of the most interesting aspects of shamanist activity was the intense activities they were involved in during periods of critical social change. Hori cites the fall of the Soga clan as a typical example among many, concluding, "Later at moments of anxiety connected with social change or crisis, shamanistic mass hysteria frequently occurred."[19]

Hori traces the phenomenon of shamanist activity during periods of change or crisis up through the post-World War II era, when new religions arose (often through shamanic-type activity) "as a response to the acute 'anomie' into which the Japanese people were thrown by defeat and occupation."[20] This association of shamans with periods of suffering and dislocation, and their role as harbingers of change, suggests the potential of their symbolic role as catalysts for "systems shifts." This role as catalyst offers a helpful model for Asian American women who seek through both spiritual and other means to be agents of transformation in Church and society.

To enrich our understanding of shamanism, particularly as it relates to women, there are many more resources available from the Korean context. Youngsook Kim Harvey points us toward the role of shamans in Korean society.[21]

There seems to be evidence that shamans manifested a non-patriarchal understanding of the world, and thereby provided an alternative system to Confucian-based male dominance. Harvey tells us that the Yi (Cho Sun) dynasty (AD 1392–1910) chose shamans and shamanistic cults as their chief targets of attack because this regime "saw shamanism as appealing to non-rational aspects of humanity; thus for a rational society to be achieved, it had to be eradicated."[22] Unable to totally suppress shamanism because neo-Confucianism "could not minister to the emotional and religious needs of the people,"[23] the Yi (Cho Sun) government institutionalized shamanism through licensing, taxation, and giving shamans and their families official social status as outcastes.

Harvey describes the historical and contemporary role of shamans as "religious functionaries and ethnopsychiatrists,"[24] who serve as intermediaries between the spirit world of the ancestors and the individual and family. In view of the official low regard for shamans and their work, the physical, mental, and emotional strain of the *sinbyong* or state of possession, we may associate shamans with the biblical symbol of the "suffering servant." According to Harvey:

> Koreans believe that when spirits are searching for humans to possess and use as their mediums, they are particularly attracted to individuals whose *maum* (heart/soul) has been "fractured" by experiences of exploitation and tragedy caused by others. . . . Families of *sinbyong* victims may have predisposed them to possession by mistreating them.[25]

It may be that the shamans are associated with conflict or abusive situations precisely because of their "suffering servant" role; Harvey also observes in the case of two shamans that their families could see that "their suffering had a purpose."[26]

Another way in which the shaman often reverses patriarchal values is that she often holds a power position in the family. "She bargains with her family from a position of strength based on her earning power, spiritual superiority and recovered health and self-confidence."[27] It is unfortunate that Harvey's study does not explore more fully the spiritual power of shamans within the community; he is primarily concerned to demonstrate that spirit possession may be a successful, if costly, coping mechanism for women who find themselves in conflict with their families or society in general. However, a study by Laurel Kendall[28] presents a more complex understanding of Korean shamans and their relationship to their community. According to Kendall, shamans *and* the women who represent the household in shamanic rituals of folk religion maintain cosmic harmony as they complement the roles males have in the Confucian-based family rites (family includes extended family and ancestors). She describes the women's roles as "a flourishing of the positive powers women wield on behalf of husbands and children."[29] Additionally, in Korean patrilocal society, women change their primary family relationships and responsibilities at the time of marriage; in effect, they pass between two kinship groups, while men remain only in one.

It seems reasonable to assume shamans may offer Asian American women the possibility of being a symbolic resource for spiritual and mystical exploration of the non-patriarchal, non-rational religious experience; deepened understanding of the relationship between personal and communal suffering, and the power for transformation effected by the "suffering servant," and the role of initiator of a system shift. With the translation of more ethnographic materials on shamans and the development of feminist research on this topic, Asian American women will be able to claim (or reclaim) the image of shaman in their spiritual identities and practice of ministry.

The role of shaman, and the symbolic power of Kuan Yin and the goddess, offer Asian American women a rather "mixed bag" of spiritual resources. The question remains as to if, or how, individual women will be able to integrate these resources into the spirituality. One problem is cultural distance from the symbols. Although Asian American women are familiar with Asian cultures, their knowledge and understanding of those cultures tends to be limited to interactions within the family, or at most within a small ethnic community. Also, many of us have very limited contact with Asia itself; some of us immigrated to the USA as children or teenagers; others, born in the USA, have never had an opportunity to visit Asia. Given this experience, it is difficult to apprehend or identify, for example, with a Buddhist goddess whose manifestations and functions cross boundaries of distant cultures and histories. From a personal point of view, although the desire is strong, the distance is too great. Without the benefit of long-term exposure to the living context of Buddhism and Kuan Yin in Asia, I am painfully aware that I can only appreciate her in the most superficial way. Hopefully, feminist-oriented scholars from Asia will begin to provide an analysis of the meaning and religious function of Kuan Yin (and the many other Asian goddesses/female emanations, etc.), which will make her more accessible to women (and men) in the West. Shamans who are able to penetrate the languages and cultures of rural Asia—a social context that is under rapid transition.

Asian American Christian women find themselves in the midst of a patriarchal culture and patriarchal Church that marginalizes them and others through the oppressions of racism, sexism, classism, and so on. As we continue to explore spiritual resources from our distant homelands and past, we will need each other as never before—to act as spiritual guides, translators, cultural interpreters, and wise women. Together, in our "theological home," we can encourage each other to embrace the radical transformation made possible through incarnation. This transformation has begun, and calls out our commitment to its fulfillment.

❖ ❖ ❖

☐ *In a study of Asian women's spirituality, Virginia Fabella and Sun Ai Lee Park concluded their discussion with the following words:*

> The emerging spirituality of women shows the characteristics of the original meaning of salvation, namely, its totality and concreteness. The release of women's creative energy and new insights have resulted in a refocusing of the different elements of spirituality, which tend to converge in a certain trend that draws its vitality from creation as contrasted with the traditional spirituality that focuses on the fall and redemption.
> Spirituality is a process. It is not achieved once and for all. It does not become congealed. It is not even a smooth, continuous growth. There can be retrogression or quantum leaps. It has peaks and abysses. It has its agonies and its ecstasies. The emerging spirituality of women promises to be vibrant, liberating, and colorful. Its direction and tendencies seem to open up to greater possibilities of life and freedom and therefore to more and more opportunities to be truly, intensely, and wholly alive! (Quoted from Virginia Fabella and Mercy Amba Oduyoye, eds., With Passion and Compassion: Third World Women Doing Theology, *Maryknoll, NY: Orbis Books, 1988, p. 87.)*

*A fine example of the extraordinary liveliness and power of this spirituality, and an excellent piece with which to conclude this Reader, is the Plenary Address that the South Korean woman theologian Chung Hyun Kyung gave at the Seventh Assembly of the World Council of Churches in Canberra, Australia, in February 1991. The full text "Come Holy Spirit — Renew the Whole Creation" can be found in the official Assembly Report (Michael Kinnamon, ed.,* Signs of the Spirit, *Geneva: WCC Publications, 1991, pp. 37–47), whereas in chapter 38 only the invocation at the beginning of the address and its concluding section are reprinted (pp. 37–9, 46).*

*To situate Chung Hyun Kyung in her own context, here is how she describes the experiential background of her presentation in the same address:*

### A Newly Emerging Spirituality

*I come from Korea, the land of spirits full of* Han. Han *is* anger. Han *is resentment.* Han *is bitterness.* Han *is grief.* Han *is brokenheartedness and the raw energy for struggle for liberation. In my tradition people who were killed or died unjustly became wandering spirits, the* Han-ridden spirits. *They are all over the place seeking the chance to make the wrong right. Therefore the living people's responsibility is to listen to the voices of the* Han-ridden spirits and to participate in the spirits' work of making right whatever is wrong. These Han-ridden spirits in our people's history have been agents through whom the Holy Spirit has spoken her compassion and wisdom for life. Without hearing the cries of these spirits we cannot hear the voice of the Holy Spirit. I hope the presence of all our ancestors' spirits here with us shall not make you uncomfortable. For us they are the icons of the Holy Spirit who became tangible and visible to us. Because of them we can feel, touch and taste the concrete bodily historical presence of the Holy Spirit in our midst. From my people's land of* Han-*filled spirits I come to join with you in another land of spirits full of* Han, *full of the spirits of the indigenous people, victims of genocide. Here in Australia, we are gathered together from every part of our mother earth to pray for the coming of the Holy Spirit to renew the whole creation (Michael Kinnamon, ed.,* Signs of the Spirit, *Geneva: WCC Publications, 1991, p. 39).*

❖     ❖     ❖

# Come, Holy Spirit—Break Down the Walls with Wisdom and Compassion

## (1) Invocation

My dear sisters and brothers, welcome to this land of the Spirit. We are gathered here together today to be empowered by the Holy Spirit for our work of renewing the whole creation. Let us prepare the way of the Holy Spirit by emptying ourselves. Indigenous people of Australia take their shoes off on holy ground. When an Australian Aboriginal woman, Anne Pattel-Gray, came to my church in Korea to preach she took off her shoes, honoring our holy ground. Returning her respect for my people and land, I want to take off my shoes, honoring her and her people's holy ground. For many Asian and Pacific people, taking off our shoes is the first act of humbling ourselves to encounter the Spirit of God. Also in our Christian tradition God called Moses to take his shoes off in front of the burning bush to enter the holy ground—so he did. Do you think you can do that too? I would like to invite all of you to get on the holy ground with me by taking off your shoes while we are dancing to prepare the way of the Spirit. With humble heart and body, let us listen to the cries of creation and the cries of the Spirit within it:

Come. The spirit of Hagar, Egyptian, black slave woman exploited and abandoned by Abraham and Sarah, the ancestors of our faith (Gen. 21.15-21).

Come. The spirit of Uriah, loyal soldier sent and killed in the battlefield by the great king David out of the king's greed for his wife, Bathsheba (2 Sam. 11.1-27).

392

Come. The spirit of Jephthah's daughter, the victim of her father's faith, offered as a burnt offering to God because he had won the war (Judg. 11.29-40).

Come. The spirit of male babies killed by the soldiers of king Herod upon Jesus' birth.

Come. The spirit of Joan of Arc, and of the many other women burnt at the "witch trials" throughout the medieval era.

Come. The spirit of the people who died during the Crusades.

Come. The spirit of indigenous people of the earth, victims of genocide during the time of colonialism and the period of the great Christian mission to the pagan world.

Come. The spirit of Jewish people killed in the gas chambers during the holocaust.

Come. The spirit of people killed in Hiroshima and Nagasaki by atomic bombs.

Come. The spirit of Korean women in the Japanese "prostitution army" during World War II, used and torn by violence-hungry soldiers.

Come. The spirit of Vietnamese people killed by napalm, Agent Orange, or hunger on the drifting boats.

Come. The spirit of Mahatma Gandhi, Steve Biko, Martin Luther King Jr, Malcolm X, Victor Jara, Oscar Romero and many unnamed women freedom fighters who died in the struggle for liberation of their people.

Come. The spirit of people killed in Bhopal and Chernobyl, and the spirit of jelly babies from the Pacific nuclear test zone.

Come. The spirit of people smashed by tanks in Kwangju, Tiananmen Square and Lithuania.

Come. The spirit of the Amazon rain forest now being murdered every day.

Come. The spirit of earth, air and water, raped, tortured and exploited by human greed for money.

Come. The spirit of soldiers, civilians and sea creatures now dying in the bloody war in the Gulf.

Come. The spirit of the Liberator, our brother Jesus, tortured and killed on the cross.

## (2) Break down the wall with wisdom and compassion

I want to close my reflection on the Holy Spirit by sharing with you my image of the Holy Spirit from my cultural background. This image embodies for me the three changes of direction I have described as necessary for metanoia: life-centrism, the habit of interconnection, and the culture of life. The image does not come from my academic training as a systematic theologian, but from my gut feeling, deep in my people's collective unconsciousness that comes from thousands of years of spirituality.

For me the image of the Holy Spirit comes from the image of Kwan Yin. She is venerated as the goddess of compassion and wisdom by East Asian women's popular religiosity. She is a bodhisattva, enlightened being. She can go into nirvana any time she wants to, but refuses to go into nirvana by herself. Her compassion for all suffering beings makes her stay in this world, enabling other living beings to achieve enlightenment. Her compassionate wisdom heals all forms of life and empowers them to swim to the shore of nirvana. She waits and waits until the whole universe, people, trees, birds, mountains, air, water, become enlightened. They can then go to nirvana together, where they can live collectively in eternal wisdom and compassion. Perhaps this might also be a feminine image of the Christ who is the first-born among us, one who goes before and brings others with her.

Dear sisters and brothers, with the energy of the Holy Spirit let us tear apart all walls of division and the "culture of death" that separate us. And let us participate in the Holy Spirit's political economy of life, fighting for our life on this earth in solidarity with all living beings, and building communities for justice, peace, and the integrity of creation. Wild wind of the Holy Spirit, blow to us. Let us welcome her, letting ourselves go in her wild rhythm of life. Come Holy Spirit, Renew the Whole Creation. Amen!

# Notes

## Introduction

1. Philadelphia: Westminster Press, 1988. Cecily P. Broderick y Guerra has provided a helpful annotated bibliography for this volume that lists publications on African and African-American women, Asian and Asian-American women, Latin American/ Hispanic women, white American women and the Third World, global resources, and periodicals related to Third World feminist theology.
2. Ibid., p. 13.
3. London: Zed Books, 1986.
4. See Katie Geneva Cannon, "The Emergence of Black Feminist Consciousness," in Letty M. Russell, ed., *Feminist Interpretation of the Bible*, Philadelphia: Westminster Press, 1985, pp. 30-40; also, Susan Brooks Thistlethwaite, *Sex, Race and God: Christian Feminism in Black and White*, New York: Crossroad, 1989; London: Geoffrey Chapman, 1990.
5. Rev. Cao Shengjie, Associate General Secretary of the China Christian Council, wrote in 1991 that in thirteen Chinese theological training centres women make up nearly half the student body. She also mentioned that by the end of 1989, there were ninety women pastors in China, nearly all ordained after 1981 and representing just under 10% of the total number of pastors in China. The information given by Dr. Kwok Pui-lan after a visit to China is somewhat different, for she writes, "Female students make up about one third of the student population in the seminaries and Bible schools. Some are preparing themselves for ordination while others will work as female evangelists." She also stresses how one of the biggest problems of the Chinese Church is how to provide adequate pastoral care for the rapidly growing number of Christians. See Cao Shengjie, "Chinese Women's Status in the Society and in the Church," *In God's Image*, vol. 10/3, 1991, pp. 10-11; and Kwok Pui-lan, "Bridge Building and Barrier-Breaking," *In God's Image*, vol. 10/3, 1991, pp. 3-9. For the situation in India, see Prasanna K. Samuel, "Women in Theological Education," *The Asia Journal of Theology*, vol. 2/1, 1988, pp. 79-82.

For the first Western Samoan woman to be accepted as a student in the Bachelor of Theology program at Pacific Theology College, see the brief report by Tessa Mackenzie, "Roina Pioneers Theological Education for Samoan Women," *Pacific Journal of Theology*, series II/4, 1990, pp. 38-40, reprinted in this Reader (chapter 15).

6. For example, in the Philippines this happened in 1979, in Indonesia in 1983, in South Africa in 1992.

7. Details can be found in the publication *Sexism in the 1970s: Discrimination Against Women.* A Report of a WCC Consultation, West Berlin, 1974, Geneva: WCC Publications, 1975.

8. Here, and in some of the following accounts, I rely on the brief history of the WCC's work for women told by the African feminist theologian Mercy Amba Oduyoye, *Who Will Roll the Stone Away? The Ecumenical Decade of the Churches in Solidarity with Women,* Geneva: WCC Publications, 1990.

9. The distribution is as follows: Africa—71; Asia—64; Latin-America—41; Pacific—26; Caribbean—17; Middle East—5; Europe—5; North America—1.

10. Geneva: WCC Publications, 1990. Ranjini Rebera's description of the program is taken from her Introduction, p. xi. The book beautifully weaves together all the aspects of the program by referring to women's work and togetherness as a powerful and empowering dream: the chapter titles speak of unfolding, birthing, nurturing, empowering, sharing, and renewing the dream of women. The Preface to the book was written by Brigalia Bam, who had earlier been in charge of the WCC's department of Co-operation of Women and Men in Church and Society and was at the time of writing Deputy General Secretary of the South African Council of Churches.

11. See Constance Parvey, ed., *The Community of Women and Men in the Church. The Sheffield Report,* Geneva: WCC Publications, 1983.

12. *Ecumenical Decade 1988-1998: Churches in Solidarity with Women. Prayers and Poems, Songs and Stories,* Geneva: WCC Publications, 1988, third printing 1991. This resource book contains many contributions from women in the Third World.

13. Virginia Fabella is a Maryknoll Sister who, at the time of publication, was Academic Dean of the Sister Formation Institute in Quezon City/Philippines and EATWOT Asia Co-ordinator, while Mercy Amba Oduyoye from Ghana was already Deputy General Secretary of the WCC in Geneva.

14. Published by the Asian Women's Resource Center for Culture and Theology and the EATWOT Women's Commission in Asia. The Asian Women's Resource Center was first established in 1988 in Hong Kong, and is now based in Seoul. Besides collecting resource material on culture and theology as these relate to women, one of its major activities is to organize and coordinate women's theological programs and consultations.

The Asian Women Theologians Conference in Singapore (November 20-29, 1987), from which some papers are included in *We Dare to Dream*, brought together thirty-two women from sixteen countries. The conference has been fully documented in *Asian Women Doing Theology: Report from the Singapore Conference*, Hong Kong: Asian Women's Resource Center for Culture and Theology, 1989.

15. The quotations are from Chung Hyun Kyung, *Struggle to be the Sun Again: Introducing Asian Women's Theology*, London: SCM, 1991, p. 20. By the end of 1990 more than 2,200 copies of *In God's Image* went out to readers in ninety countries worldwide.

16. See Marianne Katoppo, *Compassionate and Free: An Asian Woman's Theology*, Geneva: WCC Publications, 1979. To cite some examples of women's theological associations: the Philippine Association of Theologically Trained Women (PATH-TWO) was founded in 1978 and renamed Association of Women in Theology (AWIT) in 1983. There is the Korean Association of Women Theologians (KAWT) founded in 1983, the Association of Indonesian Theologically Trained Women, and the Malaysian Women in Ministry and Theology (MWMT) where, uniquely among these associations, women and men work together in partnership. There is the All India Council of Christian Women and, most importantly, the Women's Desk of the Christian Conference of Asia (CCA), which links seventeen Asian countries. Elizabeth Tapia of the Philippines laid the groundwork for this in 1980-81, and under her leadership two important meetings were held: the Conference of Theologically Trained Women of Asia (Subami/Indonesia, January 1981) and the Asian Women's Forum (Bangalore/India, May 1981). These led to the setting up of the Women's Desk of the CCA and Mizuha Matsuda from Japan became its first executive secretary (1982-6). This shows that Asian women theologians had established a viable network, and were already working closely together, before the foundation of the EATWOT Women's Commission in 1983.

17. See her chapter "Towards an Asian Feminist Theology," in

Sr. Mary John Mananzan, osb, ed., *Woman and Religion*, Manila: The Institute of Women's Studies, St. Scholastica's College, 1988, repr. 1992, pp. 92-102. This is an updated version of an article that appeared some years earlier in German as "Theologie aus dem Blickwinkel asiatischer Frauen. Das Frauen-Projekt der Ökumenischen Vereinigung von Dritte-Welt-Theolog/inn/en EATWOT im asiatischen Kontext," in C. Schaumberger and M. Maassen, eds., *Handbuch Feministischer Theologie*, Münster: Morgana Frauenbuch Verlag, 1986, pp. 51-60. Sr. Mary John Mananzan, a Benedictine nun, is the director of the Institute of Women's Studies (founded in 1985-6) at St. Scholastica's College in Manila and also National Chairperson of GABRIELA, a national federation of women's organizations in the Philippines, and Asian coordinator for the EATWOT Women's Commission.

18. The Claremont Graduate School, Claremont, California, 1989.

19. Maryknoll, NY: Orbis Books, 1990, and London: SCM, 1991. The book is based on her Ph.D. at Union Theological Seminary, New York, where the black theologian James Cone was her major adviser. More details are found in the Preface of the book. On the development of feminist theology in Asia, see chapter 1, "The Historical Context of Asian Women's Theology," pp. 11-21. Professor Chung teaches systematic theology at Ewha Women's University in Seoul, but has also held a visiting appointment at Harvard University.

20. The WCC has produced a video cassette on Chung's work entitled "Gentle But Radical." Available from the WCC, Visual Arts Section, 150 route de Ferney, BP 2100, 122 Geneva 2, Switzerland.

21. See n. 16 above for details.

22. This is the general average. Given the religious and cultural pluralism of Asia, the exact percentage varies greatly from one Asian country to another. The Philippines, for example, stands out as the only country in Asia that is 92% Christian.

23. See *Faith Renewed: A Report on The First Asian Women's Consultation on Interfaith Dialogue*, November 1-8, 1989, Kuala Lumpur, Malaysia, Hong Kong: Asian Women's Resource Center for Culture and Theology, 1989.

24. Chung Hyun Kyung draws on the indigenous tradition of Korean shamanism in her work; see her book and also her article "Opium or the Seed for Revolution? Shamanism: Woman Centered Popular Religiosity in Korea," *Concilium*, 199, 1988, pp. 96-104. Hispanic and Latin American women theologians take up themes from indigenous Indian and Central American traditions. For example,

Elsa Tamez from Costa Rica gave a lecture at the American Academy of Religion in 1992 entitled "'Quetzalcóatl Challenges the Christians' Bible," where she developed the theme of the Bible in encounter with indigenous religions and the need for an "Indian hermeneutic" in order to uncover how "God reveals Godself in other cultures." The need for more interfaith dialogue within the context of religious pluralism is also discussed by Kwok Pui-lan in "The Future of Feminist Theology: An Asian Perspective," reprinted in this Reader (chapter 6).

25. The Circle for Concerned Theologically Trained Women was founded in South Africa in 1992. It grew out of the Center of African Religion and Culture set up in 1989. For South African contributions on feminist theology, see Denise Ackermann, Jonathan A. Draper and Emma Mashinini, eds., *Women Hold Up Half the Sky: Women in the Church in Southern Africa*, Pietermaritzburg: Cluster Publications, 1991; W. S. Vorster, ed., *Sexism and Feminism in Theological Perspective*, Pretoria: University of South Africa, 1984.

26. See Susan Hill Lindley, "Feminist Theology in a Global Perspective," *Christian Century*, vol. 96, 25 April, 1979, pp. 465-9. The global dimensions of the feminist theological challenge found early expression in the work of both Mary Daly and Rosemary Radford Ruether.

27. Delores S. Williams in J. Plaskow and C. Christ, eds., *Weaving the Visions*, San Francisco: HarperCollins, 1989, p. 180.

28. Ada María Isasi-Díaz and Yolanda Tarango, *Hispanic Women: Prophetic Voice in the Church. Mujer Hispana—Voz Profética en la Iglesia*, Minneapolis: Fortress Press, 1992 (first published by Harper & Row, San Francisco, 1988). The book is unusual in that it addresses the problem of language and communication inherent in making oppressed women's voices heard by presenting the experiences of Hispanic women in both English and Spanish.

29. Orbis Books is the publishing arm of the Maryknoll Fathers and Brothers, a Roman Catholic congregation officially known as "The Catholic Foreign Mission Society of America."

30. The richness of encountering women from different faiths and cultures is already visible in earlier publications, such as Yvonne E. Haddad and Ellison B. Findly, eds., *Women, Religion and Social Change*, New York: State University of New York Press, 1985; Diana Eck and Devaki Jain, eds., *Speaking of Faith: Cross-Cultural Perspectives on Women, Religion and Social Change*, New Delhi: Kali for Women, and London: Women's Press, 1986.

For more recent publications, see Virginia Ramey Mollenkott, ed., *Women of Faith in Dialogue*, New York: Crossroad, 1988; Maura O'Neill, *Women Speaking, Women Listening: Women in Interreligious Dialogue*, Maryknoll, NY: Orbis Books, 1990; see also Paula M. Cooey, William R. Eakin, Jay B. McDaniel, eds., *After Patriarchy: Feminist Transformations of the World Religions*, Maryknoll, NY: Orbis Books, 1992. I have discussed the international and crosscultural dimensions of feminist spirituality and women's interfaith encounter in my book *Women and Spirituality: Voices of Protest and Promise*, London: Macmillan, 1989; 2nd edition Macmillan and Pennsylvania State University Press, University Park, PA, 1993; see also my edited book *Women in the World's Religions, Past and Present*, New York: Paragon House, 1987, and my article "Women in Dialogue: A New Vision of Ecumenism," *The Heythrop Journal*, vol. 26/2, 1985, pp. 125-42.

31. In Sr. Mary John Mananzan, OSB, ed., *Women and Religion*, Manila: Institute of Women's Studies, revised edition 1992, p. 99.

32. See Curt Cadorette, Marie Giblin, Marilyn Legge and Mary H. Snyder, eds., *Liberation Theology: An Introductory Reader*, Maryknoll, NY: Orbis Books, 1992.

33. The sustaining strength of this empowerment has been well expressed by Rigoberta Menchú in what she has said about the inspiration and support given to her in her struggles for greater justice for her people. See her *I, Rigoberta Menchú—An Indian Woman in Guatemala*, London: Verso, 1984, from which an extract describing the importance of the Bible for her work has been reprinted in this Reader (chapter 17).

**Chapter 1**

1. In Asante fables, Anase (the Spider) is the chief "human" character, whereas Ananse Kokroko (the Great Spider) is the name of God. It serves the same purpose as Adonai in biblical narrative.

2. Maryknoll, NY: Orbis Books, 1980.

3. Susannah Herzel, *A Voice for Women*, Geneva: WCC Publications, 1981, p. 64. Brigalia Bam, a South African woman, directed the WCC subunit on "Cooperation of Men and Women in Church and Society" from 1967 and is now on the staff of the World YWCA.

4. See Letty Russell, "Women and Unity: Problem or Possibility," in *The Unity of the Church and the Renewal of Human Community*, Geneva: WCC, Faith and Order study document no. 81, 1981.

5. See Herzel, *A Voice*, p. 9. For this and other historical references I have depended on this work, which is less than 200 pages. It provides a chronological account of the subunit ("the desk" of this paper) as well as interviews with the women involved and a valuable bibliography.
6. Ibid., pp. 6-13, 23-4.
7. A number of these concerns are gathered in the recommendations of the Sheffield Consultation held in August 1981. See Doc. CWMC03/1 (WCC/FAO) and *Ecumenical Review*, Geneva: WCC Publications, October 1981.
8. *Orita-Ibadan Journal of Religious Studies*, vol. 10/2, December 1976, carries the papers given at this conference.
9. Papers from this conference are yet to be published, but are available at the University of Ibadan Conference Center.
10. Herzel, *A Voice*, p. 78.
11. Mary Tanner, "The Issue of Scripture in the Community Study" (FOCL (WCC), 82/2/12, unpublished paper). For hermeneutical principles that demand our taking up the subject of this paper in EATWOT, see J. Severino Croatto, *Exodus: A Hermeneutics of Freedom*, Maryknoll, NY: Orbis Books, 1981, pp. 1-11.

### Chapter 4

1. "Candomblé" is an African-Brazilian religious ceremony composed of prayers, dances, and offerings led by a priest (Padre Santo) or a priestess (Madre del Santo) with the purpose of invoking the good spirits and expelling the bad ones.

### Chapter 6

1. See Marc H. Ellis and Otto Maduro, eds., *The Future of Liberation Theology: Essays in Honor of Gustavo Gutiérrez*, Maryknoll, NY: Orbis Books, 1989.
2. See S. J. Samartha, *One Christ—Many Religions: Toward a Revised Christology*, Maryknoll, NY: Orbis Books, 1991, p. 3.
3. Refer to the presentation of Chung Hyun Kyung and other commentaries in *Christianity and Crisis*, vol. 51, nos. 10/11, July 15, 1991, pp. 220-32. See also chapter 38 in this Reader.
4. Jeffrey Gros, "Christian Confession in a Pluralistic World," *Christian Century*, vol. 108, no. 20, June 26-July 3, 1991, p. 645.
5. The idea of multiple and simultaneous identities in the African-American female interpretive community is discussed in Renita J.

Weems, "Reading Her Way through the Struggle: African American Women and the Bible," in Cain Hope Felder, ed., *Stony the Road We Trod: African American Biblical Interpretation*, Minneapolis: Fortress Press, 1991, p. 70.

6. See for examples, John Hick and Paul F. Knitter, eds., *The Myth of Christian Uniqueness: Toward a Pluralistic Theology of Religions*, Maryknoll, NY: Orbis Books, 1987, and Gavin D'Costa, ed., *Christian Uniqueness Reconsidered: The Myth of a Pluralistic Theology of Religions*, Maryknoll, NY: Orbis Books, 1990.

7. Marjorie Hewitt Suchocki, "In Search of Justice: Religious Pluralism from a Feminist Perspective," in Hick and Knitter, *The Myth of Christian Uniqueness*, pp. 150-54.

8. From the transcript of conference, "The Sound of Women's Voices," held at the Claremont Graduate School in Claremont, California on April 16 and 17, 1988, quoted in Maura O'Neill, *Women Speaking, Women Listening: Women in Interreligious Dialogue*, Maryknoll, NY: Orbis Books, 1990, p. 57.

9. Langdon Gilkey has suggested that the nearest analogue to Buddhism is neither Whitehead nor Hegel, but Dewey. David Tracy argues that Buddhism sounds more like Gilles Deleuze or Jacques Derrida. See David Tracy, *Dialogue with the Other: The Inter-Religious Dialogue*, Grand Rapids, Michigan: W. B. Eerdmans, 1990, pp. 69-71.

10. See Dulcie Abraham, Sun Ai Lee Park, and Yvonne Dahlin, eds., *Faith Renewed: A Report on the First Asian Women's Consultation on Interfaith Dialogue*, Hong Kong: Asian Women's Resource Center for Culture and Theology, 1989, p. 121.

11. See Paula M. Cooey, William R. Eakin, and Jay B. McDaniel, eds., *After Patriarchy: Feminist Transformations of the World Religions*, Maryknoll, NY: Orbis Books, 1991.

12. Judith Plaskow, *Standing again at Sinai: Judaism from a Feminist Perspective*, San Francisco: HarperCollins, 1990.

13. Ibid., p. xi.

14. Wilfred Cantwell Smith, "Idolatry: In Comparative Perspective," in Hick and Knitter, *The Myth of Christian Uniqueness*, pp. 54-5.

15. See Carol P. Christ, "On Not Blaming Jews for the Death of the Goddess," in her *Laughter of Aphrodite: Reflections on a Journey to the Goddess*, San Francisco: Harper & Row, 1987, pp. 83-92.

16. Audre Lorde delivered the paper at the Fourth Berkshire Conference on the History of Women, Mount Holyoke College, August 25, 1978. The paper is reprinted in Audre Lorde, *Sister Outsider*, Trumansburg, NY: The Crossing Press, 1984, pp. 53-9.

# Notes

17. See, for instance, Rita Nakashima Brock, *Journeys by Heart: A Christology of Erotic Power*, New York: Crossroad, 1988, and Carter Heyward, *Touching our Strength: The Erotic as Power and the Love of God*, San Francisco: HarperCollins, 1989.

18. Delores Williams, "Black Women's Surrogacy Experience and the Christian Notion of Redemption," in Cooey, Eakin, and McDaniel, *After Patriarchy*, p. 4.

19. See Thanh-dam Truong, *Sex, Money, and Morality: Prostitution and Tourism in South-East Asia*, London: Zed Books, 1990.

20. Tonette Raquisa, "Prostitution: A Philippine Experience," in Miranda Davies, ed., *Third-World—Second Sex*, vol. 2, London: Zed Books, 1987, p. 221.

21. *Chiao Pao* (Overseas Chinese News), October 2, 1991.

22. See Tonette Raquisa, "Prostitution: A Philippine Experience," p. 222, and the special issue on Filipino women in *In God's Image*, March 1989.

23. See Lauran Bethell, "New Life Center," *In God's Image*, June 1990, pp. 21-2, and Niramon Prudtatorn, "Women's Human Rights in Thailand," *In God's Image*, June 1990, p. 18.

24. Yayori Matsui, "Asian Migrant Women Working at Sex Industry in Japan Victimized by International Trafficking," *In God's Image*, June 1990, pp. 6-13.

25. Elizabeth Dominguez, "Biblical Concept of Human Sexuality: Challenge to Tourism," in Virginia Fabella and Sun Ai Lee Park, eds., *We Dare to Dream: Doing Theology as Asian Women*, Maryknoll, NY: Orbis Books, 1990, pp. 86-90.

26. Rosemary Radford Ruether, "Feminism and Jewish-Christian Dialogue: Particularism and Universalism in the Search for Religious Truth," in Hick and Knitter, *The Myth of Christian Uniqueness*, p. 142.

## Chapter 8

1. Gustavo Gutiérrez, *A Theology of Liberation*, Maryknoll, NY: Orbis, 1973; London: SCM, 1974, pp. 36-7.

2. This sense of the divine is very, very often expressed by Hispanic women. We have often heard it at home from our mothers and grandmothers.

3. Sebastian Kappen, "Orientations for an Asian Theology," in Virginia Fabella, ed., *Asia's Struggle for Full Humanity*, Maryknoll, NY: Orbis Books, 1980, p. 118.

Notes

4. Carlos H. Abesamis, "Faith and Life Reflections from the Grassroots in the Philippines," in Fabella, *Asia's Struggle*, p. 137. Theological technicians likewise need competence in process design and group process facilitation. Because they are part of the community, theological technicians are "real theologians."
5. William B. Kennedy, "Conversation with Paulo Freire," in *Religious Education*, vol. 79, Fall 1984, p. 520.
6. Ibid. Freire says, "The conditions, the political awareness, the social situation, the material conditions in which we are, all have to do with the reading of a book. The question is that the language is not in itself so difficult. What is more difficult sometimes to understand is the dialectical way of life. How is it possible, for example, for one to grasp reality which is moving unless with a language which also moves? That is, if you don't use a formal way of writing, it is difficult with those who have a formal way of thinking. Nevertheless, I think it does not mean that I could not write much more simply. After that first book I think that the other ones are much more simple."
7. We are grateful to Professor William B. Kennedy for the suggestions he gave us regarding some of these criteria.
8. We are here disagreeing with Gustavo Gutiérrez. See Gutiérrez, "Reflections From a Latin American Perspective: Finding Our Way to Talk About God," in Virginia Fabella and Sergio Torres, eds., *Irruption of the Third World*, Maryknoll, NY: Orbis Books, 1983, pp. 224-5.
9. See Abesamis, "Faith and Life Reflections," p. 137. This phrase was used by John Paul II during his trip to Mexico in 1979. He said that the Church should be the "voice of the voiceless." It is to his credit that he did not credit the Church as already fulfilling this task!
10. David Tracy, *Blessed Rage for Order*, New York: Seabury Press, 1978, p. 71.
11. This is an adaptation of Tracy's "criteria of appropriateness," which has to do with "appropriate understandings of the Christian understanding of existence" (Tracy, *Blessed Rage*, p. 72). Hispanic women's liberation theology has to modify his definition of appropriateness because Hispanic women's experience has not been taken into consideration when the Christian understanding of existence has been defined.
12. We were pleasantly surprised to see that Abesamis and Kappen suggest very similar "criteria of appropriateness" to the one we present here. Abesamis, "Faith and Life Reflections," pp. 123-39; Kappen, "Orientations," pp. 108-22.

13. Ada María Isasi-Díaz, "Toward an Understanding of *Feminismo Hispano* in the USA," in Barbara H. Andolsen, Christine E. Gudorf, and Mary D. Pellauer, eds., *Women's Consciousness, Women's Conscience*, New York: Winston, 1985, pp. 51-61.

14. Ada María Isasi-Díaz, "A Hispanic Garden in a Foreign Land," in Letty Russell, Kwok Pui-lan, Ada María Isasi-Díaz, and Katie Cannon, eds., *Inheriting Our Mothers' Gardens*, Philadelphia: Westminster Press, 1988, pp. 91-106.

15. I am much indebted to the work of African-American feminists who have preceded us in this struggle to name ourselves. Their use of the term *womanist* has indeed influenced me. I am particularly grateful to Katie Cannon, Joan Martin, and Delores Williams, with whom I have had the privilege of sharing much. See especially Delores Williams, "Womanist Theology: Black Women's Voices," in this Reader, chapter 7; and Cheryl J. Sanders, Katie Cannon, Emile M. Townes, M. Shawn Copeland, and Bell Hooks, "Roundtable Discussion: Christian Ethics and Theology in Womanist Perspective," *Journal of Feminist Studies in Religion*, vol. 5, no. 2, Fall 1989, pp. 83-112.

16. Rosa Marta Zarate Macias, "*Canto de Mujer*," in *Concierto a Mi Pueblo*, audio tape produced by Rosa Marta Zarate Macias, PO Box 7366, San Bernardino, CA 92411. Much of this description is based on this song, composed and interpreted by Rosa Marta. I have known her for many years. She composed this song in response to the insistence of several Hispanic women that we needed a song that would help us express who we are and would inspire us in the struggle. For the full text of her song in English and Spanish, see Ada María Isasi-Díaz, "*Mujeristas*: A Name of Our Own," *The Christian Century*, May 24-31, 1989, pp. 560-2.

**Chapter 9**

1. Ranjini Rebera, *A Search for Symbols: An Asian Experiment*, Hong Kong: Christian Conference of Asia, Women's Concerns, 1990.

2. Padmini Swaminathan, "Legislation for the Improvement of the Socio-Economic Conditions of Women: The Indian Case," in V. Kanesalingam, ed., *Women in Development in South Asia*, Delhi: Macmillan India, 1989.

3. Miranda Davies, "Women, Politics and Organisation," in *Third-World—Second Sex*, London: Zed Press, 1983.

4. Rosemary Radford Ruether, "Redemptive Community," in *Womanguides,* Boston: Beacon Press, 1985.
5. Elizabeth Gross, "What Is Feminist Theory?" in Carole Pateman and Elizabeth Gross, eds., *Feminist Challenges: Social and Political Theory*, Allen & Unwin Australia.

**Chapter 10**

1. See "Sexual Exploitation in a Third World Setting," paper by Mary John Mananzan, OSB, to be published by CTC-CCA.
2. Susan Brownmiller, *Against Our Will*, New York: Penguin Books, 1975, p. 14.
3. Cf. Frances FitzGerald, *Fire in the Lake*. As quoted by C. S. Song, *Third Eye Theology*, Maryknoll, NY: Orbis Books, 1979, chapter 6.

**Chapter 23**

1. From Miyao Ohara, trans. and ed., *The Songs of Hiroshima: An Anthology*, Hiroshima: Shunyo-sha Shuppan Co. Ltd., 1979, pp. 45, 47.
2. From Jeffrey Abayasekera and D. Preman Niles, eds., *For the Dawning of the New*, Singapore: CTC-CCA, 1981, pp. 16-17.
3. Ohara, *The Songs of Hiroshima,* p. 63.
4. From Iben Gjerding and Katherine Kinnamon, eds., *No Longer Strangers: A Resource for Women and Worship*, Geneva: WCC Publications, 1983, p. 53.
5. This poem was first read at the Divinity School poetry evening at Harvard, and is published here for the first time.

**Chapter 24**

1. "Masculine Metaphors for God and Sex Discrimination in the Old Testament," *The Ecumenical Review*, vol. 27, no. 4, October 1975.
2. "The Words of Worship, Beyond Liturgical Sexism," *The Christian Century*, December 13, 1978.
3. Cf. Philip van Akkeren, *Sri and Christ*, London: Lutterworth Press, 1970.
4. Cf. Gerhard Voss, "Maria in der Feier des Kirchenjahres," *Una Sancta*, no. 4, 1977, pp. 308-9.
5. S. J. Samartha, "The Holy Spirit and People of Various Faiths, Cultures and Theologies," in Dow Kirkpatrick, ed., *The Holy Spirit*, Nashville, Tenn.: Tidings, 1974.

# Notes

## Chapter 25

1. Padma Gallup, "Doing Theology—An Asian Feminist Perspective," *CTC Bulletin*, 4/3, Singapore: CCA, December 1983, p. 22.
2. Ibid.
3. Ibid.
4. Chitra Fernando, "Towards a Theology Related to a Full Humanity," *In God's Image*, April 1985, p. 21.
5. Virginia Fabella, "Mission of Women in the Church in Asia: Role and Position," *In God's Image*, December 1985/February 1986, p. 8.
6. Consultation Report from Theologically Trained Women of the Philippines, "A Continuing Challenge for Women's Ministry," *In God's Image*, August 1983, p. 7.
7. Ibid.
8. Ibid.
9. Rita Monteiro, "My Image of God," *In God's Image*, September 1988, p. 35.
10. Ibid.
11. Lee Sun Ai, "Images of God," *In God's Image*, September 1988, p. 36.
12. This phrase has been chosen as the WCC mission goal for the next decade. Many Asian church women welcome this direction and have had national consultations in order to carry out this goal.
13. Susan Joseph, "Images of God," *In God's Image*, September 1988, p. 37.
14. Lee Sun Ai, "Images of God," p. 37.
15. Astrid Lobo, "My Image of God," *In God's Image*, September 1988, p. 38.
16. Ibid.
17. Pearl Derego *et al.*, "The Exodus Story," *In God's Image*, September 1988, p. 48.
18. Fernando, "Towards a Theology," p. 24.
19. Hiratsuka Raicho, "The Hidden Sun," in Alison O'Grady, ed., *Voices of Women: An Asian Anthology*, Singapore: Asian Christian Women's Conference, 1978, p. 10.

## Chapter 27

1. See also Jean-Marc Éla, *African Cry*, Maryknoll, NY: Orbis Books, 1986, pp. 9ff., and F. Ebousi-Boulaga, *Christianity without Fetishes*, Maryknoll, NY: Orbis Books, 1984.

407

2. This is, of course, not to mention that missionary Christianity seemed to provide the legitimating ideology for colonization and the exploitation of Africans that went with it. The alliance apparent between missionary religion and colonialism was not lost to Africans. Among the Agikuyu, for example, a telling adage was recounted, to the effect that there is no difference between the missionary priest and the colonial settler (*Gutiri muthungu na mubea*). An African lament reflects the same perception: "When the missionaries first came, they had the Bible and we had the land. Now they have the land and we have the Bible!"

3. This kind of tendency is still implicit in the ongoing debate about the merits or demerits of the institutions of polygamy in Africa. Many of the arguments are still given over women's heads; women are hardly consulted for their views.

4. For a detailed account of the upheaval that this particular problem occasioned in the relationship between missionaries and the Agikuyu, see Kamuyu wa Kang'ethe (1981). This work also records in detail the abusive song *Muthirigu*, which was purposely composed to wage psychological war on opponents of circumcision. The girls of Protestant families were particularly targeted in this song, and the psychological torture they underwent must have been tremendous.

5. Roland Oliver, *The Missionary Factor in East Africa*, London: Longman, 1966, p. 33.

6. Ibid., pp. 31f.

7. Ibid., p. 47.

8. Robert Strayer *et al.*, *Protest Movements in Colonial East Africa*, Syracuse, NY: Syracuse University Press, 1973.

9. Robert Strayer, *Inquiry into World Cultures—Kenya Focus on Nationalism*, New York: Prentice-Hall, 1973.

10. W. B. Anderson, *The Church in East Africa, 1840-1974*, Tanganyika: Central Tanganyika Press, 1977, pp. 23ff.

11. These three perceptions of Christ are discussed by way of illustration, and do not preclude the possibility of other "images" of Christ. These are discussed because of their prevalence and direct implications for the women's cause. It is the task of feminist theologians to analyze systematically further images of Christ prevailing in Africa to see whether they are "useful" or inimical to women's search for liberation. It would be interesting to analyze, for example, the relationship between Mariology and Christology and its implications for women in African Catholicism.

12. This view is directly derived from the Gospel narratives of the life of Jesus, for they depict Jesus as a friend and a "pal" of the

marginalized in his contemporary society. In his public ministry, Jesus is also depicted as a compassionate friend of the lonely and the suffering, whose liberation he undertakes.

## Chapter 29

1. See L. Boff, *O rosto materno de Deus*, Petrópolis: Vozes, 1979, p. 15. Eng. trans.: *The Maternal Face of God*, San Francisco: Harper & Row, 1988.
2. See what Boff says in *O rosto*, p. 18: "We are probably not far from the day when women will develop systematic Mariology in light of the feminine as realized both in themselves and, in its perfection, in the Mother of God and our Mother. Surely that image of Mary will be shaped very differently from the one I will sketch." The section on dogma that follows is based, sometimes with literal quotes, on *Nuovo dizionario*, followed by a rereading based on the presuppositions set out above. Dealing with official church teaching as we are here, it seemed wise to follow a good accepted version of the dogmatic formulations. It might seem strange that, after criticizing traditional Mariology for being based virtually exclusively on texts written by men, we should use them so widely here. This is partly because there are no Mariological works written by women or from a different viewpoint, but mainly because the texts used here come not from men or women but from Scripture and the tradition of the Church, and therefore belong to the whole church and the whole of humanity. We therefore feel quite justified in using this work extensively in this section, rereading it later with our own eyes.
3. Boff, *O rosto*, p. 138.

## Chapter 30

1. M. Furlong, ed., *Mirror to the Church—Reflections on Sexism*, London: SPCK, 1988, p. 132.
2. Phyllis Trible, *God and the Rhetoric of Sexuality—Overtures to Biblical Theology*, Philadelphia: Fortress Press, 1978, p. 49.
3. Ibid., p. 202.
4. Rowan Williams, *The Wound of Knowledge*, London: Darton, Longman & Todd, 1979, p. 1.

## Chapter 31

1. See chapter 19 for the study on the Magnificat.

# Notes

### Chapter 34

1. Sr. Mary John Mananzan, editorial in *Conversatio,* September 1975.
2. Sr. Mary John Mananzan, "Woman and Religion," in F. Carino, *Religion and Society,* Manila: Fides, 1988, p. 119.
3. Ruben Habito, "Zen Spirituality: Attuning to the Breath of God," in *Total Liberation,* Maryknoll, NY: Orbis Books, 1989, p. 105.
4. Sr. Elaine MacInnes, "What Is Oriental Spirituality?" in *Asia's Gift to a Total Christian Spirituality,* p. 5.
5. Ibid.

### Chapter 36

1. Elizabeth Amoah, "The Vital Aspects of Women's Experience of God," paper presented to Continental Consultation on Theology from the Third World: Women's Perspective, August 19-23, 1986, CIWA, Port Harcourt, Nigeria.
2. See n. 1 above.
3. Adebisi Sowunmi, "Where Is Theology in Nigeria?" in Mercy Amba Oduyoye, ed., *The State of Christian Theology in Nigeria,* Ibadan, Nigeria: Daystar, 1986, pp. 1-13.
4. Afua Kuma, *Jesus of the Deep Forest,* Peter Kwasi Ameyaw, Fr. Jon Kirby *et al.,* trans. and eds., Accra, Ghana: Asempa, n.d.
5. Interview at Union Theological Seminary, New York, 1986.
6. J. S. Mbiti, *The Prayers of African Religion,* London: SPCK, 1970, p. 148.
7. Mercy Amba Oduyoye, *Hearing and Knowing,* Maryknoll, NY: Orbis Books, 1986. This lyric is from the repertoire of the Dwenesie Singers of Accra, directed by Dinah Reindorf, a Ghanaian Methodist.
8. John S. Pobee and Bärbel von Wartenberg-Potter, eds., *New Eyes for Reading: Biblical and Theological Reflections by Women from the Third World,* Geneva: WCC Publications, 1986.
9. Huda Shaarawi, *Harem Years: The Memoirs of an Egyptian Feminist,* New York: Feminist Press, 1987.
10. E. A. Adegbola, ed., *Traditional Religion,* Maryknoll, NY: Orbis Books, 1973, pp. 203-34.

### Chapter 37

1. Naomi Southard and Rita Nakashima Brock, "The Other Half of the Basket: Asian American Women and the Search for a

Theological Home," *The Journal of Feminist Studies in Religion*, Fall 1987, pp. 135-50.

2. As in the article in n. 1, the term "Asian American" includes women born both in Asia and in the USA: the main identifying factor is that they see their lives and ministry, present and future, based in the USA. Because of this commitment, they have reflected on their experience, particularly as it relates to their Asian historical, social, and cultural heritage.

3. Anne Wilson Schaef, *When Society Becomes an Addict*, New York: Harper & Row, 1987.

4. Sandra Schneiders in Joann Wolski Conn, ed., *Women's Spirituality: Resources for Christian Development*, New York: Paulist Press, 1986, pp. 38-9.

5. Ibid., p. 13.

6. Rosemary Radford Ruether, *Sexism and God-Talk: Towards a Feminist Theology*, London: SCM 1983, p. 135f.

7. Christin Lore Weber, *Woman Christ*, San Francisco: Harper & Row, 1987.

8. Ibid., p. 17.

9. Ibid., p. 46.

10. Anne C. Klein, *Knowledge and Liberation*, Ithaca, New York: Snow Lion Publications, 1986, p. 106.

11. Ibid., p. 107.

12. Kuan Yin was originally identical with the male Avalokita bodhisattva in India. (Amitabha Buddha embodies the primary liberating energy of compassion; Avalokita embodies its secondary emanation.) The worship of Avalokita reached China as early as the first century AD, still in male form. Scholars disagree as to the approximate date that Avalokita took female form as Kuan Yin in China; it is not likely that this change occurred before the eighth century, or later than the relevant (Blofeld, 1977, p. 40). Avalokita was and continues to be depicted as male in Tibet, Mongolia, and Nepal; however, in these areas, they also revere a female emanation of Avalokita who is called Tara. She was "born by a tear shed by Avalokita in pity for the sufferings of sentient beings" (Blofeld, 1977, p. 53). In general, Tara is associated with protection and generosity, is funloving and mischievous, often pictured as a young girl. "Stories of her exploits, sometimes amusing, always merciful, are legion and very similar in content to Chinese tales of Kuan Yin" (Blofeld, 1977, p. 54). These strong connections between Tara and Kuan Yin may suggest that the Chinese used Avalokita and Tara as sources for Kuan Yin; also qualities of the legendary

Chinese princess Miao Shen are thought to have been added to Kuan Yin's character.

13. John Blofeld, *Compassion Yoga: The Mystical Cult of Kuan Yin*, London: George Allen & Unwin, 1977, pp. 20, 24.
14. Ibid., p. 36.
15. Klein, n. 10 above, p. 214.
16. Ichiro Hori, *Folk Religion in Japan: Continuity and Change*, Chicago: University of Chicago Press, 1968.
17. Ibid., pp. 202-3.
18. Ibid., p. 187.
19. Ibid., p. 197.
20. Ibid., p. 218.
21. Nancy A. Falk and Rita M. Gross, eds., *Unspoken Worlds: Women's Religious Lives in Non-Western Cultures*, San Francisco: Harper & Row, 1980, pp. 41-52.
22. Ibid., p. 42.
23. Ibid.
24. Ibid., p. 43.
25. Ibid., p. 45.
26. Ibid., p. 50.
27. Ibid., p. 51.
28. Laurel Kendall, *Shamans, Housewives and other Restless Spirits: Women in Korean Ritual Life*, Honolulu: University of Hawaii Press, 1985.
29. Ibid., p. 164.

❖ ❖ ❖

# Bibliography

ACKERMANN, Denise, DRAPER, Jonathan, MASHININI, Emma, eds., *Women Hold Up Half the Sky: Women in the Church in Southern Africa*, Pietermaritzburg: Cluster Publications, 1991.

AMOAH, Elizabeth, and ODUYOYE, Mercy Amba, "The Christ for African Women," in V. Fabella and M. A. Oduyoye, eds., *With Passion and Compassion: Third World Women Doing Theology*, Maryknoll, NY: Orbis Books, 1988, pp. 35-46.

ANDREWS, William L., ed., *Sisters of the Spirit: Three Black Women's Autobiographies of the Nineteenth Century*, Bloomington: Indiana University Press, 1986.

APPIAH-KUBI, Kofi, and TORRES, Sergio, eds., *African Theology En Route*, Maryknoll, NY: Orbis Books, 1979; Ghana: EATWOT, 1977.

AQUINO, María Pilar, "Perspectives on a Latina's Feminist Liberation Theology," in A. Figueroa Deck, ed., *Frontiers of Hispanic Theology in the United States*, Maryknoll, NY: Orbis Books, 1992, pp. 23-40.

ARELLANO, Luz Beatriz, "Women's Experience of God in Emerging Spirituality," in V. Fabella and M. A. Oduyoye, eds., *With Passion and Compassion: Third World Women Doing Theology*, Maryknoll, NY: Orbis Books, 1988, pp. 135-50.

*Asian Women Doing Theology*, Report from the Singapore Conference, November 20-27, 1987, Hong Kong: Asian Women's Resource Center for Culture and Theology, 1989.

ATEEK, Naim S., ELLIS, Marc H., RUETHER, Rosemary Radford, eds., *Faith and the Intifada: Palestinian Christian Voices*, Maryknoll, NY: Orbis Books, 1992.

BARTON, Mukti, *Creation and Fall and the Women of Bangladesh*, Dhaka: Netritto Proshikkon Kendro, 1992.

BECHER, Jeanne, ed., *Women, Religion and Sexuality: Studies on the Impact of Religious Teachings on Women*, Geneva: WCC Publications, 1990; Philadelphia: Trinity Press International, 1991.

BINGEMER, María Clara, "Reflections on the Trinity," in E. Tamez, ed., *Through Her Eyes: Women's Theology from Latin America*, Maryknoll, NY: Orbis Books, 1989, pp. 56-80.

413

## Bibliography

BINGEMER, María Clara, "Women in the Future of the Theology of Liberation," *LADOC* (Latin America Documentation), vol. 20/6, 1990, pp. 7-15.

BINGEMER, María Clara, "Women and the Theology of Liberation," *LADOC*, vol. 23/2, 1992, pp. 19-28.

BROCK, Rita Nakashima, ed., "Asian Women Theologians Respond to American Feminism," *Journal of Feminist Studies in Religion*, vol. 3/2, 1987, pp. 103-50.

BRODERICK y GUERRA, Cecily P., "Annotated Bibliography," in Letty M. Russell *et al.*, eds., *Inheriting Our Mothers' Gardens: Feminist Theology in Third World Perspective*, Philadelphia: Westminster Press, 1988, pp. 165-81.

BROWN, Kelly D., "The Emergence of a Black Feminist Theology in the United States," in S. Maimela and D. Hopkins, eds., *We Are One Voice: Black Theology in USA and South Africa*, Braamfontein/South Africa: Skotaville Publishers, 1989, pp. 61-71.

BUHAY, Sister Hilda, "Who is Mary?" in Sr. Mary John Mananzan, OSB, ed., *Woman and Religion*, Manila: Institute of Women's Studies, St. Scholastica's College, 1992, pp. 52-9.

CADORETTE, Curt, GIBLIN, Marie, LEGGE, Marilyn, SNYDER, Mary H., eds., *Liberation Theology: An Introductory Reader*, Maryknoll, NY: Orbis Books, 1992.

CANNON, Katie Geneva, "The Emergence of Black Feminist Consciousness," in Letty M. Russell, ed., *Feminist Interpretation of the Bible*, Philadelphia: Westminster Press, 1985, pp. 30-40.

CANNON, Katie Geneva, *Black Womanist Ethics*, Atlanta/Georgia: Scholars Press, 1988.

CANNON, Katie Geneva *et al.*, *God's Fierce Whimsy: Christian Feminism and Theological Education*, New York: Pilgrim Press, 1985.

CAO, Shengjie, "Chinese Women's Status in the Society and in the Church," *In God's Image*, vol. 10/3, 1991, pp. 10-11.

CARROLL, Theodora Foster, *Women, Religion and Development in the Third World*, New York: Praeger Publishers, 1983.

CHATTERJI, Jyotsna, *The Authority of the Religions and the Status of Women*, WCSRC-CISRS Home Women's Program and the William Carey Study and Research Center, 1989.

CHO, Wha Soon, *Let the Weak Be Strong: A Woman's Struggle for Justice*, ed. by Lee Sun Ai and Ahn Sang Nim, Oak Park, Il: Meyer Stone Books, 1988.

CHUNG, Hyun Kyung, "Opium or the Seed for Revolution? Shamanism: Women Centered Popular Religiosity in Korea,"

*Concilium*, 199, 1988, pp. 96-104. Special Issue on *Theologies of the Third World*, eds. L. Boff, and V. Elizando.

CHUNG, Hyun Kyung, *Struggle to be the Sun Again: Introducing Asian Women's Theology*, Maryknoll, NY: Orbis Books, 1990; London, SCM, 1991.

CHUNG, Hyun Kyung, "Come Holy Spirit—Renew the Whole Creation," in M. Kinnamon, ed., *Signs of the Spirit*, Geneva: WCC Publications, 1991, pp. 37-47.

COOEY, Paula M., EAKIN, William R., McDANIEL, Jay B., eds., *After Patriarchy: Feminist Transformations of the World Religions*, Maryknoll, NY: Orbis Books, 1992.

CULPEPPER, Emily Erwin, "New Tools for Theology: Writings by Women of Color,' *Journal of Feminist Studies in Religion*, vol. 4/2, 1988, pp. 39-50.

ECK, Diana L., and JAIN, Devaki, *Speaking of Faith: Cross-cultural Perspectives on Women, Religion and Social Change*, London: Women's Press, 1986; New Delhi: Kali for Women, 1986.

EDET, Rosemary, "Men and Women Building the Church in Africa," *Voices from the Third World*, vol. 8/3, 1985, pp. 78-81.

EDET, Rosemary, and EKEYA, Bette, "Church Women of Africa: A Theological Community," in V. Fabella and M. A. Oduyoye, eds., *With Passion and Compassion: Third World Women Doing Theology*, Maryknoll, NY: Orbis Books, 1988, pp. 3-13.

EJIZU, Chris I., "African Widows: An Agonistic Definition," *The Asia Journal of Theology*, vol. 3/1, 1989, pp. 174-83.

EKEYA, Bette, "Woman, For How Long Not?" in J. S. Pobee and B. von Wartenberg-Potter, eds., *New Eyes for Reading: Biblical and Theological Reflections from the Third World*, Geneva: WCC Publications, 1986, pp. 59-67.

ELLIS, Marc H., and MADURO, Otto, eds., *The Future of Liberation Theology: Essays in Honor of Gustavo Gutiérrez*, Maryknoll, NY: Orbis Books, 1989.

ENEME, Grace, "Women as Living Stones," in J. S. Pobee and B. von Wartenberg-Potter, eds., *New Eyes for Reading: Biblical and Theological Reflections from the Third World*, Geneva: WCC Publications, 1986, pp. 28-32.

FA'ATAUVA'A, Roina, "Samoan Women: Caught in Culture Change," *Pacific Journal of Theology*, series II, no. 7, 1992, pp. 15-27.

FABELLA, Virginia, ed., *Asia's Struggle for Full Humanity: Towards a Relevant Theology*, Maryknoll, NY: Orbis Books, 1980.

FABELLA, Virginia, "A Common Methodology for Diverse Christologies," in V. Fabella and M. A. Oduyoye, eds., *With Passion and*

*Compassion: Third World Women Doing Theology*, Maryknoll, NY: Orbis Books, 1988, pp. 108-21.

FABELLA, Virginia, and ODUYOYE, Mercy Amba, eds., *With Passion and Compassion: Third World Women Doing Theology*, Maryknoll, NY: Orbis Books, 1988.

FABELLA, Virginia, and PARK, Sun Ai Lee, eds., *We Dare to Dream: Doing Theology as Asian Women*, Hong Kong: Asian Women's Resource Center for Culture and Theology and the EATWOT Women's Commission in Asia, 1989.

FABELLA, Virginia, and TORRES, Sergio, eds., *Irruption of the Third World: Challenge to Theology*, Maryknoll, NY: Orbis Books, 1983.

*Faith Renewed: A Report on the First Asian Women's Consultation on Interfaith Dialogue, November 1-8, 1989, Kuala Lumpur, Malaysia,* Hong Kong: Asian Women's Resource Center for Culture and Theology, 1989.

FARIA, S., ALEXANDER, A.V., TELLIS-NAYAK, J. B., eds., *The Emerging Christian Women's Church and Society Perspective*, Indore: Satprakashan Sanchar Kendra, 1984.

FENTON, Thomas P., and HEFFRON, Mary J., eds., *Women in the Third World: A Directory of Resources*, Maryknoll, NY: Orbis Books, 1987.

FERM, Deane William, *Profiles in Liberation: 36 Portraits of Third World Theologians*, Mystic, Connecticut: Twenty-Third Publications, 1988.

FIGUEROA DECK, Allan, sj. ed., *Frontiers of Hispanic Theology in the United States*, Maryknoll, NY: Orbis Books, 1992.

FINSON, Shelly Davis, *Women and Religion: A Bibliographic Guide to Christian Feminist Liberation Theology*, Toronto, Buffalo and London: University of Toronto Press, 1991.

FURLONG, Monica, *Mirror to the Church—Reflections on Sexism*, London: SPCK, 1988.

GEBARA, Ivone, "Women Doing Theology in Latin America," in V. Fabella and M. A. Oduyoye, eds., *With Passion and Compassion: Third World Women Doing Theology*, Maryknoll, NY: Orbis Books, 1988, pp. 125-34.

GEBARA, Ivone, and BINGEMER, María Clara, *Mary, Mother of God, Mother of the Poor*, Maryknoll, NY: Orbis Books, 1989.

GNANADASON, Aruna, ed., *Towards a Theology of Humanhood: Women's Perspectives*, Delhi: ISPCK, 1986.

GNANADASON, Aruna, ed., "Feminist Theology: An Indian Perspective," *The Asia Journal of Theology*, vol. 2/1, 1988, pp. 109-18; reprinted in *In God's Image*, December 1988, pp. 44-51.

# Bibliography

GNANADASON, Aruna, "Women and Spirituality in Asia," *In God's Image*, December 1989, pp. 15-18.

GNANADASON, Aruna, *No Longer a Secret: The Church and Violence against Women*, Geneva: WCC Publications, 1993.

GOVINDEN, Betty, "No Time for Silence: Women, Church, and Liberation in South Africa," in D. Ackermann, J. Draper, E. Mashinini, eds., *Women Hold up Half the Sky: Women in the Church in Southern Africa*, Pietermaritzburg: Cluster Publications, 1991, pp. 274-97.

GRANT, Jacquelyn, *White Women's Christ and Black Women's Jesus: Feminist Christology and Womanist Response*, Atlanta, Georgia: Scholars Press, 1989.

HADDAD, Yvonne E., and FINDLY, Ellison B., eds., *Women, Religion and Social Change*, New Delhi: Kali for Women, 1985; London: Women's Press, 1985.

HAMMAR, Anna Karin, "Forty Years—Churches in Solidarity with Women?" *Ecumenical Review*, vol. 40, nos. 3-4, 1988, pp. 528-38.

HERZEL, Susannah, *A Voice for Women: The Women's Department of the World Council of Churches*, Geneva: WCC Publications, 1981.

HEYWARD, Carter and GILSON, Anne, eds., *Revolutionary Forgiveness: Feminist Reflections on Nicaragua*, Maryknoll, NY: Orbis Books, 1987.

HINGA, Teresa M., "Jesus Christ and the Liberation of Women in Africa," in M. A. Oduyoye and M. R. A. Kanyoro, eds., *The Will to Arise: Women, Tradition, and the Church in Africa*, Maryknoll, NY: Orbis Books, 1992, pp. 183-99.

HONIG, A. G., "Asian Women's Theology," *Exchange: Bulletin of Third World Christian Literature*, vol. 16, 1987, pp. 49-67.

HOOKS, Bell, *Ain't I a Woman: Black Women and Feminism*, Boston: South End Press, 1981.

HOOVER, Theressa, "Black Women and the Churches: Triple Jeopardy," *Voices from the Third World*, vol. 8/2, 1989, pp. 77-87.

HUSSEY, Pamela, *Free from Fear: Women in El Salvador's Church*, London: Catholic Institute for International Relations, 1989.

ISASI-DÍAZ, Ada María, "Defining Our *Proyecto Historico: Mujerista* Strategies for Liberation," *Journal of Feminist Studies in Religion*, vol. 9/1-2, 1993, pp. 17-28.

ISASI-DÍAZ, Ada María, and TARANGO, Yolanda, *Hispanic Women: Prophetic Voice in the Church. Mujer Hispana—Voz Profética en la Iglesia*, Minneapolis: Fortress Press, 1992.

ISASI-DÍAZ, Ada María *et al.*, "*Mujeristas*—Who We Are and What

We Are About," Roundtable Discussion, *Journal of Feminist Studies in Religion*, vol. 8/1, 1992, pp. 105-25.

JAYAWARDENA, Kumari, *Feminism and Nationalism in the Third World*, London: Zed Books, 1986.

JORDAAN, Roxanne, "Black Feminist Theology in South Africa," in S. Maimela and D. Hopkins, eds., *We Are One Voice: Black Theology in USA and South Africa*, Braamfontein, South Africa: Skotaville Publishers, 1989, pp. 51-9.

*Journal of Feminist Studies in Religion* (1987). Special section on Asian and Asian-American women, vol. 3/2, pp. 103-50.

*Journal of Theology for Southern Africa*, Special Issue on feminist theology, no. 66, March 1989.

KANONGATA'A, Keiti Ann, "A Pacific Women's Theology of Birthing and Liberation," *Pacific Journal of Theology* series II, no. 7, 1992, pp. 3-11.

KANYORO, Musimbi R. A., and ROBINS, Wendy S., eds., *The Power We Celebrate: Women's Stories of Faith and Power*, Geneva: WCC Publications/Lutheran World Federation, 1992.

KATOPPO, Marianne, *Compassionate and Free: An Asian Woman's Theology*, Geneva: WCC Publications, 1979; Maryknoll, NY: Orbis Books, 1980.

KING, Ursula, "Women in Dialogue: A New Vision of Ecumenism," *The Heythrop Journal*, vol. 26/2, 1985, pp. 125-42.

KING, Ursula, ed., *Women in the World's Religions, Past and Present*, New York, Paragon House, 1987.

KING, Ursula, "World Religions, Women and Education," *Comparative Education*, vol. 32/1, 1987, pp. 35-49.

KING, Ursula, *Women and Spirituality: Voices of Protest and Promise*, London: Macmillan (2nd edn), 1993; University Park, PA: The Pennsylvania State University Press, 1993.

KINNAMON, Michael, ed., *Signs of the Spirit: World Council of Churches Official Report Seventh Assembly*, Canberra, Australia, February 7-20, 1991, Geneva: WCC Publications, 1991.

KWOK, Pui-lan, "God Weeps with our Pain," *The East Asia Journal of Theology*, vol. 2/2, 1984, pp. 228-32.

KWOK, Pui-lan, "Worshipping with Asian Women: A Homily," *The Asia Journal of Theology*, vol. 1/1, 1987, pp. 90-5.

KWOK, Pui-lan, "Discovering the Bible in the Non-biblical World," in R. S. Sugirtharajah, ed., *Voices from the Margin: Interpreting the Bible in the Third World*, London: SPCK, 1991, pp. 299-315.

KWOK, Pui-lan, "Bridge-Building and Barrier-Breaking," *In God's Image*, vol. 10/3, 1991, pp. 3-9.

KWOK, Pui-lan, *Chinese Women and Christianity 1860-1927*, Atlanta,

Georgia: Scholars Press, 1992.

KWOK, Pui-lan, "The Future of Feminist Theology: An Asian Perspective," *The Auburn News*, New York: Auburn Theological Seminary, Fall 1992, pp. 1-9.

KWOK, Pui-lan *et al.*, "Suggested Readings on Asian Women and Theology," *In God's Image*, April 1986, pp. 47-51.

LEE, Oo Chung *et al.*, eds., *Women of Courage*, Seoul: Asian Women's Resource Center for Culture and Theology, 1992.

LEE, Sung-Hee, "Women's Liberation Theology as the Foundation for Asian Theology," *The East Asia Journal of Theology*, vol. 4/2, 1986, pp. 2-22.

LEE-LINKE, Sung-Hee, *Frauen gegen Konfuzius: Perspektiven einer asiatisch-feministischen Theologie*, Gütersloh: Gerd Mohn, 1991.

LEWIS, Nantawan Boonprasat, "Asian Women's Theology: A Historical and Theological Analysis," *The East Asia Journal of Theology*, vol. 4/2, 1986, pp. 18-22.

*Lila: Asia Pacific Women's Studies Journal*, published by the Institute of Women's Studies, St. Scholastica's College, Manila, 1992.

LINDLEY, Susan Hill, "Feminist Theology in a Global Perspective," *Christian Century*, vol. 96, 1979, pp. 465-9.

LITTLE, Jeanette, "Feminist Bibliography for Theological Education: Women—the Missing Element in Theological Education," *Pacific Journal of Theology*, series II, no. 4, 1990, pp. 27-37.

LOADES, Ann, ed., *Feminist Theology: A Reader*, London: SPCK, 1990; Louisville: Westminster Press/John Knox Press, 1990.

LOYA, Gloria Inés, PBVM, "The Hispanic Woman: *Pasionaria* and *Pastora* of the Hispanic Community," in A. Figueroa Deck, ed., *Frontiers of Hispanic Theology in the United States*, Maryknoll, NY: Orbis Books, 1992, pp. 124-33.

MACKENZIE, Tessa, "Roina Pioneers Theological Education for Samoan Women," *Pacific Journal of Theology*, Series II, no. 4, 1990, pp. 38-40.

MAIMELA, Simon, and HOPKINS, Dwight, eds., *We Are One Voice: Black Theology in USA and South Africa*, Braamfontein: Skotaville Publishers, 1989.

MANANZAN, Sr. Mary John, OSB, "Theological Perspectives of a Religious Woman Today," in M. Ellis and O. Maduro, eds., *The Future of Liberation Theology: Essays in Honor of Gustavo Gutiérrez*, Maryknoll, NY: Orbis Books, 1989, pp. 420-32.

MANANZAN, Sr. Mary John, ed., *Women and Religion: A Collection of Essays, Personal Histories and Contextualised Liturgies*, Manila: Institute of Women's Studies, St. Scholastica's College, 1992, first edition 1988.

# Bibliography

MANANZAN, Sr. Mary John, "Education to Femininity or Education to Feminism," *Concilium*, Edinburgh: T & T Clark, 1992, pp. 28-38.

MARTINEZ, Dolorita, "Basic Christian Communities: A New Model of Church within the United States Hispanic Community," *New Theology Review*, vol. 3/2, 1990, pp. 35-42.

MATSUI, Yayori, *Women's Asia*, London: Zed Books, 1989.

MATSUI, Yayori, "Asian Migrant Women Working at Sex Industry in Japan Victimized by International Trafficking," *In God's Image*, June 1990, pp. 6-13.

MATSUI, Yayori, "Violence Against Women in Development, Militarism and Culture," *In God's Image*, Winter 1991, pp. 22-8.

MENCHÚ, Rigoberta, *I, Rigoberta Menchú: An Indian Woman in Guatemala*, edited and introduced by Elisabeth Burgos-Debray, London: Verso, 1984.

MIZUNO, M., and BECHER, J., eds., *Women of Africa Speak Out*, Geneva: WCC Publications, Sub-unit on Women, 1989.

MOHANTY, Chandra Talpade, RUSSO, Ami, and TORRES, Lourde, eds., *Third World Women and the Politics of Feminism*, Bloomington and Indianapolis: Indiana University Press, 1991.

MOLLENKOTT, Virginia Ramey, ed., *Women of Faith in Dialogue*, New York: Crossroad, 1988.

MOORE, Robert L., and MECKEL, Daniel J., eds., *Jung and Christianity in Dialogue: Faith, Feminism and Hermeneutics*, New York: Paulist Press, 1990.

MPUMLWANA, Thoko, "My Perspective on Women and their Role in Church and Society," in D. Ackermann, J. A. Draper and E. Mashinini, eds., *Women Hold Up Half the Sky*, Pietermaritzburg: Cluster Publications, 1991, pp. 369-85.

MUSTO, Ronald G., *Liberation Theologies: A Research Guide*, New York: Garland Publications, 1991.

NASIMIYU-WASIKE, Anne, "Christology and an African Woman's Experience," in R. J. Schreiter, ed., *Faces of Jesus in Africa*, Maryknoll, NY: Orbis Books, 1991, pp. 70-81.

ODUYOYE, Mercy Amba, "The Value of African Religious Beliefs and Practices for Christian Theology," in K. Appiah-Kubi and S. Torres, eds., *African Theology en Route*, Maryknoll, NY: Orbis Books, 1977, pp. 109-16.

ODUYOYE, Mercy Amba, "Women and the Church in Africa: Perspectives from the Past," *Voices from the Third World*, vol. 3/2, 1980, pp. 17-24.

ODUYOYE, Mercy Amba, "Feminism: A Pre-condition for a Christian

# Bibliography

Anthropology," *Africa Theological Journal*, vol. 11/3, 1982, pp. 193-208.

ODUYOYE, Mercy Amba, "Reflections from a Third World Woman's Perspective: Women's Experience and Liberation Theologies," in V. Fabella and S. Torres, eds., *Irruption of the Third World: Challenge to Theology*, Maryknoll, NY: Orbis Books, 1983, pp. 246-55.

ODUYOYE, Mercy Amba, "Church Women and the Church's Mission in Contemporary Times: A Study of Sacrifice in Missions," *Bulletin de Théologie Africaine*, vol. 6/12, 1984, pp. 259-72.

ODUYOYE, Mercy Amba, "Women Theologians and the Early Church: An Examination of Historiography," *Voices from the Third World*, vol. 8/3, 1985, pp. 70-2, 92.

ODUYOYE, Mercy Amba, *Hearing and Knowing: Theological Reflections on Christianity in Africa*, Maryknoll, NY: Orbis Books, 1986.

ODUYOYE, Mercy Amba, "Be a Woman, and Africa Will Be Strong," in Letty M. Russell *et al.*, eds., *Inheriting our Mothers' Gardens: Feminist Theology in Third World Perspective*, Philadelphia: Westminster Press, 1988, pp. 35-53.

ODUYOYE, Mercy Amba, "The Empowering Spirit of Religion," in S. B. Thistlethwaite and M. P. Engels, eds., *Constructing Christian Theologies from the Underside*, San Francisco: Harper, 1990, pp. 245-58.

ODUYOYE, Mercy Amba, *Who Will Roll the Stone Away? The Ecumenical Decade of the Churches in Solidarity with Women*, Geneva: WCC Publications, 1990.

ODUYOYE, Mercy Amba, and KANYORO, Musimbi R. A., eds., *The Will to Arise: Women, Tradition and the Church in Africa*, Maryknoll, NY: Orbis Books, 1992.

O'NEILL, Maura, *Women Speaking, Women Listening: Women in Interreligious Dialogue*, Maryknoll, NY: Orbis Books, 1990.

PARK, Sun Ai Lee, ed., *In God's Image*, Seoul, Asian Women's Resource Center for Culture and Theology, 1982-  .

PARK, S. A. L., ed., "Asian Women's Experience of Injustice and Reflection," *The Asia Journal of Theology*, vol. 3/1, 1989, pp. 118-31.

PARVEY, Constance, ed., *The Community of Women and Men in the Church: The Sheffield Report*, Geneva: WCC Publications, 1983.

PATHIL, Kuncheria, ed., *Socio-Cultural Analyses in Theologizing*, Bangalore: Indian Theological Association, 1987.

PEIFEN, Jiang, "Women and Evangelism in the Chinese Church,"

# Bibliography

*Chinese Theological Review*, 1987, pp. 144-8.

PINEDA, Ana María, "Pastoral de Conjunto," *New Theology Review*, vol. 3/2, 1990, pp. 28-34.

PLASKOW, Judith and CHRIST, Carol P., eds., *Weaving the Visions: New Patterns in Feminist Spirituality*, New York: HarperCollins, 1989.

POBEE, John S., and VON WARTENBERG-POTTER, Bärbel, eds., *New Eyes for Reading: Biblical and Theological Reflections by Women from the Third World*, Geneva: WCC Publications, 1986; Bloomington, IN: Meyer Stone Books, 1987.

PRABHAKAR, M. E., ed., *Towards a Dalit Theology*, published for the Christian Institute for the Study of Religion and Society (CISRS) and Christian Dalit Liberation Movement (CCDLM), Delhi: ISPCK, 1989.

*Reading the Bible as Asian Women: Twelve Bible Studies on Mobilizing Women in Struggles for Food, Justice and Freedom*, Singapore: Women's Concerns Unit, Christian Conference of Asia, 1986.

REBERA, Ranjini, ed., *We Cannot Dream Alone: A Story of Women in Development*, Geneva: WCC Publications, 1990.

REBERA, Ranjini, ed., *A Search for Symbols: An Asian Experiment*, Hong Kong: Women's Concerns Unit, Christian Conference of Asia, 1990.

REBERA, Ranjini, "The Feminist Challenge," in M. R. A. Kanyoro and W. S. Robins, eds., *The Power We Celebrate: Women's Stories of Faith and Power*, Geneva: WCC Publications, 1992, pp. 37-50.

RITCHIE, Nelly, "Women and Christology," in E. Tamez, ed., *Through Her Eyes: Women's Theology from Latin America*, Maryknoll, NY: Orbis Books, 1989, pp. 81-95.

ROBINS, Wendy S., ed., *Through the Eyes of a Woman: Bible Studies on the Experience of Women*, London: World YWCA, 1986.

ROBINS, Wendy S., and KANYORO, Musimbi R. A., eds., *Speaking for Ourselves: Bible Studies and Discussion Starters by Women*, Geneva: WCC Publications, 1990.

RODRÍGUEZ, Raquel, "Open Our Eyes," in M. R. A. Kanyoro and W. S. Robins, eds., *The Power We Celebrate: Women's Stories of Faith and Power*, Geneva: WCC Publications, 1992, pp. 53-61.

RUSSELL, Letty M., ed., *Feminist Interpretation of the Bible*, Philadelphia: Westminster Press, 1985.

RUSSELL, Letty M. *et al.*, eds., *Inheriting Our Mothers' Gardens: Feminist Theology in Third World Perspective*, Philadelphia: Westminster Press, 1988.

# Bibliography

SAMUEL, Prasanna K., "Women in Theological Education," *The Asia Journal of Theology*, vol. 2/1, 1988, pp. 79-82.

SANDERS, Cheryl, "Christian Ethics and Theology in Womanist Perspective," *Journal of Feminist Studies in Religion*, vol. 5/2, 1989, pp. 83-102.

SCHREITER, R. J., ed., *Faces of Jesus in Africa*, Maryknoll, NY: Orbis Books, 1991.

SEN, Amartya, "More than 100 Million Are Missing," *The New York Review*, December 20, 1990.

SOELLE, Dorothee, *Celebrating Resistance: The Way of the Cross in Latin America*, London: Mowbray, 1993; published in the USA as *Stations of the Cross: A Latin American Pilgrimage*, Minneapolis: Fortress Press, 1993.

SOON-HWA, Sun, "Women, Work and Theology in Korea," *Journal of Feminist Studies in Religion*, vol. 3/2, 1987, pp. 125-34.

SOUGA, Thérèse, and TAPPA, Louise, "The Christ-Event from the Viewpoint of African Women," in V. Fabella and M. A. Oduyoye, eds., *With Passion and Compassion: Third World Women Doing Theology*, Maryknoll, NY: Orbis Books, 1988, pp. 22-34.

SOUTHARD, Naomi P. F., "Recovery and Rediscovered Images: Spiritual Resources for Asian American Women," *The Asia Journal of Theology*, vol. 3/2, 1989, pp. 624-38.

SOUTHARD, Naomi P. F., and BROCK, R. N., "The Other Half of the Basket: Asian American Women and the Search for a Theological Home," *Journal of Feminist Studies in Religion*, vol. 3/2, 1987, pp. 135-50.

SUGIRTHARAJAH, R. S., ed., *Voices from the Margin: Interpreting the Bible in the Third World*, London: SPCK, 1991.

SWARNALATHA, Devi, "Some Perspectives on the Dalit Women's Question in Andhra Pradesh," in M. E. Prabhakar, ed., *Towards a Dalit Theology*, Delhi: ISPCK, 1989, pp. 151-4.

TAMEZ, Elsa, *Bible of the Oppressed*, Maryknoll, NY: Orbis Books, 1982.

TAMEZ, Elsa, "The Woman Who Complicated the History of Salvation," *Cross Currents*, vol. 36/2, 1986, pp. 129-39.

TAMEZ, Elsa, *Against Machismo*, Ruben Alves, Leonardo Boff, Gustavo Gutiérrez, José Miguez Bonino, Juan Luis Segundo, and others talk about the Struggle of Women, New York: Meyer Stone Books, 1987.

TAMEZ, Elsa, "Women's Rereading of the Bible," in V. Fabella and M. A. Oduyoye, eds., *With Passion and Compassion: Third World*

*Women Doing Theology*, Maryknoll, NY: Orbis Books, 1988, pp. 173-80.

TAMEZ, Elsa, *Las mujeres toman la palabra*, En Dialogo con Theologos de la Liberacion Hablan sobre la Mujer, San Jose: DEI—Departmento Ecumenico de Investigaciones, 1989.

TAMEZ, Elsa, ed., *Through Her Eyes: Women's Theology from Latin America*, Maryknoll, NY: Orbis Books, 1989.

TAPIA, Elizabeth, "The Contribution of Philippine Christian Women to Asian Women's Theology," Ph.D., The Claremont Graduate School, 1989.

TARANGO, Yolanda, "The Hispanic Woman and Her Role in the Church," *New Theology Review*, vol. 3/4, 1990, pp. 56-61.

TELLIS-NAYAK, Jessie B., "The Women's Movement and the Church in India," *In God's Image*, December 1987-March 1988, pp. 32-41.

TELLIS-NAYAK, Jessie B., "Efforts at Women's Development: A Professional and Personal Perspective," *Journal of Feminist Studies in Religion*, vol. 7/2, 1991, pp. 139-48.

THETELE, Constance Baratang, "Women in South Africa: The WAAIC," in K. Appiah-Kubi and S. Torres, eds., *African Theology En Route*, Maryknoll, NY: Orbis Books, 1979.

THIAM, Awa, *Black Sisters Speak Out: Feminism and Oppression in Black Africa*, London: Pluto Press, 1986.

THISTLETHWAITE, Susan Brooks, *Sex, Race and God: Christian Feminism in Black and White*, New York: Crossroad, 1989; London: Geoffrey Chapman, 1990.

THISTLETHWAITE, Susan Brooks, and ENGEL, Mary Potter, eds., *Lift Every Voice: Constructing Christian Theologies from the Underside*, San Francisco: HarperCollins, 1990.

TRIBLE, Phyllis, *God and the Rhetoric of Sexuality—Overtures to Biblical Theology*, Philadelphia: Fortress Press, 1978.

VERGHESE, Jamila, ed., *Wake Up and Live: Dramatic Readings for Young People*, Delhi: SPCK, 1988.

VORSTER, W. S., ed., *Sexism and Feminism in Theological Perspective*, Pretoria: University of South Africa, 1984.

WARTENBERG-POTTER, Bärbel von, *We Will Not Hang Our Harps on the Willows: Global Sisterhood and God's Song*, New York: Crossroad, 1990.

WCC, *Sexism in the 1970s: Discrimination Against Women*, A Report of a WCC Consultation, West Berlin, 1974, Geneva: WCC Publications, 1975.

WCC, *Ecumenical Decade 1988-1998: Churches in Solidarity with Women. Prayers and Poems, Songs and Stories*, Geneva: WCC Publications, 1988.

# Bibliography

WEBSTER, John C. B., and WEBSTER, Ellen Low, eds., *The Church and Women in the Third World*, Philadelphia: Westminster Press, 1985.

WEEMS, Renita J., *Just a Sister Away: A Womanist Vision of Women's Relationships in the Bible*, San Diego, CA: Lura Media, 1988.

WEEMS, Renita J., "Reading Her Way through the Struggle: African American Women and the Bible," in C. H. Felder, ed., *Stony the Road We Trod: African American Biblical Interpretation*, Minneapolis: Fortress Press, 1991.

WEEMS, Renita J. *et al.*, "Racism in the Women's Movement," Roundtable Discussion, *Journal of Feminist Studies in Religion*, vol. 4/1, 1988, pp. 93-114.

WILLIAMS, Delores S., "Womanist Theology: Black Women's Voices," in J. Plaskow and C. Christ, eds., *Weaving the Visions*, New York: HarperCollins, 1989, pp. 179-86.

WILLIAMS, Delores S., *Sisters in the Wilderness: The Challenge of Womanist God-Talk*, Maryknoll, NY: Orbis Books, 1993.

WILLIAMS, Rowan, *The Wound of Knowledge*, London: Darton, Longman & Todd, 1979.

*Women to Women: Asian Women in Solidarity: Mobilising Women in Struggles for Food, Justice and Freedom*, Singapore: Christian Conference of Asia, 1988.

ZAPATA, Dominga, "Ministries Among Hispanics in the United States: Development and Challenges," *New Theology Review*, vol. 3/2, 1990, pp. 62-71.

ZARU, Jean, "The Intifada, Nonviolence, and the Bible," in N. S. Ateek, M. H. Ellis, and R. Radford Ruether, eds., *Faith and the Intifada*, Maryknoll, NY: Orbis Books, 1992, pp. 126-9.

ZOE-OBIANGA, Rose, "The Role of Women in Present-Day Africa," in K. Appiah-Kubi, and S. Torres, eds., *African Theology En Route*, Maryknoll, NY: Orbis Books, 1979, pp. 145-9.

❖   ❖   ❖

# Index

Abraham (biblical character), 303, 392
Achebe, Chinua, 263
Ackermann, Denise, 149, 282
African culture, ch. 13, 165–7, ch. 20, ch. 27. *See also* missionary Christianity
African Instituted Churches (AIC), 361, 363–5, 370, 372, 373, 374
*African Literature Today*, 284
African National Congress, National Executive Committee of, 288
"African Widows: An Agonistic Definition" (Ejizu), 138
"After Forty Years—Churches in Solidarity with Women?" (Hammar), 44
AIC. *See* African Instituted Churches
American Academy of Religion, 7
Amoah, Elizabeth, 269
Andrews, William L., 76
anthropology, theological, 31, 34, ch. 25, 275, 279
apartheid, 285–9, 292. *See also* feminist theology, South African
Aquino, Maria Pilar, 87
Arai, Paula K. R., 236
Arellano, Luz Beatriz, ch. 33
*Asia Journal of Theology, The*, 46, 138, 177, 377
Asian American Women in Ministry and Theology, 17
Asian Regional Consultation on Justice, Peace, and Integrity of Creation (Bangkok, 1986), ch. 16
*Asian Women Doing Theology*, 270, 299–301
Asian Women's Association, 123, 124
Asian Women's Network (East Coast, USA), 15
Asian Women's Resource Center for Culture and Theology, 13, 270, 350
Assaad, Marie, 201, 204–6
Association for Promotion of the

Status of Women, 73
Association of Nicaraguan Women to Deal with National Issues, 325
Ateek, Naim S., 230
*Auburn News, The*, 47
Augustine, St, 115

Bâ, Mariama, 284
Bai, Anne Grace, 136
Balasuriya, Tisa, 217
Bam, Brigalia, 9, 27, 28
Bangalore, consultation (1978), 33
Bano, Shah, 358
Barreda, Don Ramón, 330
Barreda, Mary, 329, 330, 331
Barthianism/neo-orthodoxy, 252, 255
basic ecclesial communities, 40, 190, 192, 193, 275
Bathsheba (biblical character), 392
Becher, Jeanne, 103
*Beyond God the Father* (Daly), 63, 74
*Bhagavad Gita*, 249
Bible, the. *See* feminist theology: and Bible; hermeneutics of suspicion; missionary Christianity
*Bible of the Oppressed, The* (Tamez), 189
biblical authority, 193–6, 197
Biko, Steve, 393
Bingemer, María Clara, 244, ch. 29, ch. 32
black feminism. *See* womanist theology; feminist theology, South African
"Black Feminist Theology in South Africa" (Jordaan), 149
black folk culture, 79, 80
black theology, 41, 149, 296
*Black Womanist Ethics* (Cannon), 76
Boniface, St, 250
Bonino, José Míguez, 263
*Book of Negro Folklore, The*, 78, 79
Braide, Elijah Garrick, 364

426

Brock, Rita Nakashima, 72, 377, 378
Buhay, Hilda, 270
Burgos-Debray, Elisabeth, 183

Calvin, John, 248
Cannon, Katie Geneva, 1, 47, 76
Catholic Action, 184, 186
Catholic sisters, role of, 50, 51
CCA. *See* Christian Conference of Asia
Center for Women Resources, 344
"Child Prostitution and Tourism" conference, Chiang Mai, Thailand, 126, 127
*Chinese Women and Christianity 1860–1927* (Kwok Pui-lan), 47
Christ, Carol P., 76
"Christ for African Women, The" (Amoah and Oduyoye), 269
"Christ the Liberator," concept of, 151
"Christ-Event from the Viewpoint of African Women, The" (Tappa and Souga), 269
Christian Conference of Asia (CCA), 8
Christian Conference of Asia, Women's Desk of the, 14
Christian Dalit Liberation Movement, 135
"Christian Ethics and Theology in Womanist Perspective" (Sanders), 76
Christology. *See* feminist theology, and Christology; Jesus
Chui, Jane C. N., 377
Chung Hyun Kyung, 14, 21, 64, 65, 114, ch. 25, 259, 269, ch. 38
church. *See* feminist theology: and ecclesiology; and women's participation in church life; missionary Christianity; WCC
"Church Women of Africa" (Edet and Ekeya), 46, 138
classism. *See* feminist theology: and class
Coakley, Sarah, 294
colonialism, 6, 36, 38, 128, 263, 287, 291
"Come Holy Spirit— Renew the Whole Creation" (Chung Hyun Kyung), 14, 64, 65, ch. 38
"Common Methodology for Diverse Christologies, A" (Fabella), 269
"Community of Men and Women in the Church, The". *See* WCC
*Compassionate and Free* (Katoppo), 12, 14, 25, 114, 244
Cone, James, 152
consultation on interfaith dialogue, Kuala Lumpur, Malaysia (1989), 14, 70, 350

"Continuity and Change in the Status of Women" (Solanke), 32
"Contribution of Philippine Christian Women to Asian Women's Theology, The" (Tapia), 14
Council of Konstanz (1414–18), 115, 116
creation narratives, biblical, 194, 211

dalit, 114, 134, 135, 359
*Dalit* Christian women, ch. 12
Daly, Mary, 63, 74, 262
Dannett, Sylvia, 80
David (biblical character), 183, 184, 392
Deborah (biblical character), 36
Deck, Allan Figueroa, 87
Deleuze, Gilles, 69
Derrida, Jacques, 69
development, 9, 10, 19, 32, 33, 123, 127–9, 202–4, 207–9, 303
Devi, Swarnalatha, ch. 12
Dewey, J., 69
Dominguez, Elizabeth, 73, 253
Dorcas (biblical character), 380
"dowry deaths", 106, 107, 109, 110, 132, 301
Draper, Jonathan, 149, 282
Dussel, Enrique, 116

*East Asia Journal of Theology*, 114
EATWOT, 12, 13, 308: and First World theology, 12; founding of, 11, 26; and liberation/emancipation, 28, ch. 35; and the non-Christian world, 12; and the poor, 12; and religious language (God-talk), 25; and sexism, 12, 26, 27, 28, 29; and Third World theology, 12, 28, 29, chs 1–2; and women's quest for equality, 31. Conferences: New Delhi (1981), 12, ch. 1; Geneva (1983), 12
EATWOT, Women's Commission of, ix, 3, 12, 14, 20, 35, 299. Conferences: Buenos Aires (1985), 12; Manila (1985), 12, 13; Port Harcourt, Nigeria (1986), 13; Yaoundé, Cameroun (1986), 13; Oaxtepec, Mexico (1986), 13, ch. 2; Singapore (1987), 13, ch. 28, 299–301
Eck, Diana L., 350
Ecumenical Decade of the Churches in Solidarity with Women. *See* WCC
ecumenical movement, the. *See* EATWOT; feminist theology: ecumenical dimension; WCC
*Ecumenical Review*, 44

Edet, Rosemary N., 46, 138, 363, 365
Edsa Event, Philippines, 341
Egyptian midwives (Exod. 1), 312
Ejizu, Chris I., 138
Ekeya, Bette, ch. 13, 149, 168, 169
Elizabeth (biblical character), 205, 206, 208, 272
Ellis, Marc H., 230, 339
"Empowering Spirit of Religion, the" (Oduyoye), 169, ch. 36
Eneme, Grace, 182, ch. 20, 220
Engel, Mary Potter, 88, 102, 361
Esther (biblical character), 380
exclusivism, theological, 68
Exodus, biblical book of, 183, 256
Exodus, the, 24, 191, 198, 254, 347

Fa'atauva'a, Roina, ch. 15
Fabella, Virginia, 46, 138, 189, 253, 269
*Faith Renewed*, 350
*Far Eastern Economic Review*, 116–18
Federal Theological Seminary, 153
*Feminism and Nationalism in the Third World* (Jayawardena), 3
feminism, general, 112, 128, 133, 292
feminism of color. *See* feminist theology: and women of color; womanist theology
*Feminist Theology* (Loades), 2
"Feminist Theology" (Gnanadason), 46
feminist theology (*see also*: EATWOT; EATWOT, Women's Commission of; gender; hermeneutics of suspicion; Jesus; Kuan Yin; liberation theology oppression; patriarchy; racism; Shakti; subordination of women; "theological technicians"; WCC): African, 46, ch. 13, ch. 15, ch. 27, ch. 36, 269, 299; African-American, 72, 76; American, 5, 6; Asian, 46, 47, chs 5–6, chs 9, 10, 12, 17, 23–5, 26, 31, 34–5, 38; Asian-American, ch. 37; and the Bible, 4, 24, 26, 31, 33, 34, 36, 37, 38, 39, 42, 43, 85, 104, chs 17–23, ch. 29, 295, 297, 298, 303–7, 311–13; its challenge to traditional theological thinking, 4, 5, 11, 18, 21, 34, 41, 89, 100, 310, 311, 394; characteristics of, 2, 3, 4, 6, 17, 22, 38, ch. 4; and Christology, 20, 37, 40, 76, 243, 251, 259, ch. 27, 269, 270, 365–7, 381; and class, 11, 21, 97, 98, 277; and collaboration/consultation, ix, 1, 5, 6, 15, 20, 21; and community, 19, 20, 25, 27, 28, 31, 34, 40, 81, 87, 89, 90, 91, 92, 93, 94, 95, 96, 99, 100, 102, 253, 254,

273, 282, 295, ch. 31; and the concept of God, 63, 74, 76, 136, ch. 24, ch. 25, 280, 294, 314–16, 318, 319, 336, 374, 377, 379, 381, 388; and conscientization, 4, 8, 9, 15, 90, 93, 100, 101, 103, 106, 286; and creation, integrity of 10, ch. 16, 254; crosscultural context of, 75, 76; and cultural/racial diversity, 64, 65, 66, 67, 181, 282, 297; cultural critique of, 4, 15, 18, 29, 33, 89, 100, 262, 295; definitions, 2, 3, 4, 6, 21; and ecclesiology, 19, 37, 39, 40, ch. 30; ecumenical dimension, 4, 10, 11, 181, 289, 326–8; and empowerment, 5, 7, 9, 15, 18, 19, 20, 21, 103, 104, chs 17–23; and eucharist, 316, 317; and exploitation, 6, 15, 24, 32, 103, 106, ch. 10, ch. 14; future of, ch. 6; and gender discrimination, 164, 165, 166, 268, 282, 286, 292, 293, 296, 297; and "the goddess", 377, 379, 381–5, 388, 394; and historical consciousness, 53, 54, 90, 97, 254; historical development of, 1, 2, 6, 7, 8, 9, 11, 12, 13, 14, 15, 17, chs 1–2; and the Holy Spirit, 38, ch. 24, 254–6, 266, 267, 270, 273, ch. 36; Indian, 46, ch. 5, ch. 26; and interfaith dialogue, 14, 21, 39, 42, ch. 34, 350, 377; and Jewish–Christian dialogue, 64, 70, 71, 72; and justice, 10, 17, 21, 36, 40, 42, 88, 89, 103, 108, 109, 134, ch. 16, 254, 277, 298, 331–2; and language, 4, 6, 15, 17, 21, 26, 27, 31, 33, 34, 83, 245, 282, 297; and the language of the erotic, 64, 72, 73, 74; Latin American, x, 1, 6, 7, 15, 17, 18, 20, 21, ch. 2, ch. 4, 138, ch. 18, 259, 275, chs 32–3; and liberation theology, x, 3, 8, 11, 20, 21, ch. 8, ch. 30; and liberation/emancipation, 3, 15, 21, 25, 34, 37, 38, 40, ch. 8, 135, 254, 261, 269, 282; and liturgy, 4, 9, 27, 347; and Mariology, 20, 31, 243, 251, chs 28–9, 336–8; and motherhood, 208, 315, 316, 356; and oppression, 1, 2, 3, 4, 6, 8, 15, 17, 18, 20, 21, 27, 28, 29, 32, 33, 34, ch. 2, 76, chs 8–16, ch. 22, 251, 254, 261, 262, 270, 271, 272, 277, ch. 30, ch. 33; and the ordination of women, 11, 31, 162, 290, 291; Pacific, 1, 175; Palestinian, 1, ch. 22; and patriarchy, 65, 68, 70, 71, ch. 9, 192, 193, 194, 195, 252, 253, 256, 257, 262, 271, 272, 274, 276, 286, 287, 295; and peace, 10, 45, 88, ch.16, 181, 254; and personal

transformation, 3, 8, 21, 101, 378; and the poor, 11, 12, 18, 21, 27, 37, 38, 39, 40, 43, 98, ch. 18, 204–9, 274, 275, ch. 33; and power, 5, 7, 9, 15, 18, 19, 20, 21, 92, 103, 104, 106, 108, 109–11, chs 17–23, 267, 287, 296, ch. 31, chs 35–6, 378, 379, 382; and praxis, 3, 4, 8, 17, 18, 21, 40, 89, 90, 91, 92, 95, 97, 98, 100; and prayer, ch. 36; prophetic dimension of, 87, 92, 296; publishing/dissemination of, 17; and racism, 12, 27, 28, 65, 69, 72, 76, 97, 98, 274, 282, 286, 293, 296, 297; relationship between First World and Third World, ix, 1, 2, 3, 4, 5, 6, 7, 8, 12, 15, 17, 18, 19, 20, ch. 1, 292; and religious language (God-talk), 12, 20, 25, 83; and religious pluralism, x, 4, 11, 14, 21, 42, 244, 246, 247, 249, 250, ch. 25, 285, 299, 357, 358, 364; and sexism, 12, 26, 27, 28, 29, 97, 98, 262, 268; and sexual abuse (*see also* violence against women), 73; and social analysis, 20, 164, 165, 301, 304, 340, 355; and social transformation, 3, 6, 19, 20, 21, 37, 40, 42, 88, 100, 101, 108, 109, 111, 112, 128, 133, 254, 262, 267, 268, 285, 297; and solidarity among women, 10, 11, 18, 19, 20, 36, 37, 43, 109–11, 289; South African (*see also*: womanist theology), 1, ch. 14, ch. 30; and spirituality, 61, 76, 251, 270, 290, chs 31–8; tasks of, 4, ch. 8; themes in, 1, 12, 17, 18, 19, 20, 21; and theological education, 5, 7, 8, ch. 15; theological method of, 17, 18, 21, 162, 282, ch. 29, 309–11; and theological reflection, 2, 3, 4, 5, 6, 8, 10, 18, 20, 21, 89, 91, 92, 93, 94, 95, 96, 285; and theological tradition, 4, 5, 11, 18, 21, 34, 41, 89, 90, 100, 294, 295; and traditional conceptions of place and role of women, 4, 18, 26, 27, 32, 33, 37, ch. 9, 253; and the Trinity, 243, 244, 245, 247, 315, 316, 385; and women of color, 1, 3, 15, 18, 28, ch. 7, 308, 309; and women's experience, ix, x, 1, 2, 3, 4, 6, 18, 21, 95, 96, 103, 277, 278, 283; and women's participation in church life, 7, 8, 10, 24, 25, 31, 33, 37, 39, 40, 90, 108, ch. 30; and women's participation in social life, 3, 10, 11, 24, 33, 37, 89, 93, ch. 30; and women's voices, 61, 67, ch. 7, 88, 93, 94, 95, 103, 109, 133, 134, ch. 30, 309
"Feminist Theology as the Fruit of

Passion and Compassion" (Tepedino), 189
Ferm, Deane William, 170, 189
FIDES group, 345
*Filipina*, 344
Fiorenza, Elisabeth Schüssler, 195, 262
*Folk Religion in Japan* (Hori), 386
folk/primal religion, 358, 359, 362, 363, 377, 386
Foundation for Women, 73
Friends of the Workers, 342
*From Margin to Center* (Hooks), 78
"From the Goddess of the Chinese Folk Religion to See the Necessity of Developing the Goddess Tradition in Christianity" (Chui), 377
*Frontiers of Hispanic Theology in the United States* (Deck), 87
fundamentalism, religious, 132, 234, 357, 358
Furlong, Monica, 294
*Future of Liberation Theology, The* (Ellis and Maduro), 339

Gabriel (angel), 204
GABRIELA (Philippine women's groups), 73, 344
Gallup, Padma, 252, 253
Gandhi, Mahatma, 134, 393
Gebara, Ivone, ch. 4, ch. 29
gender, 4, 5, 27, 47, 61, 66, 108, 268, 282, 286, 292, 293, 296, 297. *See also* feminist theology: and gender discrimination
gifts, spiritual, 91, 92. *See also* Holy Spirit
Gilkey, Langdon, 69
Gnanadason, Aruna, 46, ch. 35, 377
*God and the Rhetoric of Sexuality* (Trible), 295
*God Struck Me Dead* (Johnson), 84
*God's Fierce Whimsy* (Johnson), 86
Goliath (biblical character), 184
Govinden, Betty, ch. 30
Granson, Milla, 80
Grant, Jacquelyn, 76
Gutiérrez, Gustavo, 339, 354

Habito, Ruben, 348
Hagar (biblical character), 85, 303, 392
*Hakbang* (alternative retreat), 343, 346
Hammar, Anna Karin, 44
"han"/Han-pu-ri, 354, 355, 391
Hannah (biblical character), 206, 272, 372

# Index

Hanson, Paul D., 246
Hara, Tamiki, 240
Harper, Frances W., 81
Harvey, Youngsook Kim, 387, 388
Hassan, Riffat, 68
healing, 364, 365. *See also* Holy Spirit
Hegel, G. W. F., 69
HELP (women's shelter, Japan), 126
hermeneutics of suspicion, 34, 199, ch. 29, 355. *See also* feminist theology: and Bible
Herod (biblical character), 393
Herzel, Susannah, 44
Heyward, Carter, 72
Hill, Anita F., 72
Hinga, Teresa M., 261
Hiroshima, 237, 240, 393
Hispanic Theology Institute at Drew University, New Jersey, 15
Hispanic theology. See *mujerista* theology
"Hispanic Woman, The" (Ines), 87
*Hispanic Women* (Isasi-Díaz and Tarango), 87
Holocaust, the, 393
Holy Spirit, 14, 38, 42, 205, 206, 225, 229, ch. 24, 254–6, 266, 267, 270, 272, 278, ch. 31, ch. 36, ch. 38. *See also* feminist theology: and the Holy Spirit
Hooks, Bell, 78
Hopkins, Dwight, 149
Hori, Ichiro, 386
Hosea (biblical character), 222
Hus, John, 115

*I, Rigoberta Menchú*, 183,
Ibadan, University of: conference on religious studies ("Women from the Perspective of Religion"), 32; national conference ("Nigerian Women and Development in Relation to Changing Family Structure"), 32, 33
ICT. *See* Institute for Contextual Theology
image of God, the, 37, 55, 231, 243, 245, ch. 25, 323
*In God's Image* (journal), 46, 123, 201, 270
inclusivism, theological, 68, 69
Indian Theological Association, 46, ch. 5
*Inheriting our Mothers' Gardens* (Russell, Kwok Pui-lan, Isasi-Díaz, and Cannon), 1
Institute for Contextual Theology (ICT), 153
Instituto de Teologia Hispana

(Hispanic Theology Institute), Drew University, New Jersey, 15
Interfaith Theological Circle, 341, 342
Intifada, 15, ch. 22
*Irruption of the Third World* (Fabella and Torres), 23
Isaac (biblical character), 303
Isasi-Díaz, Ada María, 1, 15, ch. 8
Iteso culture, 139–43

Jacob (biblical character), 221, 223
Jain, Devaki, 350
Jara, Victor, 393
Jayawardena, Kumari, 3
Jephthah's daughter (biblical character), 393
Jesus: and Bartimaeus, 372; cross of, 40, 41, 213, 234, 296, 297; incarnation of, 281; his interpretation of marriage, 143; life of, 185, 191, 198, 254; Nazareth sermon of, 24, 154; and prostitutes, 115; resurrection of, 40, 145, 146, 209–13, 333, 334; suffering of, 41, 333, 334; and the Syrophoenician woman, 201, 202–4, ch. 23, 315; and the ten lepers, 372; and the woman at the well, 74, 115, ch. 21; and woman caught in adultery, 74, 143; and woman who anointed his feet, 43, 145, 310, 311, 315; and the woman with hemorrhage, 143, 315; and women (general), 145, 312, 314, 315, 380. *See also* feminist theology: and Christology
Joan of Arc, 393
Joanna (biblical character), 217, 273
Johnson, Bess B., 86
Johnson, Clifton, 84
Jordaan, Roxanne, ch. 14
Joseph (biblical character), 205, 272
Joseph, Susan, 255
*Journal of Feminist Studies in Religion*, 76, 87, 378
Judith (biblical character), 183, 184
Julian of Norwich, 380

*Kairos* Document, 293
*Kairos* theology, 296
Kanongata'a, Keiti Ann, 175
Kanyoro, Musimbi R. A., 46, 105, 138, 220, 261
Katoppo, Marianne, 12, 13, 14, 25, ch. 10, 123, ch. 24, 251
Kendall, Laurel, 388
Kesaya, Noela, 236
King, Martin Luther, Jr., 80, 393

Kingdom of God, the, 40, 41, 42, 183, 185, 187, 198, 276, 278, 279, 281
Kinnamon, Michael, 390, 391
Kuan Yin, 377, 379, 381–5, 388, 389, 394. *See also* feminist theology: and "the goddess"
Kuma, Afua, 362, 365–7
Kurihara, Sadako, 238
Kwan In. *See* Kuan Yin
Kwannon. *See* Kuan Yin
Kwok Pui-lan, 1, ch. 6, 76, 114, 236, 242, 350

Lambeth Conference (1988), 292
"Lapin case, the" (Nagoya, Japan), 126
Latino theology. *See mujerista* theology
Levite's concubine (Judg. 19), 36
liberation, concept of, ch. 2, 49, 53, 54, 57, 63, 64, 79, ch. 8, ch. 12, 254, chs 27–8, 282, ch. 33
liberation theology, ch. 1, 63, ch. 8, ch. 14, ch. 18, ch. 30, chs 32–3, 339, 345, 346. *See also* feminist theology: and liberation theology
*Lift Every Voice* (Thistlethwaite and Engel), 88, 102, 361
Loades, Ann, 2
Lobo, Astrid, 255, 256
Lorde, Audre, 72
Loya, Gloria Inés, 87
Luther, Martin, 248, 294

Machel, Samora, 32
machismo culture, 36, 329
MacInnes, Elaine, 348
Mackenzie, Tessa, 169
Maduro, Otto, 339
Magnificat, the, 24, 31, 152, 204–6, 207–9, 269, 271, 272, 274, 275, 281
Maimela, Simon, 149
Malcolm X, 393
Malibongwe Conference, Amsterdam (1990), 288
Mananzan, Sr. Mary John, 14, 20, 117, 270, ch. 34
marginalization of women, 191, 192, 193, 312, 358
Mariology: and ecumenism, 270; and theology of liberation, 313; 271–74, 275–81, 299, 408, 409. *See* feminist theology: and Mariology; Mary, mother of Jesus
martyrdom, 331–2
Mary, mother of Jesus, 51, 85, 151f., 201, 204–9, 243, 248, 251, 269f., 275, 313, 315, 318, 337, 384. *See also*

feminist theology: and Mariology
Mary Magdalene, 26
*Mary, Mother of God, Mother of the Poor* (Gebara and Bingemer), 275
Mashinini, Emma, 149, 282
Matsui, Yayori, ch. 11
Menchú, Rigoberta, ch. 17, 189
militarism, ch. 11, 178, 228
*minjung*, 113, 114, 354
*minjung* theology, 41
minority groups: African-American, 15, 76; Asian-American, 15, ch. 37; in Australia, 3; in First World, 7; Hispanic/Latino, 15, ch. 8, 377; in Israel, 3; in Japan, 3; in New Zealand, 3; Palestinian, 15; in South Africa, 3, 15; in USA, 1, 3, 5, 12, 15; worldwide, 2, 18, 301
missionary Christianity, ch. 13, ch. 27, 393
Mollenkott, Virginia Ramey, 350
Moltmann, Elisabeth, 262
Montanism, 248
"More than 100 Million Women are Missing" (Sen), 177
Moses (biblical character), 137, 222, 256
Mother Teresa of Calcutta, 380
Mpumlwana, Thoko, 149, ch. 14
*mujerista* theology, 15, 18, ch. 8, 377

Naaman (biblical character), 372
Nachisale, Annie, 367
Nagasaki, 393
Najlis, Michele, 324, 325
Naomi (biblical character), 71, 72
National Conference of Religious of Nicaragua, 334
neo-colonialism, 6, 36, 123, 128
"Network Against Violence to Women", 125
*New Eyes for Reading* (Pobee and Wartenberg-Potter), 138, 181, 201, 214
New Life Centers, 73
*New York Review of Books*, 177
Nicene Creed, 248, 249
Niles, D. T., 30

Oduyoye, Mercy Amba, ch. 1, 46, 138, 169–70, 189, 261, 269, 292, ch. 36
Ogunseye, Professor, 32
Okinawa, Japan, 130, 131
Okure, Teresa, 189
O'Neill, Maura, 350
Onimode, B., 32
oppression, 1, 2, 3, 4, 6, 8, 15, 17, 18,

20, 21, 24, 27, 28, 29, 32, 33, 34, ch. 2, 76, ch. 2, chs 9–16, 204, 216, ch. 22, 239, 251, 254, 261, 262, 270, 271, 272, 277, ch. 30, ch. 33. *See also* feminist theology: and oppression
"Other Half of the Basket, The" (Southard and Brock), 377, 378

*Pacific Journal of Theology*, 169, 175
Pacific Theological College, 172–5
'Pacific Women's Theology of Birthing and Liberation, A' (Kanongata'a), 175
Park, Sun Ai Lee, 13, 19, 255
Parks, Rosa, 80
Pastoral Institute, Multan, Pakistan, 209
Pathil, K., 46
patriarchy, 4, 8, 29, 37, 39, ch. 9, 252, 253, 256, 257, 262, 271, 272, 274, 276, 286, 287, 295. *See also* feminist theology: and patriarchy
Pattel-Gray, Anne, 392
Paul (biblical character), 231
Peninnah (biblical character), 372
Pentecost, story of, 24, ch. 31
"Perspectives on a Latina's Feminist Liberation Theology" (Aquino), 87
Philippine society/culture, 12, 13, 14, 118, 119, 130, ch. 34, 358
Plaskow, Judith, 70, 76
Pobee, John S., 138, 181, 201, 214
*Power We Celebrate, The* (Kanyoro and Robins), 105, 220
Prabhakar, M. E., 134, 135
*Profiles in Liberation* (Ferm), 170, 189
*Profiles in Negro Womanhood* (Dannett), 80
prostitution, 72, 73, 74, 103, 107, 108, ch. 10, 123, 125–7, 134, 352, 393
Provincial Council, Milan (1665), 115

racism, 5, 12, 27, 28, 45, 65, 69, 72, 76, 97, 98, 274, 282, 286, 293, 296, 297. *See also* feminist theology: and racism
"Racism in the Women's Movement", 76
Rahab (biblical character), 74
Ramphele, Mamphela, 287
Rebecca (biblical character), 304
Rebera, Ranjini, 9, 10, 19, ch. 9, 201, 303
Rendra, W. S., 116
*Religion and Society* (FIDES), 345
Ritchie, Nellie, 259
*River Between, The* (Thiongo), 263
Robins, Wendy S., 105, 182, 220

Rodriguez, Raquel, ch. 21
Rogers, Carolyn, 82
Roman Catholicism, 8, 50, 51, 91, 99, 115, 142–8, 184, 186, 265, 269, 271, 318, 374, 384
Romero, Oscar, 393
Ruether, Rosemary Radford, 75, 111, 230, 262
Russell, Letty M., 1, 47
Ruth (biblical character), 71, 72, 380
Ryan, Samuel, 305

Salome (biblical character), 201
Samartha, Stanley, 250
"Samoan Women" (Fa'atauva'a), 175
Samuel, Prasanna K., 169
Sanders, Cheryl, 76
Sandinistas, 328
Sang, Kim Hee, 236
Sarah (biblical character), 303, 392
Schaef, Anne Wilson, 380
Sen, Amartya, 177
*Sex, Race and God* (Thistlethwaite), 76
"sex tourism". *See* prostitution
sexism, 4, 9, 12, 26, 27, 28, 29, 30, 31, 97, 98, 262, 268. *See also* EATWOT: and sexism; feminist theology, and sexism
*Sexism and Feminism in Theological Perspective* (Vorster), 149
"Sexism in the 1970s". *See* WCC: consultations, Berlin (1974)
sexuality, female, 10, 26, 27, 103, 106, 107, 271, 295
*Shakti*, ch. 35. *See also* feminist theology: and "the goddess"
shamanism: in African culture, 141–2, 147; in Asian culture, 355, 358, 377, 379, 385–9
"Sheffield Report, The". *See* WCC: "Community of Men and Women in the Church, The"
*Signs of the Spirit* (Kinnamon), 390, 391
*Sisters of the Spirit* (Andrews), 76
Smith, Wilfred Cantwell, 71
*Socio-Cultural Analyses in Theologizing* (Pathil), 46
Sojourner Truth, 81, 85
Solanke, Folanke, 32, 33
Souga, Thérèse, 269
South African Council of Churches' Women's Desk, 289
Southard, Naomi P. F., ch. 37
Sowunmi, Bisi, 365
*Speaking of Faith* (Eck and Jain), 350
stereotyping of women, 60, 62. *See also*

432

# Index

feminist theology: and traditional conceptions of place and role of women
*Struggle to be the Sun Again* (Chung Hyun Kyung), 14, 251, 259, 269
subordination of women, 144–5, 152, 194, 195, 198, 323, 345, 379
Suchocki, Marjorie Hewitt, 68
Susanna (biblical character), 217
Sutherland, Stewart, 296
Swaminathan, Padmini, 106

Tabitha (biblical character), 380
Taizé, 249
Tamar (biblical character), 73, 312
Tamez, Elsa, 13, 138, 182, 189, ch. 18, 259
Tapia, Elizabeth, 14, 241
Tappa, Louise, 269
Tarango, Yolanda, 87
Tellis-Nayak, Jessie, 46
Tepedino, Ana Maria, 189
Terrell, Mary Church, 81
Thennavan, Kurinji, 102, 239
"theological technicians", 90–7. *See also* feminist theology: theological method of
*Theology of Liberation, A* (Gutiérrez), 63
Theresamma (Dalit poet), 134
*Things Fall Apart* (Achebe), 263
Thiongo, Ngugi wa, 263
Thistlethwaite, Susan Brooks, 76, 88, 102, 361
Thomas Aquinas, 115
Thomas, Clarence, 72
*Through Her Eyes* (Tamez), 13, 138, 244, 259
*Through the Eyes of a Woman* (Robins), 182
THRUST group, 345
Torres, Sergio, 23
"Toward a Jewish Feminist Theology" (Plaskow), 70
*Towards a Dalit Theology* (Prabhakar), 134, 135
Tower of Babel, the, 24, 306
Tracy, David, 69
Trible, Phyllis, 262, 295, 297
Tubman, Harriet, 79, 80, 82, 85, 86

United Nations Decade for Women (1975–85), 10
Uriah (biblical character), 392
"Uses of the Erotic, The" (Lorde), 72

violence against women, 103, 106, 107, 117, ch. 11, 262
"Violence and the Community" (forum held in Canberra, Australia), 107
Vivekananda, Swami, 352
*Voice for Women, A* (Herzel), 44
*Voices from the Third World* (journal), 3
Vorster, W. S., 149

Walker, Alice, 77, 78, 79, 80, 81, 82, 85, 86
Wartenberg-Potter, Bärbel von, 138, 181, 201, 214
WCC, 8, 9, 10, 11, 12, 17, 30, 170: "Community of Men and Women in the Church, The" (worldwide study, 1978–81), 10, 31; Department of Co-operation of Women and Men in Church and Society, 9, 30, 31; Ecumenical Decade of the Churches in Solidarity with Women (1988-98), 10, 11, 44, 45, 201, 289; evaluation conference (1988), 9; meeting (1953), 31; "Programme on Women and Rural Development", 9, 201, 202–4, 207–9, 303; and role of women in the church (*see also* feminist theology: and women's participation in church life), 30, 31; Sub-Unit on Women in Church and Society, 9; women's involvement in, 44. Assemblies: Amsterdam (1948), 30, 44; Canberra (1991), 14, 64, 390. Conferences: Sheffield (1981), 10, 32; Venice, 344. Consultations: Berlin (1974), 9, 31
WCSF. *See* World Christian Students' Federation
*We Are One Voice* (Maimela and Hopkins), 149
*We Cannot Dream Alone* (Rebera), 10, 19, 201, 303
*We Dare to Dream* (Fabella and Park), 13, 19
*Weaving the Visions* (Plaskow and Christ), 76
Weber, Christin Lore, 382, 383
*When Society Becomes an Addict* (Schaef), 380
White, James, 246
*White Women's Christ and Black Women's Jesus* (Grant), 76
Whitehead, A. N., 69
"Who is Mary?" (Buhay), 270
"Who is Mary for Today's Asian Woman?" (Chung Hyun Kyung), 269
*Who Will Roll the Stone Away? The Ecumenical Decade of the Churches*

*in Solidarity with Women* (Oduyoye), 201

*Will to Arise, The* (Oduyoye and Kanyoro), 46, 138, 261

Williams, Delores S., 15, 72, ch. 7

Williams, Rowan, 297

*With Passion and Compassion* (Fabella and Oduyoye), 46, 138, 189, 269

*Woman Christ* (Weber), 382

womanist theology, 15, 18, ch. 7, 87, 377

"Women and Christology" (Ritchie), 259

*Women and Religion* (Mananzan), 14, 270

"Women as Living Stones" (Eneme), 182, ch. 20

*Women Hold Up Half the Sky* (Ackermann, Draper, and Mashinini), 149, 282

"Women in the Bible" (Okure), 189

'Women in Theological Education' (Samuel), 169

*Women of Faith in Dialogue* (Mollenkott), 350

*Women Speaking, Women Listening, Women in Interreligious Dialogue* (O'Neill), 350

*Women's Asia* (Matsui), 123

Women's Desk of the Christian Conference of Asia, 14

"Women's Movement and the Church in India, The" (Tellis-Nayak), 46

women's rights, 9, 33, 344

World Christian Students' Federation (WCSF), 8, 31, 170

World Council of Churches. *See* WCC

Young-Hak, Hyun, 354, 355

YWCA, 8, 30, 31, 233

Zaru, Jean, ch. 22

Zechariah (biblical character), 205, 272

❖   ❖   ❖